A Never-ending Groove

MERCER
UNIVERSITY PRESS

Endowed by
TOM WATSON BROWN
and
THE WATSON-BROWN FOUNDATION, INC.

JOHNNY SANDLIN'S MUSICAL ODYSSEY

AN EVER-ENDING GROOVE

ANATHALEE G. SANDLIN

MERCER UNIVERSITY PRESS   MACON, GEORGIA

MUP/ H839

Mercer University Press
1400 Coleman Avenue
Macon, Georgia 31207

First Edition

Books published by Mercer University Press are printed on acid-free paper that meets the requirements of American National Standard for Information Sciences—Permanence of Paper for Printed Library Materials.

Mercer University Press is a member of Green Press Initiative (greenpressinitiative.org), a nonprofit organization working to help publishers and printers increase their use of recycled paper and decrease their use of fiber derived from endangered forests. This book is printed on recycled paper.

CIP Information
    Sandlin, Anathalee.
    A never-ending groove : Johnny Sandlin's musical odyssey / Anathalee G. Sandlin. -- 1st ed.
        p. cm.
    Includes index.
    ISBN 978-0-88146-276-0 (hardback : alk. paper) -- ISBN 0-88146-276-4 (hardback : alk. paper) 1. Sandlin, Johnny. 2. Rock musicians--United States--Biography. 3. Sound recording executives and producers--United States--Biography. I. Title.
    ML419.S198N48 2012
    781.66092--dc23
    [B]
                                                2011050966

"I've found the key that opens the door

The beginning of a path

That's a never ending groove."

—Johnny Sandlin, c. 1960s

Dedicated with love to our children,

Leigh, Kristin, Heidi;
our grandchildren,
Sandlin, Ella, Reid, Avonlea, Gray, Noah;
and our great-grandson,
Grayden Graham:

Life's never-ending groove

Contents

1: The Impacts / 1

2: Mark V / 11

3: The Five Men-Its / 15

4: The Minutes / 20

5: The HourGlass / 26

6: California / 34

7: The Fillmore / 43

8: *Power of Love* / 50

9: FAME / 61

10: The Allman Brothers Band / 69

11: Macon / 78

12: *Ton Ton Macoute* / 86

(*There is no thirteen—don't ask why*)

14: Cowboy / 97

15: Alex Taylor / 104

16: *Live at the Fillmore* / 113

17: *5'll Getcha Ten* / 119

18: October 1971 / 126

19: *Anthology* / 133

20: November 1972 / 137

21: *Brothers and Sisters* / 142

22: *Laid Back* / 149

23: The Warehouse / 256

24: Live / 163

25: Gregg Allman Tour / 172

26: *Highway Call* / 178

27: *Win, Lose or Draw* / 183

28: *Lady's Choice* / 190

29: Leaving Capricorn / 195

30: Going Independent / 199

31: *Saturday Night Live* / 207

32: Decatur / 215

33: The Decoys / 221

34: *Mom's Kitchen* / 226
35: *All My Friends* / 233
36: Aquarium Rescue Unit / 237
37: *Everyday* / 244
38: *Mirrors of Embarrassment* / 249
39: Back Door Records / 254
40: *Rendezvous with the Blues* / 258
41: *Searching for Simplicity* / 264
42: *Hard Luck Guy* / 270
43: *Blessed Blues* / 274
44: Second Street / 277
45: The Party / 284
46: Capricorn Rhythm Section / 291
47: Phil / 296
48: Rockin' Camel / 301
49: Final Thoughts / 305
Discography: Albums and 45s / 311
Index / 355

Acknowledgments

To Bill Thames, who kept me going with our motto, "P.A.D.," thank you for all those times you wouldn't let me throw in the towel.

A huge thank you to the master of punctuation, Mitch Lopate, for making me look so much better than I am, and to Bonnie Vogel, who patiently proofed the early drafts.

A very special and heartfelt thanks to the Dirty ½ Dozen: Renee Wilson, Skip Littlewood, Dave and Janet Caplice, Candace Oakley, and especially Sharon Crawford, who saw to it there were no unnecessary hyphens in the story. And to Buford and Sherry who left too soon.

Thank you to becksbolaro (James Monica), bendaway, bigdaveonbass (Dave Pierson), bluedad (John Howard), bluefox (Carol Smith), buppalo (Randy Stephens), Carlos Rivera, C. W. Moss, Lespaul71, MichaelP (Michael Phillips), PattyG (Patty Goddard), PeachNut, Rottinpeach (James Taylor), skypuppy (Vincent Lanza), and Stephen Garfield for the questions that helped keep me on course.

But mostly, I want to thank Johnny for sharing his wonderful, interesting life with me and for loving me all these years.

Young Johnny *Photo courtesy of Johnny Sandlin*

Johnny circa 1967 *Photo courtesy of Johnny Sandlin*

Above, The 5 Men-Its; below, The Men-Its *Photos courtesy of Johnny Sandlin*

Minutes *Photo courtesy of Johnny Sandlin*

Above, The Minutes; below, The Secrets *Photos courtesy of Johnny Sandlin*

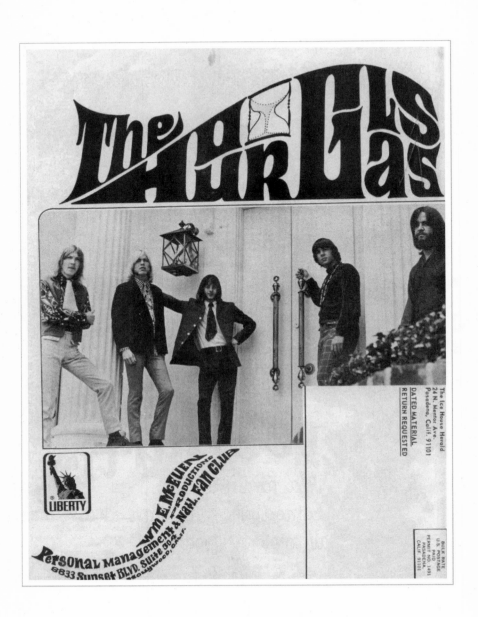

The HourGlass *Photo courtesy of Johnny Sandlin*

Johnny with HourGlass *Photo courtesy of Johnny Sandlin*

Johnny, Arthur Connley, and Phil Walden *Photo courtesy of Johnny Sandlin*

Chuck Leavell, David Hood, Bill Stewart, Johnny, and Scott Boyer
Photo courtesy of Anathalee Sandlin

Berry Oakley, Duane Allman, Arthur Connley, Johnny, and Paul
Photo courtesy of Johnny Sandlin

Capricorn Rhythm Section *Photo courtesy of Anathalee Sandlin*

Basement Bathroom at Capricorn *Photo courtesy of Anathalee Sandlin*

Johnny with bass *Photo courtesy of Anathalee Sandlin*

Oteil with Johnny's bass *Photo courtesy of Anathalee Sandlin*

Johnny and Johnny Jenkins *Photo courtesy of Johnny Sandlin*

Johnny playing drums on Eddie Hinton's Hard Luck Guy
Photo courtesy of Anathalee Sandlin

Johnny in the Studio *Photo courtesy of Johnny Sandlin*

Johnny with Decoys *Photo courtesy of Johnny Sandlin*

During a recent Cowboy session *Photo courtesy of Anathalee Sandlin*

Johnny *Photo courtesy of Anathalee Sandlin*

Above, Kunio Kashida session in Muscle Shoals; below, Akbar with Diana and Peter Thompson *Photo courtesy of Anathalee Sandlin*

Ann Sandlin, Johnny, and Hank Crawford *Photo courtesy of Anathalee Sandlin*

Scott Boyer, Johnny, and Bryan (B.W.) Wheeler *Photo courtesy of Anathalee Sandlin*

Grandson Gray Cauthen *Photo courtesy of Carolyn Bild*

Granddaughter Ella Cauthen and Grandson-in-law Zach Graham
Photo courtesy of Anathalee Sandlin

Johnny in session *Photo courtesy of Anathalee Sandlin*

The Impacts

By 1970, Johnny Sandlin and the Allman Brothers Band were well on their way to creating music that was to define the South as the birthplace of Southern Rock. But in the early fifties, Johnny was still in grade school, and a hodgepodge of country and popular music ruled the airwaves in his hometown, Decatur, Alabama.

With a population of around 25,000, life in Decatur then wasn't much different from life in any other small Southern town. You could stroll from one end of the town to the other to do all your shopping, and friends gathered at the movie theater to watch the newest release.

Against this idyllic backdrop, there had been a Sandlin in the hardware business on Second Avenue, the main street in town, since the late 1800s, first as half of Sively & Sandlin, then as Sandlin & Son, and finally as Sandlin Hardware, the store owned by Johnny's parents—his father, Big John Sandlin, and his mother, Lucille. It was Johnny's mother who helped create the environment in which his love for music began to flourish.

My mother loved music, and while I was growing up, she always had the radio on in the kitchen. One of the earliest songs I can remember is the one that begins with "Put another nickel in, in the nickelodeon." I believe the title is "Music! Music! Music!" She would listen to Perry Como and other popular singers of the time, and it's where I first heard a lot of the standards I later ended up playing in various bands.

In the first hardware store my parents owned on Second Avenue, there was a balcony that was used mainly for storage and additional stock. I had a little place up there with a rocking chair and a record player that played 78s. The hardware store carried needles for the player that came in a paper sack with ten to fifteen needles, since they wore out quickly. Eventually I upgraded to a little 45 rpm player, and with that one, I could play the 45s with one needle and then turn it over to play 78s.

Just across the street and down a ways was Hornbuckle's Records, where I spent a lot of time looking through records. One of the first ones I ever bought was a 78 by Teresa Brewer; of course, having only one record, I listened to both the A and B sides over and over so it wore out pretty fast. Shortly after I got the new player, I went with my cousin, Tom McCutchen, to Grant's Five and Dime a couple blocks up from the hardware store and saw the Sun label in the record bin. I remember thinking what a neat name Sun was for a label. I bought a Carl Perkins record, "Your True Love," "Rock around the Clock" by Bill Haley, and a Jerry Lee Lewis record. Elvis was on the Sun label, and later I got really hung up on listening to him. One day the record store was having a close out on 78s and I thought, "Oh boy, I'll buy these 'cause they'll be collectors' items someday," and I was right. Elvis and Carl Perkins were a big influence when I started trying to play.

When I was about ten, my folks and I went to a hardware convention in Memphis. In the diners during those years there were little boxes at the table where you could select songs on the jukebox for a nickel or dime. My parents let me pick one out to play, so I selected "Tutti Frutti" by Little Richard, and they weren't too crazy about that. They didn't know what to think because that was wild-sounding music to them then. Of course it's tame now, but unless you've lived it, it's hard to imagine the kind of effect that style of music had on people. Jerry Lee, Little Richard, Chuck Berry—that music was getting right down to it!

Back then you could buy 45s for a dollar each, and when I was eleven, my folks would give me money once in a while to get a record; however, if I wanted to buy more than one or two at a time, they'd find something for me to do around the hardware store to earn the money. I'd spend a Saturday waiting on customers, checking inventory, or doing whatever other job they could come up with, and at the end of the day they'd pay me five dollars. I'd take the money to the record store and buy the records I'd picked out a few days earlier. Then, I would go up to the balcony at the store and sit in the rocking chair and rock while I listened to them. Rocking seems kind of odd, I suppose, but it was natural to me. I had trouble being still when I listened to music. I still do.

I'd always wanted to play a musical instrument and I'd tried playing the trumpet, but that didn't work out because I had asthma. After that, I tried to play the piano, but that didn't work out either because I didn't like the music you had to play to learn it. I didn't want to practice scales; I wanted to play music I enjoyed. After that my folks kind of gave up. Then I saw Elvis playing guitar on *The Ed Sullivan Show*, and I knew the guitar was an instrument I wanted to play. When I was about twelve, my folks ordered a Kay acoustic guitar out of a catalog for me. It had strings on it that must have been an inch high, and after a few days of trying to play the thing, I was soaking my hands in turpentine to ease the pain. My fingers were so sore I wasn't certain I'd ever be able to play the guitar again, but I wasn't about to give up. It was almost like I knew from the time I got that guitar that music was what I was going to be about—it what I was going to do. Or at least I was going to give it everything I had.

I remember listening to Johnny Cash's "I Walk the Line," and it's the first song I ever tried to play on the guitar. Of course, I played it a little differently from Johnny Cash; I didn't change chords. I didn't realize you needed to do that. I played the song and asked my mother, "How does that sound?" She kind of looked at me a little funny and answered, "Something doesn't sound right." I was just holding a C chord and strumming, but it wasn't long afterward I figured out what I was doing wrong.

One of the first guitar teachers I had was Frankie Starr. He'd been on the *Grand Ole Opry* and knew a lot of famous people, but by the time I met him, he was living in Decatur where he and his wife ran the record store. Frankie taught me the first few chords that got me started playing. One day he introduced me to George Jones—but it was early in his career, and I didn't know who George Jones was.

One day a kid came in the record store with a '57 Stratocaster. It was probably the first electric guitar I'd ever seen, and it looked so strange my first thought was, "Boy, this is ugly!" Then I looked at it again and kept staring—I was actually almost afraid of it. It looked really expensive, and I thought it had to cost at least a thousand dollars. There weren't many bands around Decatur at that time, and I'll bet there weren't more than handful of electric guitars in the whole town.

The first electric guitar I ever had was a Gibson 175 my folks bought for me at Forbes Music store in Decatur a year or so later. After I'd seen the '57 Strat, I started noticing people playing them on television, and once in a while I'd see a musician playing one at a live gig. By the time I got ready to buy my next guitar, I selected a '59 Fender Stratocaster. There weren't guitar stores in town like there are now, so I picked it out of a catalog and my dad placed the order through a jeweler in Scottsboro. It was an incredible blonde guitar with gold hardware. I wish I still had it today.

My first introduction to playing with a band came through childhood friends. Joe Walk, who was a few years older, had lived across the street from me when I was about three, but after my family moved we lost touch for a while. Pruett Masterson lived up the street from me when I was in the fifth or sixth grade, and we entered a talent show at one of the schools. Joe had entered the talent show playing trumpet with his group, and we invited him to play with us, which he did. We didn't win, but I got re-acquainted with him. Joe was a really good trumpet and piano player, and I'd go over to his house where we listened to Carl Perkins, Johnny Cash, and Jerry Lee. I'd try to play with him whenever I got the chance. Joe was the hero in Decatur because he played like Jerry Lee and, of course, we all wanted to play the guitar parts.

Joe had a band called the Rhythm Rockets, and I eventually worked my way into being an unpaid part-time member by hanging around and annoying them until they let me play. In 1958, when I was thirteen, we got a gig opening for Jerry Lee Lewis at a fair in Cullman, Alabama, and this particular night, Jerry Lee's guitar player didn't show up. Since most of what we played were his songs anyway, Jerry Lee figured I could play them and he let me sit in. I was scared to death, and it's not an understatement to say I was terrible.

In the middle of the whole thing, somebody from the audience hollered something that offended Jerry Lee, and when he pushed back the piano bench and stood up, it appeared he was a little loaded. I'd never seen anyone from the stage talk back to the audience (and back then you never heard anyone use even "damn" or "hell" in polite company), but Jerry Lee called the guy a son-of-a-bitch, which shocked everybody in the place and made me about ten times as nervous as I already was just trying to play with him. Whoever it was had hollered out, "Play 'Wild Wood Flower,'" an old country song. After Jerry Lee finished shouting back at the heckler, he sat back down at the piano and just tore it to pieces playing "Wild Wood Flower." It was my first—but not my last—experience with over-the-top behavior of musicians. Eventually, Joe went on the road to play bass with Jerry Lee, so it wasn't his last experience with that kind of behavior either.

I played another interesting gig with Joe a couple of years later. Patsy Cline was booked to play in Priceville, Alabama, at the high school just outside of Decatur, and they needed back-up musicians. It wasn't uncommon for performers to travel from town to town and use local pick-up bands rather than touring with a band of their own, and Joe and I ended up getting the gig to play with her. The thing was, they couldn't find a drummer. I'd never played drums before anywhere other than in the house to practice, but that didn't stop me. I made my drumming debut with Patsy Cline. I wasn't very good, but I was there.

I don't recall the first time I ever got booked for a gig, but I remember the first time I made any money. Jeriel Parker was a guitar teacher in town who, at one time or another, probably taught guitar to everyone in North Alabama, including me. He hired me to play with him at a gig at the county fair in Athens, Alabama, another small town about fifteen miles from Decatur. All the bands had a standard repertoire, so I either knew most of the songs or could fake my way through them. We just showed up and played, and if I didn't know the song, I just watched Jeriel's hands and followed along. I made ten dollars and thought it was a fortune; I had a great time, people were applauding, and I made ten dollars! I thought, "I've got to do this! Why would anyone do anything else?"

One of the earliest bands I was in was with some friends from junior high school called the Secrets, and we were a pretty well-kept one. Billy Smith played drums, I played guitar, Jackie Whitley was the singer, and eventually Jackie's brother, Johnny, joined to play piano. We practiced over at Jackie's house a lot of the time. We never made any money playing, or if we did, it wasn't much. We were only together about a year and a half.

At some point during that period I participated in my first recording session. Hollis Champion, a local singer and guitar player who'd had some success in Nashville, took me, Dwight Shirley, Butch Owens, and Billy Smith up to a radio station in Tennessee to cut some tracks. The place wasn't really set up for recording—it was just a radio station with a recorder. There was only one microphone, and the guitar and bass were run through the same amp. We recorded "That Old Red Devil," along with "Let Our Conscience Be Our Guide," and Hollis had the tracks pressed into 45s. I don't think there are any copies still around, which might be a good thing for me because I really wasn't used to playing that style music. I was happy to hear it on the radio at the time, though.

A few years later, Butch Owens also went out on the road with Jerry Lee for a while and ended up part of a Jerry Lee legend. Butch had gone over to Jerry Lee's house in the country, and during the visit, Jerry Lee accidentally shot Butch and almost killed him. Jerry Lee wouldn't give anyone his address so they could call for help. Finally, Butch got a helicopter transport, but he barely made it to the emergency room in time. He spent seven weeks recovering in the hospital.

The band I probably had the most success with in high school was the Impacts when I was in the tenth or eleventh grade. I played guitar, Buddy Thornton played bass, Jimmy Ray Hodges was the saxophone player, Barry Smith was the drummer, and Van Rudolph sang and played sax and harmonica. Jimmy Ray's brother, Robert, played trumpet with us part time when we could afford him. We had a pretty rocking cover band and played regularly in Fayetteville, Tennessee, and at various local proms and fraternity parties at the University of Alabama, Auburn, and at the University of the South in Suwannee, Tennessee. We also had a regular gig at the *Am Vets* club in Huntsville Wednesdays and Fridays. On Saturday night the club had more of a dance band playing standards, and I got some pick-up gigs there. I wasn't totally ready to be playing them, but I loved learning those old songs, some of which I used to listen to on the radio with my mom.

The Impacts played a lot of Jimmy Reed and some Bo Diddley. Our set list included songs like "Road Runner," "Stay Just a Little Longer," "Twist and Shout," "Love Light," "I Got a Woman," "Johnny B. Goode,"

"Crawdad," "Who Do You Love," "Suzy Q," and "Dimples." A gig that stands out in my memory is one we played in Athens, Alabama. Jimmy Ray lived over there and had gotten us a job playing for the opening of the new Texaco filling station where we stood outside and played to entice people into stopping by to fill up. For our efforts, all we got was a tank of gas, and back then gas was going for only about thirty cents a gallon!

Van had a real wild side that came out once in a while. One night, we were in my car returning from a gig at the University of Alabama in Tuscaloosa, and Van was driving. In Birmingham, he pulled up alongside a guy who was gunning his motor. Van started to drag race with him. There were five of us in a two-door car pulling a trailer, and I asked, "What in the hell do you think you're doing?" After the second red light, he stopped, and I was relieved because I was sure he was going to jerk the rear end out of my car.

By this time my parents' hardware store had moved to the building right across the side street from the old one, and it had a nice, large basement. When we didn't have a place to practice, we practiced in the basement of the store and learned several songs down there after the store closed for the day. For a while my dad hired Buddy and Van to work for him at Christmas time, and we'd all work during the day and practice at night. The Impacts lasted most of high school.

I played in a band every chance I could or at pick-up gigs that sometimes got interesting. When I was thirteen or fourteen, I was hired for a gig at a club in Tennessee. I had been playing just a little while when the bartender told me the cops were about to raid the place. He said since I was underage, I couldn't be there, but the warning came a little too late—the police had already arrived. The cops made me leave, so I had to go sit in the car until the they left.

Another time, Boyce Dilbeck, a musician who also used to give me music lessons, wanted some time off from his gig at the Pine Villa, a pseudo-legal after-hours club in Triana, Alabama, so I filled in for him. While we were playing, about fifteen cops came in, turned the lights on, and made everybody sit still while they walked around and took pictures of what was on each table. I was seventeen, underage, and totally freaked out. The raid was a big-time deal, and I didn't want to explain to my folks about getting busted at an after-hours club. I sort of crouched down behind my amp, but they didn't mess with the band. Fortunately, the cops just took their pictures and escorted one or two of the guys who ran the club outside. The next thing I knew, the lights were back off and we were playing again.

Decatur High School was built in the '50s and was a long, two-story building with a lot of windows and no air-conditioning. By 1961, when I was a sophomore, not much had changed. It was still as uptight and straight-laced as it had always been. There was a dress code of sorts: guys couldn't wear t-shirts, and girls wore skirts or dresses. Of course, we didn't have cell phones or soft drink machines, and if you got caught chewing gum, you had to go to the principal's office. You didn't even want to think about a teacher walking in on you smoking in the bathroom. Sporting events were the main activities for students, but sometimes the school would loosen up and host a band for special occasions. It was at one of these school functions I heard a band that changed my life.

Charlie Campbell was a good friend of mine who played saxophone in the school band, and we used to hang out a lot playing guitars as often as we could. Charlie and I hadn't started playing in a band together yet, but we were huge music fans. I don't remember if Charlie was playing in a rock 'n' roll band then, but if not, he definitely wanted to. We heard about a band, the Mark V, that was going to play in the school cafeteria. Since we were sophomores, we had to sneak in to hear the band because it was a school function for seniors only. The Mark V was from Florence, Alabama, and its members were Jerry Carrigan, David Briggs, Norbert Putnam, Marlin Greene, Dan Havely, and Jerry Saylor. Everybody in the band was already playing on recording sessions and were the best musicians I'd ever heard. As it turned out, they were the cream of the crop and went on to make a name for themselves in the music business.

Jerry Carrigan, from Florence, is one of the best drummers ever. He was *the* drummer in Muscle Shoals, Alabama, at that time. He later moved to Nashville where he played on hits for Charlie Rich, Ray Stephens, George Jones, Tammy Wynette, Elvis, and Johnny Cash, to name a few. He toured with Elvis and toward the end of his career was on the road with John Denver for a long time career. Unfortunately, he developed carpal tunnel syndrome and had to retire several years ago.

David Briggs, from Killen, Alabama, played keyboards. After his session work in Muscle Shoals, he and Norbert Putnam opened Quad Studios in Nashville before he struck out on his own and opened his own studio, the House of David, in Nashville. He was the first-call piano player in Nashville for about twenty years or longer, and during the '70s, he toured with Elvis. I cracked up when I saw a movie about Elvis several years ago that had a character playing the part of David.

Norbert Putnam was from Muscle Shoals, Alabama, and the bass player in the band. After leaving the Shoals and moving to Nashville, he did a lot of session work with Elvis, Roy Orbison, Linda Ronstadt, and J. J. Cale, to name a few. He also produced albums for Joan Baez, Jimmy Buffett, John Hiatt, and a lot of others.

Marlin Greene, from Town Creek, Alabama, and played electric guitar. Marlin had a big role in Percy Sledge's career. He had a lot to do with the writing and recording of "When a Man Loves a Woman" and, along with Eddie Hinton, was co-writer of "Cover Me." He was a truly great guitar player and played sessions for Rick Hall. He was and is an extremely creative person and I wish he was still in the area but, last I heard, he was working for Bill Gates in Seattle.

The singer in the band, Jerry Saylor, was very gifted, but he passed away before his career could really take off. Jerry was older than I was, but we were friends in high school, and I always looked up to him. He was a popular guy who loved music. I spent a lot of time with him and he helped me get several gigs. Dan Havely, on trumpet, later found a career as the band director for Athens High School in Athens, Alabama.

After seeing this band, I felt totally inadequate. Those guys made a lot of musicians feel inadequate. People who heard them would say, "That's the best drummer/bass player/guitarist I ever heard. . . ." They made me want to work harder, and I knew I wanted to play in that band some day.

2

Mark V

In 1958, Tom Stafford and James Joiner opened a small recording studio, Spar Music, above the City Drug Store at the intersection of Tennessee and Seminary streets in downtown Florence, right next to the Alabama Theatre. Today the only thing left is a sign in the parking lot where it used to be. David Briggs, Dan Penn, Donnie Fritts, Rick Hall, Bill Blackburn, and Arthur Alexander were a few of the musicians who spent their time there writing and recording demos. The early studio equipment consisted of a mono tape recorder and a piano, and there were egg cartons stapled to the walls to baffle the sound. Less than a year later, Joiner sold his interest in the studio back to Stafford, and in 1959, Rick Hall and Billy Sherrill joined Spar Music.

When things didn't work out for him at Spar, Rick left to start his own studio in Muscle Shoals using the name they'd all come up with, Florence Alabama Music Enterprises, or in short, FAME. In 1961 Hall leased a tobacco warehouse on Wilson Dam Highway and cut "You'd Better Move On" with Arthur Alexander. Using the money he made from that recording, he moved his studio to its current location on East Avalon in Muscle Shoals. The first rhythm section at FAME included David Briggs, Norbert Putnam, and Jerry Carrigan, all members of the Mark V, Terry Thompson, and sometimes, me. Of course, you can't talk about anything musical in Muscle Shoals without mentioning Spooner Oldham and Peanut Montgomery. Peanut played bass or guitar on a lot of the sessions, and Spooner's career is legendary. He's written hit songs and played with just about anyone you can imagine—from Aretha Franklin and Bob Dylan to Janis Joplin, Neil Young, and the Drive-by-Truckers.

Around 1962, the Impacts were trying to find a place to do some recording, and Van Rudolph either knew someone or found a connection that could get us to Spar Music in Florence. We went there one night to record, and I clearly remember seeing Donnie Fritts with a set of

Slingerland Green Sparkle drums, along with Spooner, and, of course, Tom Stafford. It was the first time I'd ever been in a real studio, and it was shocking in certain ways. The egg cartons on the walls were makeshift, but then again, many things during this time were.

I'm not certain how it happened, but later in '63, Rick called me to come over to FAME and play guitar on some demos. I was excited about it because I'd be playing with members of the Mark V, the same group I'd seen at Decatur High School. I met Terry Thompson, another guitar player on the session, and he showed me a lot of things on the guitar. I remember he had this beautiful Gibson ES-345 with a gold-plated Bigsby tremolo. I freaked out over the guitar, and he told me how much better he liked it than the Fender Strat I was playing at the time. It wasn't too long before I went down to Forbes in Florence and bought a guitar exactly like it. Terry was such a hero to me that I even had the Bigsby installed.

Terry was an amazing person, and he was playing things very few other guitar players in blues and rock and roll were playing at that time. He's another one who passed away too soon. Terry's death was a big loss to the music community because he was a nice guy and gifted player. If you listen to the Jimmy Hughes intro to "Neighbor, Neighbor," you'll hear some really great playing. Terry came up with that; it was his lick.

I got to do a few sessions with Rick and play on the back side of some of the stuff. I rarely made it on the A side since I was the back-up in case Terry wasn't able to make it, but I was happy to have the experience. I got to meet Jimmy Hughes and had a chance to play on a Tommy Roe session one time, but I had other commitments the night Rick called me in '63. I wish I'd been there, though, because they cut a hit record.

Back then, I preferred playing live. I was proud of the fact I was in the studio and doing something not many people were getting to do, but I loved the freedom of playing live rather than being in the studio where everything was so controlled. Rick's a wonderful guy, but working for him is challenging. He challenged me to the point he drove me crazy, and I finally had to leave.

When I'd go play sessions for Rick, I'd start out playing guitar. If Terry was there, it would be the two of us on electric guitar. Quite frequently Rick would tell me to get the bass. He'd say, "Why don't you try the six string bass? Get that thing out of the closet there." Rick had a six string Danelectro bass I didn't want to have to play, and I'd think, "Aw, shit, I have to go get that thing." So I'd go into the closet and get the bass, but I couldn't play it very well. It wasn't any fun to begin with, and then Rick would want to double the bass…the tic tac sounds. I'd go out and try, then after about twenty minutes he'd say, "Why don't you try acoustic guitar on this?" I felt like that was even a further demotion for me from electric guitar. I don't think I even owned an acoustic at this time. Rick had a large, old acoustic Gibson, but I wasn't an acoustic player at all, so that would last about five minutes. It was awful. If you were an acoustic player back then, you knew you weren't going to be heard on the record with the country stuff we were doing. Finally, Rick would say, "Hey, why don't you come up here and help me listen?" I'd hang my head with shame and walk up the stairs to the control room. Sometimes I'd get to play on a song, but about half the time, I'd end up in the control room with Rick. I felt totally deflated and half embarrassed, but I guess that's how I got used to being in the control room.

I'll say this about Rick: when you get a record produced by him, it's his record. More than likely he told everybody in there what he wanted played and insisted that they do it his way. If it worked, it's his record, and if it didn't, he wasn't afraid to take the blame. Nobody doing records in Alabama has had more commercial successes than Rick, but I wanted to play live.

Charlie and I were friends with Jerry Saylor, and the first night I heard the Mark V play, Jerry introduced us to the rest of the band. I got to know them all better later on through my session work at FAME, and eventually they hired Charlie to play sax with the band. When guitar player Marlin Greene left, I was asked to join. When I first started playing with them, Jerry was the singer, and then when he left, Dan Penn joined the band. I was familiar with Dan because I'd seen him do demos over in the Shoals, and I may have even played on some he and Spooner Oldham were doing at the time.

Dan was a hero of Muscle Shoals and people wanted to be like him. He had confidence—and with good reason—he knew more than everybody else about what he was doing. When he was sixteen he wrote "Is a Bluebird Blue?," which was a hit for Conway Twitty. I asked him about it once and he said, "Yeah, it was so easy. I thought I had it made, but it was a long time before another hit came around." He had an incredible voice and could sound a lot like Ray Charles. It was great to hear a white guy singing like that, but nobody knew what to do with him as far as making a record. Even now he still has the most soulful voice I've ever heard and is my favorite singer. There's something special about Dan's writing and singing, and he's the nicest guy in the world.

By the time I joined the Mark V, Roger Hawkins had replaced Jerry Carrigan on drums. Jerry's dad was booking the band, and Jerry had gotten upset with him and quit. Roger was another incredible drummer. He was a member of the FAME rhythm section and later went on to be one of the founders of Muscle Shoals Sound Studios. He, along with David Hood, Jimmy Johnson, and Barry Beckett became known as The Swampers. During his career, he's co-produced albums with Paul Simon, Bob Seger, and others, and drummed on sessions with Aretha Franklin, Wilson Pickett, Cher, Rod Stewart, Eric Clapton, and a long list of others. He played a few shows with us, but then Jerry made up with his dad and wanted his gig back. Roger was out, and Jerry was back in.

When I'd played with the Impacts, we'd drive several hours to the gig, play until two in the morning, pack up and drive back home on two lane roads. The Mark V would play a gig, spend the night in a motel, and drive home the next day. It was the first time I'd ever done that with a band, and I thought we were pretty high class. We played a lot in Mississippi at officers' clubs on bases and at several of the universities in the Southeast. We played at the National Guard Armory on the river in Sheffield that eventually turned into the second Muscle Shoals Sound Studios. With Jerry's dad booking the band, we got some pretty good gigs. I played with the Mark V for about nine months, after graduation and during my first year at college, and I loved it.

My folks always wanted me to get an education so I'd have something to fall back on. In fall 1963, I went to Athens College in

Athens, Alabama, about fifteen miles from Decatur, and majored in music. I guess that was a stupid thing to do if I was trying to have something to fall back on. They didn't teach commercial music in those days; the program was designed to prepare you to be a church choir director or a band director for a high school. While both are good professions, I knew that wasn't where my future was. I did, however, learn theory and about various instruments and orchestration that helped later on when I was working in the studio. College was okay and I enjoyed it, but when summer of 1964 came, I got hooked up with the next band that was a major influence in my career, the band that became the 5 Men-Its.

3

5 Men-Its

It's kind of strange the way the 5 Men-Its came together. It was the summer of 1964, and I'd just finished my first year of college. Charlie was at his house rehearsing with a new band, and he called and said, "These guys are here from south Alabama and they need to get a band together for a gig in Panama City. They're looking for a horn player and a drummer." Charlie knew I had a set of drums I'd fooled around with over the years, and he told me to come over and bring them. I loved playing the drums, and watching Jerry Carrigan in the studio had really inspired me. Since Mark V didn't play every weekend, I thought, "Shoot, I'll just go and play drums." It was simple as that. I went over to Charlie's house, and it was there I first met Paul Hornsby, Fred Stiles, and Paul Ballenger. Hornsby played guitar, Paul Ballenger played keyboards and sang, and Fred was on bass. We set up in Charlie's living room to practice for the gig and learned as many songs as we could in a day. Then we packed our equipment in a couple of cars, and I rode with Charlie six hours down to Panama City.

Charlie and I thought the guys already had the gig, but when we got there, we discovered it was more of an audition at this club called the Old Dutch Inn. We went in, set up, and played, but we were exhausted. I guess we weren't very good because when we finished, they said they didn't need us...thank you very much.

Charlie was smooth and could talk almost anyone into doing about anything, so he started going up and down the strip looking for work. He found a club and told them about the band, how we'd just come off the road. We ended up getting a gig there for a few nights. It was just a little bar, and I think the main reason we got the job was because Charlie could play "Red Sails in the Sunset" on the saxophone, which happened to be the bar owner's favorite song. The rest of the band decided the gig was no good and didn't want to play there. After three or four nights, the bar didn't want us there either. We couldn't find anything else in

Panama City, so I found a ride back to Decatur and Charlie went on over to Pensacola.

He drove to the Casino—a place with a ballroom, a bar, games, and pinball machines—on the beach near the long pier. Charlie went in and met the manager and told him, "Yeah, we've got this band, we just got off the road with the Beach Boys," and was spinning this huge yarn about us. Finally the guy said, "That's good, you all come on down and let me hear the band." So Charlie got us a gig playing in the bar area of the Casino. He was kind of excited about it and told us we'd play in the bar a couple of nights during the week, then on Sundays we'd be in the big ballroom. We got together and rehearsed a couple of days, then drove back down to audition. After the manager heard us, we ended up with the gig. I think we played three or four nights a week, and we played anything from rock and roll to old standards.

We spent the summer just having fun, and it was one of the best summers of my life. I had no responsibility and was carefree in the sun and sand; we were just a bunch of guys were acting crazy and having a good time. We rented a house for the whole band down the road from the Casino, but it wasn't very big and didn't have a lot of amenities—like furniture. The house didn't have an air conditioner, and summer in Pensacola is pretty hot. Since we didn't have much to do and we didn't want to stay in the house all day, a lot of the time we'd hang out at the Casino or on the beach.

Fred had a good friend who was a pilot stationed at the naval base in Pensacola, and he came over to the Casino to see him one day. Now, Charlie had a way about him that if you had one thing, he had two just like it, only better. If you said you'd shot big game in Africa, he'd say he'd done it twice. Back then we didn't realize it, but in retrospect, it was probably his way of joking about stuff. Fred introduced Charlie to his pilot friend, and Fred's friend was talking about all the training he'd gone through. Charlie started telling him about how the Air Force wanted him and he'd been flying…he made up all kinds of bizarre things. Charlie had been flying before and maybe had his pilot's license, but he'd only just finished his freshman year of college and was a long way from being a pilot in the Air Force. He kept going on about the flying stuff, but I knew it wasn't true.

We decided to teach Charlie a lesson. We convinced this guy to take Charlie up and give him a rough ride to see how much he liked it. The band chipped in and bought an hour of flying for one person, and when Charlie said he wanted to go we said, "Okay, you can do it."

The pilot was going to fly over the Casino where we'd be hanging out, and he was going to do a lot of loops and upside-down flying with Charlie in the plane. Up they went, and the pilot gave Charlie a wild ride while the rest of us were on the ground going nuts laughing because this guy was really putting on a good show. Later, we asked him how Charlie did, and he said Charlie was about to turn green, as I imagine just about anyone who'd gone through that would have been. (Charlie loved flying, though, and had a career as a pilot for a commercial airline and later with Hooters, but it killed him in the end. On April 1, 1993, I turned on the television to pictures of a plane crash that had killed Alan Kulwicki. Only later did I learn that Charlie was the pilot of the plane and it was him, along with Kulwicki, that day in the smoking wreckage.)

After spending the summer in Pensacola, we went home and I returned to school at Athens College.

The 5 Men-Its had gained a bit of notoriety in Pensacola that first summer, and during the fall of '64 we thought the next step would be to put out a record. I'd worked on sessions for Rick and knew about FAME, so I called and made arrangements for us to record there. I'd played guitar on sessions before but wasn't that good or comfortable in the studio playing drums; still we had fun and made a record. One of the songs, "Growing Old before My Time," was one we played at the gigs. Since we'd all picked up nicknames in Pensacola and Paul Ballenger was known as The Old Man, that's what we called the song. The backside was an R&B song, "I Don't Love You No More." We had five hundred or a thousand 45s pressed up on our own and sold them at gigs. It got a little local air-play, but nothing ever happened with it to amount to anything.

During the first year of the 5 Men-Its, everyone was always trying to put each other down in a joking manner; it was one of those inside things. If you saw a picture of the band back then and you asked "Who doesn't belong in this picture?" it would have been Hornsby. We were all college age or ready for college, and very preppy looking, but

Hornsby had long, slicked back hair. So Hornsby first became the Greaseball, but that didn't have a very good ring to it so we named him The Dingleberry, which we shortened to The Berry in polite company. Finally The Berry became Paul's name. Because of his way of taking liberties with the truth, Charlie became The Lying Lip, which was eventually shortened to The Lip. Fred Stiles was named The Pooh because it just sounded good and fit him, and Paul Ballenger was The Old Man because he was the oldest member of the band. After a few other names, I became The Duck. It certainly was a providential name since my studio today is named Duck Tape Music and is near a wildlife refuge. Later, when Eddie joined the band, we called him High School Hinton and later, The Bear. He ended up as Eddie Bear.

I'd left the Mark V to take the 5 Men-Its gig because I wanted to do something different over the summer, but I couldn't get the Mark V job back during the winter because they'd hired Joe South to do some gigs with them. After that, I was kind of intimidated to go back anyway. It was rough having them run somebody like that in on you. Joe had a reputation as an excellent guitar player, and I'd heard some of the great things he'd done on records. I didn't feel I was worthy as a guitar player to go back and try to fill what had been Marlin Greene's-shoes-turned-into-my-shoes-turned-into-Joe South's-shoes. I was afraid to step back into them because they'd have been way too big for me after Joe. I think he played some with them for a while until Dan eventually put together the Pallbearers with Norbert Putnam, David Briggs, and Jerry Carrigan with Dan singing. It was an amazing band with just the four of them, and they didn't need a guitar player.

After the summer, we tried to keep the band together, but Paul Ballenger decided to quit at some point in the fall. Hornsby, Charlie, Fred, and I still wanted to play. We needed a singer, and Eddie Hinton was Fred's roommate at the University of Alabama. I'd heard a lot about Eddie, so we went to rehearse with him to see how that worked out. Eddie was already in a band called the Spooks (which had a good reputation), but he decided to join our band. For a while, Eddie played electric guitar and sang, Paul Hornsby had switched from guitar to keyboards, Fred Stiles played bass, Charlie was on sax, and I was on drums. I think we tried to make something happen during the off season by playing some fraternity parties, but that didn't work for a lot of reasons. Then, in the summer of '65, we returned to Pensacola with Eddie Hinton as the 5 Minutes.

In the fall of '65, Charlie and I left the band, and Bill Connell took my place. I made two hundred dollars a week at a club gig in Huntsville where I played seven nights a week (and went to school during the day). I worked with Chuck Rhoden and Butch Owens, the guitar player who eventually ended up playing bass with Jerry Lee Lewis. I stayed in the Huntsville gig for maybe eight months, but it was long enough. Losing the gig was the best thing that could have happened, but I was distraught at the time. It was a lot of money, and I hadn't ever made that much money before, but you don't get anywhere playing cover songs every night in the same place for the same people.

I went to see the 5 Minutes to get caught up because Connell was quitting the band in order to join the Allman Joys, and there was talk about my rejoining. Even though there were only four members in the band, they were still called the 5 Minutes, which I thought had to cause trouble once in a while. I found out they had a cardboard cut-out of Colonel Sanders they took around with them. When someone asked why there were only four members in the 5 Minutes, they'd get out the cut-out and set it on the stage, which I thought was amazingly creative. In summer 1966, Connell left and I rejoined the band.

4

The Minutes

We returned to Pensacola as the Minutes and played at a club called The Spanish Village that was down the road from the Casino and across the street from the beach. We had a cheap hotel room right on the other side of the bridge going into Pensacola where, as I remember, we stayed too long. The TV was terrible, and there were only the barest of necessities. Since it cost as much to rent the room for a week as it did for a couple of nights, a lot of the time we rented a room for the whole week and went back home rather than stay there when we weren't playing.

We often finished playing early, and sometimes after we were through, we'd go to a club in downtown Pensacola called The Tail of the Cock and listen to the band. Jerry Woodard owned the club and was the singer in the band; Barry Beckett was the piano player, and Ronnie Eads played the saxophone. That was the first time I met Barry and Ronnie. They were a cover band like we were, but they played to an older audience.

We'd go down and listen to them, but that's about all we did. I guess they might have heard of us since we had some notoriety playing at the beach, but theirs was a year round gig, so they probably met a lot of bands. Occasionally they'd let one of us sit in. If they did, it was because someone was tired and needed a break, not necessarily because it would bring anything new or different or creative to their band. Everyone in our band was still a kid at that time, maybe around twenty years old on average.

Eddie was fronting the Minutes, doing all the singing and playing guitar, and sometimes Hornsby played guitar and we'd have two guitars. We did Beatles' tunes, a lot of blues, some John Lee Hooker stuff...Eddie loved John Lee Hooker. The Spanish Village had a patio where bands geared to younger people played on the weekends, so we'd play inside for the people over twenty-one while the teenagers were out on the patio. That's where I first saw the Allman Joys with Duane and

Gregg Allman. Hornsby had heard them when they played in Birmingham, and he'd been telling me how good they were. Bill Connell, who'd taken my place for a while in the 5 Minutes, was from Tuscaloosa and friends with Hornsby and Fred Stiles, and he was playing drums with the band. I finally saw them for myself one night when the Minutes played at the Spanish Village. We were playing inside and the Allman Joys were outside on the patio. When our band took a break, I went out to hear them. They were just incredible.

They were playing very different music from what we were: English stuff, Yardbirds, and Beatles' music. We had a lot of songs in common, but they were playing the Blues Magoos, "We Ain't Got Nothin' Yet" and "Give Me Some Lovin'." It was great. Duane had a Vox distortion booster that was maybe six or eight inches long, a couple of inches wide and a quarter of an inch deep; a little metal thing with an off and on switch he had mounted on a Telecaster with some clamps like we used to sell in the hardware store. I don't remember how the clamps were normally used, but I know it was something totally different from how Duane was using them. I'd never seen anything before like that distortion booster. Most people would just plug into the amp, but Duane wanted it where he could hit it with his little finger to go into that extreme overdrive. It was a cool sound. He'd just hit it and work the volume control, and it would go into complete overdrive on the front end of the amp. It sounded as if he were playing backwards. It looked cool, and you've gotta say something about anything that looks that cool and sounds so good; plus, Duane looked incredible playing it, which is not in any way to take away from his playing. He was just a cool guy in general, and he used amazing gear. I've never seen another guitar player that good.

Gregg was one of the best singers I'd ever heard. At eighteen he was close to being in the same league as Dan Penn, just amazing. He was playing a Vox keyboard with the black and white keys reversed, which was popular with a lot of the English bands. I thought it was a pretty cool thing to be playing, especially considering the band played a lot of English songs. The Allman Joys consisted of Duane and Gregg, Bob Keller on bass and singing background, and Bill Connell on drums. They were as tight and exciting and different a group as I'd heard. They left a deep impression on me, and I hoped one day we'd get a chance to play together. The timing wasn't right at that moment, but eventually it all worked out.

The next day I got to meet Gregg and Duane when they came over to our hotel room for a visit. They were both incredibly thin, and I'd never seen any guys with beautiful shoulder length blond hair like that before. Gregg, of course, is a natural blond, and Duane's hair was kind of a reddish blond. I almost started laughing, not out of derision, but amazement because it was Pensacola in the mid-'60s! It was almost a cardinal sin to go around with long hair at the time, and I couldn't believe they hadn't gotten killed. I was very concerned about it because Pensacola is a conservative military town and sometimes sailors didn't like long hair.

For a while the Minutes was managed by Papa Don Schroeder, a disc jockey in Pensacola who promoted dances and bands. While he was managing the band, we played various places in the area. Papa Don went on to produce some great records with the Muscle Shoals guys. He cut the hit song, "I'm Your Puppet," written by Dan Penn and Spooner Oldham and recorded by James and Bobby Purify, two guys from Pensacola, and he brought Barry Beckett to Muscle Shoals for the first time.

After we spent the summer with Eddie in Pensacola, we wanted to go on playing, but Fred left the band because he wanted to go back to school. So it was just Eddie, Paul Hornsby, and me and of course, after Fred left the band, we had to have a bass player. I had a couple of lifelong friends, Jimmy and Price Mitchell, brothers who played the clubs in Huntsville a lot, and frequently I'd fill in for someone in their band who couldn't make it or just didn't show up. Whatever the reason, they'd call me and I'd fill in. I'd heard their bass player, and although I'm not proud to admit it, we stole their bass player, Mabron McKinney. Mabron wasn't used to playing the style music we were doing because he'd been playing a lot of country music over in the Huntsville clubs. We didn't play any country songs, but he was a talented musician who could adapt very quickly. He joined the band and became known as the Wolf because of his beard and hair.

We got hooked up with 1-Nighters booking agency and hit the road for six or eight months. We'd only played in Pensacola for summer gigs, but when we went on the road, it was a whole different trip. The first gig we had was in Louisville, and I'd never been that far north before. The first thing they did when we got there was insist we all have matching blazers. We said, "We don't have matching blazers." They told us, "Well, you'd better be getting them if you want to play here." I mean, we were booked there and counting on the money, so we had to get matching blazers or matching coats of some sorts. The thing was, they wanted us to dress up, but the place was a dive. For $150 a week we not only had to play six nights a week, but we had to play a jam session on Sunday too. So, for thirty dollars a night, we'd play about eight p.m. to one a.m. or later. We played the popular songs in front of audiences younger than we were used to, but I'll tell you, playing like that will get a band tight if it doesn't burn out first. I don't know if we even made it through the whole week.

I remember playing in Burlington, Iowa, in the middle of winter, which was, I believe, the worst place I'd ever played. Burlington's claim to fame was being the closest "wet" city to Illinois, so people from Illinois would come to Iowa to drink. It was cold and snowing and, of course, the club was another dive. They told us, "Now if any blacks come in here, you play some country and western music where they'll leave." That really rubbed us wrong because most of the stuff we played was black music. It was everyone's influences; it was what we were about. The first night we kind of tried to do what we'd been told, and when a few black people walked in, the band started playing some country song. Finally we looked at each other and said, "We can't do this." We started playing our regular stuff and the club fired us. We had a good band, but the club wasn't going to encourage blacks to come into the place. They were going to do everything they could legally do to run them out, and we knew it wasn't right. Blacks were the people we wanted to play for; they appreciated what we were doing more than a bunch of rednecks in Iowa.

After that gig and a few more like it, Eddie decided he wanted to quit the band and go to Muscle Shoals to write songs and play sessions. Of course, we didn't want that to happen, and it was kind of sad. It wasn't like we were mad at him; we were just ticked off because he was leaving and because we were going to miss him. Where would we find someone else who could play guitar and sing like Eddie? The rest of us ended up going back to Decatur to my parents' house and started working on putting another band together.

I knew for certain by then I was going to stick with music: the bug had bitten and it wasn't going to let loose. Sure, I had dreams of being hugely successful and making enough money to be able to do what I wanted, but the reality was we were making enough money to just get by without getting ahead at all. However, regardless of the money, or lack thereof, I was a musician, and I was going to stay with it.

It wasn't too long after I first met Gregg and Duane that Eddie decided to leave. Since we were left looking for a guitar player and a singer, we contacted them hoping maybe they'd be available and if not, they might know someone who'd be good. As it turned out, they weren't available, but they recommended Pete Carr, a good guitar player. He was only about fifteen years old. We were all young, but Pete was especially young. He came over and played great. We were going to use him, but we had to find a singer. Pete brought Don Bailey with him, and Don sang, but really wasn't physically able to do it with the band. I think he had just one lung, and you can imagine what a disadvantage that would be for a singer.

We played a gig with Don in a gymnasium somewhere in south Alabama for some young people at a prom and some of them seemed to like us, but in general we were getting mixed reviews from the audience. Still, it was going along pretty well, and we were going for this big climactic song to end the first set when Don got down on his knees, then he kept getting lower until he was almost lying on the stage. I was thinking, "Man, this guy is getting into it. He's really putting on a show. Maybe if the music isn't doing it for the crowd, the showmanship will get them." Unfortunately, Don was really ill at the time because he couldn't breathe. We didn't realize he was sick until the set was over and we were taking our bows and people had to help him off the stage. I don't believe he was able to do the second set. It was sad, and I felt terrible about it. Hornsby sang a little bit, so we finished the night with him and a Ventures instrumental. We could tell this wasn't a band that was going to happen until we found someone to replace Eddie.

It was a bleak time without Eddie, and after we'd heard Duane and Gregg, we knew we'd never be happy until we found someone like them. In the meantime, we stayed in touch, and while our band was breaking up again, they lost their bass player and drummer. We called and said, "This kind of works out. Why don't you all come up here and let's see what happens." It was perfect. We needed a singer and guitar player, and Duane played guitar and Gregg sang, played guitar and the organ, so the two of them came up to Decatur to rehearse in my parents' garage. That was the start of the band eventually known as the HourGlass.

5

The HourGlass

My folks lived up the street from where I'm living now, and we all gathered at their house and set up in the garage for a week of rehearsal. When we were playing, I was sitting in a corner with my back to the rest of the house facing towards the entrance of the garage. Paul and Gregg were sort of in front of me and to my left with Duane next to them, and the Wolf to my right. We were in a semi-circle so we could all see each other. Paul had his cut-down A-100 Hammond organ and Leslie speaker, and we were using one of our guitar amps for a public address system. It was loud! The house is located near the Wheeler Wildlife Refuge, and there weren't a lot of neighbors around at that time, but we managed to annoy most of them while we were practicing. I'd bought a tape recorder at Mock's Electronics in Decatur, and it was a nice little ¼ track machine. I didn't know anything about tape at the time other than some sounded better than others, so I picked out some good tape to use and recorded most of the rehearsals. I had the recorder sitting behind me so I could turn it on and off as we went through the songs.

The band clicked right from the beginning and, after only a few minutes of rehearsal, we knew it was going to be good—it just felt right. I can't remember what all we played at first, but they were songs everybody already knew and had been playing. We'd already learned a lot of the ones the Allman Joys did because we were fans of theirs, and they knew some of the songs we played. We'd count off the song and play it and if there was a problem, we'd stop and start over. We'd get one worked up and then move on to the next song. Back then, bands had to play at least three or four hours a night, sometimes longer, and we didn't want to have to start repeating songs in the second set, so we learned as many as we could to have at least two or three hours of material.

I'd played "Dimples" in the Impacts, and then in the Minutes we refined the arrangement. Paul was an excellent guitar player who ended up playing keyboards by default, and he and Eddie came up with a guitar riff that Duane and Paul played in the HourGlass. After the HourGlass, Duane and Dickey Betts played the same twin guitar parts to "Dimples" with the Allman Brothers Band.

The Minutes had been playing mostly blues and R&B, while Gregg and Duane had been playing music mainly from English bands like the Who and the Yardbirds. Duane was really influenced by Jeff Beck, Peter Green, and Clapton, who had all played in the Yardbirds. With the HourGlass we played the Blues Magoos "We Ain't Got Nothin' Yet" and a lot of those kinds of songs just because we liked them. I liked the Allman Joys version of the songs better than the records. I'd heard all those records but hadn't cared for them until I heard their version. The Allman Joys without a record deal was much better than the bands they were covering who had deals, and it seemed wrong.

We were all good players, but the band was even more special with Gregg's singing and Duane's playing. We did guitar rock and a lot of rhythm and blues, and for that type music I can't imagine a better or more tasteful guitar player than Duane. He would play to the song and, as great a soloist as he was, he never minded playing a less significant part if that's what fit. Gregg just absorbed the blues, and it seemed extremely natural and real to him. To play with musicians that good had always been my dream, and when we all played together, it was nothing but joy for me. Wolf was an extremely good bass player and we would "lock" in together. Duane and Gregg were just flat out exciting, and Paul always played great and had his parts down pat. I can't say enough good things about the band.

Eventually we acquired a following of people who came to the rehearsals, much to the chagrin of some of the homeowners in the neighborhood. A lot of our friends and people who'd heard about the band started showing up to listen. We'd raise the garage door and there'd be anywhere from five to fifteen people, sometimes more, outside the garage listening to our essentially private rehearsal. Some of the local musicians came by: my wife Ann's brothers, Byron and Randy Gray, were there, as were Mike Acker and Tommy Compton, to name a few.

I don't remember if Buddy Thornton was there or not, but I'm sure if he was in town, he would have dropped by. He may have been off at school. Buddy was real straight at that time, but we jerked him back from his day job later on and took him to Macon. He did some engineering at Capricorn and often had the task of repairing the equipment. He later went on the road with the Brothers and did front of house mixing, then on to Miami to work for Bill Szymczyk before going to work for the government in a job so secret he could never tell anyone. He recently retired with a top level security clearance.

At first we thought about keeping the name "Allman Joys," but Duane and Gregg didn't want to use the name. We had difficulty coming up with one and finally ended up with Allman-Act, a play on the word "almanac," a pretty dumb name that seemed good at the time. Bands tend to get a little crazy when trying to pick out a name, and that was the least offensive one we could think of.

Gregg and Duane had played as far North as New York and as far west as St. Louis. Pepe's a Go Go in St. Louis loved the Allman Joys, so Duane called the club. Pepe's wanted us but the place was booked, so we headed to St. Louis, played at a club right across the street for a few nights, and then moved across the street to Pepe's.

As I said, the band cooked from the start. We played both blues and the psychedelic stuff, getting crazy at times. Every once in a while Duane would throw his guitar over his shoulder, and one night at Pepe's, we thought we were The Who or something and were playing "Tobacco Road" to end the set. It could have ended our career. We'd really gotten into the vibe of the song and had a lot of feedback going. Gregg had an Echoplex on the p.a., and he used to set it until it started feeding back and going nuts, then he'd keep adding to it. He'd holler or make some additional noise, and it would keep repeating with an awful, psychedelic sound. We did what we thought was our best version of the song, then, after we finished, we were walking toward the bar when a guy who was either the club owner or owned some other club asked, "What's the name of that song?" Duane told him and he said, "Don't ever play it again." And from looking at this guy, I'd say it's probably a good thing we never played the song again in that particular club because it could well have ended in disaster.

We played in an area called Gaslight Square and didn't get nearly as good a response as we'd hoped for playing in St. Louis, but there were a lot of tourists who came to see us. The whole place fell victim to urban blight in the '70s and was eventually demolished, but back then there was just club after club. There'd be a band next door and another one up the street, and it reminded me of New Orleans where there was club after club with go-go dancers and a band sitting up high. It was at one of those clubs I first met Bonnie Lynn, later known as Bonnie Bramlett. Gigging in those clubs was a means to an end; it certainly wasn't a lot of money, but we made enough to get by.

Duane and Gregg were staying in a room over the club where we were playing and wanted to use my tape recorder. I had a bunch of tapes the band had recorded in my folks' garage while we were first rehearsing and some from a few of the live gigs we'd done at Pepe's. While I was gone somewhere, the tapes got stolen from their room along with my tape machine and my '60 Precision bass we carried with us as a backup for Mabron. The tapes were the earliest recordings of the band and the songs were all cover tunes, but they were good and they were gone. I was pretty upset, and for about thirty years, I thought those were the only recordings I'd had of the early band; however, a few years ago, when our garage was being cleaned out, I found some that had been put in a trunk and stored in the back corner of the building.

One of the defining moments for the band came about when Mabron's wife flew into St. Louis and he went to pick her up. Back then there weren't many people with long hair or a full beard like Mabron had, and he ran into a long-haired group at the airport, the Nitty Gritty Dirt Band, who was playing in town at Kiel Auditorium. Everybody said, "Hey Bro', how ya doin'?" and started talking. He also met their manager, Bill McEuen, who also managed the Sunshine Company and later, Steve Martin. Mabron invited him drop by to hear us when the Dirt Band finished playing at the auditorium, and he did. He kind of freaked out over our band and called Los Angeles right then to say he'd found the next Rolling Stones or whatever.

He told us, "You all gotta go to California." It was scary because I'd never been anywhere close to California. About the farthest west I'd been was Memphis. I wanted to do it and *didn't* want to at the same time.

It was one of those things where you were scared but knew if we were gonna get anywhere with the band, we had to go.

Bill asked us to send him some demos, but the band was so new we hadn't done any recording other than the live stuff we'd done in my folks' garage and Pepe's in St. Louis, so we decided to go to Boutwell Studio in Birmingham and cut a demo tape to send out to California before we went. We cut three songs written by Gregg, "Whacha Gonna Do," "Changin' of the Guard," and "Richmond." Eddie was working at Boutwell at the time, so it seemed like a good place to go, and Ed Boutwell engineered the session. It was the first time I'd ever recorded anything you could overdub on. Ed had modified this stereo machine so it enabled you to listen to what you'd recorded and then add something on the other track. That was an eye-opening experience. Ed later became famous for the "rolling punch." If you're listening to something on your multi-track machine and have the proper track armed, you can listen all the way up to when you punch the record button and the track will go into record. It's something we take for granted today.

We had a lot of fun making the recordings, but it sounded a lot better when we were in there playing than it did when we listened back. It didn't matter—we were excited about getting to record and we felt there was no limit to the potential of the band. Looking back, the demos weren't very good, and they didn't really represent the band. The songs Gregg was writing at the time were more country and folk, and we hadn't quite figured out how to adapt them to the style of music we were playing. However, we sent the tape to Bill anyway. After hearing the demos, I'm surprised McEuen still wanted us to come out there, but he did. Eventually we got it together to go.

None of us had been to California before. We convened again at my parents' house in Decatur and headed out. I was driving my car, and Gregg and Duane, who by this time had picked up the nicknames "Coyote" and "Dog" respectively, were in a van with the equipment. Initially we called Gregg "Harlow" because his long blond hair seemed reminiscent of Jean Harlow, but the name never caught on. We tried it for a while and you know how it is with nicknames: you try them on for a while and if they don't sound right or you get tired of them, you go to something better. The idea was to pick a name that needles the person a little bit, and if what you picked wasn't doing it, you had to find something else. We all had different names at various times before the right one stuck, except for me. I didn't have any nicknames other than "Duck."

We didn't have any gigs along the way, so we drove straight through to California, and everything went along without too much hassle until we got to Texas. We pulled into a gas station where some of the locals saw us. We all had long hair, but Gregg and Duane had shoulder-length hair. A guy came out with a baseball bat and threatened us, and it was obvious that he and his friends were planning to "beat our ass." We got back in the car and got the hell out of there as fast as we could. I figured they'd kill us and no one would ever hear of us again. I didn't like Texas for a long time because of that incident.

We were actually afraid to pull in to buy gasoline after that because people hated long hair so much. They either thought you were un-American or they called you every ugly name for a homosexual they could think of. After what happened in Texas, when we needed gas, we'd have to get the least freaky looking of us—either me or Paul—to drive that particular car to the pump to gas it up. It was uncomfortable, and we didn't know what we were going to meet up with after Texas, but that's the only place we met with any "armed" resistance.

When we first got to California, we were going directly to meet with Bill McEuen, so we stopped at a little cheap motel outside of Los Angeles to let everyone get cleaned up. We'd been on the road for a couple of days without stopping anywhere except to get gas and something to eat, so we were a little road rank. We checked into the room long enough for everyone to take a shower. With our long hair, we had to have crème rinse to keep it looking good; however, back then, it didn't come together with the shampoo like it does today and had to be mixed in a glass with water. Gregg showered before me and left the glass he'd used for mixing the crème rinse sitting in the shower, but I didn't see it when I got in, and I kicked it. The glass broke and cut my right foot really bad. There was blood everywhere, and when we left the place, it looked like someone had been slaughtered in the bathtub. We kept the cut together with Band-aids, wrapped my foot in a towel, then went on into L.A to meet Bill. His first job as our manager was to get me to a clinic to have my foot sewn up.

I owned several sets of drums over the course of the time we were in California, but when we first got there, I was playing a set of Ludwig Ringo drums with an 18-inch bass drum and large 13- and 16-inch toms, which is a pretty ridiculous-looking set with a tiny bass drum and normal size toms. The more I played them, the more I realized the bass drum couldn't be heard since for the most part, drums weren't mic'd—certainly not the way they are now for a p.a. After that, I had a Leedy set that was stolen from the parking lot of the apartment complex where we lived at the time. Next, I had a Rogers set for a short period of time. They were nice, red and black checked, and I ordered the set from a Rogers catalog. I remember looking back through the catalog after I got them and discovered they were the Dave Clark signature model. I thought, "Oh Lord, what have I done?" No offense, but Dave Clark of the Dave Clark Five was not my favorite drummer, and the thought that someone might think I was aspiring to be like him made me want to get rid of that set as soon as I could. All I could think of was how to get rid of them, and I ended up swapping them for another set of Ludwigs that I played until I came back from California. It was a mod orange set with a 22-inch bass drum and 13- and 16-inch toms. I always preferred a Ludwig super-sensitive snare with the long snares on the bottom, mainly because of Roger Hawkins. That's what he used, and it always sounded wonderful. I still have one that I use in my studio today.

Duane was playing a Telly with a Strat neck, and he and Gregg both had Super Beetle Vox amps. I had an old Fender Bassman amp with four 10-inch speakers that Duane really liked, so we took it out to California with us. As loud as we were playing at that time, the speakers in the amp were not quite loud enough, so we put JBL speakers in it. I kept that amp until my friend, Butch Owens, borrowed it and it was stolen. He later replaced it with another old Bassman amp with the original speakers. It's a good amp he got from Joe Walk, and I still have it today. Paul played an A-100 organ with a Leslie cut down to be portable. It wasn't a B-3, but it was close to it, and we had a Wurlitzer piano that Gregg played. Later, when Pete Carr joined the band, he played a Jazz bass with a custom amp that had belonged to Mike Acker, who lived in Decatur.

We had an acoustic/electric guitar and a Fender 12-string Gregg would play sometimes. Gregg didn't play guitar very often, but he wrote a lot of songs on one. He became friends with Jackson Browne when we were in California and Gregg learned a lot from him; I think they learned from each other. Gregg went through a folk phase with his writing, but his style changed with different instruments.

I've still got the Wurlitzer from the band, and it has a story that came with it. Several of us went to Wallach's Music Center on the corner of Hollywood and Vine in Los Angeles. Wallach's was a well known music store that sold equipment and records and was the first to have a demo room. We bought a lot of our instruments there while we were in California. When we played live, Gregg and Paul set up close together so they could swap between the Wurlitzer and B-3 when they needed to, but Paul picked out this particular Wurlitzer to play since he was most concerned with the action on the keyboard. The salesman showed us how to hook it up to an amp, which was essential, because on stage you couldn't hear it off the little speaker that came in it. Once we figured it out, it sounded great. The Wurlitzer is still my favorite keyboard.

Duane had borrowed a '59 Les Paul Goldtop from my friend, Tommy Compton, who still lives in Decatur, and he didn't want to give it back to Tommy. And Tommy definitely wanted it back. Eventually Gregg traded the Wurlitzer for the guitar. The guitar was worth more than the piano, but Tommy had a use for it and was trying to keep Duane from getting busted because Tommy's dad was ready to go after him to get the guitar back. So, the piano was sent back to Decatur, and Duane kept the guitar. Of course, that guitar would be worth a fortune now, certainly more than the piano is worth. Tommy eventually sold the piano to Henry Lowery, who sold it to Eddie Hinton, then, after Eddie died in '95, his mother sent the piano back to Henry, and I bought it back from him a year or so later to use in my studio.

6

California

The Nitty Gritty Dirt Band had rented a nice big house in the Hollywood Hills known as the Dirt House, but they had to give up the house two or three weeks after we arrived. Some of the band members had already moved out, but some of them were still living there. When we got to town, they told us some bedrooms on the lower level weren't being used and invited us to stay there and hang with them. It was a beautiful three story house with bedrooms everywhere and a big living room upstairs where they let us set up our equipment to rehearse and learn some new stuff. We heard the first Cream album in that period, and it was pretty amazing. As soon as we got the album, we freaked out and listened to it over and over. It was a huge influence on our music.

Because my right foot was still healing, I had to play the bass drum left footed when we rehearsed and until the accident, I didn't realize my feet are the only ambidextrous parts of my body. It was slow going, but after a while, my foot started to get better and I could play bass drum again with my right foot.

Everyone said the house was haunted and I believed it. The house had a vibe, especially in the downstairs bedrooms. Of course, that's the first thing the guys in the Dirt Band told us, so that's what I believed. When they told us to be careful because we might see something in the middle of the night, sure enough, I'd wake up and see a figure in the room. Who can say whether or not I really saw something? It fit my way of thinking, and I thought I heard very odd noises at all hours of the night. We weren't there long enough to get familiar with the house, maybe just a couple of weeks until we moved into an apartment. I really hated to move because it was a beautiful place.

We moved into two apartments at the Mikado on Cahuenga Boulevard right across the street from the big wooden Hollywood sign that is in all the movies. In fact, if you crossed a four lane road and walked up a steep hill, you'd be at the sign. It wasn't too far from the

Hollywood Bowl, and sometimes we could hear music from there at night. Each apartment was extremely small. When you walked in the front door you were in the living room or the not-so-great room (or whatever you call it) that was barely partitioned off from the kitchen. You could sit on the couch and see the stove and refrigerator. There was a door to the single bedroom, and off the bedroom was the lone bathroom.

Originally, Gregg and Duane shared an apartment, and Paul, Mabron, and I were in one, so we were a little more crowded. There were only two beds in the bedroom, and we took turns sleeping on the couch in the living room. It was crowded, and with three guys living in the same apartment it could get a little edgy at times. After a few weeks, we could spread out more when we each got our own place at the complex. Other than the Dirt Band and McEuen, we didn't know a soul out there, but we were intoxicated just being in California and meeting all new people. We were going to be stars, so it was all wonderful.

California was strange but enjoyable, and we kind of fit in after a while even though everyone kidded us about our Southern accents. It seemed like there was a more caring spirit about each other out there than in the South, which was still in the middle of the civil rights movement. Los Angeles was wild. People hitchhiked everywhere, especially downtown if they wanted to go a few blocks, and we didn't see that where we were from. Life on the street was peace, love, flowers-in-your-hair type stuff all up and down the Sunset Strip.

When I first arrived in California, I wasn't doing any drugs. I took speed when I was in school, but that was because I was overweight and the doctors prescribed amphetamines to curb my appetite. I wasn't totally ignorant of what drugs would do, but pot was a whole different trip. Gregg and Duane fell right into it and so did Mabron, which kind of left Paul and me. We were both from the Deep South where people just didn't do drugs. Eventually, I tried marijuana. My first experience with it was both eye-opening and a little scary, but I liked it a lot. After that it was no big deal, but by that time most of the other guys had moved on to acid.

I was interested in acid, but I never did want to try it. Even though a lot of people were doing it, you don't need to be working when you're on acid because it changes things. One day I was talking with one of the background singers on the first HourGlass album and I asked her what she thought about people dropping acid. She told me she thought people don't have as much "soulfulness to their playing" after they do it. I don't know if that's a valid observation, but it was a good enough reason for me. I didn't think acid was safe; I was afraid I'd go to a place and never get back. As I've grown older, I've seen people who ended up in one of those places and *didn't* ever make it back. It was the right choice for me.

When we first met Bill, the Dirt Band had a top ten record, "Buy for Me the Rain," with Liberty Records. He also had another band he managed called the Sunshine Company that eventually had a top-twenty national record with Liberty, so I guess that's where his connections were. But Liberty wasn't nearly as excited about us as Bill had led us to believe, and it took some doing for him to get us on the label. I don't think the demos we sent had impressed the record company, but Bill had ties with Dallas Smith, producer of the Dirt Band, Sunshine Company, and Bobby Vee, and between Bill and Dallas, they put together a deal and twisted some arms to get us signed. I honestly believe Liberty didn't want the band—they wanted Gregg. While Bill was busy working on the deal, there was nothing to do and no place to rehearse, so we just sat around the apartment. It seemed like it took a long time, but in retrospect it was just a few weeks from when we got there until we signed with Liberty.

The record company didn't want us using the name Allman Joys or Allman-Act or any of the ones we'd used before, so the five of us gathered around a table and tried to think of a name for the band. It got goofy. Someone said HourGlass and I said, "That's not too bad" and someone else said, "No, that sucks too," so we kept looking for a name. When no one came up with anything we liked any better, HourGlass became the name by default.

One of the conditions of the deal was we had to do two songs: "Silently," which we didn't like and definitely didn't want to do, and a song called "Bells," which we just really, really, *really* didn't want to do. It was almost at gunpoint that we finally agreed to record it. Evidently, some deal was cast among the various people involved in getting us signed, so there was no way we could get around doing either of these songs. Believe me, we tried.

Before we recorded "Bells," we rehearsed it and had been kidding Gregg about the very dramatic way he sang the word "bells." When he was in the studio recording his vocals, the rest of us were standing in the control room making faces and doing everything we could to distract him, and Gregg kept cracking up. Finally, they threw us out of the control room and told us to leave, so we left. Later, Duane went in to overdub, and after a while working on the song wasn't funny to him any longer, and he copped a real attitude. He didn't want to have anything to do with the song. You can only have someone embarrassing you for so long before you get mad, and Duane's tolerance for bullshit was a little lower than the rest of ours. "Bells" wasn't a hit song and, to this day, I don't know why Liberty made us record it. Maybe someone won a bet.

When we began to work on our first album, the record company wanted to select the songs we recorded. The only writer in the band, at least the only one who attempted to write at that time, was Gregg. A lot of his songs were good, but they were more folk sounding when he played them on the guitar, and we really had a problem, or at least I did, trying to make them work in the context of our playing. On the first album, Gregg had a grand total of one original song, "Gotta Get Away." Liberty gave us a box of demos and told us to select songs for the album from those. There were a few good ones in there, including a couple of Gerry Goffin and Carole King songs we ended up recording, but overall, we weren't happy with what they gave us to work with and wouldn't have chosen any of them except under duress. So, the first problem we had with Liberty was that they didn't like any of our material and didn't know what to do with us.

The next problem was they didn't even want the band to play on the record. They wanted to get studio musicians and thought maybe they'd let Duane play some guitar stuff and then overdub it with a studio player, or let him play some rhythm, with Gregg in there singing, but the rest of us weren't included. The record company wanted to make it Gregg with his backup band, and that wasn't our idea at all. That was kind of a deal breaker for us, and we told them no, if that's the way it was going to be, we weren't doing it. If we couldn't even play on the record, it wasn't going to happen. We were good enough to play because most of us had already recorded with our bands. I'd done sessions off and on for a long time, so it just didn't make sense to us as a band to have other musicians play on our album. We really had to fight them over that.

The story is, if Patty Hearst had been on Liberty, they'd have never found her. I think by the time we got there, Liberty was in its declining years and was used to having nice pop hits. They had Johnny Rivers, Gary Lewis, and other pop acts, and the label wanted to make us into a band like Gary Puckett and the Union Gap. They wanted to turn Gregg into a Gary Puckett. We'd seen them on television, and eventually did some shows with them, but they were the polar opposite from where we were musically.

As a producer, Dallas was indifferent to us, and we returned the sentiment. It was the first time we'd recorded with an official record company producer who answered to the record company. Dallas was employed by Liberty and had his office at the record company, but in the pecking order of things, we were far below him. We were used to producers back home like Rick or Eddie, who contributed ideas, wanted to work with us, and wanted to make us better. Dallas didn't work like that. He was a producer used to working with the best session musicians in Los Angeles and getting a singer in with songs that had been pitched by other writers for that particular singer. He'd pick out the songs he liked and thought would fit the artist, then go in and record them. It was a cut-and-dry way of doing things.

We started out trying to do what was asked of us, but it seemed Dallas kept adding more and more things we had to get over. For instance, the song "Heartbeat" stuck in our craw. I'm not saying it was a bad song, but it certainly wasn't a song for us. By the time it was done, it had horns and female background singers—and the band was incidental. Since Gregg's vocal was the only thing the record company was interested in, Dallas worked it around to where the band was essentially backing up Gregg on the song. That's not the way we thought it should be. Everyone was part of our band. Gregg was the singer, but Duane, with his amazing solos and playing, was just as important a part of the act as Gregg. What they tried to makes us wasn't who we were.

To be honest, the whole recording process was a shock. Gregg and Duane had recorded in Nashville with John D. Loudermilk, and I'd worked with Rick and Eddie in Muscle Shoals, and we learned how things worked in our area. When we went to Los Angeles, it was totally different, and it seemed like they were working on a whole different clock. In the South we'd go in and work on a song and try different things until something just clicked, and you'd say, "Yes! This is it! This feels good. This is the right groove for the song. Now we're hitting on it!" It was different with Dallas. We had to get a certain number of songs in a certain amount of time in the studio, and that's just how it had to be. It went against what we could do, and it just didn't work.

Dallas added an additional keyboard, Mike Melvoin, who played on most of the first album and when he couldn't make it, a guy named Mac Rebennack came in to play. It was twenty years later when Dr. John was living in Macon and we were friends before I learned he was the Mac who'd played on the record. Back then, he was just another fellow with a funny accent. Both of them, Mike and Mac, were great guys. Mac was real "greasy," and Mike was more of a straight ahead player.

We also had a good horn section for the album, and the horns were cut live. Armin Steiner was the engineer and saving grace of the sessions. He made us sound good. If it hadn't been for him, recording would have been much harder. The studio was Sound Recorders, and it had a great West Coast drum sound. It wasn't my favorite bass drum sound, but Hal Blaine was a wonderful musician. I got to play his bass drum on our album, which was good because I was still learning to tune mine and they kept rushing us. They kept telling us to hurry because the cartage people might be there any minute to pick up the equipment.

It didn't take all that long to record *The HourGlass*. We had the songs, and we'd go in and cut two or three one day and two or three the next. There was very little of Duane's guitar on the album. It's not that Duane didn't want to play a solo, but the songs they wanted us to do and the way they wanted us to play them didn't leave much room for him. Duane showed up a little loaded to record a couple of times, and he didn't hang around the studio like we were used to doing. We didn't mind hanging around when we were excited about our record and trying to see what we could add to it, but recording there was a "get in and get out" situation that didn't sit well with Duane. Everyone else was just happy to have a record deal, but he had a larger vision. I guess the rest of us were just holding on, hoping things would get better.

During this time, Armin had kind of taken me under his wing and said I might be able to play sessions out there. He wanted to know if I could read music, and I told him I could because I *thought* I could. I knew I wasn't up to what a regular session guy could do, but I thought if they'd try me on some demos, I could work my way up and learn what I needed to know. The next thing I knew, they called me for a session with Bobby Vee because the regular drummer wasn't available. Of course, it was Dallas Smith producing. Jimmy Webb was the arranger and probably the writer of the songs we were doing that day, and everything was written out. I faked my way through most of the stuff, but there was a song with a lot of accents and kicks here and there and different parts he wanted accented, and there was no way I could read it. This was a three-hour session, and I had to get it right then. Everyone in there was a first call player except me. I got through the session, but I probably went from a "maybe call" to a "never call." If I'd been allowed to listen to the demos first, I'd have been okay, but without hearing the song I couldn't just read and play it. Still, they kept my parts, and the Bobby Vee album was the only hit record I'd played on up to that time.

Armin was really nice to me, and I liked him a lot. He and I related on how things should sound, and I learned a lot from him about how things worked in Los Angeles. I think we were both going for the same things, but he knew quicker ways to get there and I was kind of riding along with him. About that time, Dallas Smith helped me realize I might have the ability to be a producer. When I saw the way the HourGlass was being guided and how different my thinking was from Dallas's, I came to believe that if he could do it, so could I. I thought I might even have a better shot at it because I was a little more empathetic with the artist, certainly more than he ever was.

The cover of that album was a mystery to all of us. I don't know who thought of the picture, but Liberty wanted us to dress up in what appeared to be costumes. The thing is, much of what seems like costumes *now* was what a lot of the hippies were wearing back *then*. Everyone was an Indian or a cowboy or whatever, dressing like some character. So, they sent us to a costume shop in Hollywood—out there you could find one on every block—and we went in and picked out costumes we liked. I was from the South and proud of it, so I chose a Confederate uniform. To be honest, it was kind of fun at first. Then, whoever was in charge must have been higher than we were because someone said, "Oh, let's double expose the photo" and then, "Hey, let's put it on the album upside down to catch people's eye." It looks like a misprint. I didn't realize at the time we'd look a little goofy, and when I look at it today I think, "Who are those idiots on the cover?" When it was all said and done, we may not have liked the costume idea overall, but it had little to do with our troubles with Liberty.

When the album was released, of course, we were happy to have a record out. That was a big accomplishment back then, but it wasn't one we were going to tell people "this is us," and I didn't want to give a copy to all my friends. I just knew when they listened to it, they'd be surprised and wonder what happened. I listened to the record and thought at first it wasn't too bad. Then I listened again and got used to it, but down deep, I knew it was pretty awful. A person can only rationalize so long before the truth hits you in the face and you're snapped back to reality.

I don't remember the response we got from the people here at home, but I think everyone was pretty surprised. I know I would have been if I'd seen us play live and then bought that album. We left home sounding like one band and, after a few months out there, a record comes out sounding like something totally different. It didn't represent what everyone had liked about the band. Sometimes people's short-sightedness is kind of amazing. If you looked at Gregg and Duane, they looked like stars, and I still can't believe no one at Liberty could see that. Evidently, that's what Bill McEuen saw in the band in St. Louis, but then Liberty put out an album that, other than for Gregg's vocals, didn't feature what made us strong as a band. I never heard what Bill thought of the album, but I can't believe he would think it was great. He'd taken a band he'd fallen in love with, and the record company and producer had given him something he hadn't bargained for.

After we finished the album, we played around California to tour the record, mainly at the different clubs in Los Angeles, but we had to be careful because Liberty didn't want us to be seen out playing at a lot of other places around town as we'd like to have done. The whole business is different today, but back then, it was more the regimented "suit" way of doing things—and we weren't a suit band. We did a few TV shows and Gregg would lip-sync to the record, which was never fun, especially with the one they released as the first single. It was the song "Heartbeat," with the horns and female background vocals. Their parts were good and they were top players, but it looked silly for us to be performing as a five piece band with horns and chick singers in the background when they weren't around. At the time the record was mixed, they were definitely out front in the mix. We felt like it wasn't genuine; it wasn't what we were planning to do, and the whole thing was kind of trying.

We did the *Merv Griffith Show*, and I'll never forget the guy at the station. We were running the song down during rehearsal and he said, "How you gonna to do this? You've got all these horns, where are they?" Then he wanted to know what kind of visual they were going to get with just the five of us up there and background singers coming in. That's the moment I had my suspicions confirmed that what we were doing was totally wrong. It's when we decided it wasn't going to happen again.

Everyone in the band was kind of in shock. We didn't know what to expect next. Most of us had wanted to give Los Angeles a shot and see what they were going to do with us. This was supposed to be the place to go, but instead of going there, I think now we'd have been better off to go about three hundred miles north to San Francisco. We might have had better luck there. Los Angeles wasn't right for us, and it affected everyone's morale.

7

The Fillmore

The thing we hadn't figured out when we first got to California was that we were popular in the South because we did cover songs and played what people wanted to hear. When we got to California, no one cared if you could play a certain song. Chances were, the band that had originally recorded it was right around the corner. We were in Los Angeles, the center of music, and we had to find something that fit what we were doing and make it our own. It took a while before I came to that realization. We never thought about doing that when we were playing around the South. I'd played the club circuit for years but had never done original songs, except for maybe when the singer would write one or perhaps the occasional novelty song. Out there in California, we had to start incorporating original material into our sets.

After the album was finished, the record company sent us out in the area to tour the record. We'd been used to playing three or four hours a night, sometimes four or five nights a week, but at least every weekend. Out there, we might play an hour on the weekend, and a lot of the gigs were just showcases, designed for the right people to see us in the proper place and to get some press. There wasn't a lot going on the rest of the week. We had photo shoots and whatever else the record company might want us to do, but for a long time, there wasn't a place we could rehearse. I think that really slowed the development of the band. If we'd had a place to practice sooner, we'd have improved a lot quicker because we all loved to play. There was very little money in it for us, and Bill was paying for most of our necessities, a place to live, and some money for food. So, other than the small advance we received each week, we didn't have a way to make money. We were sinking into debt.

Clubs there didn't seem quite like the clubs I'd been playing back home. They were listening venues as well as clubs and people went there to listen, or at least act like they were listening. We played the Hullabaloo Club on Sunset in West Hollywood a few times; in fact, the first gig we played was at the Hullabaloo shortly after we arrived in California. The club had a regular show that ended about midnight, but several nights a week there'd be an after-hours show. Bill had gotten us on the after-hours gig. We were a new band and no one had ever heard of us, but it was fun. We came on first and did our little psychedelic show. People were always kidding us about our accent, and when they'd come up and ask what kind of music we played, we'd pronounce it "*sackadilic*," which seems kind of funny now. The night we played, the Doors were also on the after-hours show and went on after our band.

Gregg and Duane knew a lot more about the Doors than I did. I didn't know what to think of them, but I was impressed by the mood they created. Their music was drastically different from the blues and R&B I'd been listening to, and the way they set up a mood before they played was ominous and scary and left an impression on me. The band would start playing a really slow guttural sounding music and keep it up for about five minutes, then Jim Morrison would come out and do his thing. I was a Muscle Shoals and Stax guy, and I didn't care for what the Doors were doing at first. I like it better now and realize how much they were influenced by the same music I liked. After the gig, Morrison and Gregg got to be friends and would go out together and get high.

The Hullabaloo was an old movie theater with a big stage and a screen in back where they would show movies. Eventually, they started letting us in for free, and we'd go kill time at the late night movies. The Hullabaloo also hosted events, and on June 4, 1968, I went to a Pat Paulson for President rally at the theater. Pat Paulson was a comedian who had gained notoriety from his appearances on the *Smothers Brothers Show,* and he was making a light-hearted run for the presidency. Politics wasn't really our thing, but I'd started getting interested because of the Vietnam War. I went to the rally and was having a great time because he was always so funny, then there was a little break. Shortly after midnight, someone went up and announced that Senator Robert Kennedy had just been killed. It was a shock and I couldn't believe it. I wasn't able to process it at first, and then it took me back to the time of the JFK assassination, which was the beginning of my skepticism of government. Robert Kennedy's death was the confirmation of what I believed. Everyone sort of drifted away after hearing the news, and I left to go home and watch the coverage on television.

Bill got us opening up for different people at the Whiskey, and we ended up playing there a lot and developed a following. At first, we'd be the opening or middle act of a three act show and then worked into being the headliner. It was a neat gig, a lot of fun, and we felt comfortable. We hadn't been in California too long and were just getting used to the freedom out there, where people didn't judge you by the length of your hair and speech was freer than back home.

Usually during our gig at the Whiskey, Duane would talk some over the microphone on stage and maybe introduce Gregg or the rest of the band. One night Duane was feeling good. After not working for a while, we were finally playing, and he was really happy. He stepped up to the mic and said, "It's just free out here. I love the freedom. You can even say *'fuck'....*" And then the whole p.a. went dead. Someone came up and took the mics off the stage, and then someone else came up and said a few words to the effect of "No, you *can't* say that, and if you ever say it again, there'll be dire consequences." They brought the mics back out, power was restored, and we continued our set. We were shocked. I'd never seen anything like that before and haven't seen anything like it since. Turned out you couldn't say *fuck* after all.

During our later gigs at the Whiskey, it got to be where a lot of people would come and sit in with the band. One night Eric Burdon, Janis Joplin, and Paul Butterfield sat in, and all three were on the stage with us at the same time. Janis sang several songs and was out there riffing. They were famous even back then. Their legends, especially Janis's, continue today, so it was a pretty heady experience. Eric hung around for a while afterward and seemed to like the band.

Being a drummer means you have more stuff to pack up after a gig than everyone else, and I was running late after the show. I went upstairs to the dressing room where Janis was just sitting by herself. I nodded to her and then Paul Butterfield came out and was talking to her. I guess he was going to help her get home or was seeing if she needed a ride or something. I just remember looking at her and she seemed kind of lonely. At least that's how she struck me.

It wasn't long after the album was finished that Mabron left the band. I don't know what happened with Mabron, but he became interested in ideas about space travel and anti-gravity. It went from, "well, that's interesting" until he started contacting people at the University of Southern California, and it kind of got out of hand. I was a sci-fi fan, so I understood the idea, but he was more interested in it than he was in the band, and it was hard to pry him loose from it. Mabron was a great bass player, but sometimes he was hard to deal with because of his intense interest in this other stuff when the rest of us were focused on the music.

There came a point when it became obvious we needed to get someone else to play bass. Bob Keller had been playing bass with Gregg and Duane the first time I'd ever seen the Allman Joys, and he was in California with us hanging around and kind of looking for a gig. They said Bob was a good player but a little flaky. He seemed normal and together, he got along with Gregg and Duane, and Paul and I liked him, so he started playing with the band. He already knew a lot of the songs from having played them in the Allman Joys. He was quick to learn the newer stuff we were doing and sang background, which was a big help. I thought maybe, finally, *this* was the band.

The first big gig we had after the record was released was October 15, 1967, at the First Annual Pop Music Festival in Sacramento at Hughes Stadium. The line-up included Jefferson Airplane, Strawberry Alarm Clock, the Nitty Gritty Dirt Band, and the Sunshine Company. We played right before Jefferson Airplane, and they were big heroes then. They'd had a hit with "White Rabbit" and were hugely popular. It was nice playing in a big venue like that, and I think people liked us. The staging was on a football field, and it was the biggest crowd we'd played in front of at that time. We still hadn't figured out where we fit musically at the time of the Pop Festival and were just happy to have a good gig and be out of Los Angeles for a while.

However, the best gigs of all in California were at the Fillmore. There was nothing to compare with those. Shortly after we finished our first album, we got a gig at the Fillmore Auditorium located on the corner of Fillmore Street and Geary Boulevard in San Francisco. We'd heard a lot about the Fillmore and were pretty nervous. We didn't know how we'd be accepted there, but we were hoping people might like us. We went in the afternoon of the show to set up, and it was a nice place with a big stage. It was a big room without any chairs where people stood and listened to the band. I was excited about the gig, and it was better than I even imagined. A lot of things that happen in your imagination are better than the reality, but getting to the Fillmore, setting up on stage, and playing for that audience was wonderful. They were very attentive, and I felt as at home there as I felt at any place I've played.

We'd heard stories about Bill Graham, owner of the Fillmore, and were kind of in awe of him and his power, but he was always nice to us. He genuinely liked both the HourGlass and, of course, later the Allman Brothers Band. Every time we played the Fillmore, Bill said nice things about us when he introduced the band, and after a while, other bands would come out to hear us. Neil Young and Stephen Stills of Buffalo Springfield liked us, and Duane would go and sit in with them at their gigs whenever he had the chance. One time, either Stephen or Neil had to leave a gig for some reason and got Duane to sit in for him.

Before the end of the year, we had a gig at the Santa Monica Civic Auditorium, and we played the Cheetah along with the Standells. The Cheetah was a strange place with a lot of flashing strobe lights, the kind where if you moved your hand in front of your face, it would look like an old movie and make you kind of crazy—at least it did me. They would cycle the lights on and off and, about every five minutes or so, the lights would turn on for thirty seconds, and it drove me nuts. There was a lot of stainless steel in the club, and it seemed as if the whole décor was metallic and reflective. It was nice looking, but it sounded like being inside a big tin can. One night, we were playing and I had a Vox amp on either side of me. Drums weren't mic'd back then, and we didn't have monitors. Gregg and Duane were both playing pretty loud and, although I was playing as hard as I could, I couldn't even hear the drum heads. I was playing by visual cues because I couldn't hear anything. I thought it was too damn loud, and it was killing me.

We were playing at the Cheetah the night Otis Redding died. We were on a break when we got the news, and the next set we played an Otis song, "Can't Turn You Loose," and I missed one of the stops. Otis was my hero and I felt doubly bad about screwing up the song the night he died. I remember it vividly.

We played with the Electric Flag at the Cheetah, and I got to know Buddy Miles pretty well. It seemed drummers back then were all influenced by each other, and you'd have your favorites. There was the "Buddy Miles camp" and the "Ginger Baker camp." Baker had a unique style and was an extremely talented drummer, but Buddy Miles had a lot of soul in his playing. A few years ago, I got to work with him one more time when I did a record with Spoonful James, a group from Auburn, Alabama. They'd met Buddy and asked him to come to the studio to play and sing on one of the cuts. He was easy to work with and was very nice to me. Buddy went through some rough times toward the end of his life, and I'm glad I got to see him that last time.

We played a lot of different clubs during that period: the Blue Law with Canned Heat, the Avalon Ballroom, the Kaleidoscope, and the Troubadour. The Troubadour was a folk club, and the acoustics were excellent. There was a lot of wood in the club: both the floors and the stage were wood, and it was a great- sounding place. We needed somewhere to rehearse and rented time at the club in the afternoon to practice. Finally they hired us to play there. They had a lot of acoustic acts, and later on we were one of the electric acts that played there. It was a great gig.

We thought we were all set with the band, but Bob Keller was only good for a couple of months. A lot of times the Whiskey would let us in early so we could work up some new material for a show. One night in January '68, we went to rehearse for our gig there the next day. Everyone showed up on schedule except for Keller. No one could find him, and we were freaking, afraid something had happened. It was during a time when lots of crazy shit was going on in Los Angeles. There was peace and love, but there was also a dark side. We went back to where we were living and called everyone who might know Bob, but we couldn't find him. We thought he'd been acting a little down, and it crossed our mind he might have taken his own life or had been injured somehow. We just didn't know.

Sometimes during that period, we'd go up to the Hollywood sign and just sit and look at the city. Right behind the sign there was a valley, and we thought maybe he'd gone up there and jumped and killed himself, or maybe he'd slipped and fallen off and was lying down there, hurt. We thought of all the things you think of when someone important in your life goes missing. We went up there to search for him with no luck. Finally, we gave up. We didn't know what happened to him, but we had a show to do the next day and no bass player.

Fortunately, Pete Carr was out there and had been hanging out with us for a while, so we asked if he knew how to play bass. He said he had never played bass, but we told him it was time to learn. We needed him the next night. He knew most of the songs already and could easily have played them on the guitar, but he hadn't played bass on any of them. We ended up spending all night going over the material until we just couldn't work any longer. Pete literally learned to play the bass overnight, and he did just fine. Before long, he had it all down and was the best bass player yet. Bob Keller wasn't with us long enough to get a nickname, but Pete, because of his young age, quickly became The Beaver, or The Beav for short.

About three months after Keller disappeared, he called me like nothing had happened, just to see how things were going. I was glad to hear from him to know he was okay, but I was still pretty pissed at him and didn't really have much to say.

8

Power of Love

The HourGlass recorded two albums for Liberty. It wasn't too long after the first album came out that the record company decided it was time for the band to do another one. We'd done our share of bitching about the first record because the songs weren't ours and weren't reflective of our music, so for the second album, we were given more choice in selecting material. We mostly selected songs we played live: a couple of Eddie Hinton and Marlin Greene songs, "Down in Texas" and "Home for the Summer," one of Dan Penn and Spooner Oldham's songs, "Power of Love," (the title cut). Except for those three and "I'm Hanging Up my Heart for You" and "Norwegian Wood," the rest of the songs were Gregg's. Gregg was writing more, and although we had a difficult time before figuring out what to do with his songs, the band was getting better at adapting them to our style. For the second album, we were going to try to do something better, something that captured what the band was all about. Honestly, though, we were still trying to find out what we really were about as far as recording. We could play songs live, but we still had some work to do learning to play in the studio, and we needed a producer who understood where we were coming from.

Both of our albums on Liberty were produced by Dallas Smith, and we weren't happy about it, but we weren't given a choice of producers. It was going to be Dallas, but since we didn't know other producers, we wouldn't have known who to ask for anyway. He was okay, but he wasn't someone who understood where we were trying to go. The chemistry just wasn't there.

The first album was done at Sound Recorders with Armin Steiner as the engineer in charge of the sessions, and that record sounded better than second album. The second album was done at the newly remodeled Liberty Studio. The engineers did an okay job, but it didn't have the color of sound like the record done at Sound Recorders. It was another case of not knowing exactly what to do with us, so both albums were learning experiences for us in all kinds of ways.

Dallas didn't have much to do with the second record. He generally set up and arranged the session and consulted with us on the material. Sometimes he sat in the control room and listened, but other times he was on the phone or in the other room, so it was pretty much just us and the engineers. We'd go in and listen, and he might say it was good. We'd all make comments and then get a general consensus as to the best cut. Other than Dallas just being there, I can't remember anything else he did on the album.

When we first started recording the album, we'd been rehearsing at the Troubadour. I had a little 2-track recorder I set up with a couple mics to record us. It's another one of the tapes I found out in my garage a few years ago. At the time, everybody in the band thought the rehearsal tape sounded pretty good. In fact, when we listened and compared it with our first record, the recording we did on the 2-track sounded like us, and we liked it. That was our "sound," and we thought if we could get that overall sound in the studio, then we had it.

We thought it was good enough that some of us in the band went down to the record company studios and caught a couple of Liberty staff engineers in the office who weren't doing anything and asked them to listen to the tape. Back then, I didn't know what a quarter-track tape was, and they told me it was kind of weird playing it back on a half-track machine because of the head alignment. I asked, "Well, can you play it at all?" They did, and we told them *that's* how we wanted to sound. They responded, "Yeah, that's not what we do. We want to get something better." If it was something better, we were all for it, but as it turned out, we got in the studio and there were complications.

Soon after the album started, maybe after the first session, Duane quit the band and went back to Daytona. He said something to the effect, "I'm getting out of here" and then left. We were all having our own share of personal problems, so I was never clear on what happened. It appeared he and Gregg had a big blow-up, and Duane decided to leave. It took everyone by surprise. We were out there recording an album and we lost *the* essential member of the band. He was not only our friend; when you live in such close proximity with someone for that long and go through all the good and bad stuff we had together, there's a closeness nobody can fill. Our friend was gone. It was like a relationship breaking up and it was all bad.

We went through a lot of different emotions when Duane left. We were mad at him for leaving and confused why it had to happen, but it was just one of those things. We did our best to muddle through. Duane was the one who inspired us and lit the fire under us to keep it exciting. Everyone in the band was good, but without him, the super hot talent in the band was gone. We thought about getting someone else, but before we could say it out loud, we knew there wasn't anyone who could replace Duane. If we weren't making it in Los Angeles with Duane, we certainly weren't going to make it without him. There weren't any better players around then or now.

We didn't want to hire anyone else. The best guitar player we knew other than Duane was Pete, and he was playing bass with the band. Having Pete with us was really a good thing. Mabron and Bob were good players, but Pete had positive energy. He was fun to be with, and having people in the band who are not only talented but fun always invigorates everyone. We started recording some of the tunes without Duane. Pete would play bass when we cut the track, and then he'd do some overdubbing with guitar. However, as good as Pete was at that time, he still wasn't Duane, and we weren't getting the sound we wanted.

We kept thinking Duane would be back. Without him there, we didn't sound as good as we could and our playing suffered. From all the work I've done since then, I know it takes a lot of things to make a good sounding record. It takes a good environment and a certain comfort level with the band. They need to know they're going to sound good, and we were never that confident. We were in a situation where everyone was uptight with a lot of the personal stuff going on, and it was probably the worst time we could have picked to do our second album. We might have been able to get by in the studio without Duane, but we couldn't play live. It was a frightening time.

Three or four weeks later, right after we'd recorded all the songs, Duane came back. There was a little awkwardness when he returned, but everyone was glad he was back, and we went on and did what we had to do. He went into the studio and added his parts, but it never was right. We'd have gotten better tracks to begin with if he'd been there, and we wanted to re-cut some of the tracks with Duane when he returned. We'd already spent time overdubbing on the tracks we already had, and Liberty didn't want to put out any more time or money to re-record them. I can understand the decision, but this was another example of the record company's short-sightedness.

We felt Duane had deserted us at what appeared to be the moment we had a chance to get something really good going, but as it turned out it wouldn't have made any difference. I've never thought about what might have happened had Duane been there for the whole album because I don't think it would have mattered who was playing on the record. This was a time when we were unsure about everything. We thought we had a good band, but it was hard to know for certain, and we were around a million other bands that seemed to be getting ahead quicker than we were. There are a bunch of reasons we didn't make it big—but the bottom line is we didn't.

Shortly after we started working on the second album, Buffalo Springfield's Neil Young and Stephen Stills came by when we were recording, and the session inspired them to write liner notes for the album. When they wrote about the session, they were talking about Duane and how inspirational he was and how he led the band; however, after Duane quit, Liberty got in touch with them and told them to substitute Gregg's name in the story instead of Duane's. After Duane returned to the band a few weeks later, we tried to get them to change the notes back to what was originally intended, but we couldn't get them to do it.

Neil and Stephen told us we were one of their favorite bands; they may have told that to all the bands, but it meant a lot that they respected what we were doing. Believe me, when things were tough and we didn't have a lot of money, respect from people we admired meant a hell of a lot and kept us going. Sometimes we'd have photo shoots or do press interviews, but we weren't busy enough. It was better when we were able to find a place and practice.

A thing about California: if you've got money, it's a great place to be because there's everything in the world to do. If you don't have a lot of money, you can't afford to go anywhere or do much except drive around at night and look at the beautiful views. We made a few friends out there, and some of the guys in the Dirt Band were also living at the Mikado, so we'd go and talk to them, maybe watch television, whatever, smoke up and get high.

One afternoon while we were still living at the Mikado, I'd gone out for some reason and Duane had company up at my apartment. When I returned, someone stopped me before I got there and said, "Man, the cops were at your place," and I asked, "What for?" All I could think about was some Mexican amphetamines I had in the drawer by the bed. They were called Mexican Whites that came in packages like a roll of Tums and cost five dollars. I'd gotten them from a friend who brought them back from Mexico.

I walked up to the apartment and asked Duane what happened. He said, "Man, the cops came here and went all through the house and scared us before they realized they were at the wrong address." The warrant was for an apartment two doors from mine. Meanwhile, they'd gone through the apartment and found the amphetamines, but didn't say anything about them. I guess they were looking for bigger things and realized it wouldn't be much of a bust to arrest a guy with five Mexican Whites. That wouldn't have been anything to be proud of: five or six cops wasting their time on some musician with a few uppers. We were relieved there wasn't pot in the place.

Back then, everyone took amphetamines because they weren't illegal. You had to have a prescription for them, but all the truck drivers, and I'm sure anyone who had to work nights, would take them every once in a while. Cops going through the apartment scared both Duane and me. After that, I went and flushed them. Right after I flushed them I thought, "You know, they saw these and didn't say anything. That's pretty stupid of me to flush them now." But it shook me up.

In early '68, everyone started receiving their draft notices. It was the height of the Vietnam War, and our nerves were on edge. We thought it was a bogus war waged for money and political reasons, and no one I knew wanted to go. When you got your notice, you had to go back to the draft board where you were from. Since we were far from home, it took a lot of effort to get there. The only way we could get back from California was to either drive for a couple of days or fly, which wasn't cheap. When Gregg got his notice, he and Duane flew back to Daytona to prepare for Gregg's physical. Of course, we'd already had long discussions about what was going to happen when we got our notices. Gregg had decided he was going to shoot his big toe. We'd heard that if your big toe was missing or damaged to where you couldn't keep your balance, you could get out of the draft.

So, Gregg and Duane returned to Daytona for the physical. From what Gregg told us when he returned to California, he, Duane, and some friends had a big party, and he shot his foot with a .22 rifle. I don't remember all the details of the story other than it involved a party, a lot of alcohol, and a gun. When he returned to HourGlass, he used a crutch for a while and played some with his foot propped up. Then, he hopped around with a cane as his foot started to heal. If you look at the reissue of the Whiskey a Go Go poster dated June 6–9, 1968, you'll see Gregg had his picture taken with the cane. I don't know how badly he damaged his big toe. I never especially wanted to look at it to find out, but it was enough to keep him out of the army. Then I got my draft notice, and my folks sent me a ticket so I could return for my physical. For good or bad, I had high blood pressure, and the draft board passed on me at the time.

In summer '67 we'd met Angela Cartwright and Billy Mumy at the Whiskey. Both were actors on *Lost in Space*, a big television series at the time. A few months later, June Lockhart, who played the part of the mother in the series, hired us to play at a party she was giving. They were fans of The HourGlass and invited us to go to the set and see where they filmed the show. I'd never been on a Hollywood set before, and we had fun having our pictures taken with some of the cast and the sets they used for some of the scenes.

Another time we got an invitation to the premier of John Lennon's first movie. We decided to chip in and rent a limo to go down to the theatre and make a big entrance. However, there was a long line of limos, and we couldn't afford to have the limo driver sit around and wait, so he dropped us off about a block from the theatre and that was it. It wasn't a very successful limo trip or impressive arrival. The rest of the band left before the end of the movie and had rides back with friends, but I decided to stay. I remember walking out after the movie and I had one penny in my pocket. I'd left my wallet at home, and I was nervous because it was a part of LA I wasn't familiar with. I can't even remember how I got back home.

We were all trying to find a way to save money. Finances compelled us to move down the hill from our apartment on Cahuenga to another apartment complex on Lash Lane, which was not only down the hill, but down the economic chain as well. We hadn't exactly been living the life of luxury, but at least I had my own place. By that time, all our wives or girlfriends had split, so Gregg, Duane, Pete, and I moved out of our apartments at the Mikado and into the cheapest place we could get at the time. It had one bedroom with two double beds, a kitchen, and a furnished living room; that was all there was to it for four people. We'd take turns sleeping on the couch, and the other three would take turns sleeping two to a double bed and one in the other.

Actually, that apartment was more fun than the other place and provided a certain degree of closeness in the band. We were definitely physically close and we got along pretty well. Sure, we'd have disagreements here and there, but they were nothing we couldn't resolve. A little later, Duane got an apartment round the corner on Yucca Boulevard, and Pete stayed with him there while Gregg stayed with some friends.

While we were living on Lash Lane, one of our roadies we called The Ghoul had a little Yamaha motorcycle Duane would sometimes take out for a ride, and once in a while I'd go riding with him. The motorcycle wasn't very fast, and it was a dubious thrill riding on the interstate with the traffic speeding past us. The homes and scenery in the Hollywood Hills are beautiful, and one night we wanted to go for a ride to take a look around. I was on the back of the motorcycle with Duane driving, which seemed like a good idea at the time.

The road going up into the hills was curvy and winding, and we were just riding along looking at houses and really enjoying ourselves. There were nothing but curves and a lot of cars parked on either side of the road, so there wasn't a place to go too fast. Even going ten or fifteen miles an hour the bike can slide out from under you, and Duane was kind of hot dogging it up the mountain. We came to a curve he took a little too fast and sure enough, the bike slid out from under us and we were both thrown. We got up with our knees, arms, and faces bleeding from where we had hit and skid along the pavement.

I told Duane, "Damn, you kind of took that curve a little fast, didn't you?" He kind of shrugged it off, saying, "Naw, something must be wrong with the bike." I told him I thought we should go on back down to Hughes Market to get some bandages and something to drink. He started to get on the bike and I told him, "I'm gonna drive. You scared me enough already—I'm not going to let you drive back down there." We went down to Hughes Market and walked in all skinned up and bleeding. We got some strange looks, but it was Hollywood and they'd likely seen a lot worse. We bought bandages and a gallon of Red Mountain wine that cost a dollar and left. We lived right around the corner from the market, so we went on home. I never liked motorcycles much to begin with. I like the *idea* of them, but I'm not comfortable on them. After that night, I never went riding with Duane again.

About this time we went to a club called the Magic Mushroom near where we lived and saw Taj Mahal with Ry Cooder and Jesse Ed Davis. After that, Duane started learning to play slide and practicing in his apartment. He'd had a cold and bought a bottle of Coricidin, took the pills, and started using the bottle as a slide. I can remember going by his place and hearing him practice and wondering what on earth he was doing. When someone is learning to play slide, it's more than a little grating to people who have to listen to it—sort of like someone learning to play the violin. For a while it was driving me nuts, and I didn't understand why he wanted to do it.

We never talked a lot about his slide playing, and in my shortsightedness, I thought at first it was a losing proposition, but Duane was not to be outdone at anything. When he set his mind to something he'd conquer it, just as he did the slide. However, it was a sore subject at times. Duane is always credited with being a great slide player, but before he was a great slide player, he was a great guitarist. He was incredible, and I didn't understand why he wanted to play slide. Now I do, but back then, my imagination was limited. As the story goes, I asked him, "Why don't you get that bottle off your finger and play right?" But I don't know if I really want to own up to that lack of foresight.

It was a while before he introduced the slide to the band, and then he played it on "Statesboro Blues," which was the arrangement we got from Taj's record. When Duane started playing slide with the band, it wasn't all that good—not for someone who ended up being what I consider the premier slide player of all time. The problem was mainly tuning, and it was really annoying. He had all the licks down, but playing all that stuff in tune took him a while to conquer. He played slide on about three or four songs, and we'd try to avoid them when we could. It got to be where Hornsby and I would give each other a look when Duane went for the slide and try to call another song that didn't have a slide part on it. It's funny when I think back on it now because I remember how I dreaded hearing him play when he picked up that bottle, and then it was like something just clicked and he was incredible.

We didn't have a whole lot of dealings with the record company other than going to Liberty for a meeting once in a while. When it looked like the record might do well, they sent us on a short tour that was mainly in the Midwest, which was a wonderful place to be in winter. Then we went to St. Louis, where we had a small following from our time in Gaslight Square. Once we developed a following, we got a kind of celebrity treatment, people asking for our autographs, asking us to sign the records, posters, and that sort of thing. I remember being in a record store to promote the album and no one showed up. We were sitting in the back part of the store with a Sharpie ready to sign the album, or at the very least give an autograph. Other than maybe a couple of people who knew us, nobody came to see us. We ended up walking around looking at records and acting like we were customers instead of the band. It was kind of embarrassing.

Eventually, when we returned to California, we started rehearsing a lot because we were going nuts. We'd gone out there ready to play, and it seemed as if we were always waiting to play instead. Bands need to work and play music or things don't work out, and I was really having a problem sitting around with nothing to do. Then we started worrying about everything, and that just made it worse.

The band was disgusted with Los Angeles, and overall we were unhappy. We didn't like the way the second album sounded, and we didn't know what to do about it. The record company was fixated on

Gregg, and I think they'd just as soon see us go. They saw him not only as a way to bail out their investment in the band, but to make a fortune with him as a new pop idol. I can understand them wanting Gregg, but they overlooked Duane's playing most of the time. He was too good to be overlooked by anyone who was supposed to know something about music.

I recently acquired a press release put out by Liberty dated 3/20/69 that illustrates what we had to deal with. Neither Paul nor I were ever Nashville studio musicians. By the time of the release, Bob Keller was long gone and Pete was the bass player. Not much else is very accurate either.

The Hour Glass
Liberty Records
In the Hour Glass, it's a wise instrument that knows its own father.

All five members of this ensemble are excellent musicians and a couple of them can play every instrument in the band.

New sounds and new tonalities are something the Hour Glass is always seeking. It is this spirit of musical exploration which has given them proficiency in many moods of music, ranging from rhythm and blues through psychedelic rock to romantic balladry.

The founding fathers of the band were Duane and his brother, Gregg Allman, who played guitars and sang in small Southern taverns and clubs of varying elegance from their boyhood days.

"Once we were on the road with a couple of other musicians," Duane recalls, "and we showed up at this Southern Louisiana town. It was going to be a Saturday night dance patronized mainly by Cajun shrimp fishermen and roughneck oil field workers. We worked before roughneck audiences before but when we showed up and went on the stand, we were behind chicken-wire screen, floor to ceiling, separating us from the dance audience. I went to the owner of the joint and said, 'What's with this chicken-wire?'

"He said: 'I'm doing you a favor. Sometimes our patrons get to drinking a little too much and throw things like empty bottles at the bandstand. Don't let it hurt your feelings.'"

Allman would have felt bad except that he later heard that Red Nichols and many of the finest and most expensive bands in the country had also been booked back of that chicken-wire.

It was only a small incident in a long career in which the Allman brothers were learning their profession the hard way—in one-night stands.

Today, on their Liberty records, the Hour Glass shows that polishing.

Duane is usually—but not always—the lead guitarist. Brother, Gregg, is lead singer. He also writes many of the songs used by the group.

The Allmans are frequently joined in their vocals by Bob Keller, the bass player whose voice fits in perfectly with the Allmans to create their far-out harmonies.

Johnny Sandlin, whom the band for some reason or other calls T.H.E. Duck, is a wide-swinging percussionist. As a kid he had wanted to become a scientist, but somehow that became forgotten as he moved into music. At the time he joined the Allmans he was a studio musician in Nashville, Tennessee.

Also a native Alabama musician is Paul Hornsby, who decided he wanted to be a musician when he was only six years old, and has never changed his mind. He is very valuable in the quintet since he plays drums, guitar, bass, organ piano and violin.

He also was once a studio musician in Nashville, and in that league you have to be able to move fast and well.

He enjoys the Hour Glass game of Musical Chairs. "Keeps you out of a rut," he says.

9

FAME

The saving grace for me during this time was playing at the Fillmore. There wasn't a better place to play and I've never seen anything even close to it since. Not only was it the way everything was set up, but it was the audience and how they responded to us. It just felt right playing there. The Whiskey wasn't quite the same because of the club atmosphere, but it was great playing there too. We were living in Los Angeles, so it was like our hometown and the fans were good to us. Plus, we got to interact with some of the bigger acts; the stars like Janis, Eric Burdon, Paul Butterfield and those folks. But after a year and a half everything was going downhill and it didn't feel like we were getting anywhere.

As far as our dealings with the record company, as I said, the whole problem we had with Liberty was they didn't know what to do with us and we didn't know how to help them. What got me is how they were so concerned with image. They didn't want us going out and playing just anywhere or sitting in with certain people. They wanted us seen in the "right" places, which was an odd way of looking at it. I understand the reasoning, but it just wasn't for us. We weren't into playing the Hollywood games of being seen in the right places; we wanted to play music. There didn't appear to be any other way we could make any money to get ahead, at least nothing we were willing to do. None of us wanted to go to work at McDonalds.

We were at odds with management because we weren't the type band who was going to have a top twenty hit. There was also general mistrust developing between the band and Bill McEuen. For one thing, we were going deeper and deeper in debt because Bill was basically paying for our upkeep. The gigs we had didn't pay that much, and he'd get the gig money and dole it out to us for our food and rent. I've never seen an accounting of how much money we owed. I never tried to figure it out, but it had to be a considerable amount because at one time Bill was paying for three apartments and food for all of us. I think we might have earned our food money, but I doubt if we earned our rent or the advances we'd gotten to buy equipment. Bill and Liberty were spending the money to keep us alive out there, so I think it was only right for him to receive the money for the gigs; I know we certainly couldn't have supported ourselves under the conditions imposed by Liberty. I don't know if it was justified or not, but when the band isn't working and you're sitting on your ass most of the time, you tend to sit and think bad things. Sometimes it's because they're true and sometimes it's just because you don't have anything else to do.

Power of Love started to get a little bit of recognition, and Liberty sent us out again to tour the album. We headed to the Midwest, which was relatively close to home, and I remember playing at one of the gigs where we were put up in an extra nice hotel. Usually we were only given a couple of rooms for the whole band, but this time we had our own rooms. Still, everyone came down to mine and we all ended up sleeping in one room anyway.

I was going to go on to Decatur after the tour, and someone suggested we all pool our money and go to FAME to cut something. If we could get our sound there, then Liberty would know what we were supposed to sound like. We were unhappy with both our records; the only studio I thought could capture our sound was Rick Hall's place in Muscle Shoals. Arthur Conley's "Sweet Soul Music" was a huge hit at that time. and if there was any hope of us making a good sounding record, FAME would be the place to do it. Because I'd worked some for Rick, I knew who to call to book the studio. We decided to head to Muscle Shoals.

We took five hundred dollars and met up with Eddie Hinton, who agreed to produce the recordings. Jimmy Johnson was working for Rick and engineered the session. It was pretty much just Eddie, Jimmy, and the band. Eddie met us at FAME one Sunday in April and we set up in Studio A the way the musicians did when cutting a session for Rick. And it worked. I mean *everything* worked. The drums sounded great, the bass, the piano, the B-3, the electric piano and Duane's guitar all sounded incredible.

I can still envision where we were set up, and I can remember playing the drum parts. If you were looking out from the control room, I was on the left side of the room against the left hand wall about a third of the way down from the control room playing my mod orange Ludwigs with the 22-inch bass with 13- and 16-inch toms and Roger's super-sensitive Ludwig snare. Pete was playing a white jazz bass right beside me, since bass and drums usually work together. I was looking at him and he was looking at me and it was a stone groove. Duane was playing a Strat with his Fender Twin sitting on a shelf facing away from us in the back of the room and it was loud even with a baffle around it. You could hear it in all the mics, but it sounded great. Paul and the piano were up on the right side, almost in front of the control room close to Gregg and the B-3 so they could switch places depending on the track.

We did some of the songs that went over well at the gigs, "Ain't No Good to Cry" and the "B. B. King Medley," which was one of our most popular songs at gigs, and about the best thing we ever recorded. "Been Gone Too Long" was a fairly new song of Gregg's. Not only is it a pretty song with Gregg singing well, but Duane's doing some Curtis Mayfield stuff on guitar through the whole thing that's just beautiful. We played these songs live every night, so we were able to cut all the tracks in one evening. Gregg overdubbed a few vocals and added a nice Wurlitzer piano part on "Ain't No Good to Cry"; otherwise, it was pretty much straight to tape with very little, if any, sweetening.

We were having a good time; it was a fun night, and we felt good playing. I could tell everyone was enjoying it and we got something we were proud of, something I'm proud of to this day. We knew then the problem we had with Liberty wasn't us. We proved we could get our sound, that it could be done and done simply.

After we finished recording at FAME, Eddie gave us a copy of the tape and we came back to Decatur. We were just blown away with it. It was good then and it still holds up today; that was the band. That was the closest thing ever recorded as to how the band sounded live. If you like it, it's what we were, if you don't, it's still what we were. We called Bill and played the stuff for him over the phone, but of course he couldn't tell anything. He told us to send him a copy and he'd get it over to Liberty, so we got a copy of the tape ready to go and sent it out there the fastest way we could at the time. Instant transfer wasn't available back then; it was just a slow day's mail.

We thought Liberty would want to record us down at FAME, but, after they received it in California, Bill called us back. The news was shocking. He said Liberty didn't like it; it wasn't the direction they wanted us to go, and if that was where we were headed, they were going to drop us. Talk about the bubble bursting. We just felt totally hopeless. What they essentially said was they didn't like *us*, and what do you do about that? We were obviously wrong for them. It was definitely the best stuff we ever recorded and we were really up...until the record company kicked us in the teeth.

After Liberty rejected our tape, we all got both bummed and pissed. We knew in our hearts they were wrong, but didn't know what to do about it. They still had us under contract, so we couldn't take the tape and shop it anywhere else. What could we do? We knew at that point we'd never make it with Liberty. I think Bill knew what we could do and knew that we hadn't been handled right, but I guess he'd felt we had to have the recording deal and we just got caught up in things. Whatever, it wasn't going to work with Liberty no matter what.

After what went down with the demos, we knew the band recording for Liberty was over. Our clothes and equipment were still out there (and we had a few more gigs booked), so we had to return to California. We went back, and for the next month or two after we returned, we played again at the Whiskey and Fillmore. We hadn't decided what we were going to do, but we were sick of Los Angeles; of not being able to play and not making any money since the good-paying gigs we'd had were few and far between.

We had all the pieces in place for it to happen, it just didn't. We all decided to do what we were doing before we ever went to Los Angeles: go home and play clubs again. We made calls trying to get booked back in the South, and a lot of where we ended up playing was based on the popularity of the Allman Joys. One place we played was the Comic Book Club in Jacksonville. That's where we met Ronnie Van Zant and the One Percent, the band that eventually became Lynyrd Skynyrd.

A funny thing happened...well, it wasn't funny to us at the time, but in July '68, One Percent opened for us at the Comic Book Club and played all the songs off our newest album. What's worse, for the most part, they may have played them better than we did. We were sitting out there in amazement because they'd actually learned the songs off the album. They'd been fans of the Allman Joys prior to the HourGlass and had learned the same songs they did, but those were mostly cover tunes. This was different. They had our album and were doing a damn good job of playing our songs. So, they played them and then we went up and played the same songs.

On August 9, 1968, we played one of our last gigs at the Kiel Auditorium in St. Louis. The Allman Joys had been popular in St. Louis, and we'd been booked with Janis Joplin, Iron Butterfly, and some other bands. The auditorium was a beautiful place and we had a good time. The gig got cut short that night and not all the acts got to play, so the bands played in the park the next day for free. It was one our best paying gigs, about a thousand dollars or something, which was just huge for us at the time.

I'm not certain if this happened after the gig at the Kiel or one of the other times we played there, but I do remember we got ready to leave St. Louis one time and we'd been at someone's house "smoking." We wanted to take some of it with us, but we were really afraid to because the cops back then would throw your ass in jail for pot. I definitely didn't want my parents to find out I was a "dope smoker." The five of us were riding together, and the agreement was that if we were stopped by the cops, whoever had a joint left had to eat it so we wouldn't have anything in the car. Gregg was driving. As we were pulling out of town, Duane fired up his and we smoked it, so his was all gone. I don't know the order of whose was smoked when, but I ended up still holding mine because I was saving it for down the road. We were on the interstate out of St. Louis heading south and, believe it or not, we got pulled over. I saw the flashing lights, took my joint, and started eating it.

The highway patrolman came up, and got Gregg out of the car. As I said, there was a war going on and we all had long hair…. It's difficult now to understand what long hair really meant back then, but it was a pretty strong statement being made in a very uptight country. Some cops would hate you because of your long hair. The officer was fairly nice to Gregg, but when he asked him for his license, Gregg said, "I don't have a license." I didn't know that. He was driving my car without a license, and there I was eating a joint and couldn't even talk. It was a full, rolled up joint, and it tasted just awful. Then the cop asked Gregg, "Who owns the car?" And that was me. So he starts questioning me, and I could barely speak because I was still chewing part of the joint. The cop said he'd let us off with a warning, but Gregg couldn't drive. I couldn't believe it and felt incredibly relieved. I'd been scared out of my mind thinking of what the headlines might be in the local newspaper back home. We got in the car and made a hasty exit. It took a long time for my nerves to settle down after the experience, but as the pot was digested, I started feeling pretty good on down the road.

We played Daytona at the Pier, which was a good gig because that's where Duane and Gregg were from and we always had a good crowd. The band was at its best then—really cooking—but after a few of the gigs we played at the bars, it was like starting over. Then the gigs were harder and harder to come by. Paul was getting tired of it, and I'd about had enough myself. We'd been so hopeful and tried so hard again and again only to have our hopes dashed. First it was not having the right recording, or the record wasn't just right, or we didn't do the right material. After we cut at FAME and did it our way with Eddie producing and Jimmy engineering, it still wasn't working. We knew we couldn't keep it up.

There was an incident that stands out as a pivotal moment for me. The band played one club that was just awful. We were doing our own material (not playing cover songs anymore, which was all anyone really wanted to hear in bars down south), and I saw the way the audience was acting. They didn't care for us and weren't interested in the original material or what little stage show we had. We were playing for people who didn't appreciate or want us. After coming from the Fillmore it was like, "Damn, what are we doing here in this bar? We know we're better than this." We didn't need to be the background music for guys trying to pick up chicks, and it was a frustrating time. If no one liked the band, what the hell were we going to do? I felt like we'd failed. We'd gone to California to do great things, but it hadn't happened. I wasn't up for going on. It was just one of those things where you can't go back after you've been out and seen what it could be, where people accept you for who you are. So the band split up. It's a shame because at that time the band was really good. I don't think any of us realized it then, but I can reflect now how tight and organized we were and what great players we had.

None of us was going to quit playing, but I felt we'd gone as far as we could together and I was ready to try something else. I never even thought about quitting music since there was no doubt in my mind I was going to stay in the business, and I didn't want the band to break up. It was a hard time, but I can't say it was a wasted experience because everything leads you to the next step. Still, it was sad.

I saw how different sessions in Los Angeles were from sessions in Muscle Shoals, and I thought we had a better way of doing things here. We gave it time to happen, which is the way that seemed to create the best music even if it wasn't always as efficient. I became more confident about becoming a producer from watching people who weren't very good at it and thinking I knew as much or more than they did. That doesn't include Rick; I'd learned Rick's way, and Rick understood the type musicians we were. In his case, he developed a lot of them. He'd tell you right where to hit the drum and go out, take a quarter or half dollar and draw a circle in the center of the snare drum and tell you to hit it right there every time. Then he'd go out and check to see if there were any little dings outside the circle. If your guitar sound wasn't right, he'd have you change it and try this or that until you got it. He's done more hit records than any ten producers.

There never was any discussion with the label about a third album. Compared to the music business now, though, I admit they at least gave us two records with only minimal sales before they pulled the plug. We still had a while to go on our contract with Liberty, and I guess that's why they wanted Gregg to go back to California. Liberty finally figured how to get what they'd wanted all along: Gregg as a solo artist. They eventually cut some sides with him using studio players as the HourGlass after we left. It still didn't work out, and I don't think Gregg was too happy about the recordings either. He never would play any of it for the rest of us. In fact, I never heard what he'd done until later when there was a re-release and someone sent me a CD.

There wasn't any formal pronouncement that the band was breaking up. Everybody just decided to go their separate ways. To the best of my memory, it was a friendly parting. Duane and Pete went back to Florida along with Gregg (who eventually returned to California); Paul went to Tuscaloosa, and I came back to Decatur to look for work as a session player in Muscle Shoals.

10

The Allman Brothers Band

When the band first got together to rehearse in my parents' garage, some of the neighbors had complained we were too loud and the singer "sounded like he was black." It bothered my folks that people were complaining, so they built what we referred to as the "little house," down the road and around the curve from their house. The thought was that I could live there, and the band could practice there. Originally it had one large den with a Murphy bed in the corner, a kitchen, laundry room, and bathroom.

From the beginning I wanted a studio there someday even though it wasn't feasible at the time; there's a twelve-foot-high slant in the ceiling for that reason. I didn't know anything about building a studio, but I did the best I could in trying to imagine how it might look one day based on what studios looked like in the '60s (which was a lot different than they look now). I guess I had some insight because I've made records there for the last twenty-five years.

While the HourGlass was in California, my folks sold their house and moved down the street into a new one they'd built in front of the little house. Theirs was called the "big house" and was connected to the little house by a carport. After the HourGlass broke up, I moved into the little house while trying to find work. I knew I wanted to go to Muscle Shoals to play sessions, and living as close to the Shoals as I did, it seemed like the perfect thing to do. I was hoping to get a job playing over at FAME again. By that time, Quinn-Ivey Studio had opened in the Shoals. I figured through one of those connections I could get a job, but it turned out there really wasn't much work for me at either place.

I saw Eddie Hinton and talked with him a lot during that period. Every once in a while, he'd use me on a session. At that time Roger Hawkins was playing drums on all the sessions in the Shoals. Sometimes, though, Eddie would want two drummers, and he'd use Roger and me. Roger had his hands full trying to find out which beat I was going to land on, but it was special for me to be playing with him because he was and still is one of my three drum heroes: Roger, Jerry Carrigan, and Al Jackson, Jr. It doesn't get any better.

I didn't have any regular club gigs during that period, so I'd sit in with a band once in a while if someone needed a drummer for a week or even a night—it didn't matter. If I had a chance to play a gig I would, but I didn't have much else to do. My dad was still in decent health, so we went hunting about every day during the season. While I'd been in California, Dad had closed the hardware store and he and my mother had retired, so I got to spend more time with him, just the two of us together. For me, that was the best part.

After the HourGlass broke up, everyone sort of scattered. Paul went back to Tuscaloosa and worked with some really good musicians down there: Chuck Leavell, Charlie Hayward, Lou Mullenix, Joe Rudd, Tippy Armstrong—all of them great players. Gregg had gone back to California, but after he returned, he and Duane were living in Daytona when they hooked up with a band from Jacksonville called the 31st of February—Scott Boyer, David Brown, and Butch Trucks. The band was just guitars, bass, and drums with Scott and Butch singing. Butch actually can sing, but you don't get to hear him very often. I think you can hear him singing background on the Allman Brothers "Revival." With Gregg and Duane, the 31st of February made a great recording of "Melissa." Duane played beautiful slide on it. To me, it's the quintessential recording of that song.

Jimmy Johnson, a fine guitar player himself, had heard Duane play when he was engineering the HourGlass recordings. As with just about everyone who'd heard him play for the first time, Jimmy was blown away. Jimmy mentioned Duane to Rick Hall and Rick got in touch with him. Rick was working with Wilson Pickett and hired Duane to come to Muscle Shoals and play on the session. Duane was the one who suggested recording "Hey Jude" and then ended up playing guitar on the song. His playing on that song caught the attention of people all over the world, including Eric Clapton.

Rick eventually signed Duane to an artist's contract and then tried to figure out what to do with him. He wanted him to cut some demos, so Duane called me, Hornsby, and Berry Oakley, a bass player from

Jacksonville he'd gotten to know from sitting in with Berry's band, the Second Coming. The plans were to cut a Duane Allman solo album, and we spent three or four days recording whatever songs we could think of. Some were songs we'd done in the HourGlass and others we all knew. We cut "Goin' Down Slow" with Duane singing. I thought it was really moving. Then, at some point during the course of doing the album with Duane, Phil Walden came over to talk with Rick. I think Rick asked him to come over and see about managing Duane.

This was in 1969 and after Otis Redding was gone. I didn't know Phil Walden, but I knew of him because he either managed or booked all the artists I really loved from Percy Sledge to Otis; all the Stax artists and just about all of Rick's. I thought at the time he was very personable, and he certainly generated high energy and excitement. I don't know who did what where or when, but somehow, between the connection with Rick, Jerry Wexler and Phil, Phil ended up with Duane's contract.

After the Wilson Pickett sessions, Duane moved to Muscle Shoals and got a place by the lake. Phil had introduced Duane to Jaimoe, who was living in Macon, Georgia, at the time, and Jaimoe would drive up and stay with Duane. Usually after the sessions, they'd both come over to the little house in the afternoon or evening and we'd spend the night listening to music. I remember when the Beatles' *White Album* came out. We'd have a smoke and listen to it. Duane had a habit that if something wasn't happening, or if what was happening didn't interest him, he didn't waste the time. He'd take a nap. So, he might be up all night having little cat naps here and there. I was never an early riser. One of the reasons I liked being a musician was I didn't have to get up too early, but sometimes Duane would come over knocking on the door at 7 a.m. It was a great time, and I was glad Duane was back.

While we were working on his solo album, Duane started trying to put another band together. Berry was already there, as was Jaimoe. Duane asked Paul and me to join the band. I thought about it for a while. Paul and I talked about it, but neither of us wanted to go on the road again. We were so burned from Liberty and the whole Los Angeles experience that we weren't ready to jump back into it. I wanted to play drums on sessions and thought that would be the best thing for me to do. Later Duane asked Eddie to join. By then Duane was jamming with

Berry, Jaimoe, Butch, and Dickey, who was also in the Second Coming with Berry. Duane didn't have a singer for the band, and Eddie was a great singer. Eddie wanted to write and produce rather than join the band and turned down the offer. If Eddie had agreed to join the band, I probably would have said yes, too.

It would have been interesting if all of us had done it, and I sometimes wonder what would have happened. I was honored that Duane asked me, but I didn't have it in me to go back on the road. If I'd known it wouldn't involve having to live in California again I might have reconsidered. Don't get me wrong—I liked it when I went out there for Capricorn later and wasn't so broke, but it's not a good place to be without money and we never had any when we were in the HourGlass.

While I was trying to get something going in Muscle Shoals, Eddie and I cut a couple of instrumentals, the Canned Heat song, "Goin' up the Country" and Johnny Otis's "Hand Jive." We had a great band with David Hood on bass, Barry Beckett on keyboards, Eddie on electric guitar, I played drums, and Duane played slide. In the old Muscle Shoals studio on Jackson Highway, the bathroom was located in the studio, and Duane's amp was set up in the bathroom—which was next to where I was playing drums. Then Eddie and I went to Memphis to finish the tracks with the Memphis Horns that included Wayne Jackson and Andrew Love. That was the Duck and the Bear 45 Eddie leased to Atlantic. I had co-production on the record, but it was mostly Eddie.

If you think about the Memphis horn section, it was pretty evenly black and white. Booker T. and the MGs were evenly mixed, two blacks and two whites, and they were great. A mixture of races seemed to be where the best music was coming from, and everybody I grew up playing with idolized black musicians. The biggest compliment someone could have given you was that you sounded like a black band.

Although my plans were to do studio work, I did very few sessions. Mostly, I'd go over to the Shoals to spend some time with Eddie, and we'd talk about record production and listen to music. I wanted to produce records and had ideas of how I wanted to do it, but Eddie was a lot further along in knowing how to produce. I probably learned more about record production from him than anybody else. He was incredibly smart, and he wasn't afraid to jump into something and just do it.

Bottom line, there wasn't room in Muscle Shoals for me anymore. Eddie knew Steve Alaimo in Miami, and Steve was partners with Henry Stone, who owned the biggest one stop record distributorship in the Southeast. They had a little studio upstairs in the corner of their record distributorship called Tone and Steve wanted to put together a studio band. Eddie was making pretty good money at the time, and he bought a ticket for me to fly to Miami with him to check on a job for me at Tone. It was the first time I ever flew first class. Steve Alaimo was a celebrity of sorts, and we stayed at his house while we were in Miami. He'd been the host of *Where the Action Is*, a daily television show back then, and we were staying at his house. It was a pretty heady feeling.

The studio was a little funky (most of them were back then), but I thought it sounded good. When Eddie and I got there they were cutting a thing with Betty Wright and that's where I first met Butch Trucks, who was playing on the session. Steve wanted to hear me play, so I went out and played on the track. They liked what I was playing and kept my part. I ended up on the track of "I Love How You Love Me," which turned out to be Betty Wright's first nationally released single. That was kind of exciting, but it didn't sit too well with Butch, and after a while of sitting there while I played, he left. Steve Alaimo sang on it with her which was kind of a unique thing. Betty is black and Steve is white, and as far as we knew at the time, there weren't any other black and white pairings. I wasn't hired right then; they said they weren't ready to have a full time rhythm section. I returned to Decatur, but shortly thereafter I got a call offering me a job, and I moved to Miami.

I played quite a few sessions in Miami doing demos of music I really liked. Eddie was down there when I played on a song he'd written the day before, "Sweetheart Things." He'd just written the song and wanted to give me writer's credit, but I didn't feel right taking it because I didn't do anything except stay up with him while he wrote it. Clarence Reid was a writer there along with several others who were excellent R&B writers. There was one top-forty song that came out of it called "I'm Doin' My Real Thing" by Clarence.

The studio rhythm section was David Brown (who had been with the 31st of February) on bass, Bobby Birdwatcher on piano, and I played the drums. After I was hired, I called Pete Carr and got him to come down and play guitar. He took to it right away. He's a great player and had great ideas for what to do, and it was a pretty good rhythm section.

We did so much work that it made me want to start doing my own productions. Brad Shapiro was the studio producer and I'd talk to him saying, "Come on, and let me do something. I really want to take a song." Finally he said yes, and I worked with a married couple who were really good. I loved their voices and harmonies and cut a couple of songs with them using the rhythm section where I was in charge of the session. I worked on the arrangement and called the shots. It was my first introduction to solo production, and though it didn't happen often, every once in a while I'd get to do a song or two. I don't think any of the demos I produced ever made it to an album or were even released, but it was my ambition to produce all the time and get to play some too. Whereas Dallas Smith was the executive guy in Los Angeles, coming in and getting the arrangers, calling the contractors and booking the time, he wasn't musically involved in the recording. Brad was a little more musical, but not as much as I wanted to be. I learned a lot watching Brad produce, and it bolstered my confidence that I could be a good producer.

I remember we used to give Brad a lot of grief. We all still acted like kids; everyone had their nicknames. In fact, we called the rhythm section the Zoo, and we were merciless to each other. One day, before we got to the studio, Pete and I worked out something to pull on Brad. When we first got in, I told him, "Man, don't be too rough on Pete. He's got this condition where he can have a seizure if he gets upset. Just be nice to him and keep it on the level. It hasn't been a problem so far."

During the day I'd say little things to him to set him up then finally Brad made some comment and Pete hit the floor with foam coming out of his mouth. I told Brad, "Oh no, you've done it now." Thinking Pete was about to die, Brad was trying to shove his wallet in Pete's mouth, and finally we had to tell Brad he'd been set up. It was crazy stuff, but it did break the tension. He took it well, but since the rest of us couldn't stop laughing, I guess there wasn't a whole lot he could do other than join in.

The studio was only open for a few hours a day, so we'd go in about eleven or twelve and record until five or six. Then they'd lock up the place, and we were gone. I guess Henry didn't want any one in the distributorship at night, which is understandable with everybody's love for records. We could buy them for two dollars apiece, and I spent a lot of money on records during that period. Every once in a while Henry and Steve would take us out to eat at a nice restaurant.

Bobby Birdwatcher had a big house, and David Brown and I ended up living with him. We'd go home after work and David and I would sit up drinking and arguing all night. It didn't matter what the subject was; David was one to argue about anything—and he still is. He'd argue with a tree. I'd met Scott Boyer on my first trip to Miami, and once in a while Scott had some gigs lined up. Some nights, I'd go out with him, David, and Pete to play bar mitzvahs at some of the big hotels along the strip at the beach. The band was like a babysitter for the folks who'd go out on the town and leave their kids with us, but I enjoyed it. I liked Scott, and I've worked with him in some way or another ever since then.

It was during this time I really started to hear about the Allman Brothers. One day I got a call from Duane. He told me about the band, how they were getting together, and how he was in Macon and would see Phil Walden, who was putting a studio together. He wanted me to hear the band. He told me they were playing in Daytona and, after he called a couple of times, I decided to go on up to see them. It was a pretty good drive from Miami to Daytona, but Pete went with me to take a listen.

It was a relatively small place where they were playing, but it was packed. The room had a high ceiling and a high stage. It may have been two or three feet high when most stages, especially in clubs, might have been six inches off the floor. They played what would become the opening song from their first album, "Don't Want You No More," then "Dimples," and one of Gregg's songs I remembered hearing before. When I first heard it in California, it was a folk song, but believe me, it wasn't then. It was probably "Dreams."

I was surprised it was such a big band; there were two guitars, a keyboard, bass, and two drummers. When we were in the HourGlass, there was an excellent band we used to go see called Clear Light. They had two drummers, and Duane really loved the idea of having two drummers. He liked the sound and wanted to incorporate it into the band. He talked to me about getting a second drummer, but I wasn't crazy about the idea. In fact, I never liked the idea of two drummers until I heard Butch and Jaimoe together, and that was the first time it ever made sense to me.

Jaimoe is not a conventional rock drummer. He was a very fine jazz drummer, and the fact that he was doing other colorful things to Butch's more solid groove is what made it work so well. I don't know if any other bands could pull that off to where two drummers were much more than just an increase in volume. Butch had a unique way of playing a high hat. A lot of times, other than just opening and closing it, he'd use his right hand on the ride cymbal and play eighth or even sixteenth notes by opening and closing a hat with his left foot. It was an interesting sound, and I'd never even thought about doing that. Usually you just close the hat on two and four and there he was playing eighth notes on it. He did a lot of really great things. By the end of the HourGlass days, Duane was getting a whole lot better on the slide. By the time the band ended, he was great on it. It had only been a few months since the last time I'd seen him play, but I could tell that night he'd gotten even better.

In the HourGlass, Paul played guitar some, and he and Duane would play harmony, but it was never taken to the extent Duane and Dickey did it with the Brothers. It was something I'd never heard before—some of the harmonies were Western Swing-sounding—but the music was definitely not Western Swing. This was a rock idiom with the guitars twinning and sometimes the organ adding a third part. That was the first time I'd met Dickey, and there was no denying him. He's always been an excellent player, and together he and Duane created a whole style of music.

I guess what hit me more than anything was the whole band; they were amazing. You could pick out any guy in the band—each one was a superb musician—but put them all together and they were even better than they were individually. I loved hearing them.

When I go back and listen now to the old tapes, I think of the HourGlass as part of the evolution to the Allman Brothers Band. On the tapes you can hear how they morphed from the HourGlass into the Brothers, but I never thought much about it then. I ended up sitting in for a song or two that night, and it was exciting. I was just sitting there blown away by the band, and then they asked me to play. I wasn't expecting to sit in and was unprepared, but I'll remember forever the impact the band had on me and getting to play with my old band mates.

I'll never forget that night. They were still in the rough phase but, man, they just blew me away. The band was electric, and the crowd was in love with them. They were in Daytona (their crowd to begin with), but I couldn't imagine anyone not loving them. Everybody there had the sense this was a real happening; that you were seeing the future and they were going to be big. You knew they were going to do it; it was just a matter of time and they did. For a while the Allman Brothers Band became the biggest band in the world.

11

Macon

After Duane got the band together in Jacksonville, everyone moved to Macon. Phil Walden called to ask me to come up and put a rhythm section together for the studio he was opening. It was kind of appealing. I'd met Phil before and liked him, plus Duane had called several times saying, "Man, you gotta be up here. We need you to come up here." Finally I told him I'd go check it out and then took off. When I got there, I liked Macon immediately. It's one of the few towns where I got off an exit and eventually found where I wanted to go without too much trouble, which seemed like a sign since I have such a terrible sense of direction.

I managed to find Phil's office and went in and talked to him about putting the studio rhythm section together. I told him I also wanted to be a producer and asked what kind of deal he could offer me. He said he'd pay me a salary of $175 a week for a month or two to put together and play in the studio band, and then it would be raised to two hundred dollars, depending on what happened. He would also pay me a percentage for the records I produced, so I accepted the offer and gave notice in Miami.

Steve Alaimo was really pissed off. He hadn't told me anything about it beforehand, but, when I returned from my trip to Macon, they were installing an 8-track machine. We'd only had a 4-track in the little studio and they'd bought a new Ampex 8-track. He told me they wouldn't have bought it if they'd known I wasn't going to be there, and he was mad as hell but I told him I wanted to move on and be a producer.

When I moved to Macon in July 1969, Capricorn Records was an idea that Phil was still putting together. Phil Walden & Associates managed most of the Southern black R&B acts, which, of course, had included Otis Redding. Phil was handling the management, Alan Walden was doing the booking, and Bobby Wallace worked with Phil in the management company. Carolyn Brown was the receptionist and Phil's private secretary, and she took care of everything. She was the person to see when you went to talk with Phil. Today, if anyone ever wants to know anything about Capricorn, Carolyn is the one to talk with because she was there from start to finish.

I arrived in Macon around the time the Brothers were working on their first album. It was being recorded in New York because the studio in Macon wasn't quite ready. The first Capricorn release was the Allman Brothers Band on the Atco/Capricorn label in November 1969. Phil believed the record company was about to happen, and he needed a record company person with experience. Atlantic was where his connections were because of the success he'd had with the black artists on that label and through his relationship with Jerry Wexler. In fact, Phil and Jerry were both Capricorns and that's how the name Capricorn came about for the record company. Phil had met Frank Fenter through Jerry and knew he was head of Atlantic Records in the United Kingdom, and he wanted Frank to work for the label. I remember meeting him shortly after I moved to town when he was in Macon for a couple of days talking with Phil. Phil told me Frank would be working with him, and shortly before the first Allman Brothers Band record was released, Frank and his wife moved from England to Macon.

Frank ran the nuts and bolts of Capricorn. He knew everybody in the music business and knew the record business from the ground up. He really got things started to help us sell a lot of records. Overall, I had a good relationship with Frank. We certainly had some disagreements at times, but I liked him and respected what he did. He was extremely sharp, and I appreciated what he knew about the record business. He was optimistic, had a good attitude, and could help keep everyone enthusiastic about things.

There were two guest houses behind a large house right off Ridge Avenue, and Phil lived in one of them. When I got to Macon, I moved into the other one and my house was comfortable, but not nearly as nice as Phil's. Living that close I'd see him a lot and we'd talk and listen to music some, but he was going with Peggy about then and they were pretty serious. Bunky Odom, who worked with Phil in booking, was my roommate for a while in the guest house and it was like the *Odd Couple* with two Oscars living there. Bunky read a lot of newspapers and he'd drop them where he sat. I didn't know there were that many newspapers published. Eventually they spread out and we had a whole carpet of them.

Bunky was the most competitive person I know. Right across the street from where we were living was a school with a softball field in the school yard and a lot of times on the weekends the Capricorn employees would get together for a game that would almost always end up with a trip to the emergency room. We were playing a friendly softball game one day when Bunky slid head-first into first base and nearly killed himself. Everyone was telling him, "Bunky, it's just a game!"

When I first started working at Capricorn, the name of the studio was the Otis Redding Memorial Studio. When you walked in the front door, it looked like a vacant building with a whole bunch of lumber and other stuff lying around. Down the hallway was the door to the studio. It seemed the studio would be a wreck, too, but then you opened the door and there was this beautiful studio. The contrast was shocking.

During a later remodeling, the front was made into a reception area and some offices were added. We had a game space where we could eat and musicians could sit around while someone was in the studio overdubbing, a copy room, and a side room that served as a shop for any repairs that needed to be done. It was nicely laid out and a comfortable place to spend a lot of time. The original bathroom at the studio was way back down in a corner of the basement and I don't think it had a door on it. The basement always felt haunted to me, and I'm not the first person to say that. Maybe it was just scary looking, but it was a frightening trip when we had to go to the bathroom. Later, when the front was remodeled, the bathroom was moved upstairs and I felt like we'd entered the twentieth century.

Jim Hawkins built the original studio in Macon. I think he designed the big room after the RCA or CBS recording studios that were state of the art back then. There was a huge 16-input Universal Audio all tube console Jim had put together like everyone was doing at Stax and Muscle Shoals Sound. I remember how we couldn't wait to get rid of it and get something new, but now they've reissued all the modules and they cost a fortune. What was a two- or three- hundred-dollar module then is now about a thousand or twelve hundred dollars. Bill Putman, who was the man at Universal Audio, and later on Urei, designed the modules. Each one was three or three and a half inches wide and had big, stove-top style knobs, a mic pre and a tone control/equalizer with a high frequency and a low frequency boost or cut. I think it had three or four busses, and it was just amazing how good it could sound. It was designed for 3-track recording, and when we went to 4-track, we had it modified to work as a 4-track.

The studio had a big control room with three speakers. We had four tracks to work with, and if we had something on track one it automatically played back on the left speaker. If we recorded on track two, it played on the right, etc., and we only had one pan pot. It was basic stuff based around mono. Stereo was happening, but it wasn't big the way mono was. We'd concentrate on a mono mix and then do a stereo mix to save in case the song made it to an album. Everyone was doing mono mixes because without stereo radio, the 45 was what was going to be heard on the radio. At the time, FM was just for classical music; AM was the only popular format, and the frequency response of AM was limited. It depended on the station, but there was and still is a lot of compression. Everyone was mixing to the market where we were going to sell our records, so we ended up mixing on one speaker. (For additional information on the studio equipment, check out Jim Hawkins's website at www.electroacoustics.com.)

There wasn't any digital echo in the late '60s, so in the beginning about the only thing we had by way of effects were three little rooms in the basement of the studio Jim built to use as echo chambers. Each was a small, oddly shaped room with bathroom-style tile on the floor, ceiling, and sides that made the rooms amazingly reverberant. The echo chamber was set up with a speaker facing one corner and a mic at the opposite corner. If you wanted reverb on something, you sent the sound to the speaker and monitored the return of the mic. The more of the signal sent to the speaker, the more reverb would be picked up on the mic to bring back to the mix. It didn't sound bad, but it was a little cranky at times. If someone was down there—for whatever reason—making very much noise, we could hear it in the studio monitors upstairs, which made for some very interesting eavesdropping.

Like any other studio, ours had problems from time to time. Jim would be down there fixing it, going by Pick-up Meals (a meat and three), then heading back to the studio to work some more on whatever was wrong. Things didn't always work like they were supposed to, and we were lucky to have eight channels working at one time on the Scully 8-track. Now, with the way things are with computers, you have unlimited tracks and can go until your computer runs out of power. Back then, though, you had to be quite conservative with tracks. You had to plan ahead and know how many instruments there would be and have an idea of what to put on the record because there were only eight channels to work with. We were working a lot, but we enjoyed it. Whatever problems I had with the studio, Jim was able to chase them down and get them fixed.

I must admit I'm impatient about technical things, or at least I was then. After I started doing more producing I think I got on Jim's nerves because if any little thing was wrong, I'd try to get him to fix it immediately. But he tolerated me, and by the time we got through, it was a great sounding studio; in fact, it was better than we realized at the time. Later on we'd get newer stuff that was supposedly better but sometimes the older stuff sounded better. Having good equipment makes some things go smoother, but it's not up to the equipment to be successful. If you're recording an artist and don't get in the way, you can cut a hit on any equipment.

After the studio was finished, the hope was to record a lot of the acts Phil was managing. It would save money, they'd have a home base, and it would consolidate what Phil was doing for the management company. I think the idea behind it was to emulate Stax and Muscle Shoals. The studio band wanted to be like Booker T and the MGs and the Muscle Shoals Rhythm section.

Starting out, we had a heck of a time putting the rhythm section together. Paul Hornsby played keyboards, and Pete Carr, who'd been in Miami, moved up to Macon about the time I did. Pete and I had several months experience playing together in Miami. Of course, I'd recorded with Paul, but we went through several bass players. One of the bass players who didn't work out at first was Charlie Hayward. I think he was probably good enough to do the job, but he was a little nervous and younger than the rest of us. We really liked him a lot and liked working with him, but he needed a little more experience. We had to get someone else, but a few years later, he came back and re-joined the rhythm section. I liked his playing and, after a while, I used him on everything.

Duane hooked us up with Robert Popwell, who was like James Jamerson or someone in that style. The stuff we were playing was very basic R&B, but Popwell was one of those bass players you had to wear out in order to get him to play something simple. He wasn't sure what simple and basic *was*, and Hornsby would get so mad he'd go over and dog cuss Popwell because he was playing so busy. It would take all of us getting on to him and threatening to kill him to get him to settle down. I'd look over and tell Popwell to play just on the one and the three beat. I can listen to some of the old records where I played very simply, which left plenty of room for him and he took it. It still sounds good. After Popwell left the band, he went on to play with the Crusaders, a great band from California with amazing players.

For a while we had a hell of a time getting the rhythm section to jell. We'd cut stuff and it just wouldn't be that good. At times the studio didn't sound exactly right. It took a lot of effort to get it to work like we wanted, but eventually both the band and the studio improved. (I've noticed that when the band plays better the studio sounds better.) The first things we played on in Macon were for Jackie Avery, a great guy and excellent songwriter. Phil had signed him to his publishing company, so Jackie would come down to the studio to record his songs. In fact, most of the songs we cut during that period were demos for Jackie because we couldn't rent out the studio. Later, Phil signed all the members of the different bands to writing contracts with his company No Exit Music. Gregg, Dickey, and the rest of the Allman Brothers were signed to the company, as were the guys in Marshall Tucker, but I think Avery was the only staff writer he had who was a writer and not a signed artist.

One of the few outside projects we did during that time was when Phil would rent the studio to Jerry Williams, a.k.a. Swamp Dogg. Pete and I had worked with him in Miami, and he kept the studio busy doing records for different artist or groups. Capricorn wasn't cutting a record with him, but Phil and/or Frank Fenter would sometimes rent the studio to Swamp Dogg for a weekend. For two or three days in a row we'd go in and record maybe fourteen, fifteen, or sixteen hours a day with Swamp Dogg until we were so tired we couldn't see straight. He'd start on Friday and come out Monday morning with a mixed record. Of course, there were only eight tracks to mix; back then mixes were pretty basic, but he'd do a whole record. He'd find some of the local horn players around, and we'd have horns and background singers—and the whole thing was done in a weekend.

Jerry was the funniest person I ever worked with in the studio. He had a wonderful sense of humor, but he was a little sarcastic at times. The only way an artist in the studio could hear you was if you pushed the "talk back" button in the control room. There's a little switch on the console you hold down, and when you're through talking, you release it. Someone would be out there singing, and maybe they wouldn't be doing a very good job. Jerry would hit the talk back and say, "Hey man, you're killing us. You need to take it from the top, but just give it just a little more of what you've got...." Then he'd release the talk back, look back at us, and make some remark or comment like "You sick bitch!" that kept us in stitches.

I'd been interested in engineering from the time of the HourGlass days, and I'd done a little bit at Tone Studio with Terry Kane, the man who built their studio. Jim Hawkins began teaching me the basics of engineering and showed me a lot about how things worked in the studio. He showed me how to use tape machines and how to do editing, which always amazed me. After I learned to do it, it wasn't quite so amazing, but the more involved you get into it the more difficult it is. If Jim was there, he'd engineer the session. Sometimes he wouldn't be available, so I'd cut the track. I'd turn the recorder on, then run out and play drums. Sometimes I was the only guy there doing all the recording.

I did some demos with Floyd Miles, a singer from Jacksonville who sounded a little bit like Otis and was a good friend of Gregg's. He was another reason I was glad to be in Macon rather than Miami. Floyd had written some songs that I thought were going to be great. After we finished recording, I took them to Phil and was really disappointed because he wasn't interested. I kept trying though and took them back up to him every chance I could, but I never had any success in getting Phil's interest.

When we were working, Phil would stop by the studio to check on things, but there wasn't all that much interaction with him in the beginning. Once I got involved in producing, I'd see him more. If I got something that was really hot, I'd call him and play it over the phone. That was a big deal back then. You'd call up him and say, "Hey, listen to this!"

Phil was always inspiring. He'd say, "Oh man, we're gonna do this...we're gonna do that" and we would. He'd get you all fired up to do whatever it was, and you really believed you could do it. He would always say, "We can do it, we can do it, come on, I can make it happen, I've got this guy, I've got this guy...he's gonna help us." He'd plan the whole thing and he'd make it work. I came to love and respect him.

Phil had a legendary temper, but he never directed it towards me. I'm not sure I could have taken it if he had. Someone would make him mad and he'd go nuts. He'd get on the phone and start cussing someone, and it would just go on and on. I was in the office a couple of times when those calls came in; I'd sit there almost afraid to move. I'd be afraid he was going to kill himself because his face would turn red and I thought he was about to have a heart attack. He'd get up, pace, and pound on the desk.

Phil was with his anger like Duane was with his guitar. Duane would be playing intensely until he'd about wear you out with his intensity, and just when you thought you couldn't take it any longer, he'd hit an even higher gear. Phil was the same way when he got mad. Just when you thought he couldn't get any more intense, he'd hit another gear and it would be just unbelievable. You didn't want to be in there and you couldn't leave. A lot of times some of the staff would gather outside his office door just to listen.

12

Ton Ton Macoute

About the time Capricorn was getting starting, there had been racial tension between some of the black acts and the record companies. Phil told me about being at the 1968 NATRA (National Association of Television and Radio Announcers) R&B disc jockey convention in Miami and having his life threatened. Some of the black acts had invited white record company executives to go for a drink…then threatened their lives because they felt the record companies had cheated them out of their money. Jerry Wexler was hung in effigy at the same convention.

Phil had done a lot to help close the racial divide. Believe me, working with a close black friend in Macon, Georgia, in the sixties was not what the Chamber of Commerce was looking for. A lot of the "establishment" didn't know which way to jump. Phil was the first high profile person I knew of who didn't let race get in the way of business. While I lived in Macon, I didn't get hassled too badly by the police, but I remember taking Floyd Miles home after working on some demos one night when I got stopped by the cops. The mayor of Macon even bought a tank for use in case of civil unrest due to racial tension. They called him "Machine Gun" Ronnie Thompson, and he actually had a machine gun and a tank.

For at least the first couple of years I was in Macon, I spent about all my working time in the studio, pretty much going home long enough to sleep and then heading back to the studio again. In addition to playing in the rhythm section, I began producing almost as soon as I arrived at Capricorn. I'd go into the studio to play drums on albums Jerry Williams was recording, and then I'd play on and produce other projects. I was fortunate enough to work with Arthur Conley on a few singles during this time.

Phil managed Arthur Conley when he'd had the big hit "Sweet Soul Music." The studio was coming into its own, and since I was starting to produce, Phil agreed to let me do a couple of sides on Arthur. I liked him a lot—he was nice and a really neat dresser. It took him a while to learn a song, but he had a marvelous voice and always memorized the lyrics. In addition to his being a great singer, one of the reasons I wanted to do a record with Arthur was that he was Otis Redding's protégé. In fact, Otis had cut "Sweet Soul Music" with him over at FAME in Muscle Shoals. I went about choosing some songs for him. Arthur said he wanted to record "They Call the Wind Mariah." It is a song from a musical, which I thought was weird, but it was one Sam Cooke had done. I'd always liked that song, but I knew it from the Sam Cooke version on the radio—not the musical.

I figured out an arrangement to do with just strings for the intro. We didn't have anything like the digital metronomes you can plug in now. The traditional metronomes would have to be put in a separate room with a mic, which would have been a little more trouble than we wanted to go to anyway. Since I was playing drums on it, I did clicking sticks to set the beat and told Hornsby to play just a single note melody on the piano to be a guide for the strings. It was kind of silly sounding with me sitting there going "click, click, click" with the drum sticks and Paul playing the melody to the intro one note at a time. After quite a few takes we got through it, and it came out pretty good.

I talked to Eddie and sent him a track of what we'd done, and he wrote the string parts for me. I went to Muscle Shoals to pick him up, then he and I went up to Memphis and recorded the strings at the old Ardent studio. I think Terry Manning, who subsequently worked with Z. Z. Top and numerous other major acts, was the engineer. I always liked the record. It got some play and made the charts, but it never was a hit.

Atco pulled the record and stopped promotion just as "They Call the Wind Mariah" started up the charts because it was time to release the next single. It was a Jerry Williams song called "God Bless" that we'd originally cut with Swamp Dogg. I'd picked it as one I wanted to do with Arthur. It was one of those pull-at-your-heartstrings songs, and Arthur, of course, did a good job. That song also had mixed success and got some airplay. It made it to number thirty-three on the R&B chart and was in the top fifty on the pop chart. None of the singles were hits, but they kept the flame burning.

When the song was on the chart and looked like it was going up, Frank called to tell me how pumped he was. He told me, "Johnny, you might as well go ahead and order that Lincoln or something else nice to drive 'cause you've got a hit record." A new car was a sign of success, and I was really excited and thought that wasn't a bad idea. I even called the Lincoln dealer but was put on hold while they were putting me through to the salesman. Before the guy picked up, I came to my senses. I thought there was a good chance it wasn't going to be a hit, and I certainly couldn't afford a new Lincoln on a salary of a hundred and seventy five dollars a week!

I cut another single on Arthur with a song Jackie Avery had written. Avery came in one day and started playing a song I fell in love with called "Your Love Has Brought Me a Mighty Long Way." Pete and Paul were at the studio, so Popwell and I worked up a groove to the song and then recorded it. It was one of those magic days in the studio when everything seemed to come together, and we cut a great track. Avery had a really gruff voice that just fit the song and he sang great on the vocal. Pete was doing some of the background vocals and, if you listen to that version of it, you can hear what sounds like a woman screaming in the background going, "hey, hey" or something like that. It was Pete using his falsetto voice to sound like a black soprano lady, and it freaked everyone out. The whole group was gathered around the microphone with a gospel sound going on. When Pete hit that, everyone started looking around. We stopped to find out who was doing it; and Pete admitted it was him and asked if he should stop. I told him no, that it was great. Nobody believed Pete could make that sound.

We finished recording the track that afternoon and did all the background vocals. I was excited about it, so I took it over to Phil's place and left it on his doorstep. When he listened to it, he liked it but wasn't nearly as excited about it as we were. He said he thought it was a good song for Arthur Conley. I told him Avery was perfect on it, but Phil said no, he wanted to do it on Arthur. Eventually we put Arthur's voice on the track and it came out well. I was proud of it then and still am.

The first single on the Capricorn Records label was from Johnny Jenkins's *Ton Ton Macoute* album. Right after I got there, Phil started telling me about Johnny Jenkins. The first thing he had in mind was for me to record an album with Johnny. Phil had been booking Johnny all across the South when Otis Redding was just a singer in the band and Johnny was the star. Even when I was in a band in high school back in Decatur, I'd hear something about Johnny once in a while long before I got to meet him.

Since Johnny had been an influence on Jimi Hendrix, Phil wanted to do something similar to Jimi, which I took to mean that Voodoo Child image, and to cut something in that vein because blues wasn't selling at all. I was introduced to Johnny and talked with him; then, I started looking for songs. When Phil bought Duane's contract he got some of the tracks we'd cut at Rick Hall's FAME studio. I thought we could use a few of them since that album was suspended. The Allman Brothers were starting to happen, and there was no need for a Duane Allman solo album.

I was a huge fan of Dr. John and had worn out several copies of his first album, *Gris Gris,* so I thought I'd do something in that swampish, New Orleans vibe and decided to cut a track of a Dr. John song, "I Walk on Gilded Splinters." Duane wanted to play on it, and I was fortunate enough to get Butch and Jaimoe to play on it too. Duane was on dobro, a featured part of the song; Butch played drums; Jaimoe was on timbales; Popwell played bass; Paul played keys; and Pete played electric guitar on the track.

It was a magic night in the studio when we cut the track. Duane was set up behind a couple of baffles with the dobro, Popwell was in a little bass area of the studio, Jaimoe was out on the floor, and Butch was in the semi-drum booth. I showed Butch a beat I wanted him to play; then he took it and did something else in the general vicinity of what I wanted— but better than I had in mind. The track grooved from the beginning. We cut two or three really good takes, and I chose one for the album, made a copy of the track, and took it back to my house. I just knew there was something special to that track. Duane got excited about it and called Phil next door and told him, "Man, you gotta hear this." I don't know if the call woke him up or if he was doing something else, but he told Duane he'd listen to it the next day. When Phil finally heard it, he was equally excited.

Johnny wasn't involved with the tracking of the song because he didn't want to come in and play much with the band. He didn't know the song, so the job then was to get Johnny's vocals on the track. The lyrics were difficult to dig out to begin with; there were some French-Cajun words that weren't easy to pronounce, so I wrote it all out phonetically. Johnny wasn't really crazy about that song and stumbled through it. Mainly his goal in a record was to do a more traditional blues thing, which I wasn't especially interested in doing at that time.

We did record two or three more conventional blues songs for the album that Johnny was used to playing. The blues things were fairly simple; there wasn't all that much production on them since they were songs everyone either knew or were familiar with, and we cut them in an afternoon. We also cut three songs that were on the 1997 re-release of the *Ton Ton Macoute* album. One of my favorite cuts on the record was "I Walk on Gilded Splinters." Since then, the drum track on it has been sampled on the Beck single, "I'm a Loser" and the Oasis song "Go Let it Out." It really was a magic track.

I was sitting in my studio a few years later watching MTV while changing strings on a guitar when I first heard Beck's "Loser." I thought, "Damnation! That sure sounds familiar." Then I blew it off thinking it was just something similar. After hearing the song three or four more times, I decided to get the record and listen more closely. When I did, I realized it was the drum track to the Johnny Jenkins's version of "I Walk on Gilded Splinters." The song starts out with about forty-five to fifty seconds of drums and they'd taken a few bars off the intro and looped them to make a track for "Loser."

I was shocked and called my lawyer at the time and asked him to check it out. He did and told me Beck had gotten a license from Polydor for the sample. Johnny ended up making some money off the track, but Butch and I weren't very happy about being excluded from the royalties.

One of the other songs on the album, "Voodoo in You," was Avery's tune. We cut it using the same line-up as "Gilded Splinters." The song contained the line, "I don't believe in hoaxes," and Johnny kept singing, "I don't believe in *hoxes*." I'd explain to him the word was pronounced *hoaxes* with the long "o" sound, but he'd still sing it *hoxes* that rhymed with *foxes*. This went back and forth for a while, and finally on the record it ended up *hoxes*. I thought it was pretty funny.

Another one of my favorite songs on the album was one Johnny called "Catfish Blues," also known as "Rolling Stone," and it was recorded one night with Johnny playing acoustic, Duane playing slide on acoustic, and Berry Oakley playing bass. It was just those three instruments with Johnny stomping his foot on a piece of 4x8 plywood we'd put down. There were two takes and we kept the track I thought was the better of the two, but they were both special. We recorded a lot of other songs I liked; one from the Taj Mahal album, "Leavin' Trunk," and we did "Sick and Tired," a Chris Kenner song I'd played in a bunch of bands. Then Jackie wrote "Blind Bats and Swamp Rats" and "Voodoo in You," which was the first single. I was really proud of the drum part I played on "Blind Bats and Swamp Rats." It's the only track I feel I've ever played completely right.

Naming the album *Ton Ton Macoute* was Frank Fenter's idea. He'd either just been to Haiti or was familiar with the goings on down there from the news. Ton Ton Macoute was the name of the evil police force in Haiti that was controlled by Papa Doc. They had a horrible reputation and Frank thought since we were doing this album with all the voodoo-sounding stuff, having something that related to Haiti would be a good idea, hence, the name *Ton Ton Macoute*. I didn't like the name at first but grew to love it.

That album has surprised me. It was one of those that garnered a lot of attention and great reviews, but only very few were purchased. I've gone to New York and been introduced to people who'd say, "Oh yeah, you did that Johnny Jenkins album." These are people I'd have never thought even had a way of ever hearing it. Obviously, more people heard it than I realized.

For all intents and purposes, that album gave me validity as a producer. After that, people considered me as a realistic possibility to produce their albums. *Rolling Stone* liked the album, mentioning it several times over the years and comparing other subsequent albums to it, but originally it didn't hurt having some of the Brothers playing on two of the tracks.

I was proud of the album until I heard that Johnny Jenkins didn't like it at all. Then it totally blew my groove and freaked me out because I loved it. I finished it up and took him a copy, and all I heard about was how much he hated the record. Johnny didn't even want to tour the album. I didn't want to do records the artist hated, and I re-evaluated my production style after that. Before then, I'd have an idea and go until it got done. I wasn't demeaning to anyone...I just knew what I wanted, whether it was good or bad and would push things until I was satisfied with it. After that album, I tried to be more sympathetic to the artists and their styles.

When you have something the artist needs to do, there are times you need to insist they do it and make it as palatable as possible because as a producer you should have a better idea how the recorded media will attract the most interest from the public. I've learned, though, not to push things to the bottom line if the artist is adamant. Sometimes, if an artist is indifferent to a song, I'll try to get them to cut it and listen to it again after it's been recorded. Occasionally they'll change their opinion, but I never wanted to do another record for anyone who hated or was embarrassed by their album. When I worked with Johnny again years later I think his opinion of the album had mellowed a little bit. Because the track to "Gilded Splinters" has been sampled, it's one of the few albums that made him some money.

I always liked Johnny. He was eccentric and at times acted like he didn't trust me or Phil Walden or anyone. While we were working on *Ton Ton Macoute*, I used to go up to Johnny's apartment in Macon to pick him up. Every time I'd go there he'd tell me, "Phil's supposed to send me some money for the babysitter." I don't know that he had a babysitter or even a baby, but I assume he did. So I'd give him whatever he and Phil had agreed on or I'd say, "Come on down to the studio and we'll get you your money," and we'd take care of him that way. I don't think he really trusted white people at the time, but I'd go down and get him, and he was always nice. He was a good guy, and in '96 when we did *Blessed Blues* together, we got along really well.

The second Atlanta Pop Festival was held July 3–5 right outside of Macon in Byron, and the Allman Brothers were going to be on it. Phil had made arrangements for Johnny to play, so we thought we'd put a band together like we had for the *Ton Ton Macoute* album and have this dynamic band with a dream line up to back him up. We had two sets of drums for Bill Stewart and me. Jaimoe was playing congas; Lou Mullenix, a great drummer and good friend who is no longer with us, was playing timbales; Chuck Leavell was playing piano; and Hornsby was playing organ. Popwell played bass, and Pete was on guitar with Ella Avery, Jackie's wife, singing back-up. The line-up, especially with the percussion section we had, sounded like a train coming down the tracks. It was the most powerful thing I'd ever heard. I couldn't believe it; it was just thrilling and gave me a rush. It was hard to get Johnny there because he didn't want to rehearse, so we only managed to get a couple of rehearsals with him before the show.

We were scheduled to play late Saturday night, but everything kept getting pushed back later and later until we went on just as the sun was coming up. There was a sea of people; some were sleeping while others were just waking up and crawling out of their sleeping bags or make-shift shelter for the night. It was freaky to look out and see the crowd. There were so many people that once we started playing and the crowd began moving around, it looked a little like a sea. I'd never played before that many people, and it was kind of scary and awe inspiring to look out over a crowd that big. We woke them up though—at least a few of them anyway.

The stage at the festival was twenty-five feet up and to get there, you had to climb a long staircase. The set-up was Bill and me in the back, Chuck, Popwell and Ella Avery to the left, and Paul and Lou to the right. I don't remember where Pete was, but the stage was balanced.

So we went on with this big band and played one or two songs, then all of a sudden we saw Johnny walking off the stage. He'd broken a guitar string, and we figured he was going over to get it fixed. The next thing we knew, he was down the long stair case and about fifteen feet behind the stage area, heading for the road. We only had about seven songs worked up to play with him and that was it. We weren't a regular working band and had nothing to play, and there he was leaving with Phil chasing after him. We called a shuffle in G and played that for a few minutes, then Johnny came back. His guitar was fixed and we finished out the set.

There was a not-so-funny story about my name as producer on the single, "Voodoo in You," that was released before the album came out. Phil was down at the studio and told me they'd gotten the records in. It was being released in England first because Jimi Hendrix was breaking big in England. Also Frank Fenter, originally from South Africa, had lived in England for a long time and been head of Atlantic, so that's where his connections were. I went to the office to get a copy and it read, "Produced by Jackie Avery." I wanted to cry. I never have felt so many strange emotions at once—anger, sadness, confusion. It turns out Frank thought that Avery, since he was the writer of the song, was the producer. I wondered why he'd thought that, but it didn't matter. My name wasn't on it. The single with Jackie Avery's name was a white label disc jockey copy, so I don't know if it got much farther than that, but it broke my heart at the time.

The credit was corrected on the album, but another odd thing happened in connection with the record. Somehow before the release of the album, the left and right channels of the stereo mix were reversed. I'd put a lot of energy into making the album sound the way I thought it should, and it was correct until someone plugged the wrong plug into the wrong hole while it was being mastered at Atlantic. I suppose to most people it's not that important, especially if you don't know which way it's supposed to be, but a lot of thought was given into how things were panned, how the music moved from left to right. I could have spit nails after hearing that.

It took a while to finish *Ton Ton Macoute*. We'd cut the tracks and Johnny would come in later and do vocals, so I was working on several things at once. There was always something going on at the studio. Stax used to farm out tracks, some to Muscle Shoals and a few to Capricorn, and their producer would come down to work on them. Don Davis was one who came down to cut some tracks and, for some reason, Alan Walden was involved and wanted me to produce it. I was all for that, but I told him if I was going to do all the work, I wanted production credit. We got into a little tiff about that. He didn't think I deserved any credit if I took charge of the session and I disagreed. He thought I was the studio drummer and should do what I was told. I can't remember how it was resolved, but we came to an understanding and never had that problem again. The tracks got cut and one of them was ultimately used for an Eddie Floyd record.

Around this time there was a single released with the studio band going by the name Macon. Booker T would do a lot of instrumentals around dance grooves or songs that were made for this or that particular dance and Phil got the word from Jerry Wexler there was a dance called the Chicken. He thought we should do an instrumental for it and put us to work writing and recording one and we came up with a song called "Pulley Bone." The band was Popwell, Paul, Pete, and me and was recorded a la Booker T and the MGs. Of course they were our heroes and still are. Since it was going to be released as a 45, we needed a back side and came up with a song we named "Ripple Rap." We weren't making a whole lot of money back then, and Ripple was a cheap wine that was a cheap way to get a buzz, hence "Ripple Rap."

We played it for Tom Dowd, a well respected producer and engineer with Atlantic, and he pointed out that the song had different sections and kind of jumped around a lot, something we'd missed. He told us we needed to elongate some of the sections. I always remember that as a king piece of advice from Tom. We made the changes and the song came out better, but I don't know that we completely implemented what he suggested. It was a very limited release, more like it just kind of escaped.

I stayed pretty busy most of the time. The Brothers were gaining national recognition and there were all kinds of people wanting to work in Macon. Jon Landau was a writer and publisher who'd been at *Rolling Stone*, and he and Phil met and became friends when he'd interviewed Phil for the magazine. He came down to Capricorn to record Livingston Taylor, and at first Phil arranged for Jon and me to co-produce the album. I think the world of Jon, but we were both novices, and he had his own ideas about recording. He finally talked to me one day and said he wanted to do it by himself. He wanted me to play on the record, but he didn't want me to be involved in the production. I told him, "Sure." To be honest about it, the album was coming off okay, but I heard things differently and felt kind of useless. I suppose he was more insistent than I was about certain things, and he understood Livingston a lot better than I did. I loved Livingston and his music and enjoyed just playing on the record, and Jon and I remained friends.

Livingston's brother, James Taylor, was just starting to happen big and was playing all over. His other brother, Alex Taylor, came down during the recording and that's when I first met him. Alex and I hit it off right away, and Phil signed him for me to produce his album.

14

Cowboy

Duane told Phil about a band from Jacksonville, Florida, called Cowboy with Scott Boyer, whom I'd known from my days in Miami when we'd go play gigs along the beach, and Tommy Talton, another writer and guitar player. In addition to playing guitar, Scott and Tommy were the lead singers in the band; Pete Kowalke was on guitar; George Clark played bass, Bill Pillmore was the piano player, and Tom Wynn was the drummer. Phil sent me down to Jacksonville to listen to them and let him know what I thought. I have to admit, it was a weird experience.

The band was holding the audition in the middle of nowhere, back in some woods I didn't even know existed in Florida. We took a four-wheeled drive vehicle into the woods and had to walk the rest of the way to get to this guy's place. It was a very nice cabin with a swimming pool, and there were a bunch of naked people swimming and walking around. Evidently clothing was optional. I've never been too wild about guys walking around naked, and it certainly was eye opening. It wasn't a bad thing, just a very weird vibe.

The whole gig had been arranged specifically for me to listen to the band, and all the members were set up inside the cabin ready to play. About two or three times in my life I've gotten so sleepy nothing could keep me from drifting off and this was one of those times. I don't know if I hadn't had enough rest or if I was getting sick, but by the time the band got around to playing, I was so drowsy I couldn't keep my eyes open. I was having one of the "Sorry, it's time for you to shut off" moments. I'd be listening and have my eyes closed and then suddenly be jerking awake. It was embarrassing because the band was good, but I just couldn't stay awake. By the time they got through the first few songs I knew I wanted to work with them, however I don't think I even made it through the first set.

I went back and told Phil I totally concurred with Duane and thought we should sign them. The band came up to Macon to meet with

Phil but before they did, they stopped by to see me at the studio, and I did something I learned never to do again. While talking about their upcoming meeting with Phil, I advised them to try to keep at least half their publishing rights when they made the deal with Capricorn. I gave them the advice but also said, "Please, *please* don't tell Phil I made this suggestion." Later, Scott told me right after the meeting started one of the guys in the band said, "Johnny told us we should ask about keeping half our publishing." I felt pretty betrayed by the artist and wasn't very happy at all. I hadn't been at Capricorn very long, and it wasn't good for me to go against the company employing me. I never, *never* did it again or ever will. After meeting with Phil, the band moved to Macon and signed with Capricorn. In fact, after the Brothers, Cowboy was the next band signed by the label.

When we began recording, everyone in the band was up for the project. They had an album's worth of material they'd been playing live. They were well rehearsed, and the songs were fun, light, hippie, good feeling music; innocent folk with a little country rock flavor and great harmonies along the lines of the Eagles. A lot of their heroes were more like Jesse Winchester and the Band.

One afternoon in the studio, I got the sounds as best I knew how at the time and we started recording. Tom was set up in the drum booth; George, on bass, was in the booth next to the drums; Scott was on acoustic with his back to the control room surrounded by two large baffles, and the piano was more or less in the center of our set-up. Tommy was to Scott's left out in the room with his amp next to him, and Pete was sort of in front of the drum booth with his amp. We recorded the first two or three songs on the album the first day and cut everybody all at once.

There wasn't all the over-dubbing there is now. We had eight tracks with one track for drums, one track for the bass, one track for the piano. After that, we had to start figuring out what we wanted to do next. Sometimes we'd put the piano on with the guitar and after we recorded it, we might think, "I've got to bounce this rhythm track," or "I've got to bounce this guitar track and get the piano down to one track to make room on the eight-track to get the rest of the stuff." Occasionally when we filled up six tracks, we'd bounce them down to one or two tracks or we'd keep the drums and bass on discreet tracks and bounce the rest down to one or two. Sometimes I'd do some of the mixing down as we recorded live. Everyone in the band was an excellent singer, and they had beautiful harmonies.

The band sounded good. They were playing well, and it was all recorded live. There may have been a punch in or two, or someone might have missed a chord. If it was on a separate track it could be fixed. Of course, if it was mixed with something else going down, you either had to do them both over or do the whole track over. Most of the people making records during that time really could play and sing, and it was fun to record that way because it kept everyone on their toes. Now, it's really easy to get lazy thinking if you miss a lick or two it's no big deal because you can always go back and fix it. Back then you'd have a whole bunch of people mad at you if you were the one who screwed up the track. It was a whole different mindset.

I think we were there for a couple of days straight between good things to smoke and a few amphetamines. Everything had been going well with the recording, but after a while we got a little tired. I said, "Hey, I've got some Black Beauties here." Black Beauties were an amphetamine I had at the time for weight loss, and they had all kinds of names like California Turn Around or biphetamines, and they were pretty powerful. The guys were asking, "What's this like?" I told them, "Oh, they'll just make you feel better and keep you from getting too sleepy." So everybody took one and we cut over half the album in those two days.

Towards the end of our two days in the studio, about the time the effect of the Black Beauties was starting to wear off, some of the guys got to thinking of some ways to keep the session moving along. One of them said, "Hey, let's do a track naked." I thought to myself that certainly wasn't necessary and wasn't something I even wanted to envision. I told them, "I'll turn the lights out and you can do what you want, but y'all can't come into the control room naked." All the guys took off their clothes and we cut a track or two. I could see them from the waist up, but I didn't look down.

It was early morning of the second day when Floyd, the janitor, came in. Usually he'd come in and check to see if anyone was in the control room, then he'd go on and clean the studio first but on this particular day, he walked into the studio while everyone was playing naked. He wasn't in there long. As soon as he saw one of the guys, he headed out and went on to do his work elsewhere in the building. After that, Floyd always looked in the control room and knocked to make sure it was okay to go out into the studio.

When we were finished with our two-day marathon recording session, I remember walking out of the studio and the sun was up. When I'd first gone into the studio, I'd had to park about a block away in a bank parking lot because, for some reason, Broadway had been lined with cars. As I walked down to the car I felt like a vampire with the sun beating down. I just wanted to get out of there and get home. I got in the car, cranked it up, and started backing up…right into a car in another parking space. My first thought was to just leave, but that didn't seem right, so I got out and looked at the car I'd hit. It had a minor scratch on it, so I waited around to see if the owner would come out. People gathered around, talking to me. I tried to make sense out of what they were saying, but I was still on another plane and trying to act normal. I don't remember the resolution, but it was taken care of and I made it home.

When it was time to mix the album, I'd decided to mix at Criteria because the studio B mix room had an MCI with Pentron faders and Capricorn had very few eqs, compressors, or reverb. I called Tom Dowd and asked if he would consider helping mix the record. I wanted to watch Tom mix and thought maybe if he was involved and liked the record, he might put in a good word with Atlantic and draw attention to the album. Tom said he didn't know if I really needed him, but he agreed to help me. I went to Miami to the studio and put the multi-track on, and Tom started mixing. He mixed fast and didn't use a lot of processing, but what he did sounded good. He only had time to mix three of the songs and then told me to take it from there, so I mixed the rest.

When I'd first gone to hear them, the band's name was Easy, but before the record was released, some of the guys didn't like that name and they came up with "Cowboy." Either Scott or Tommy told me opinions were mixed on that one, so finally it was decided they'd shoot hoops and whoever won got to pick the name of the band. Scott's side won, and the band became Cowboy. The album was titled *Reach for the Sky*, and there'd been a number of ideas submitted for the cover that had been turned down. Finally, one afternoon, the band went up to Phil's office and one of them, probably Tommy, drew the picture that turned out to be a really neat cover.

Cowboy didn't have anything near the commercial success they deserved, but they were popular. The first album was well received, but when they went out on the road, they never did get their live show as together as their records, at least during that time period. They played some good places and played some with the Brothers, but there wasn't a lot of continuity in their performances. Everyone was pretty young then and didn't know what to do other than the best they could by just going out there and doing it.

The album got some mixed reviews. *Rolling Stone* was the place you wanted to have your work reviewed, and I remember reading one review by Bin Edmonds that read in part, "On the surface, *Reach for the Sky*, the debut offering of a group called Cowboy, seems possessed of an energy best characterized as stationary. Nevertheless, the omens are clear; this group is one to watch." At the time it was heartbreaking to read. Capricorn was a new label, this was the second album I had released, and Cowboy was a new band. I got a lot of notice for both the Cowboy and *Ton Ton Macoute* albums, and I couldn't believe the number of people who'd heard them. They didn't sell well, but there must have been a lot of word of mouth. I remember Marlin Greene and some of the others over in Muscle Shoals loved them.

Duane was around a lot during that time. He lived in Macon, and when the band wasn't on the road he'd come by the studio to ask if I needed him for anything. He told me I could call if I needed him, and if he wasn't busy he'd come down. I couldn't ask for anything better than that; plus, the rest of the Brothers were available too. They were all good people, and there was a sense of community with the bands in Macon, at least that's what I felt. Of course, I just saw one aspect of it all. My frame of reference was mainly how they related to me in and around the studio or at my house after work.

Duane was the best kind of friend. If he liked you, he liked you and was always on your side. There's not a better friend to have than someone like that. We'd gotten to be pretty tight in the HourGlass out in California, and of course he got me involved with Capricorn while I was still in Miami. We just always got along. He liked what I was doing with recording and trusted me with it. His belief in me—believing I knew what I was doing and was going to do something well—made me even better.

Duane could be full of fire and excitable, and he could be mellow. He was a lot of fun to hang with and talk to, and we used to get albums and just sit down and listen to music. He always enjoyed hearing something different and approached everything with an open mind. He had no preconceived notions about something and would accept it for what it was; if he thought it was good, he liked it, and if he didn't like it, he didn't like it. But he didn't read about an album and make a decision before he heard it.

Duane was the boss of the band in the studio and everyone knew it. It wasn't like anyone was challenging him for the position. They all listened to him, and I always felt he gave the band stability and focus. He wasn't perfect. There were all kinds of things that would go wrong, but he would pull everyone out of whatever detour or sidetrack they got into. It was about the music with him. Duane took care of the band and kept everyone on course. They might all veer off for a little bit, but he'd drag everyone back, especially Gregg.

I had a phone in my apartment/guest house and all my friends would come and visit when I wasn't in the studio. They'd drop by and we'd smoke a joint and listen to some records. Gregg would come over a lot to make phone calls. One month I got an outrageous phone bill that was so much it freaked me out. I tried to find out why the bill was that high because if I'd made any long distance calls, there weren't many. In the '60s making a long distance phone call was a big deal, and you didn't just do it without thinking about it for a while. Come to find out, Gregg had made the calls to a girl somewhere out of state and he'd spent a long time on the phone.

I said, "Gregg, I've got this big phone bill" and he'd say, "Oh yeah, I'll get that for you tomorrow." Then I'd tell him, "I need the money. I don't have the money to pay it." We weren't making a lot of money then and none of us had much to spare. I wouldn't hear from him for a day or two and then I'd try to get it from him again. Finally Duane stopped by the house and I said, "Hey, Duane, when you see Gregg tell him I need the money for the phone bill." The next day Gregg came by and handed me the money. He'd gotten the word from Duane he needed to get the money to me right away. Duane bossed Gregg around and at times I thought he was kind of tough on him, but I guess maybe not. They loved each other, though, and everyone loved both of them. I still do.

There was something about Duane. You almost had to know him to understand what it was because I don't think I can describe it. You could tell Duane had an undeniable passion for music and something was going to happen with him; I noticed that the first time I saw him in Pensacola. All around, I think he inspired Phil Walden to do all the work he did in helping the band gain national recognition.

It was an exciting time, and Macon was the place to be. We were generating an energy that started attracting people to the area and we were getting a lot of press. Of course, being involved with Jon Landau didn't hurt because of his previous association with *Rolling Stone*. He was a good person to have in our corner, and he helped call attention to the label. Phil was the head cheerleader, the guy who knew the business and knew who to talk to. His enthusiasm could get just about anything done. You could be totally against him, yet he would make you believe what he believed because he got involved with the artists and believed in their music. He could sell it and make other people feel that way too. It was a magic feeling.

15

Alex Taylor

After the first Allman Brothers album was out in '69, we had a chart in Phil's office to keep track of the record's progress. I think it got up to fifty thousand in sales, which was respectable for that period, but it wasn't as good as we'd hoped. Then it was time for the band to record their next album. The band had started to tour a lot, but when they were in town, they'd call me. We'd go to the studio and record demos for their next album, which I thought I was going to produce. At least that's what I'd been told by Phil and Frank, as well as Duane and Gregg. I was doing most of the recording at Capricorn at the time, engineering, playing, or producing, so it was natural they'd want me to do the demos for the album. And everyone loved the demos we did.

We cut a version of "Midnight Rider" and, of course, it's a classic now. There was an earlier demo of it I didn't work on, but this particular version was more finished and featured the whole band. We cut "Hootchie Cootchie Man" with Berry singing, and I thought he sang well on the song. Berry could really sing and so can Dickey. They would have been great singers for the band if Gregg hadn't been in it, but Gregg is such a superb talent there aren't many people who can go toe to toe with him.

One of the demos, "Statesboro," eventually came out on the *Dreams* package. It's credited as "produced by Tom Dowd and Johnny Sandlin," however Tom and I never produced anything together. I think it's a track I started and he finished. We also cut "Elizabeth Reed." The Brothers would go next door to what we called the Hamlin building to practice. They were always fairly loud, so we could hear them through the studio walls. That's how I remember first hearing the strains of "Elizabeth Reed." There was something magic about it, so I walked over while they were working it up. I was sitting about ten feet from Duane and Dickey. When they hit the opening unison line and broke into harmony it gave me chills. I didn't see any way it wouldn't be a hit song, and it turned out to be one of their staples.

The Hamlin building isn't there any longer, but if you walked out of the studio and turned left, the Hamlin building was on the corner right by the alley. They tore it down a while back and it looks naked out there now. The buildings all up and down the block are gone, and the studio looks very lonely by itself. To be honest, I'm surprised it's still standing. I don't know how much longer it will be there if no one steps in to save it.

When the studio first opened it was a storefront with the studio in the back. During one of the renovations, the glass front was removed and security doors were put in place. After another renovation, the front of the studio was painted with a rainbow. The building was nondescript before the storefront was covered over. There weren't a lot of markings except for maybe just a sign. You'd really have to describe where it was for people to find it. Then we started getting some publicity, and one day there was this brilliant rainbow painted across the front of the building. It was visible from blocks away; you probably could have seen it from outer space, and I couldn't believe it. I thought someone was going to see me walking in there and ask what was going on inside, or if I had any dope I wanted to sell or if there was any I wanted to buy.

I think was Peggy Walden's idea to paint the front like that. It looked good, but it was a real shocker. The people who worked there every day didn't exactly know what to think for a while, but we got used to it. The studio was easy to find after that, though; we just told people to look for the rainbow. The rainbow didn't last all that long. I don't think Phil ever liked it, and he had it changed to something more stately looking, back to our brown and vanilla brown or whatever the color scheme was called. The stained glass window over the door came a good bit later. It's hard for me to judge when things happened because I was so busy and lost track of time.

There were all these different "stab and shoot clubs" near the studio, and most of them were a bar and grill. One in particular, across the street and down a hundred or so feet, had pretty good sandwiches. At night we'd either go over there to get our food or someone from the studio would go over and pick up our order. Finally, one night we called in an order and they volunteered to deliver it for us. When the person arrived with the food he said, "You all just call us and tell us what you want, and we'll bring it over to you and you can pay us. It would probably be better if you all didn't come back over there. A lot of the people don't like hippies." Most of us took that as fair warning and that was fine too. We could order drinks or sandwiches or whatever we wanted and they gladly delivered it.

In the daytime we used to get a lot of pick up meals from Lindberg's, a little restaurant in an alley that was a great place with an incredible luncheon. Of course, Mama Louise always had the best soul food. Then, for a while, we'd to go a boarding house where they put all the food on the table, and you'd pay three or four dollars to eat. It was like a family dinner with people you didn't know. Sometimes Phil, Bobby Wallace, Frank, and I would get into Phil's Caddy and go down to the Pig and Whistle. It was just sandwiches, and I'd always have the Pig special. We'd have our big executive lunches in the early days at the Pig and Whistle while sitting in Phil's car having window service. Everything was going well, and we were having a great time.

I remembered those executive lunches later on, much later on, when we'd made some money and were all going to lunch at a fancy Macon restaurant. Everyone would have cocktails and there was a lot of fancy food on china with cloth napkins and candles on the tables. All I could think about was the Pig and Whistle. I was much more comfortable there.

Sometimes in the early days, when I was playing drums on sessions, I'd go out at night with Duane and Berry. At one point, Frank owned an upstairs club just a block from the office on Cotton Avenue, and we'd go in and sit in with whatever band was playing. There were several other clubs in the area where we'd go and sit in; it just depended on who was playing. Boz Scaggs used to go along once in a while. It was amazing the people who were in Macon at various times. You can trace a lot of it back to the Allman Brothers Band, but more specifically, Duane; Boz was an example. Duane played on the album Boz did for Atlantic over in Muscle Shoals. Duane lived in Macon, so Boz moved to Macon and lived there for a while.

At some point during this time, I remember going down to Grant's Lounge with Phil when the Marshall Tucker Band first came to town to audition for Capricorn. Grant's Lounge was a small bar on Poplar that became kind of a hangout for the record company. The guys would go down there and jam. Grant's started hiring bands that would come to Capricorn. The first time I saw the Marshall Tucker Band, they were playing like it was an audition for us, and all the people in the office were there as were Hornsby and I. Phil and Frank really loved the band and believed in them, but I wasn't too sure what I thought when I first heard them. They were nice guys and were all very polite and said "yes sir" and "no sir" to me, which seemed a little strange because we were about the same age. I was only twenty-four or twenty-five, and being called "sir" was freaking me out a little.

I went into the studio and cut some demos with the band. I don't know what it was, but they were playing better than I was recording them, and I wasn't very happy with the demos. Phil wasn't either. They went back into the studio later with Paul and cut some more tracks that were better, and it seems they fit Paul's production style better than mine. I think Paul came more from a country and rock and roll background and then to R&B, whereas my background was mostly R&B without much country experience. Johnny Cash was about as county as I'd gotten at that point. The band worked better with him, but after they had all those hit records, I wished I'd held on a little tighter. I've thought about that decision a lot, and it was one of many I wish I could have changed.

After doing the demos with the Brothers, I worked on several other projects, one of which was with a band from up north called Melting Pot. During this time, another thing was happening with Capricorn on the business end. Capricorn was with Atco or Atlantic/Atco/Capricorn or however they wanted to put it out, but they had a deal that Atlantic would have right of first refusal on anything cut at Capricorn. However, if Atlantic passed on an album, Capricorn could do anything with it they wanted. Atlantic passed on the Melting Pot album, so Frank worked a deal with Ampex and *Melting Pot* was released on that label. It was one of the better sounding records I cut during that time.

I experimented with mics and mic placement on that album. We were limited with sixteen inputs, but that was the first time I'd multi mic'd drums. Usually drums had only two or three mics on them; one on the bass drum, one overhead and sometimes, one on the floor tom side and looking across the floor tom toward the snare. Mostly it was just the overhead and bass drum mics. I had a nice condenser, either a 47 or an 87 overhead and then probably an EV triple six on the bass. On this album, I fooled around with putting a mic on each tom. I'd heard about other people doing that, and it worked well for me. When Tom Dowd came to record the Brothers, I learned a new way to mic the drums with three mics. He used a mic on the bass drum and two 87s, one on either side behind the drummer's head, facing the drums. Tom had a very commonsense way of doing things, and he placed the mics the way the drummer was hearing the music.

I had an odd selection of mics to use. Back then when studios went into business, it seemed all of them had 87s and that's what Jim Hawkins purchased for Capricorn. I suppose we got them at the direction of Atlantic because Atlantic was who we looked to. (In the engineering department there was Phil Iehle and Tom Dowd who used 87s. Rick Hall used them at FAME in Muscle Shoals and I'm sure they had a bunch of 87s at Stax.) The 87 was an expensive mic, about three or four hundred dollars, which was a lot of money back then, but now they sell for three grand plus.

I also learned a lot from recording horns on the album. We had a big glass window between the control room and the studio, so I got the horn players to stand about five or six feet back from the glass window and put mics close to the glass. Then I added a mic on each horn and blended the results to one track for a rich horn sound. If we doubled any horns, they'd all be bounced to one track. It didn't make it easy because we were doing a lot of overdubs and needed every track we could get. On one track there'd be a piano for the intro and the first verse, then a tambourine, and then background vocals in what we called track salad. But the players were good. and I was happy with how the whole album came out. It was one of my biggest learning experiences.

Alex Taylor and I had become friends when I worked on the Livingston Taylor albums, and interspersed with all the other projects, I produced *Friends and Neighbors* with him. Alex had this big old bluesy voice, so we cut him in that style. We cut a bunch of covers including "Night Owl," written by his brother James, and a new song James had written, "Back on the Highway." I worked on that song for about fifteen hours trying to get the ultimate track to the point everyone was going crazy.

"Night Owl" was a nice rocking tune, and I wanted horns on it. The best horns I knew of at that time were lead by King Curtis in New York. He was associated with Atlantic, and with Phil's help I had the opportunity to work with him. King Curtis came in with the players and did a fantastic arrangement for the horns. All the horn players were standing around a 47 in the studio, and it was just a killer sound. King Curtis did some solos and fills, and it was a thrill to listen to him. The engineer was great; in fact, I think the engineer may have been Jean Paul, Les Paul's son.

I wanted strings on one song, and the next day I had a small string section booked for some violins. It was a very odd experience. Let's say the session was at 7 p.m. and the players were due in at 6:30 p.m. Atlantic hired the arranger because I'd never done strings before. This guy showed up with manuscript paper that I thought were the finished charts, but when I looked over, the pages were blank. I introduced myself and asked if he was the arranger and did he have the charts. He said, "I'll write 'em here." I reminded him the string players were due in fifteen minutes. He replied, "That's all right."

It was a simple song, but it wasn't *that* simple, and I was absolutely a nervous wreck because I didn't think this guy had even listened to it. He went ahead and wrote the string charts for the song, but I was very uncomfortable and never did feel good about that session. I was trying to be as professional as I knew how to be, but I hadn't seen a lot of producers work so there wasn't much to go by. However, it was an experience to remember; I got to meet King Curtis and work in the Atlantic studio to record strings and horns.

James Taylor came down to Macon and played on Alex's album. That was when James and Joni Mitchell were going together, and I got to meet her. It was the best of times. I'd be in the studio where this incredible music was being made, go out into the hall to get a soft drink, and find Joni Mitchell sitting on the steps by the Pepsi machine playing her autoharp and singing. God, I loved it! It was a hippie's paradise!

Scott Boyer played a lot on that record, and Bill Stewart played drums. When Wet Willie first came to Macon, it was with a slightly different line-up, and Bill was the drummer. I think either Frank or Phil was interested in Wet Willie, but at first they weren't signed. I heard demos the band had cut with Bill on drums. I really liked his playing and thought he had a lot of potential. By then I was busy producing, and Frank told me I was either going to have to produce or play drums because there wasn't time for both. He told me he and Phil wanted me to produce, and I needed to find and hire a drummer to take my place. Since the record company preferred I produce rather than play, I figured that's what I'd do.

I was probably better at producing. I didn't think I was going to be a good enough drummer to do what I wanted to and felt I could fake my way through producing a lot easier than I could drumming. After I heard Bill, I hired him to play drums when I couldn't. Phil started calling Bill the "assistant studio drummer." That was his official title. In retrospect, I wish I'd never quit playing the drums—or at least had kept up my chops—because I loved playing.

Sometimes I'd play bass in the studio on albums I was producing, but I wanted to get back to playing live for a while. After we'd finished recording his record, Alex was going to tour. I told Phil I'd like to go on the road with Alex and play bass. I don't know why I wanted to do it, but it seemed appropriate at the time.

Right after Alex's album came out, we went on the road for about three months up in the Northeast and Canada, which turned out to be interesting given we were there in January. His road band was me on bass, Hornsby on keyboards, Joe Rudd on guitar, and Bill Stewart was on drums. Earl "Speedo" Sims, who'd been Otis's road manager, was with us. I tell you, I'd trust that man driving at any speed anywhere. He's the best driver I've ever seen. He drove for all kinds of acts, but mainly Otis, who was everybody's hero, and we felt like we were in good hands. He's the only guy you'd feel safe with in a car going a hundred and fifty miles an hour downtown and not think anything about it. He was a good guy to be with on the road, and we used to room together. Speedo was also a songwriter and wrote part of Aretha Franklin's hit, "R.E.S.P.E.C.T."

We ended up at Martha's Vineyard, which isn't the place to be during cold winter weather. Those people don't know what cold is up there and they never met a winter they didn't enjoy and embrace. They'd be wearing T-shirts out in ten feet of snow and they'd say, "Hey, how you doin'?" and I'd answer, "Freezin', why aren't you!?"

A lot of the time on the road with Alex was fun, and a lot of it was pretty crazy. We had one really interesting show opening for the Brothers, who were playing a college gig in a gymnasium somewhere. Being on the same label tends to get you an opening slot with the top act. We had small equipment, little amps, and a normal size set of drums; I was playing bass through a little Fender amp. When we got to the gig, there was Berry's giant Ampeg bass rig sitting there along with Duane's two Marshalls and Dickey's two Marshalls—Dickey 1 and Dickey 2— too many Marshalls in my opinion. The Brothers wanted us to use their equipment instead of ours to avoid a stage change. We didn't know exactly what we were getting into because it was more equipment than we were use to…much more.

Joe Rudd could be an amazing player, or he could sound as if he hadn't been playing very long. It seemed like he was one extreme or the other. When he was great, he could make you cry, and when he wasn't great, he could make you cry for different reasons. When Joe first plugged into Dickey 2 we thought, "Hmm, this is going to be loud for Joe." When Joe was "on," he was just magic, but when he was "off," he was as far from magic as you could get. This was one of his "off" days, so he wasn't just bad…he was bad and loud. It was one of those times he looked like he'd just landed from another planet.

Joe's set-up was close to Paul, and from the audience's perspective, Paul would have been on the right. Joe was next to Paul with Bill in the middle, sort of in the back on a riser playing Butch's kit and I was on the opposite side from Paul. All during the first song, Paul was glaring at me and mouthing, "Tell him to turn down, tell him to turn down," pointing to Joe and then to the amps, just raising hell about it. I half-way understood because Joe was playing through Dickey 2, whatever that combination was, and it was really was too loud.

Suddenly, Hornsby got up from the keyboard and walked across the stage over to where I was and said, "Tell him to turn down. Tell him to turn down or I'm walking off the stage right now." I asked him, "Why don't you tell him, Paul? You've got to pass right by him going back." But he said, "You tell him or I'm off the stage." After the song was over I walked over to Joe and told him, "You know, Paul wouldn't mind if you turned down a little." I think he did, or at least made us think he did, and the band finished the rest of the show. The whole exchange just cracked me up. I could understand why Paul would want him to turn down, but I couldn't figure out why he wouldn't tell Joe himself. I guess maybe he was afraid he'd really go off on him. It was just one of those nights.

After Alex's album had been released, it got a very nice review in *Rolling Stone* and Phil called to tell me I was being promoted to vice-president and head of A & R (Artists and Repertoire). I'd gone from making $175 a week in the beginning to getting $200 a week. With my new title and promotion, my salary jumped to $350 a week. I thought I was rich.

Alex and I remained friends over the years, and I produced his album *Dinnertime*. He had his new band together by then that included Lou Mullenix and Chuck Leavell.

Shortly after Alex's album was released, it became apparent there wasn't a need for a dedicated studio band since most of the artists on Capricorn were self-contained groups. We were no longer doing records with many single artists, so it was time for Pete and Popwell to move on. It was hard to see them go because Pete was like a little brother to me and Paul. Popwell was our friend and one of the best bass players ever. Pete went on to Muscle Shoals to play in the rhythm section and formed LeBlanc & Carr with Lenny LeBlanc that had some hits. Eventually Pete produced albums of his own doing instrumental guitar records, and he played with Paul Simon on albums and at the Concert in the Park in New York. Popwell moved to California and hooked up with the Crusaders. Today he's a preacher in Nashville and still a great bass player. Of course, Hornsby and I remained in Macon.

16

Live at the Fillmore

One of my most embarrassing moments involved Tom Dowd and happened when the Allman Brothers Band was getting ready to record their second album, *Idlewild South*. It was decided I was going to produce the record, and of course I was chomping at the bit to do it. Then, about a month before they wanted to start recording, Phil and Frank told me they'd decided they wanted me to work with Tom Dowd and co-produce the album with him. The Brothers already had one record out on Atlantic, so there's a good chance Tom had already heard about the band when Phil and Frank asked him to come to Macon. I thought it was a great idea; it would be an honor to have my name listed with Tom Dowd. That was what I thought was going to happen, and no one ever told me anything different.

Tom arrived in Macon late the day before the session started, and I called the hotel and woke him up the next morning. The band wasn't scheduled to record until that evening, but the roadies came in early and set up the band's gear. I told him I was at the studio and asked if he had any preferences as to where they should set up. He didn't have a preference, so I told him I'd take care of it. That night the Brothers came in, and there was a lot of energy and electricity for the session. I think they started out with "Elizabeth Reed." I was talking to Tom and making suggestions for the first couple of songs like someone who was co-producing, but it wasn't long before I knew something wasn't right. Tom knew nothing about my co-producing with him. I said something to Gregg like, "What's wrong? Did I say something wrong? Tom was looking at me kind of weird." Gregg said, "Look, I think he's going to produce it by himself." Once I realized I wasn't going to be involved with the sessions, I left.

Boy, I felt like the biggest fool in the world. I'd been in there embarrassing myself in front of Tom and the band and everything I held sacred at the time. It was a huge letdown, and it took me a while to get over it. I thought I was going to produce the band because I'd done all the demos and they all liked the sound of them better than their first album, at least that's what everyone said. I guess Phil or Frank decided it would be best just to go with Tom and no one was willing take me aside and tell me. Tom had had hundreds of hit records. He'd produced a lot of them, and he'd engineered a lot more. Considering that I'd only done one or two that hadn't really sold, I understood their decision, but there was no excuse for their not letting me know. It just killed me. It was cold-blooded, and I felt betrayed and was deeply angry. I couldn't believe they didn't tell me, and I don't know why they didn't.

They recorded for a few days in Macon and cut a few tracks, but I can't remember which ones other than "Elizabeth Reed." I don't know if there was much overdubbing done because Duane and Dickey or Gregg, whoever, did their solos live and then Gregg would usually overdub the vocals. A lot of times he'd put down a vocal as the track went down and sometimes they were keepers, but a lot of them were overdubbed. They cut some tracks that were pretty much finished in Macon. Tom then wanted to go to Criteria in Miami where he did most of his work, and that's where the album was finished. Most of it was done in Miami; maybe twenty-five percent was done in Macon.

When I heard *Idlewild South*, "Revival" was a shock to me. It didn't really sound like anything the Brothers had ever done, and it blew me away. It was wonderful.

Live at the Fillmore, the Allman Brothers' third album, was the first one I was involved in, and I supervised mastering the album. Tom had recorded and mixed the album in New York and given the band a 7 1/2 ips (inches per second) tape, which was the medium used back then for giving the artist a pre-release copy of the album for approval. Cassettes weren't used for musical evaluation because the quality of the ones available was considered compromised, so they had a 7 1/2 tape they played for me. It sounded wonderful. The mix and everything sounded really rich, and the band loved the sound of it. Later, though, when they heard the reference disc, they didn't like the way it sounded at all. It wasn't nearly as good as the tape, and the tone and richness were gone.

We cued up both the tape and the acetate so we could listen and switch from one to the other and the tape was definitely better, especially when you listened to the tape and then heard the acetate back to back. Since the band liked the demos I'd recorded for their second album, Duane asked me to go to New York and fix it so the acetate would sound like the tape. Of course I told him I'd do it.

Everything went through Atlantic at that time, and we had to use their mastering facility. I flew to New York and went to Atlantic Studios to explain the problem to the mastering engineer who'd originally mastered the album. The people who work in mastering are usually not the type who produce records, and this guy was an older gentleman. There I was, a long-haired hippie coming out of a total music background, so at first I don't think he put a whole lot of stock into what I was saying. We did the same experiment I'd done with the band; we put the tape on, then listened to the mastered version. It was obvious the fidelity had changed, and the master wasn't as good or as rich in texture. The guy wasn't really enthralled with the idea of a 7 1/2 sounding better than the mastered version, but in this case there wasn't much denying it.

This was my first time to supervise mastering, and it was an interesting experience because there are a lot of considerations to be aware of on the technical side. You looked at the grooves on vinyl through a microscope at the mastering place in order to avoid "kissing grooves" (grooves that touch), because they're likely to cause skipping on the record. The worst thing you could have was a record that skipped because customers would return the record, costing the company and losing the sale.

Another thing that could be problematic was trying to get the record loud without getting it *too* loud. Everyone wanted to have the loudest record on radio, but if you went too loud, the record might skip. The ideal length of an album was thirty-seven or thirty-eight minutes per side, and another consideration when mastering was losing volume if the album ran too long. Since FM was just starting in radio, the volume of a record needed to be comparable to the ones played before and after it. We worked on the Brothers' album most of the day doing various things, primarily some eq and compression differences, and finally the engineer got close enough that I realized it was the best I could get there.

Fillmore East was the first big credit I was hoping to have, and I still wasn't entirely happy with what was done at Atlantic. I was responsible for making the master sound as good as the tape, and since I wanted to impress the band that I could get it done right, I decided to try another mastering place to see what the difference might be with a different facility. I'd read the Record Plant name on the back of albums I liked (and it had a great reputation), so I took a cab over to their mastering studio in New York.

When I first arrived, Chris Stone, one of the owners, met me at the door. I explained I'd been re-mastering the new Allman Brothers record, trying to make it sound like the tape, and I couldn't get the sound I wanted over at Atlantic. Chris took me to the mastering suite, which was just a small room back in the corner of the tenth floor, and I met George Merino.

Chris told me, "Here, we'll just let George cut you an acetate and you can take it back and compare it." I asked George if he would consider doing a song to let me hear what he could do with it, but he ended up doing both sides of the album. It was remarkable how easy it was to work with George. I felt at home with the Record Plant, and the songs George cut there just blew away everything I'd worked on all day long. It was a double album, and I was worn out from working on it over at Atlantic and not getting what I was after. But in less than an hour at the Record Plant, the album sounded great.

I took that acetate back to Phil and Frank, along with the one from Atlantic, and I said, "Listen, I've got two versions. Which one sounds better?" First, I played the one from Atlantic without telling them where it was from. Then I said, "This is another way of looking at it" and played the one from the Record Plant. They said the second one sounded better, a lot better, and asked me what I did. I told them it was better because it had been done at the Record Plant. The band only heard the reference disc I'd done at Atlantic, and they were extremely relieved to hear the new one because it sounded more like the tape. I told them there was still a better ref, but the release date was looming and there wasn't time to use the Record Plant master. The one from Atlantic was used, but from then on, all but one of my records and at least 99 percent of the Capricorn releases were mastered with George.

When I heard the difference between the mastering places I began to realize why some people made great sounding records and others didn't. I knew I couldn't be satisfied mastering at Atlantic after that. The mastering engineer is very important. If the guy is really good and the equipment is working, he'll get something good out of it, but the Record Plant always had the newest and best gear. They had top-of-the-line equipment and a top-of-the-line engineer, and that's the way it ought to be. It was a great thing to find a mastering engineer I totally trusted to take my record and make it come out sounding better. A good mastering engineer doesn't compromise what you've done, but if you've messed up somewhere in the mixing, they'll help correct it without totally turning your record inside out. I appreciated having found George Merino and Chris Stone, and I've valued my friendship with both of them over the years.

Atlantic wasn't crazy about our decision to change mastering studios. They wanted all the mastering done at their facility to maintain their own quality control, but Capricorn was heading in another direction from the traditional Atlantic sound. We'd all heard the difference. Once you hear that kind of difference, it's hard to think about mastering at a place that doesn't make records sound as good as another one. It was more expensive for Capricorn, since mastering at Atlantic was either part of the deal or at a reduced rate, but after that the Capricorn masters were done with George Marino at the Record Plant (until George moved to Sterling Sound, and then we mastered there).

I always went to mastering sessions, but I don't know how important it is anymore if you have someone you trust and can work with. To be honest, mastering sessions are boring. You usually hear the first song on the disc over and over while things are getting set up for the album, and you're hearing it in a different environment and over different speakers. It's hard to make an informed judgment, so you want to have the mastering engineer know what he's doing and know what you're looking for.

The number of times you hear a song from start to finish depends on the song and the intricacy of the arrangement. I think at least a hundred times would be a good starting place. You can hear it three or four times just running it down for tracking while you're working it up. If you're lucky, you get the track in one of the early takes because over all they have a better feel and it starts to change the more takes you hear.

After a while, the takes don't feel as good, but they get more accurate so you try to find that spot where they have the best of each. At least that's what I try for.

The band was happy with the new mastering, and one afternoon Duane and Berry came over to my house. They said they had something for me and gave me this beat-up, brown guitar case that was bandaged with tape. I'd never seen a Fender case like that; most of the ones I'd seen were rectangular. This one was shaped like a regular guitar or bass case. They told me to look inside, and when I opened it up there was a beautiful '57 Precision bass. I couldn't believe it. It was a valuable bass back then, and it's even more valuable now. The neck is the perfect size; it plays and sounds great, looks good, and it's still the best-feeling bass I ever played. There were a few little scratches on the body when I got it, but that stuff doesn't bother me as far as the playing and the way it sounds. It looks like one Fender has in their catalog of classic basses. I've never changed anything on the bass but the strings, but I did buy a newer and more durable case.

The whole band bought it, but Berry and Duane picked it out and presented it to me as thanks for the work I'd done on the album. I've loved it and played it both live and on a lot of records, and other people who came to record at Capricorn would use it. Charlie Hayward played it some on the *Laid Back* album. It's a great bass and records very well. I keep it around my studio now, and if I don't like the sound of the bass someone is using for recording, I pull that one out. I'm fortunate to have a wide variety of basses I've collected—maybe too many—but the bass I got from Berry and Duane is the one I love and treasure.

17

5'll Getcha Ten

A lot of people aren't really sure what a record producer does, but being a record producer is like being a contractor. You work with both the record company and the artist to handle details that range from making certain the artist and musicians have a place to stay if you have to import them, to overseeing all budget aspects of the project with the record company. The way I see it, you work with an artist you like, one whose music you enjoy, and picture their musical image and what's good for them. Then you find the right studio environment for recording. Selecting the right songs or helping the artist perfect the ones they've written determines the success of the record. A producer makes sure the keys of the songs are correct, insures the musician's instruments are in tune, and most important, tries to get a great vocal that's in tune and performed with heart so you believe the singer means what they're singing.

During the tracking you try to come up with ideas to make the tracks flow and come off like you imagine. You try to be open to ideas of musicians in the session because quite often they'll come up with something better than you've thought of. Then the challenge is to stay out of the way. Once the track is cut, you make certain you decorate it with the proper instrumentation. It's your job to see that everything is done properly and that you're capturing the best of the artist.

With just about everything I've produced, I've done some of the engineering, or in some cases, all of it. As I started producing more and more, though, I could see the benefit of having an engineer I could trust. Having someone who knew both what they were doing and how I liked having things done meant I could devote my time to thinking about the performance. Engineering is entirely different from producing in that the engineer is responsible for all the technical aspects of recording, and sometimes I felt it could take away from the production side if I tried to do both. There needs to be a flow to the session; the musicians have to be comfortable, so everyone has to be top notch at their jobs. The better the environment, the better the music is because happy people usually make better music. In the end, if things go right a producer gets some of the credit, but if things go wrong, the producer gets all the blame.

Along with my promotion at Capricorn came a lot of responsibility to make sure all the productions would go well. I also attended more meetings. I never enjoyed meetings and don't know anyone who really does. I'd meet with Phil and Frank and discuss artists they were going to sign or were thinking about signing, and they'd want to know how I felt about them. A lot of times we'd do demos of artists, and either Hornsby or I would take charge of those. The company was so new that Phil was still trying to get the structure in place, but he was the president, Frank was vice-president, and I was vice-president and head of A & R.

It wasn't all work, though. Capricorn hosted company picnics that later evolved into enormous events. While it may have seemed at times like the record company just fell together, the Capricorn picnics were run like an army drill. Someone was assigned to be in charge of the horseshoe tournament, someone else would be in charge of volleyball, someone else was in charge of potato salad, etc. The first few picnics were like a big family picnic held out at Phil's beautiful lake house. It was a large gathering and we'd go out in the afternoon and have whatever "refreshments" we'd want. It was also a time when people who stayed inside all the time would go out and injure themselves; the day sometimes ended up with a short trip to the emergency room.

The guest list included everyone from the office and some of the people Phil had invited who'd helped and been involved with Capricorn. It started out like family, but by the third picnic it was a big deal. Phil began flying in all the artists on the label and people associated with the different record labels, first from Atlantic and later on Warners, and even later, Polygram.

One year Martin Mull was flying in for the picnic, and he and Dr. John ended up sitting next to each other on the plane. Martin knew who Dr. John was, but Mac had never heard of Martin Mull and had absolutely no idea who he was or what he did. Of course Martin was being his funny self all through the flight, and toward the end of the trip Dr. John told him, "Man, you ought to be a comedian."

I remember thinking the picnics were really getting too big when Phil began using buses to transport us to the picnic because he didn't want anyone to drive afterward. The last one I went to was held at a park in Macon. The Allman Brothers, Bonnie Bramlett, and some others played. It was in the late 1970s and was a monster picnic.

But I digress. Terry Kane came to work in the studio as an engineer, and shortly afterward, Jim Hawkins left Capricorn. I wanted to redesign the control room, so Terry tried his hand and definitely redesigned it. The studio was developed in three different phases and this was what I think of as the interim design. The first one that Jim built was Universal modules and Altec 604E speakers with Mackintosh amps, which was pretty standard.

It was during this interim remodeling that the front was made for a reception area with a game space where we could eat and musicians could sit around while someone was overdubbing. There was a side room that served as a shop for any repairs that needed to be done and a copy room, and that's about the time I got an office at the studio. I never had one on Cotton Avenue because there was really no need for it.

Things didn't work out very well with Terry and the remodeling. Terry had been drafted to do the studio renovation, but things hadn't been finished on time or on budget. Phil was ranting at him, and he was standing in front of Phil's desk. Terry reached down, picked up the front edge of the desk, and leaned it on the back legs. Things started sliding back towards Phil, but it didn't slow him down at all. Terry ended up leaving town that night. I think he painted his van and left, and that was the last time I ever saw him.

Along about this time I produced an album for Whiskey Howl. Phil told me he had a gig for me with Warner Brothers Canada, which I thought was interesting, but at first I wondered if he was farming me out for good or for just this project (fortunately it was just the project). I went to Toronto where Whiskey Howl was based, and I couldn't believe how clean Canada looked. Everything was beautiful and looked freshly shined, at least it did then; I haven't been back for a long time. We recorded at Eastern Sound Studio, a great studio with a large API board that sounded rich and huge.

I'd talked with either the band or their manager and told them I wanted to use Chuck Leavell on the album, and they agreed. By then Chuck was beginning to make a reputation for himself, but he still wasn't all that well known. Chuck had a prior commitment and couldn't be there the first day, but he was supposed to arrive late that night and meet me at the hotel.

After we knocked off at the studio I went to the hotel and waited for Chuck. This was a super nice place, one of the nicest hotels I'd been in; room service was delivered on silver plates and with crystal glasses. I had two beds in my room, and Chuck was going to stay with me in the other bed. He was supposed to take a cab from the airport and everyone assured me he'd be in at the specified time, so eventually I fell asleep. About two or three in the morning I heard a lot of noise, and it was Chuck just getting in. Because he didn't have a key, he wasn't allowed to come up to the room. The people at the front desk gave him all kinds of hell until finally someone got the authorization to allow him up to my room where he told me all about his adventure with the hotel police.

We had a good time working on the album and the band played great. We did the recording in four or five days in Toronto; then I went to mix it in New York at the Record Plant. The budget was tight and I couldn't afford much time, so I booked about eighteen hours. Danny Turberville, an engineer who was working with me at the Record Plant, and I went in one afternoon and worked straight through. We did part of the mixing in studio A on a Spectrasonics console and the rest of it in studio B on a Datamix console which is like an API. It was an exhausting experience and I never wanted to mix that way again.

At that point, I was out of money. I had a plane ticket to get back home, but otherwise I was totally broke. I asked Phil to wire me some money and then took a cab to the Western Union office to pick it up. I don't know what I'd have done if the money hadn't been there because I didn't have enough with me to even pay the cab driver. I guess I'd have had to take off running. Fortunately, the money was there.

I really liked the album and thought it would be good for Capricorn. While the studio was being remodeled, I had a two-track tape recorder at my house so I could listen to masters. Phil and Frank came to my house for lunch one day and listened to the album while we ate.

They weren't interested because it was a more traditional blues record, and Capricorn was starting out in a different direction. I believed in the band and gave Phil a test pressing after the album was finished. He still wasn't interested. After the album was released, though, it did fairly well in Canada.

The next Cowboy album I did was *5'll Getcha Ten*, which is also the name of one of the tunes on it. We cut a few tracks in Macon, but the album came along during one of the times we were updating the studio, so after recording the first few tracks in Macon, I arranged to take Cowboy over to Muscle Shoals on Jackson Highway to finish the rest of the record. The old Muscle Shoals building had a good sounding room and a lot of character. They'd upgraded to a Flickenger console and I did the engineering. Boards back then were relatively simple if you had any engineering experience, so I took to that one fairly well. We had a lot of fun, and it was a good place to be. I enjoyed seeing the rhythm section again—David, Roger, Jimmy and Barry—and they were around all the time.

My favorite song on the album was "Please Be with Me." Although Scott Boyer has a different memory of the story behind the song, I remember the first time I heard it. We were in the studio one day, and Scott had his acoustic guitar and was sitting on a drum stool over by the drum booth playing "Please Be with Me." He played a verse and a chorus, and I kind of freaked out and said, "Gosh Scott, that's great. Let's cut that one." He said it was something new and that we would do it on the next project.

Just hearing that small part of the song hit me hard, and I convinced him to finish it for this album. He finished writing the song in room 13 of a hotel in Muscle Shoals. The name of the place has been changed so many times I don't remember what it was called then, but it definitely wasn't a high-end hotel. For years, every time we'd pass that hotel Scott would say, "That's where I wrote 'Please Be with Me'…in that room right over there, number 13."

Duane was between gigs with the Brothers, and we asked him to come in and play on the album. He drove over from Macon one afternoon, and we cut the take of "Please Be with Me" that ended up on the record. George Clark was on upright bass, Tom Wynn was on drums,

Pete Kowalke played guitar, and Tommy played acoustic. Duane had just gotten a new dobro and had it with him, so we put it to use and he played slide on the dobro while Scott played acoustic guitar and sang. It was a magical song and a good take that day, but I thought we had a better one in us and coerced everyone into coming in the next day to get another take. Both takes are out on records. The first one is on the original release of *5'll Getcha Ten* and the second version is on the *Duane Allman Anthology*. It was just different takes on different days with the same personnel on each of them playing the same instruments. I think that's the last session Duane ever played on for anyone other than the Allman Brothers.

I tried to get Duane to play guitar on another song that didn't go so well. The song, "All My Friends," was written with 7/4 time signatures in parts of the song. One of those 7/4 segments was where I wanted Duane to play a short guitar or slide solo, but the timing of the song just threw him that day. It's a good song, but the solo parts were difficult to play. The band learned it and had it down tight, but for anyone coming in, well, you play songs either in 4 or you play in 3 but rarely in 7, especially in pop music. It was just odd.

First Duane tried a solo, but he couldn't get it down. He got really angry and threw his guitar across the room and said, "If you wanted a steel player you should have hired one. I don't ever want to hear that song again," or something like that interspersed with some colorful language. I think he was just angry at himself because the time signature was so unnatural. Next, Tommy tried a solo in that section of the song and it didn't come out right. Then we got Eddie Hinton to try a solo, but he got flustered and it didn't work either. Scott was the only one who felt it. He'd been a viola player in school and had it with him, so he just played the melody on the viola and it worked. Actually, it was probably the most appropriate thing. We'd started out on a high note and left on a down note because of the problems we had with the song. None of the players—and they were all good guitarists—could play it with that time signature to where it flowed. Eddie and Tommy were pretty damn good, and Duane was the best there was. Scott later said about the session, "Man, I just felt like shit."

As I've said before, I had a set up at my house with a tape player and a nice stereo, and a lot of people would bring tapes over. After the *Layla* sessions, Duane brought a tape over and said, "That's me. That's my lick there." Then he played the opening lick to "Layla," which is a classic now. It was another thing I was extremely impressed with. People have tried to dissect the lick and attribute it to this or that artist, but in reality every lick is a cop of something either sped up or slowed down, consciously or unconsciously. It's weird, but I think the lick is very close to "Midnight Rider," just a different rhythm but with similar notes.

Duane enjoyed it when the music was good. He had the best band anywhere, and when it happens right, it's a wonderful experience; everybody kind of hits something at the same time and same place. Duane was magic and kept everybody invigorated when he was excited about something. If he was on fire he'd get you excited about it whether you felt like it or not. He was happy about the success the Brothers were having; they all seemed happy and were starting to get somewhere, making a few dollars and having hit records. What more could you want? It seems like that was all we'd ever dreamed of.

18

October 1971

When you're in your twenties and each day brings new adventures and exciting challenges, dying is the last thing on your mind. But on October 29, 1971, the only thing anyone was thinking about was death as it mingled with the crowd gathered at the hospital where Duane was fighting for his life. There have been several accounts of what happened that day, who was where and who did what, written by those who were there. Each is a valid memory of that time, but memories are personal. Some will remember a tragedy in infinite detail down to the light reflecting off the pop top of a soda can in the wastebasket of an emergency room, while others remember little but the kaleidoscope of emotions of the time. And recollections often differ. These are Johnny's memories in his words, the events he lived through and the way they were filtered through the shock of that day and the days that followed.

It was afternoon. I think I got a call at home from someone at Capricorn telling me Duane had been in a serious accident, so I left and drove to the office on Cotton Avenue. I really don't recall all the details. I walked out front of the office and, although I know now that he was out of town at the time, for some reason I remember Phil, Frank, and Bobby Wallace being there with me. The hospital was about a block and a half from the office so everyone decided just to walk on up there to check things out. The Brothers were home, taking a break from recording their new album, and everybody had been riding horses. There'd been several broken legs and various injuries that maybe needed a few stitches, and I thought that's all it was. I thought maybe Duane's motorcycle had flipped over and he'd broken a leg or something, so there wasn't any great concern at the moment. Still, we all thought we'd go and see what it was anyway. I'd been to the hospital several times for the stomach flu and other things around that time and it seemed like, "well, here we go again to the emergency room to see what's wrong and make sure everybody's okay."

When we started up there I had no sense of dread at all. We walked to the back of the hospital where cars pull into the emergency room and there were a few people already gathered waiting to hear something. That's where we were when one of the people who was standing around, I don't remember who, told us Duane had been in a very serious accident. There'd been a birthday party at the big house for Berry's wife, Big Linda, that afternoon. Afterward he left on his motorcycle to go home, to the apartment he shared with Dixie. Over the years there have been rumors about Duane hitting a peach truck, but it was just a truck. The truck was turning left in front of him as Duane was going over the hill, and he didn't have time to slow down when he saw it. The truck had something sticking out of the back and he swerved to avoid it. It wasn't a peach truck and *Eat a Peach* had nothing to do with it, even though there are some people who believe that to this day.

We all became very concerned. Gregg came up and was crying and being helped by a couple of friends. At that point I realized he knew more than the rest of us, and it was something very serious. We heard that Duane had been thrown from the motorcycle and had gone into the curb head first, and the doctors were trying to save his life. They didn't know what shape he'd be in if he lived—or if he'd fully recover. Even if they saved his life, he might be a vegetable. That was the way it was put. I felt numb because I couldn't believe this was happening—not after all the stuff they'd been through, the escapes they'd made, the close calls they'd had before with any number of things. It was a beautiful day with everybody straight, happy, and having a good time. And Duane was lying there dying.

I don't know if I even went inside the hospital or into the reception area of the emergency room. I think I just stood outside in the back there where the ambulances would pull in. I guess we were there an hour or so before we got word Duane would be in surgery for several hours. No one could tell us if he was going to live. It seemed like a really long time between learning he had a severe head injury and finding out he was gone.

After we heard the news, my girlfriend at the time, Dottie, and I went over to the big house with everybody. I think some of the Brothers might have been at the house, too. I don't remember. I really don't remember. I know a lot of the road guys were there. I remember Red Dog and Tuffy, and I think Twiggs and Joe Dan Petty were there too. I get to thinking about it sometimes and I see all these faces, yet I can't tell for sure who was there. I know it was all family. Kim Payne was there, and I remember that he was completely distraught. All the road crew was really dedicated to the band, and they were good, hard-working folks. When they went on the road they had a good time, but they did their job. They took care of that first. There was a strong belief in that band, a spiritual awareness of how important their music was and the road crew made sure everything was right. I couldn't imagine a better or more dedicated group of people; they took care of the band, and they treated me well and took care of me too. It was before the days of professional roadies, days when the crew was made up of friends who hung out with the band and learned the job from the ground up when there wasn't any money. When the band started taking off, they shared the perks of their success with the crew.

We were stunned. Everybody there…it was like we were dead too, and nobody knew it. Duane was the guy…there are a lot of people about whom you could say "without him, none of this would have happened," but he was definitely one of the main ones. The band just wouldn't have happened without his energy and effervescence and his "we'll get this done" attitude. Other bands had moved to Macon because of the Brothers, and Duane was *the* head brother. There was no doubt who the band leader was—it was Duane. Everyone focused on Duane, more than he wanted, I think. He was as proud of his band as he was of his own ability. And what a great band it was. In interviews, someone would mention his incredible talent, but Duane would say, "Oh that was Dickey." He'd point it out if it wasn't him, or he'd say, "Dickey's better than I am. I got the best guitar player in the world standing right beside me." Duane once said, "Every time Dickey played a good lick, I got credit."

Duane listened to everything, and he could play anything. He was never afraid. He'd get out on a limb and chop it off, then grab another one and keep going. There was never any fear in his playing, and in jam bands like that, when it works, there can't be any fear. Everybody has to know they're going to go down a road; it's going to be a fun road, and they're going to see interesting things, and it's all going to come out right. You can't be worried about whether the bass player is going to follow the change or if the drummer is going to lose it, and in that band, they don't. In "One Way Out" there are twelve bars where the beat is just twisted, it's back to right, and then it stops perfectly. The band knew they were going to come back and it would be okay. It's probably the tightest stop in the whole record and I love it.

Of the six members of the band, people focused on Duane. This was before the rift between the record company and the band. Duane kind of the kept peace there and took care of the band. The band had more or less chosen him as the spokesperson, and he'd meet with the record company, then call everyone together and explain things. If there was any interpretation to be done between the record company and the band, Duane did it. At that time the band just wanted to play music. It was so much into their heart and soul that they didn't want to have to deal with the other part of it.

As an artist you can get bogged down in the business end of music to the point that it takes something away from the music. It's not the easiest thing to deal with because you have to quantify the worth of something that you feel is your child, your life's blood. People back then played music because they didn't have a choice; that was what they had to do and, if Duane had never made it big, he'd have been playing guitar in a bar somewhere. Of course, with his abilities, there's no way he wouldn't have made it big any place you put him. He was going to shine through and anyone who first saw him knew it.

I was closest to Duane and Berry and I spent a lot of time with them. At one point Gregg and I had been really close too, but he was drifting away into this stardom thing and I wasn't on that trip. Duane and I could talk openly and we knew each other well enough to call each other on things. It was that kind of relationship that was so valuable. We didn't agree on everything, but it was okay, I knew whatever he said would be an interesting concept. I'd show him ways to look at things and he'd show me ways to look at things. There aren't many people who can be that totally honest with you and still love you and that's the way it was. When I first met him, I didn't know how to take him though. Gregg was easy to get to know, but I felt Duane was a little standoffish at first and it took time. He wasn't going to accept just anybody. He wanted to make sure you were someone he wanted to know and if so, on what level. He treated most everyone who deserved it with respect.

I don't remember a lot about being at the big house, but I remember there was food. I remember a lot of smoke, which at the time wasn't very appealing, and a lot of liquor. People were really wasted and drunk, but I don't remember what I did. I don't think I got screwed up, however I don't know. I just remember being there and not having anything to say. I was terribly numb and didn't know what was going to happen. You know, Duane's gone, what's going to happen? He was the one who made it work and all the things he'd been such a part of, the most important part, was all in peril.

You have to remember, this was '71, and the Brothers had just released *Fillmore East* which was their first million selling record. It was the one that broke them through, but the whole city hadn't realized that. The band was still working on *Eat a Peach* and not everybody in Macon knew who they were; it was just amongst this small community of musicians. It wasn't like it is now. You mention Allman Brothers Band today and everybody salutes, but back then the prevailing thought was 'let's get those people out of this town so we can go back and live like we use to.' It was kind of the attitude we dealt with for a long time. They didn't want the dirty hippies coming in to their pristine Macon community.

It could have been two days or it could have been a week before the funeral service, I don't know. I sort of have feelings and remember moments from that time, but I do remember the service and the music. The funeral home was right across from the camera shop on Cherry Street and people came from all over. Jerry Wexler was there. If it hadn't been for him I think all the Southern music in Memphis, Muscle Shoals and Macon would have had a really hard time getting noticed. He was Phil's friend and he was a friend to us. I knew about him from reading the back of the Atlantic albums long before I even thought about being a producer and, as a producer, I always wanted his approval. I wanted a pat on the back from him because I admired his taste in music so much.

He flew in, Dr. John came, Bonnie Bramlett, and maybe Delaney was with her, but I don't remember. Bobby Caldwell, a drummer I'd worked with in Captain Beyond was a friend of Duane's and he and the band came. Donna Allman, Duane's ex-wife and mother of their daughter, Galadrielle, was there, as was Dixie Meadows, who had been living with Duane. I didn't know it at the time, but people didn't treat Donna very well.

There was a stage and the band was set up and playing. All I could think of was how sad it was; this band that, for me, stood for joy, this band that made me feel so good was playing without him. There was only an empty chair that held his guitar. The Brothers played, and then other people played. When it was my turn, I didn't play. I couldn't do it. This was one of the darkest times in Macon. I was still numb, and I stayed that way for a long time.

We didn't go to the cemetery because Duane wasn't buried at that time. I didn't know he'd remained at the funeral home long after the funeral. Even though it's such a logical thought process—you have the funeral and then you go bury somebody, I hadn't been to a lot of funerals before. Ann and I had been to the funeral of a friend who had died in high school, but I didn't exactly know what the protocol was—or I didn't want to know because I wasn't ready to accept it—I never even thought about that part. I guess someone would have to hypnotize me and take me through a regression to remember details of that time because I only remember the feelings and wandering around in a daze. It was heartbreaking. I think about Duane every day, but the memories aren't sad anymore. He encouraged me in everything, and he always believed in what I was doing and in my sincerity about doing it. I miss him. I can't help but wonder what we could have accomplished over the years had he lived.

It wasn't all that long before we started back to work because everyone in the band was talking about having to play. It would have been crazy just to sit around, and, of course, Duane would have said, "Hey Man, you guys gotta play." He would have rallied everyone together and gotten them playing again. Eventually they pulled it together the best they could on their own and started practicing. But there had been so much based around Duane, I just didn't know what they were going to do without him.

19

Anthology

After Duane was gone, everyone existed in a haze. I don't remember how anyone else dealt with his passing because I was in my own fog. I've talked with several people, and looking back on it, I agree with Kathy Martin who once told me we didn't know how to grieve at the time. That's right; all we knew to do was just plod on ahead. It seemed music was the thing that made us all happy, it was what made Duane happy, and I didn't know what else to do but work and try to make more music. The band couldn't just stop playing. They had to regroup and get over the shock and move on without Duane, so that's what they did.

I was surprised when, a week or so after the funeral, I heard the Brothers were going to play in New York on November 22. I wondered who was going to play slide on the songs. I'd never heard Dickey play slide and didn't even know he could. As it turned out, he's a very fine slide player. I didn't go to the show, but everyone told me it was good. The band played three more shows and then returned to Miami to continue working on their album.

It might have been longer, but seems it was only a few days after Duane died that Phil had the idea of releasing an anthology of some of Duane's best works. There was such a large body of work to choose from it was hard to know where to begin, but Phil had some ideas. Folks at Atlantic, Tom Dowd, and I had some ideas, so I gathered the tapes of some of our favorite songs featuring Duane and used them to compile the album. A lot of tapes were already at Capricorn, I flew to New York to get the tapes at Atlantic. I got the four track master from Eddie Hinton for the "B. B. King Medley" and mixed it for the album.

The "B. B. King Medley" was one of the things we'd recorded in the HourGlass over at FAME Studio with Eddie producing. Out of the three or four tunes we cut over there, this song was the one we thought really captured the band. Liberty had thought it was just useless, so the tapes were still in Muscle Shoals. Since the band had paid for the recording, they belonged to us. We knew the recording was something Duane would be proud of, so Eddie sent me the four track masters for me to mix the song.

Along with the "B. B. King Medley" is "Hey Jude" (the first thing that garnered Duane both national and international attention), and "Road of Love," a great cut with Clarence Carter. "Goin' Down Slow" is part of the album we'd started over at FAME for Duane's solo project with just four of us (Duane, Berry, Paul and I) playing and Duane singing. There isn't a lead guitar part on the track since Duane's solo project was put on the back burner when the Allman Brothers came along and, of course, we never had the chance to finish it.

"The Weight," with Aretha Franklin, has a slide intro that's just killer, and "Games People Play" was a Grammy winner for King Curtis, who was really good friends with Duane. "Loan Me a Dime" was done over at Muscle Shoals Sound with Boz Scaggs and features a really neat jam that draws you into it. "Living on the Open Road" is a Bonnie and Delaney recording, and Duane added a lot to the song. "Rolling Stone" is an acoustic thing I produced on *Ton Ton Macoute* with Johnny Jenkins and Duane playing some great acoustic slide. "Down along the Cove" was also cut for Duane's solo album and used for *Ton Ton Macoute*. I'd taken the track, on which Berry, Paul, Duane and I play, and added a few things with Johnny singing on it.

"Mean Old World" was from the time of the *Layla* sessions when Duane was recording with Clapton in Miami; "Statesboro" and "Don't Keep Me Wondering" were from the Allman Brothers' live album. The "Dreams" cut was also from the live album. "Stand Back" was from *Eat a Peach*, and "Little Martha" was the perfect song to end the album. It was just Duane and Dickey on acoustics and Berry on bass. By the time we were finished selecting songs for the *Anthology*, we realized we almost had enough for a second album that became the *Anthology II*.

There were mixed feelings for a lot of us while putting the album together. It was exciting to be able to compile a great collection that outlined some of the best parts of a guy's career, someone I knew and loved and was proud of, but I wished Duane had still been there making more music. It was wonderful and at the same time incredibly sad. I like the album and I'm proud of my part in it; I know Duane would be proud of his.

The band was in the middle of recording *Eat a Peach* when Duane died. I don't remember how long it took, but they finally finished the album. Because the Brothers had run over on the time that he'd set aside for them, Tom had other commitments and wasn't available to mix the album. Phil and the band asked me to mix it, so I flew to down to Miami and went to Criteria. Tom was there in studio B, which had a custom MCI with Pentron faders, and had already mixed the first minute or minute and a half of "Les Bres in A Minor," so I finished mixing that song, did a few overdubs with Gregg and Dickey, and finished mixing the rest of the album.

One thing I really liked about Criteria was it's the only studio I'd worked in where you couldn't see the monitors. They were built into the wall and there was a black cloth covering them, but when you looked at the wall, you wouldn't necessarily know there were monitors there. This was before studios began using near-field monitors and the control rooms were equipped with only a single set of soffit-mounted speakers. I think that helps, in a way, when you're mixing because it's easy to fixate on monitors when you should be listening to the music. Gary Kellgren, an engineer and one of the co-founders of the Record Plant, once told me, "Don't listen to the monitors—listen to the music." In Criteria, you had a center spot that kept you from focusing on the monitors, and I always liked mixing there.

When I mix, I always try to get the rhythm section as solid as I can with the drums. The way I used to pan it with the Brothers, Butch was kind of mixed from middle to far right and Jaimoe was mixed from middle to far left so when you listen to the record, you get the feeling of how the band was set up on stage. If you were looking at the stage from the audience, it went from Gregg on the far left on the B-3 to Duane, and behind Duane was Jaimoe. Dickey was to the left of Duane; behind him was Butch with Berry to Dickey's left. The bass ended up in the center, but that's where it belongs in the mix. A bass is not very directional anyway, and for mastering you needed it in the center for vinyl. Bass frequencies contain the most energy, and if it was mixed to the side it could cause the record to skip.

Revisionists go back and say we left the bass off "Little Martha" by mistake, but it was left off deliberately. Both guitars on that song were cut in stereo. I panned one of them wide stereo and one of them in between which gave a little different blend on the sides, but more centered images. We put the bass in and it didn't sound right, so I asked Barry for ideas. He said "take it out," and we both agreed it sounded better that way. It wasn't something I forgot; it was discussed and that's the way we decided to do it. The band called the shots and we usually agreed. If I was happy with it, they were ninety percent happy with it. Whatever they wanted changed, we'd change. We had a good working relationship then. You know, I loved the guys in the band.

Up to this point I hadn't mixed but three or four albums. The record was going to ship platinum, so I didn't want to screw it up. It was very important for me to get it right, and at the very least I didn't want to hurt it. I really wanted Tom's approval on my mixes, so I left a 15 ips copy of the mixes at Criteria and asked him to let me know what he thought. It took a while for him to get in touch to tell me the mixes were fine, and by then the record was already number one. Maybe that was Tom's way of saying, "you don't need my approval."

One thing that's always stuck in my craw was the credits for the album. I was pumped up because it was the biggest record I'd worked on to that point and it was going to ship platinum. To be honest, I was proud of my mixing, and then I took *Eat a Peach* all the way through the mastering at the Record Plant with George. The band liked the work I'd done, but I ended up on the credits as a "special thanks" on the insert, not even on the album jacket. It's like I could have been the guy who scored the best pot. I've tried ever since then to get my credit on the album. Polygram owns the masters now, and I've talked with their A & R department, but even after all these years and several re-releases, they've refused to change it.

20

November 1972

Capricorn had initially been associated with Atlantic, but when Capricorn's three-year contract was up, Phil worked a new deal where they'd be a subsidiary of Warner Brothers and the first release on that label would be *Eat a Peach*. It wasn't long after the release that it was time to make another record. The band wanted to do it because they were all dedicated to keeping the Allman Brothers Band going after Duane's passing. I've heard Tom say Atlantic wouldn't let him work with the Brothers any more, but that never made any sense to me because all of the labels were part of the same Warner/Electra/Atlantic group. I imagine if Phil had wanted Tom bad enough he could have gotten him. My understanding was the band was happy with the mixing I'd done on *Eat a Peach* after Tom had to leave, and they didn't want to worry about his availability on the next album. It was decided I'd produce the album. Phil was happy it was going to be all in-house.

As the Brothers were gearing up for the next album, we were starting work on Gregg's solo album, so they were both going on at the same time. At some point, Gregg had gone to Criteria and put down three or four tunes, and when he came back to Macon, he was talking about doing a solo album. He played the songs for me and I liked his ideas, so I asked him why he didn't come back to Macon and let me do the album. He thought it was a good idea, and that was the beginning of *Laid Back*.

After that, every time Gregg came home from the road, we'd go into the studio where he'd put down song ideas and songs. A lot of the time it was just him and a piano or guitar. He'd work on songs then play them for some of the band. If they rejected it, the song was a possibility for Gregg's album. That's where a lot of the material that came out on *One More Try* originated. Some of the tracks that came out on that CD were rough mixes that maybe I'd done one night to see how a part worked, for instance, a dobro part on "Will the Circle Be Unbroken?"

Although it felt right at the time, the next day it was obvious the dobro didn't belong on the song, so I took it off.

Before the recording of *Brothers and Sisters* started, the band signed a new contract with Capricorn re-allocating percentages. I never was sure about the particulars, but part of their deal was that they got free studio time at Capricorn. The band was writing on the road, and when they were home they'd go into the studio to work on the songs. Dickey would show the song to everybody if it was his, and Gregg would show the rest of them the song if it was his. Then, using the free studio time, we'd do a rough cut to put it down. A lot of times, in the beginning, Jaimoe would just sit and listen. He was very much aware of what everybody else was doing, but he'd sit there and figure out where he fit in and what he could add to it. Then he'd strike up a groove, and they'd go from there. Most of what was recorded wasn't useful, but they'd work out the long, drawn out intricate arrangements until everyone got tired.

We cut "Wasted Words," which had more of the Allman Brothers blues sound than some of the others, and I liked the raw attitude. I always thought it was a hit song and should have been the first single, but it wasn't meant to be. I'd never heard Dickey play slide before, and I was amazed at his playing on that song. The band worked up "Ramblin' Man." I could tell there was something special about it but had no idea it would be their first hit single. Everyone in the band thought it was a hit when we got through, and everyone in the office was excited about it. The guitar playing on the song is amazing. "Ramblin' Man" got a lot of airplay, but it had a long ending and the DJs would fade it out early. I did a shorter mix and sent it out as DJ copies.

When the studio had been remodeled we'd gone from an old UA console to one of the first MCI production consoles, meaning it was a complete assembly line board. In the beginning, the tech guy would buy parts and build a console, but this one had 24 ins, the black and red ones. It was the MCI JH416, which was relatively simple to use and it sounded good; it wasn't great, but was new and it functioned okay. We were at 16-tracks then, and I think we bought a new MCI 16-track tape machine with the console. It was a little troublesome and there were a lot of snaps on punch-ins that had to be fixed by spot erasing the pops, but the machine didn't sound bad; we just had to get the bugs worked out of it.

Finally, before *Brothers and Sisters* was finished, we got a 3M 16-track machine. It had its problems too, but 3M finally got it straightened out.

One of the problems I encountered with the machine was a giant snap in the breakdown section of "Jessica," which I remedied with an edit that took several bars out of the song. I told the band about it, but no one seemed to notice what I'd done. The edit probably made the song better, but I wouldn't have made the change had the machine not malfunctioned. Tom Flye told me about a problem he'd encountered with that particular model. The machine was notorious for going into the "record" mode on its own. Once during a mix session, with the safety on, the machine went into record and erased several bars of the master tracks before it was noticed. Fortunately, that never happened to me.

Early on there were discussions about bringing someone in to replace Duane; there was even talk about bringing in Clapton. I don't know if that would have worked, but it would have been amazing to hear. I think the attitude of the band was that even though there were many good guitar players around, they just couldn't replace Duane. They had to do something, though. After several months of playing with just the five members, they ended up getting Chuck Leavell to play with them, and that was a great move.

Chuck is an incredible player. We'd already started working on Gregg's solo album earlier, and Chuck played for those sessions and for other projects. In the beginning, when I needed piano or organ I'd use Hornsby, but after he started producing, I'd get Chuck for the keyboard parts. You could tell he was going to be a star; he had that "thing" and still does. It seems every time I hear him he's better than the last. I mentioned him to the band (and probably Gregg did as well), and when the Brothers began recording *Brothers and Sisters*, they decided to try him out to add another harmony instrument. Chuck came in one night to play with the band and just stayed with them. It was interesting to hear all the Allman Brothers songs with those wonderful harmonies coming out of Chuck's keyboard.

Berry was really having a rough time and drinking heavily after Duane died, and while we were in the studio, everybody was aware it was getting close to the anniversary of Duane's death. He'd come in to work for a while, but a lot of times he'd get too messed up to play before he was done. Sometimes we'd go out at night and jam with him and have some fun, then go on into the studio. We could tell he *wanted* to be interested in the recording, but some of the fire had gone out of him. He never got over Duane's death. He took it the hardest and just wasn't ready to let go. Of course, no one was ready at the time, but Berry didn't live long enough to be able to accept it. He used to talk to me about going out with the band and he'd say, "I want you to go on the road with us, and when I get too screwed up to play, you can take over and play bass." I told him that while I was honored, he didn't need to get so screwed up he couldn't play. "The band needs *you*," I told him. But Berry needed help.

Years later I tried to learn what he played on "Stand Back," but I never could get it down. It was too hard for me to play, and I don't know if anyone has ever covered it. I know "Stand Back" was one of Duane's favorites because he brought me the rough mixes to let me hear what they were doing. I was just blown away and knew the Brothers had taken another step on the path to greatness. I never heard that Duane wasn't happy with the slide part on the song, but maybe that's because I've heard it that way all these years.

Sometimes Berry played with a thumb pick, but most of the time he played with a flat one. I remember the thumb pick more because I played with a thumb pick during that time, too. He was a guitar player before he was a bass player, and he had a very melodic sense. The band was the perfect medium for him with the low ends of the drums and the organ. I didn't appreciate his playing as much as I should have then, but as the years go by, the more I realize what a great player he was.

On November 11, 1972, Berry was out at Idlewild South where Scott Boyer and the rest of the group Cowboy lived. He called and wanted me to go out jamming with him that night at Grant's Lounge. Berry also a few other people to meet him at Grant's, however on his way home from Idlewild South he had an accident on his motorcycle; he flipped over the handle bars and hit a bus head on. Apparently he got up and said he was okay and rode off. But he wasn't okay—he was bleeding into his brain. When he got back to the big house where he was living with Big Linda; his daughter, Brittany; and sister, Candy, he went upstairs to lie down. Later, when they couldn't wake him up, they realized it was serious and got him to the same hospital where Duane had been about a year before. And then, he was gone too.

I was at my apartment when I heard. At first, I hadn't planned on going to the club that night, but then I decided it might be fun. The next thing I knew, I got a call (I can't remember from whom), and they asked, "Did you hear about Berry?" I said that we were supposed to go jam that night but they told me he'd had an accident and was dead. Oh, God, it was awful. It didn't seem real. We had been planning to go out that night, and I couldn't understand how the accident happened. I went to the big house, and it was the same thing all over again. It was incredibly sad, and we had no way to take away the pain but with liquor and music. Mike Callahan called it an Irish wake.

Berry was one of the nicest and most good natured human beings you'll ever meet. He was fun to be around and you could talk music with him. He not only played the bass, but he also played guitar and had been one of the main singers in the Second Coming, the band he was in before the Brothers. Berry was from Chicago, and his knowledge of the blues was far more extensive than mine. He was always turning me on to stuff and telling me about this or that particular artist. I didn't know him until we did some of those sessions in Muscle Shoals with Duane, but I liked him from the beginning and liked playing with him. The relationship between the bass player and the drummer is always a critical thing—it either works or it doesn't—it's both of you feeling comfortable and in turn making the band comfortable.

The night after Berry died, everyone went to Grant's Lounge. I went along and played bass. I just happened to be the one who was there. We played for a while, but I didn't know how to play a lot of their songs, at least the ones that had more than two or three chords.

I was a pallbearer at Berry's funeral. He had a Catholic service, and it was the first time I'd ever been to a Catholic funeral. My memories of the funeral are very similar to my memories of Duane's—there was numbness and haze. I don't remember who was there or how many people attended. It was a terribly sad time, and I don't have any words to describe it. We hadn't had enough time to grieve for Duane, and now Berry was gone. I wondered how much more we could deal with.

21

Brothers and Sisters

After Berry died, everyone took a break because the Brothers couldn't play without a bass player. I don't remember exactly how long it was, but after a while the band started holding auditions at the studio for a bass player. I don't think anyone thought of just quitting; music was what they did, and we all felt that it was kind of our mission. We wanted to make good music, and I was happy and proud of what we were doing.

The band heard several players before Jaimoe brought Lamar Williams into the studio to audition. He told them Lamar was his friend, and he wanted him to try out. Because Jaimoe didn't want the band to select Lamar because of their friendship (and didn't want to play a part in the decision), he introduced Lamar to the band and left. I don't remember who all auditioned, but once they heard Lamar, the band discussed it and offered him the gig.

Lamar had a good melodic sense and fit right in with the band. Insofar as their contribution and the way they played, Berry and Duane were unique and irreplaceable, but Lamar fit in amazingly well. In fact, I was extremely surprised. He was an excellent player, but he didn't play like you'd expect a black bass player to play at all. Most black bass players use the first and second fingers on their right hand to pluck the strings, but Lamar used a pick and sounded as if he could have been Berry's understudy. I think that's one of the reasons he fit in so well with the band. He'd take a used Clorox bottle and cut out different pick shaped pieces of plastic, and those were what he used.

Lamar was a nice guy and easy to be around. He seemed to fit in the band without any rough edges. I felt good about him instantly, and we never had any disagreements. He'd spent time in Vietnam before he joined the band, but for a long time I didn't know he'd been in the service. I guess he'd been Jaimoe's friend since before he went into the military.

Once the band decided to hire him, they all went to Jekyll Island to rehearse. Both Dickey and Gregg had written some new songs, and after the Brothers finished working up the material with Lamar, they came home to Macon and we went back into the studio. We recorded every night so we'd have each song in its various stages of development. That way, if something magic happened while the band was working on it, we'd have the recording. Usually a song started out as an embryo and evolved. For three or four days everyone would show up and work on a song, learning their parts and getting comfortable with them. Maybe by the fourth night, everything would have been worked out and we'd cut the master track.

When I recorded the band, I used two tracks each for Butch and Jaimoe, one track for the bass, which was direct, two tracks for the piano, two for the organ, one for vocals, one for background vocals and one for Dickey. Dickey had an amp in the studio with extra speakers placed downstairs in the basement because it was so loud. The Marshall cabinet with 412s was near the front of the building facing the street and I wondered what anyone passing by on the sidewalk might think hearing that sound.

There were several of the road crew and a number of friends around the studio; everyone had friends and hangers on who would show up, but most of the time the band came in ready to work, not to socialize. The main problem was just getting everyone together. Usually, Dickey was the last one to arrive, but once they were all there, it wasn't a lot of trouble to get to the song they were working on. Waiting on the band to show up wasn't as bad in the beginning as it got to be later on, however, it was starting to be a problem. I never had any trouble with Dickey to amount to anything other than him getting mad once in a while and walking out of the sessions, but it was never a personal thing between us. He'd either get frustrated because things weren't going right in the studio or something else had happened in his life that was frustrating him and, when he got tired, he'd get up and walk out.

We'd recorded "Wasted Words" and "Ramblin' Man" while Berry was still with us and the next songs we recorded were "Southbound" and "Jessica," the song Dickey had written for his daughter. That's the most joyful song I've ever heard, and Chuck's solo on "Jessica" is the quintessential rock and roll keyboard solo. I remember taking with T Lavitz, keyboard player with the Dixie Dreggs, some years later, and he said it was that solo that got him interested in playing.

There are very few overdubs on that album. The piano solos are mostly live and, to the best of my recollection, Dickey's tracks on most of the songs were all done live with the band. We cut one of Dickey's songs, "Pony Boy," which I think was the first acoustic song the Brothers had ever done on a record. It was a lot of fun to watch Butch ham-boning to the track.

Gregg's always been a great writer, and he's gotten better over the years. It's like anything else—if you keep doing it and work on it, you improve. His songs increasingly fit the Allman Brothers, and his writing was geared toward the band. Most of Gregg's songs were about relationships that were usually screwed up and they were obviously more popular with the Brothers then than when we were in the HourGlass. The Allman Brothers music had been mostly based on a blues and pentatonic scale, but beginning with "Blue Sky," the band began shifting into a major key. Dickey was becoming the more prolific writer in the band, and his country rock influence was taking on more prominence. Four of the seven songs on *Brothers and Sisters* were written by Dickey, and "Jessica" was the culmination of the band's embracing the major scale.

None of us handled Berry's passing very well. There was a pall over the band, the town, and the whole music thing, as far as I was concerned. Still, we had to keep going. If you put your energy into the music, for a while you could stop think thinking about other things. In a way the music was relief from the sadness we felt inside. In a little over a year, two of our friends and members of the band were gone. It was weird how close the deaths were, and everyone thought a lot about that and wondered what was going to happen or who was going to be next.

There seems to have been an evolution of drugs in Macon that started innocently with marijuana. Cocaine cam later and was expensive, and until everyone started making money, we couldn't afford to buy it. When the good money started coming in, it was easy to get and we were all doing it. Cocaine helped us stay up a long time, and we thought it gave us an edge—although the project was usually compromised because the work wasn't as good as it might have been if we'd not been doing drugs. Cocaine use had been going on for a while before *Brothers and Sisters*, but it had gotten worse since then. Gregg wasn't holding it together very well, but who could blame him? He was messed up a lot, and that never makes anything easy. In my experience, if someone wants to accomplish something, getting drunk or way too high never makes it better and this was a case of both.

It seems like it took nine months to a year to record *Brothers and Sisters* because the band would be out on the road and record when they were back in town. And, of course, there was a lot of time lost that was unavoidable. An illustration of how it was going: a lot of blues songs share the same chord changes, and "Outskirts of Town" was one of the earliest songs I'd heard the Brothers play when Duane was still alive. The band had come up with a great arrangement that changed the song, and Gregg had started writing new words to it. We cut the track, but the words weren't finished. Whenever I'd ask about it, Gregg told me, "Yeah, I got it finished. I've got three verses with a couple of extra." When it came time to sing it, though, he didn't have much at all.

Gregg was having trouble finishing the song because he was in pretty bad shape. Finally, one day he started singing the words to Bobby Bland's "Jelly Jelly." To get the album finished, we went ahead and had Gregg sing the words to that song on the track; it was the only way we could get the song recorded. As soon as Gregg finished his vocal, Bunky Odom was waiting for him and ushered Gregg off to rehab. The very first releases had the wrong title because "Jelly Jelly" was the song on the album, but "Early Morning Blues," the name of the song Gregg never finished, was listed on the album cover.

When it was time to mix the album, I'd go into the studio at night, and one of the band members would usually be in the control room with me making suggestions. When I was mixing "Ramblin' Man," Butch would be there one night and maybe someone else the next. Mixing the song was difficult because there are a lot of guitars on it. Somewhere in the middle of the mix, Dickey came in and said, "What's wrong with that?" I asked, "Is something too loud or too soft? What?" He said, "No, it sounds too fast." I told him that was the speed it had been recorded, and I looked at the machine we cut it on to make certain the vari-speed wasn't on. It was a 16-track 3M 79 machine that had a built in vari-speed, and it was set at 15 ips. I said, "No, according to the machine, that's the speed we cut it." He asked if I could slow it down, so I turned the vari-speed on and got it slowed down a little bit. He said it sounded better.

I knew how Dickey could change his mind, so I told him, "Look, Dickey, let me do this, I'll set this knob to vari and you turn it until it sounds like it's the right speed because I don't want to do it and it not be where you want it." I showed him where the knob was and told him to turn it to where it sounded right to him. He went back and fooled with the knob for a minute and said it sounded about right. I wrote down whatever the settings were and asked if he was happy because I was going to go ahead and mix it at that speed. He said he was happy and left. When I finished mixing the album, I wanted everyone to come and listen to it. Eventually I got everyone except Dickey to come by.

The album was late being finished, and I couldn't wait for Dickey any longer. It was time to master the record, so I went to New York to George Merino and had it mastered. It used to take two weeks to get the test pressing and approve it. We had to do this in plenty of time before we needed to release the record, but because the album was late, everyone was "hurry, hurry, hurry." I did the mastering and went back to Macon. I couldn't believe it when the next day there was a reference disc for me to approve, not just a ref you get when you're mastering, but a test pressing. There were times I'd had to wait two weeks and beg for those things, but there it was, overnight. I knew then the manufacturing facility could get one out faster if they wanted to.

I called everyone in the band to come by and listen to it and told them we had to do it *then* because I only had a couple of days to let the company know if there were changes. The whole time I kept trying to get Dickey to come out and listen. Finally he came by the house about a week later to hear it. I said, "Listen man, I got the test pressing and it's going to be out soon." I put it on, and when "Ramblin' Man" came on Dickey said, "That's wrong, that's wrong." I asked him what he meant and he said, "It's too fast." I told him, "I think you sped it up." He said, "Well, it's too fast. Stop it." He heard about thirty seconds of the song then was gone. He wouldn't even listen to the rest of the album.

Warners had been calling repeatedly for the album; I got more calls from them than I did from Capricorn and told them I was mixing as fast as I could. When we hit that snag with Dickey, I was really disheartened. I was tired, I'd stayed up way too long mixing, then I'd gone to New York for mastering. Once we had a test pressing, I played it for the band and everyone was happy except Dickey. To make matters worse, the people in advertising at Warners must not have gotten the memo about the album delay because they prematurely released a bunch of advertising—big buys like the backs of magazines and full page ads— almost a month before the record was out. People would go to the store looking for the album, but it wasn't there. Then Dickey wanted to delay the release even more by having me remix the song. I got a little sleep, set out to do the re-mix, and had Dickey go down to the studio to make sure it was the right speed. He came in and spent maybe five minutes adjusting the vari-speed again to what he wanted and then left. There wasn't any automation or recall on the console, so I started mixing again from scratch. I went back and put it at the original speed and remixed it.

I thought the second mix was the one the label used, but, as it turned out, they went ahead and pressed the records from the first test pressing and released the fast version anyway. I can't remember Dickey saying anything about it, but when it got to number two in Billboard and number one in Cashbox, I think he was happy. Still, it bugs me. It's too fast and makes Dickey's voice sound a little thin or high pitched.

Brothers and Sisters was my first gold record for production. I was working in the studio in Macon when Carolyn Brown called me to say the gold records were in and that I should come get mine. I thought it was kind of odd because I was looking forward to having a big ceremony with cheering crowds as Phil presented me with my gold album. I thought that was the way they were supposed to be presented. When I went to the office, I was expecting some kind of surprise, perhaps a little ceremony. When I arrived I said, "Hey Carolyn, I came for my gold record!" She replied that they were all in a corner, piled against the wall; I should just go through them and find the one with my name on it! I thought to myself that wasn't the way you were supposed to get a gold record, but it turns out it was. There was also one with my name on it for *Eat a Peach*, and I got that one too.

I went back to the studio and told Sam Whiteside and Carolyn Harris, who were working with me, "Hey look, I've got to at least have a picture of me getting my first gold record so I want you all to present it to me and have someone take a picture." I still have the Polaroid taken of the "presentation." It's a neat picture.

22

Laid Back

Laid Back began after Gregg recorded some songs at Criteria in Miami and brought them back and played them for me. We decided to re-cut the things he'd done in Miami and record enough new material to make a complete album. I'd always wanted to do a solo album with Gregg and feature him in a different light from what he was doing with the Brothers. To me, his voice sounded best on blues and on his own songs, so my idea was to focus on Gregg Allman, the great singer. Though I wasn't sure of all the particular songs we'd record for the album, I was sure of the direction I wanted to go and I had an "auditory vision" of what the mixes would sound like, i.e., reverb, panning, and such.

There was a lot of positive energy around *Laid Back* and a lot of good feeling about the record. The first thing we cut was a Jackson Browne song, "These Days" that Gregg had gotten from Jackson when we were out in California with the HourGlass and had been performing ever since. Scott Boyer ended up playing steel on the track, Tommy Talton and Gregg played acoustic guitar, Bill Stewart played drums, and I ended up playing bass. Later on, Gregg wrote the song "Multi-Colored Lady" that was in the same genre as "These Days," and we recorded that one using the same players.

Gregg and I talked about doing "Midnight Rider," and he came in with a new six beat lick intro to the song, but he was on the road when we cut the track and we ended up doing the intro with a four-beat variation. Scott's gotten blamed for screwing up the lick, but it was intentional, and he played it that way at my request. Gregg didn't say too much about the intro changes at the time; however, it kind of festered, and after a while he started bitching about it. He didn't really like the changes, and now when he performs the song, he plays it with the six-beat intro. I think both ways work fine.

Chuck Leavell played Rhodes on the track, and I remember thinking what a perfect, ominous sound it was for the song. Tommy played slide guitar I ran through a Cooper Time Cube. That made it easy to stereo Tommy's guitar with his original signal on the left and his delayed Time Cube signal on the right, making a pretty ominous sound. Personally, I like the way the song was done, but there were several things about it Gregg didn't like. Fortunately, he didn't mention most of them until years later, and by then it had been a top ten single, and the album, *Laid Back*, was a top ten on the Billboard chart. You still hear it on the radio today, and recently I've heard it on at least two different television shows and in a movie or two.

We recorded a lot of songs where I'd talk it over with Gregg and then go in and cut the tracks while he was on the road. When Gregg wasn't there, I'd get with Scott and go over the arrangements with him and Chuck, then present the song to the rest of the band. Scott was invaluable in that he not only played, but sang all of the guide vocals for the songs. I enjoyed working that way and was inspired because I was more involved in the production of the album than on a typical Allman Brothers record. With a Brothers album, the band already had everything worked up, and my job was to get the best sounds and performance.

I'd heard Gregg sing "Will the Circle Be Unbroken?" with just him and an acoustic guitar and we talked about recording the song. Gregg wasn't there when we cut the track, but I remember Chuck played an old upright piano we'd brought from a side room into the studio to use for the song. I had this idea and got just about everyone I knew of, or could get in touch with, who was a good singer to come in and sing back up on track. I tried to get the Dixie Hummingbirds, but they said they weren't going to work on any more secular music because their fans hadn't liked them recording the album they'd recently done with Paul Simon. There was a local black quartet that was quite good, and they sang on it instead. Working on that song was a joy for me.

Les Dudek asked to play on *Laid Back* and probably would have been good, but he'd played on a song or two for *Brothers and Sisters*, and I wouldn't work with him again because of his attitude. I wanted Buzzy Feiten to play on the album and was fortunate enough to get him to fly in from California to play on the record. The intro he played on "Queen of Hearts" is one of my favorite guitar parts ever.

We cut another one of Gregg's songs, "Please Call Home" off the first Allman Brothers album. It was always one of my favorite songs, and we dressed it up a little bit for Gregg's album. We cut an old R&B song "Don't Mess up a Good Thing," and he did "All My Friends," the song that had frustrated Duane earlier on the Cowboy album. As I mentioned before, Scott originally wrote the song with sections in 7/4, and Gregg told him if he'd change it to 4/4 he'd record it. The changes were fairly simple for Scott to make; he recorded a demo of it, and we went in and cut the track for Gregg.

I went to the Record Plant in New York to record strings and horns for the album and got to work with Roy Cicala, Frank Hubach, and Danny Turberville. I remembered Roy from his work on some of John Lennon's albums, and he was one of the better known engineers up there. My good friend Ed Freeman did string and horn arrangements. I loved the stuff I'd heard him do, so I called to ask if he'd write the string and horn arrangements for me. We had a seventeen-piece string section and the Johnny Carson horn players. I loved doing the strings, but it was kind of frightening. After Ed had written the charts, there was a part in "Midnight Rider" I wanted to change. I felt like a fish out of water standing before seventeen of New York's finest string players humming the new part, but they seemed okay with it as long as I didn't get too close. Ed rewrote the charts right there on the spot.

Right after that, one of the engineers at the Record Plant told me the studio had three restrooms—one for the men, one for the women, and one for string players. It cracked me up. My only previous experience with recording strings was the Alex Taylor session with four strings and an arranger I didn't know. This time the session went much better even though the viola player was reading the *Wall Street Journal* right up to when he was ready to start playing. He'd put down the paper and come in right on cue. I did backing vocals up while I was there too. I wanted eight women—and Ed contracted for them—but they sent seven women and a guy. I was a little surprised, but the guy had an amazing range and could sound like a girl. Cissy Houston was in the section, and it sounded wonderful.

Chris Stone had told me about his new studios in Sausalito and invited me to mix there, so when it was time to mix the album, I made my first trip to Sausalito. It's one of the nicest places I've ever been; the people at the Record Plant always treated me well, and I fell in love with the API console in Studio A.

I was mixing on a 16-track machine, and they had an extra 16-track machine in the room for me to use for tape effects, i.e., slap back or various delays. Unfortunately, the extra machine would sometimes run backwards, but no one had mentioned that to me. I discovered it by accident one night when I was stoned and sitting in the studio thinking of things to do. I put the machine in play, then looked over and saw it running backwards. I'd never seen a machine do that before and didn't even know it was possible. I thought I was seeing things and was afraid to mention it to anyone, so I went over to stop it and then turned it on again. That time it ran normally. I thought I was hallucinating and later got up the nerve to ask Kurt Kinzel about it. He told me sometimes the machine did that when it got near the end of the tape.

While I was out in Sausalito, I met Kurt, who worked as my assistant engineer. I liked him a lot. He's a talented engineer, and later on after clearing it with Chris Stone, I hired him to work for Capricorn. We were working in studio A, across the hall from where the Grateful Dead was recording in studio B. I'd met the Dead when I'd been at a gig they shared with the Brothers, and I became friendly with Owsley Stanley. Sometimes he would talk about very technical things I didn't understand, and other times we'd just talk about music. Soon he was hanging out with us more than with the Dead in studio B. I enjoyed his company, but when we were trying to work we would lock the doors when we went in to mix so no one would come in. However, Stanley was certainly an interesting person to talk with.

I'd been there a week and had the entire album mixed except "Please Call Home." I was just finishing it when Gregg flew out to listen to the mixes and decided he wanted to re-sing the song. It was a sixteen-track album, and I had all sixteen tracks filled with instrumentation and only one for his vocal. If I wanted to record him re-singing the song, it meant I had to erase the track we called "the vocal." Making a "safety" or back-up tape meant losing a generation, but fortunately I went ahead and made one because we tried for a day and a half to get a better vocal and ended up using the old one I'd saved.

The album was about a year-long process since the Brothers were touring a lot, and Gregg wasn't always available. Getting everything in place took a while; we were doing the *Brothers and Sisters* album during part of that time; and, of course, Gregg was working on that. So, with *Laid Back*, we'd work a little bit and then other things would come up or certain people wouldn't be available. About three-fourths through recording the album, I sent rough mixes to people I wanted to get pumped up about it—to Phil and Frank, to the Capricorn office in Los Angeles, and several other people. I'd also given Ed Freeman a copy of the rough mix I'd done after we did the strings and horns in New York, and he loved the roughs. The Capricorn guy the in Los Angeles office loved the rough mixes too.

When I was finished with the final mixes of the album, I took them to a mastering studio in Sausalito near the Record Plant and had them take a shot at it because they had electrostatic speakers I wanted to try out. I liked trying out new gear, and while I was at Capricorn, companies frequently sent me the newest equipment to try. The speakers were connected to a conventional wolfer and didn't really knock me out, but I was amazed at the sound that came out of the flat panel mid-range/tweeters.

I had some refs made and took one to the guy at Capricorn in Los Angeles I then I took the tapes to a second studio in Los Angeles and had Denny Purcell do a version with eq (elaborate tone control) and a version with no eq just to put it down that way. When I got back to Macon and listened to them at home, I liked the one without any eq better, but I wasn't really happy with either of them. The masters I had were pretty good; still, I knew I'd feel more comfortable if I took it to George and have him master the album for me.

While I was still in Los Angeles, the guy at the L. A. Capricorn office called and told me he wasn't sure about the master. He said things like, "the steel guitar wasn't as loud as it was in the roughs" and critiqued the mixes. I told him it was the final one, and I'd mixed everything to where I thought it should be with all the pieces. He replied, "Man, I don't know if I like this or not." I told him to listen to the album again.

Meanwhile, he got Phil and Frank together in a conference call and told them something to the effect of, "Look, I need to come to Macon right now. I don't want to tell you why; I just want to come and show you something." First they agreed, but then either Frank or Phil called him back and told that he could come, but he had to explain first. He said something like, "I just heard the mixes, and they sucked. I think they're just awful, and we need to have it remixed." They told him when I got back from California that they'd listen and see what they thought. Of course, I heard about this later.

I felt like the job I was doing was being challenged. At that time *Brothers and Sisters* was in the top ten on the charts, the single was in the top five, and the album shipped platinum. I'm not saying I made the Brothers. The album was going to ship platinum regardless of who produced it, but I was there and felt it was my charge to do the best work I could on the record. While I was mixing *Laid Back,* Gary Kellgren had been in the studio off and on; I trusted his ideas because he was a creative genius. I knew he wasn't the kind of guy who'd just stroke my ego. He'd tell me the truth whether I liked it or not, and he liked my mixes.

Then Ed Freeman called, and he didn't like the final mixes either. He didn't feel the string parts were up as loud as they were on the rough mixes. He was right—they weren't. The roughs Ed was talking about were done in New York right after the strings and horn tracks were finished. After I record something, I tend to do roughs with the parts I'd just recorded more prominently in the mix so I can listen to them. I want to hear what I've just done to make sure I like it. I respect Ed's opinion, but we have different tastes. I like some of the things he's done and he likes some of the work I've done, but we don't hear things the same way.

This is why I don't ever send out rough mixes now to anyone except the artist. I won't send out anything except a final mix because, while you may get opinions that can help, they usually hinder. I'd spent a lot of time and done a lot of work on the mixes, and by that time I was entrenched in them. Gregg and I liked them, and I wasn't going to budge.

When I returned to Macon, Phil and Frank listened to the ref and told the guy in Los Angeles that my mixes were fine. They told him, in effect, the mix was my call and that it was his job to promote the records. Ed was really disappointed. I'm not saying he was wrong because it's all a matter of opinion, but I've gotten a lot of compliments on the way that record sounds. Gregg loved the album when it was finished, and it's probably one of my two or three favorite albums.

23

The Warehouse

Phil had signed Captain Beyond to the label, and the band was recording out in Los Angeles. I think they were producing themselves and had gotten about 95 percent of the recording done when they asked me to mix it. I called Chris Stone to set up time at the Los Angeles Record Plant, and we went into studio B. The tapes were 16-tracks and, good golly, I'd never heard as much stuff on one tape before. It was a real challenge to mix. The band was great, but I'd be going along with a track and there'd be a lead vocal; the next thing you know, there'd be a tambourine, percussion, a finger snap, or hand claps. I'd be moving from one thing to the next every few seconds. There was so much going on that I referred to it as "track salad."

There was no automated anything at the time, so it was all done live. Without automation, mixing the album was almost like playing an instrument and with several different instruments or sounds that were in different places, so it was it an over-all challenge. Instead of mixing a whole song at once, I'd mix a minute just past an edit point before everything started changing, get that part done, and listen to it. If it sounded okay, I'd cut the tape and splice it to the ¼-inch tape. I'd hope the next edit point would match up with the previous one. Then I'd mix the next minute, and if everything worked right, I'd go on and no one could tell there was an edit. Most of the time that worked, but once in a while something would change so much I'd wonder, "what was that?" I ended up mixing the whole album a minute at a time.

Different members of the band were there at different times. Larry "Rhino" Reinhardt was there a lot, as were Lee Dorffman and Bobby Caldwell. Often they'd be looking over my shoulder, unintentionally adding to the tension. Sometimes, they'd join in to help and ride the fader of a particular instrument or background vocal while I did the rest. It took a while to finish the mixes; it was satisfying but taxing. In fact, working on that album was one of the tensest times I'd been through.

Ironically, I also had one of the most relaxing experiences of my life while working on that record. I'd gotten through eight or ten hours of mixing and was just fit to be tied. There was a room at the Record Plant with a Jacuzzi tub. I sat in the thing for thirty minutes, then went to lie down and was out like a light.

Once I finished, everyone seemed happy with the mixes, and I've had more compliments on the way that album sounded than most other things I've done. I've been asked a lot about the 3-D cover for the album, but I don't know who designed it. That came from the art department at Pacific Eye and Ear, and I was just as surprised as anyone else when it came out. The band dedicated the album to the memory of Duane.

Dinnertime was Alex Taylor's second album. When it was time to do the record, the Capricorn studio was going through the second of its renovations and wasn't available for the sessions, so we went to the old Muscle Shoals Sound. When I played in Alex's first road band it was me, Paul Hornsby, Bill Stewart, and Joe Rudd, but the members of Alex's new band were Lou Mullenix, Charlie Hayward, Chuck Leavell, and Jimmy Nalls (who was playing guitar with him then). It was a hellacious band; all of those guys were superb players, and they all went with us over to the old Muscle Shoals studio on Jackson Highway to play on the sessions. I also took Bill Stewart with us plus, Roger Hawkins and the rest of the Swampers were available if we needed them.

I remember one particular song on the album that gave me some stress. We went into the studio and started learning a new song, "Change Your Sexy Ways" that was something Alex had just written with Jimmy and Chuck. It took a while to work up. I was getting kind of concerned, thinking it was going to take forever and we'd never get the track down. The first night we worked a long time, but I didn't think we'd gotten the track. We went back the next day and finally got it. I hadn't produced too many albums at that time and couldn't sleep for about two or three days because I was so mentally wired. We finished that track and then cut one of my favorite songs, "Burn Down the Cornfields," a Randy Newman tune. For some reason it speaks to me, and I think Alex did a good job on it.

While we were in Sheffield, we all stayed at this funky motel that was just down the street from the studio and where Scott had written

"Please Be with Me." This was the early days, and we didn't have a big budget from the label. As bad as that place was, it didn't seem all that bad back then. I'd been in some worse places for sure, and most of our time was spent in the studio anyway. It was a fun album to do—Alex was in great shape and when the album came out it got pretty good reviews and even sold a few.

Alex and I used to room together when we were playing on the road, and that in itself was an adventure. He was a good guy and I loved him, but occasionally he could have a temper. I only saw him get angry a couple of times, and I can't even remember what was wrong then, but when you're on the road in a station wagon with the same people every day, things can get pretty tense after awhile and you can have disagreements even with people you like a lot. Anyone who's been in a band, or around a band much, understands that. I always liked Alex and he seemed to like working with me, however *Dinnertime* was the last album I ever did with him.

We stayed in touch over the years and, a few months before he died, he called and asked me about cutting some things with him. When he called I was over at Muscle Shoals Sound working with Panic and I told him if he could scrounge up some money so we could afford to rent the MSS studio, I was ready. He was working on getting the money together when he died, so it never did come to pass. He was in Florida, and the night he died I remember there was one of the biggest snow storms in Decatur we'd had in a long time.

Once the studio at Capricorn was put back together, *White Witch* was one of the first albums I recorded on the new MCI console and MCI machine. It was an exciting time working on the new equipment and learning how to use it, but back then things just didn't work right all the time; it took some tender loving care to keep it all going. Thank goodness Jim Hawkins was still around, and by then so was Ovie Sparks. Ovie had come to work with us and was a genius when it came to highly technical things. Between Ovie and Jim, they could fix just about anything.

Terry Kane, who, as I've mentioned, had been at Capricorn engineering and designing the studio, found the band White Witch and brought them in to the label with the idea was he was going to produce them. But Terry was a little hard to get along with, and there were all kinds of differences between him and Phil and Frank. After Terry's run-in with Phil, he left, and since White Witch was still there, I inherited the job of producing them. I really liked some of the stuff they did, but they were a little outrageous for the time. When I first went to hear them play, Ron Goedert, the lead singer, was performing in a dress. I guess I was pretty straight-laced as far as my music preferences and they were kind of pushing the envelope. Even the name White Witch wasn't something that was exactly norm, but they told me it wasn't something evil, it was a positive thing, white being the operative word, so I was okay with doing the record.

I got to experiment a lot during that album because the band was into making things sound unusual. At the time there were no digital effects or exotic stomp boxes, so you had to create the sounds you were going for using either tape machines for phasing or flanging. Eddy Offord had moved to Macon by the early '70s, and it was a blessing to be around Eddy because he was the consummate English engineer.

The English engineers knew how to do everything we'd hear on records. I'd ask Eddy how he did this or that on the Yes album *Fragile*, and he'd say, "Oh, here's how you do it," then he'd show me some involved thing with multiple tape machines. We bought a mini Moog synthesizer for the studio that had a lot of new sounds and textures, so I was exploring some different stuff that wasn't the typical instrument assonance. It was a walk on the wilder side for me at the time.

The band had some good songs, and recently I saw one on iTunes called, "And I'm Leaving," which is one of my favorites on the album. Strangely, that song would be number one in a certain area like Selma, Alabama, or some place in Utah or Idaho, and all over the country there would be these little secondary radio markets where it would be the number one song, but it never did break wide open nationally. There's an interesting thing about another song on the album titled, "It's So Nice to be Stoned." We had a section of the song where there's a repeat chorus at the end. I somehow got the speed at double time so it sounded like the Chipmunks singing, then I took a mix of the two-track and played it back double time and recorded it on the 16-track so you heard the band singing the chorus with the Chipmunks singing double time. I thought it was funny (considering the title.) The whole thing is a novelty type song, but it's good.

On the album there is an engineering credit for Carl Hornsby. Over the years, Paul and I have these friendly slights we've traded ever since we first met and were playing in the 5 Minutes together. We'd call each other names, and sometimes I'd call him Carl. There was no reason to call him Carl other than that he really hated it, so naturally I had to call him Carl all the time. Paul helped me with the engineering on the record, and I shouldn't have done it, but I listed him as Carl Hornsby. People kept asking me who Carl Hornsby was, and Paul let me know he didn't appreciate it at all.

Ron Goedert was the lead singer of White Witch; Buddy Pendergrass was the keyboard player, and Buddy Richardson was the guitar player. Beau Fisher played bass, Bobby Shea played drums, and Sammy Creason played drums on one song. Sammy was playing with Kris Kristofferson and was living in Macon, so if anyone needed a drum track, we had a great studio drummer in town. It was wonderful having all these great musicians around. The guys in White Witch were nice and always good to me, but after I started working with the Brothers I didn't do any more White Witch albums.

I really admired Eddy Offord—talk about a godsend. Eddy was an English producer and engineer who had worked on a number of great records, including the Yes albums. He had mixed a lot of the songs I'd heard on the radio, and he shared some of his stories and tricks with me. Things that can be done now with just a couple clicks of a mouse, like flanging and delays, were done with tape machines. Anyway, Eddy had cut an album with Wet Willie. Phil thought it was good but needed a couple more up-tempo songs, and he wanted me to record them. One of Wet Willie's standard songs, "Grits Ain't Groceries," is a Little Milton song I got for them. I loved the song and don't think it had been exposed to a white audience at that time. We cut "Keep a Knockin'," a Little Richard song I'd always liked, and I thought the band pulled it off well. Of course, as far as singing, Jimmy Hall can hold his own with anyone.

The Wet Willie *Drippin' Wet* album was a live recording that was done on December 31, 1972, at the Warehouse in New Orleans; Wet Willie was on the show with the Allman Brothers that night. I also recorded several of the Brothers' songs, one of which was later released on *Wipe the Windows, Check the Oil, Dollar Gas*. I'd been around during the *Fillmore East* recordings, and Tom Dowd used a truck owned by a man named Aaron Baron from Location Recorders in New York. He was an engineer Tom used for *Fillmore East* and, when the record company decided to record the Brothers at the Warehouse, I hired Aaron and the truck for the job.

In the case of most live recordings, the best trick is to get the right recording truck and the right people to do the engineering; then listen to them and not get in their way. This is something that's served me well over the years. Sometimes I'll make a suggestion or get another mic selection or change a mic here and there, but nothing major because they know what works for them and their equipment and their set-up. Other than the logistics of recording live, it's mostly getting stable electricity to the truck and getting the mic snake to the stage. A lot of that has changed now with digital recording because it's easier to have a set-up in a small area. You can have a couple of pieces of outboard gear and a computer and record the band while sitting in the club.

We had to have two 16-track machines on the truck so we could have one running and one to start running before we ran out of tape on the first one. It was the only way to have a complete show, and unfortunately there was a lot of overlap and additional tape expense. We were still running at 15 ips without noise reduction, but later it was 30 ips and that just eats up the tape. At 30 ips you've got sixteen minutes to a reel of tape, so you can imagine, if you're recording a two hour show, how much tape it would take, especially with a five minute overlap.

The construction was finished and Capricorn studio was in good shape by that time, so I took the tapes back there to mix the album. We had to do a couple of tweaks and replace some keyboard parts because Wet Willie had been using a Wurlitzer that had gone terribly out of tune during the recording. That's another difference between analog and digital. With analog the tape, speed varied ever so slightly and, when we went to overdub the piano, it wasn't in tune with the tape. I think the tape machine on the truck was running slightly off speed, probably due to the electrical feed at the Warehouse. I've worked before where I'd speed the tape up or down to try to match pitch with the piano and it'll drive you nuts. With digital, it doesn't drift; it's always steady unless there's something terribly wrong, but with tape machines, hardly any of them are the same speed all the way through the reel. It'll be the same speed for a while and then slowly drift toward the end.

When I recorded the two songs with Wet Willie in the studio, we had a lot of interaction and they were fun to work with. I think a lot of Ricky Hirsch. He was always an outstanding player, and I loved Jimmy's singing. Jack Hall's a good bass player and John Anthony and Lewis Ross were good players too. With the live album there wasn't a lot of interaction with the band. "Y'all go play good" was about it, other than a little encouragement here and there. There wasn't much I could do until I got back to do post-production when we did a few overdubs and the mixing.

About that time we'd just gotten an ITI parametric eq for the studio, which was the first type of parametric equalizer made and had been co-invented by George Massenburg and Burgess MacNeal. We got two of their stereo eqs, and I played with them a little bit, but decided not to use one on the mix. The tape itself sounded better in the truck than it did when I got it back to the studio, and I was never quite happy with the mix. I took it up to master with George Merino. He listened to it and said, "Look, this isn't up to what you usually do, and it's hard to master." I could tell George thought it needed to be remixed, so I told him I'd go back and take another try at it and returned to Macon.

I started to mix it, and thought I'd use the EQ to see what it would do. The difference was amazing. There were some real deficiencies that only a parametric equalizer like that could address. I sent the tape back to George and asked him if it sounded any better. He said it was great and thought I'd remixed it, but I told him what I'd done. He asked me about the equalizer, and the next time I was up there, he had an ITI.

24

Live

Don Kirshner was starting a new television program called *In Concert*, and the way I understood it, the Allman Brothers Band was going to be the very first recorded for the series. A call came in to the office from Kirshner's people, and Phil told me I needed to go up to Hofstra University in Hempstead, New York, and record the band for the show. This was when the Brothers were kind of peaking. Everyone was excited the band was going to be on network television, and it made me happy that Kirshner was doing good music. He wasn't just going for the showy bands; he wanted a great concert band, and the Brothers were probably the greatest.

The Kirshner people already had the recording truck set up, and the video was going to be filmed in black and white. This was when Berry was still alive, and the band set up as they always did: Berry on one side in the kind of up front stage left, Gregg at the extreme stage right and Dickey next to him. Behind Dickey was Jaimoe, and stage left behind Dickey was Butch with Chuck in the back. It was a dynamite concert, but not one of their greatest because of the constraints of T.V. There'd be applause, and then the band would have to stop while the video was being prepared for the next take. It was close to a real concert in that there was an audience, but there was still the obviousness of the television cameras and a producer telling the band when to play and when to stop.

The recording went off without a hitch, but I had to mix it immediately because the show only had a limited amount of time booked in studio B at the New York Record Plant. They said the show was going to be broadcast right away and we had to put a rush on it. I was probably the one who insisted on doing my mixing at the Record Plant because I was comfortable there, but because it was a union thing, I had to use whatever union people were connected with Kirshner to run the machines. Most of the time they'd just be standing around letting me do the work while they were officially there, I guess, to make sure I didn't screw up.

A weird thing happened, though. There wasn't time to play back the tape just because I *might* have missed something, so I was mixing the multi-track tape live as it played. It was just one long, continuous mix. There was one guy who was there as a tape operator, and his job was simple: when I got ready to put the mix down I'd say, "Okay, roll it," and all he had to do was put the machine in record mode. It was a two-track stereo mix, but it was being recorded to a four-track machine because we had to have a couple of extra tracks for the SMPTE time code (the code that allows the audio to sync with the video later). I told him to "roll it" and saw two red lights on the machine. I wasn't thinking about time code then, and when I saw two lights go on, I rolled it and did about as good a mix as I could, having only gone through it one time without a preview. I'd listened to the recording and tried to balance it before we started putting it down, but basically it was just like mixing a live show.

It was probably about as good as a mix as I could do in an hour of just sitting there going straight through with no chance to stop and go back, but when I got finished, one of the guys said, "Uh, we've had a problem." I replied, "A problem? What kind of problem? It seemed to go all right to me." He said that something happened with the four-track machine. I asked if something was wrong with it. He said, "No, nothing's wrong with it. We've got it fixed now." Frustrated, I asked, "What happened, damn it? That was a good mix." He hesitated and then reluctantly pointed to the tape operator, saying, "He forgot to put one of the tracks into record."

I was angry. I was under a lot of stress to finish, and it wasn't easy to mix under those conditions. But since I'd had to do it that way, the first time through would likely have been the best, and I felt good about the mix I'd done. Because there wasn't any more time, we just rewound the tape and started over.

Let me be clear—I was working at the Record Plant, but it wasn't Record Plant people. Believe me, Record Plant people didn't screw up; it was one of the union people there with one of the major labels. You think, "Good golly, the guy had one thing to do. All he had to do was arm the tracks on the four-track, press two buttons, wait for an hour and stop it." It was a simple thing, but it was important or the music didn't record. I guess looking back on it, it *could* be almost funny...but, come to think about it, it's still not funny.

I'd been expecting the show to be on in six weeks after the recording, given the rush on getting the mixing done. In fact, the Kirshner people in New York had told us it would be out in a couple of months, but it wasn't broadcast until more than a year later—and by then Berry was gone. I was excited about seeing it, but it had been such a long time that I'd lost some of my initial enthusiasm. I can't remember how it sounded when it aired, but it probably didn't sound great. Nothing sounded very good on television back then because the televisions all had little mono speakers.

Watkins Glen on July 23, 1973, was my third pop festival. I'd been to the first Atlanta pop festival and played with Johnny Jenkins at the second one, and Phil had scheduled me to go and record the Brothers at Watkins Glen. It was a one-day event, and I arrived the night before the concert. I had a room in a hotel located on one of the highways leading to Watkins Glen and traffic was just wild. Car traffic had stopped by then, and people were parking way back and walking to the festival; an endless stream of people all day and all night and they just kept coming. It was so crowded that I had to take a helicopter to get to the backstage area.

Trying to record that show was an absolute nightmare. Whenever you're doing a live recording, it's also a major event for sound; in fact, the live sound engineers probably have the more difficult job. All I need is a feed from the microphones to the truck while they have to do an amazing and intricate set up, especially for such a huge event.

The Grateful Dead were the best at recording live. Their shows always sounded good. I knew all the Dead sound people because the Brothers had played with them a lot. I'd talked to them some; it's how I got to know Owsley Stanley. We began negotiations over the sound for the show, and it was a fight about microphones as to who got the best split where the mics all came together. The way they recorded, one signal was sent to the sound system and one signal went to the recording. That's the only way to do it if you're going to do any recording, and the Dead didn't want to give us a feed; they didn't want to degrade the sound by going through an extra transformer. They were right on one level because sound is changed when it goes through extra equipment, but the change is usually very minor and not something a normal person would hear. The Record Plant truck was there for the recording, and Frank Hubach, the Record Plant engineer, just about got into a fight with Dan Healey, one of the Dead crew, while trying to get their individual domains set up. It was a hassle because the Dead told us they were there to do sound reinforcement for an event and weren't there to see that we recorded the show. Finally, though, they let us have the feed.

Looking out at that many people was astounding. Once you looked past the first fifty rows, all the features blended into one sea-like mass. It was like looking at a television show only you were close enough to touch them. There were about 600,000 people there, which made it the largest festival ever at that point. There have been larger ones since then, but at that time it was a little frightening. I wondered what would happen if that many people tried to rush the stage. I was glad they were peaceful.

The Band, which is one of my favorites, performed; then the Dead, who always played a long show; and finally the Brothers, who were considered the headliners. After the lengthy show, I was exhausted. Everyone had been there since early in the day and we were ready to leave. After what I thought was the end of the show, after the Brothers had done their last encore and walked off the stage, there seemed to be a jam brewing. The most colorful part of the jam was Rick Danko of the Band trying to sing Sam Cooke's "A Change Is Gonna Come." He approached the microphone and told everyone he was going to sing the song, and there was a large round of applause as he stepped up to the mic. He started to sing the opening, "I was born…" but the word "born" was an extremely high note. When he sang the word, he hit a really bad note and he knew it. He stepped back and said, "I'm going to start over." There was a smattering of applause as he reached back and sang, "I was born…" and again "born" was a terrible note.

It was obvious he was in no condition to sing, and he teetered close to the edge of the tall stage. As he was about to fall off, Bill Graham went up to try to hold him back from the edge. The third time he said, "I'm going to try again," instead of encouraging applause, the entire crowd fell silent. It was shocking to hear 600,000 people suddenly get that quiet. Undaunted, Rick started over, but he still couldn't hit the note. This time, he kept going. After a short version of the song, he was helped off stage.

When it was finally time to leave, there were four of us who got into the helicopter to go back to the hotel. Midway in the flight, the pilot says, "Guys, it looks like I'm a little low on gas, and I'm looking around to see if I can find a place to get some." I told him I didn't know what kind of fuel a helicopter ran on, but I didn't think we were we'd find gas for a helicopter where we were. He said not to worry—he could get some gas from a regular gas station and make it until he made it to a refueling station. He found one gas station and dropped down low, but he could see they were closed and took off again.

There wasn't a city around, so there weren't many options. Then the motor sputtered and quit...all we could hear was the "whomp, whomp" sound of the rotating propellers. He told us he was out of gas and was just going to set the helicopter down. I thought, "Set it down!?" We were about a hundred and twenty feet in the air, and I didn't have a good feeling. Luckily, even without fuel a propeller will turn for a while, and we landed in a Holiday Inn parking lot. It was a jarring landing, but no one was hurt—scared to death, maybe, but not hurt. The pilot told us to wait while he went to get some gas, but we told him no thank you, we'd find another way back. We caught a ride back to the hotel. I didn't think the pilot was very together, and I sure wasn't going to ride with him again.

The experience didn't turn me off of helicopters, though. I rode other ones later in New York. I thought it was pretty neat how a helicopter could take off from the airport and land on one of the skyscrapers in the middle of New York City. It was a lot better than a cab ride from the airport, which was sometimes a harrowing trip.

I don't know what happened to the recording I made the night of the Watkins Glen festival other than one of the songs, "Come and Go Blues," was released on *Wipe the Windows, Check the Oil, Dollar Gas* several years later. I'm not sure what the legalities were about releasing the entire concert, but I don't remember it being an especially great performance by the Brothers. Of course, they never played a *bad* show.

Once I started producing the Brothers, I did the rest of their live recording. They were the flagship group for the Capricorn label, and since I had the good luck to be producing them, if they needed me to record, I was there. September 10, 1973, Don Kirshner returned to Macon to record the Brothers for another show he was going to call *Saturday Night in Macon, Georgia*. A day or two before the show, Elliot Mazer's truck from Nashville was in town, and Elliot and I went to a park in Macon and recorded Wet Willie. The band was good and played one of my favorites, "Country Side of Life." There were a lot of people in the park, and it was like hippies gone wild. By then I was comfortable with engineers on the truck, one of whom was Denny Purcell. I'd met Denny in California and I really liked him. Later on when I moved to Decatur and mastered in Nashville, I worked with him at his company Georgetown Masters for about ten years. As I did with George Merino, I trusted Denny to give me something better than I'd give him. If there ever were any problems, he'd see they were corrected. Denny passed away on August 27, 2002. I now work with his protégé, Jonathan Russell, and I think about Denny every time I go to master. I miss him.

The actual show with the Brothers was at Macon's Grand Opera House and was a hectic night that turned out to be a semi-fiasco. If you were facing the Opera House, the truck was parked outside on the left side of the building where there was a door, and we had cables with everything run to the stage. The band was set up, and we put the mics around and had the roadies do a line check or sound check of sorts. It was a small place, and word had gotten out. The Opera House was filled.

When the lights went down, the band went on and played a couple of their usual songs. *Brothers and Sisters* was out at this time, so they were playing songs off that album along with some standards from their earlier albums. Gregg announced, "Now we're going to do one of my favorite songs, "Ramblin' Man." About that time Dickey kicked off "You Don't Love Me," which obviously wasn't "Ramblin' Man," so everyone in the band kind of looked around and joined in. Of course "Ramblin' Man" was a hit single, and everyone wanted the band to play it. The next song, the same thing happened again. Gregg said, "Now we're gonna do

'Ramblin' Man'," and Dickey kicked off *another* song. About midway through, Dickey put his guitar down and walked off stage while everyone finished the song. As he headed out, Phil, Bunky Odom, and a few others chased after him. The rumor I heard was that someone had slipped Dickey some acid that night and he was somewhere on the moon.

Finally Phil and Bunky got Dickey back. He went on and did a half-hearted version of "Ramblin' Man," but you could tell he just didn't want to sing. It was a rough night for the Brothers and not one of their best shows. Some of the Kirshner people had said we had to get the recording done that night because the television crew was leaving for Jamaica (or wherever) the next day. They were putting pressure on me that only television people can apply when they're in a hurry to get what they want.

It was a nightmare, and I told the television guy I didn't think the performance was good enough for what they wanted. Because Capricorn was undergoing renovations, I couldn't mix it there, so I got the Nashville truck to go out to my house. I lived a little outside of town on a two lane road, and they had an eighteen wheeler that was the longest recording truck I've seen. They maneuvered it into my driveway where we could get power from my garage. We were there for a couple of days trying to mix and match tapes to make it work. Mixing Wet Willie wasn't a problem because they played so well, but the Brothers thing just wasn't easy. It was hard to mix when I knew the band wasn't happy about it and wanted a re-do, and I felt weird because Phil was telling me I had to go ahead and mix it. We didn't have a choice except to just get it done if we wanted it on air, so we did the best we could at the time.

The Brothers played Winterland in San Francisco later in the month on September 26. We did a lot of simulcasts from Winterland, and this was one of them. There was a great Japanese hotel in San Francisco where I stayed. It was heaven being out there. By then I'd gained some notoriety as a producer and got to meet a lot of interesting people, including Tom Donahue who was the father of FM radio. The underground FM radio format was born in San Francisco, and with its great atmosphere was the perfect place for arts and music. I loved San Francisco and always enjoyed being there, even in the HourGlass days when we'd all be in one room in the cheapest hotel we could find. The town just had a vibe to it, and it seemed like everyone in the band was happier there than we were in Los Angeles.

Whenever the Brothers played at Winterland, I'd get the Record Plant truck with Tom Flye to record them. Tom is one of my favorite engineers and one of the greatest people I know, as well as one of the most talented. He'd bring the truck over to Winterland and set it up. We'd get the mics set up, hopefully get a sound check, try to cram that big band onto twenty-four tracks, and have two or three left over for the audience. Usually things went pretty smoothly.

I loved the sound of instruments live, not only because people played well, but that's the way we grew up making music. It just had a liveliness and airiness to it that's difficult to get in a studio environment. This particular gig was exciting because it was being simulcast, and people were able to get recordings of the show. One guy who had recorded the show off FM radio sent it to me, and I thought it sounded pretty good.

I finished 1973 recording the Brothers at the Cow Palace in San Francisco. The only thing I knew about the Cow Palace was that the Republican convention had been held there the previous year. I'd watched the convention on TV and was anxious to see the place in person. With any venue I'd done prior to this one, the truck would park outside, the cables would be run to the stage, and we'd sit outside in the truck. Sometimes with a loud band like the Brothers you could hear a little bit through the walls of the venue in the truck, and you kind of got an idea of what it was going to sound like on the speakers. At the Cow Palace the truck was pulled inside the building, and the place was just huge. It was a monster venue with a gigantic stage and what looked like a hundred-foot ceiling. Even parked about two or three hundred feet from the stage, we could still see it when we looked out of the truck. Tom Flye was there for that show too.

It was New Year's Eve and everyone knew it was going to be a circus. Poco was on the bill along with Santana and the Brothers, and I was there to record them. The show was being broadcast live to millions of people coast to coast and across the world on Armed Forces radio. I remember discussing the telephone lines we used to lease back then and how, for more money, we could get the extra lines at a higher resolution for audio. We always tried to get the best lines to send the show on where it would have the best fidelity.

Bill Graham introduced the Brothers. The show was exciting, and the band played really well. Bill had become good friends with the band, and I'd known him from the HourGlass days. When I started producing the Brothers, Bill and I would talk every once in a while, and I really admired him. I was a little intimidated by him, but I thought he was a great guy; he was always took my calls and was kind to me. Right at the stroke of midnight, Bill came out in a diaper. It was funny, but it wasn't pretty.

I had this little metal container about three-fourths of an inch thick that looked like a piece of jewelry. I could open the lid, put in whatever I chose to keep, and then close it. Somehow during that gig it disappeared with my "medication" in it, but by midnight I was feeling good and all of us in the truck had already had our attitudes "adjusted." I asked, "Hey Tom, if I press this button, does it go out over the air?" And he said, "Yeah." So I pressed the button and said, "Happy New Year, America!" After I did it, I wondered for about ten minutes if I should have done it, then I decided what the hell, I was just glad to be there.

Back in those days we had real hope for the future. It looked like we could do anything, and it was a magical time in a hopeful world. After Berry and Duane died, there was nothing else we could do but music. We had to pull everything back together, and it was nice to have a good gig where nothing major went wrong. Overall, despite the obvious sadness that still loomed with Duane and Berry, it felt like maybe things were going to get better. Even now at New Years, I get the feeling that the next year will be good, that I won't make the same mistakes again.

25

Gregg Allman Tour

The first Cowboy album received amazing reviews and was popular among a small niche of high profile people who paid attention to Capricorn releases, but it never did sell very many copies. The second album came out with Scott's song "Please Be with Me," that Eric Clapton later recorded. Once Clapton's version was out, we thought it would be a good idea to re-release the Cowboy album containing that song. We figured if someone saw the song listed in the credits, odds were they were going to think there might be other good songs on the album. Gregg had cut "All My Friends" for *Laid Back*, which was also on the second Cowboy album, so the first two Cowboy albums were repackaged and we named it *Why Quit When You're Losing*.

I suggested the title because it was something my mother used to say all the time and it seemed appropriate. Although both Cowboy albums had been well received, the band hadn't really broken. We thought this might be a chance to make something happen for the band since it would be a new publicity angle that would get the record out to more people. It did moderately well, but it never broke out either. I thought the album had an awful cover; it's one of two Capricorn covers I really didn't like. It was a picture of one cowboy hitting another and I wondered where they'd come up with that idea. Perhaps since the band was named Cowboy, someone thought it would be clever to depict something like a saloon brawl, but I never liked it.

Around that time, I worked on the album *Normal* with Martin Mull. Those sessions were some of the most fun I've ever had. Martin was on the label and wanted to cut a few songs with us, so I got most of the people I normally used for tracks into studio. We had a ball. Martin had one song, "Jesus Christ, Football Star" that was a little dark but funny, and Martin was also incredibly funny and great to work with.

We also cut "Ego Boogey" and "Woodshop," which was probably the most fun to record because we all got to play different tools. We were having work done in the studio, and there was a table saw lying around in the side room, so we had someone playing the table saw. I played the acoustic saw, sandpaper, and the hammer. We added other things like screwdrivers and anything else we found. We cut four songs for the album, but Martin decided to re-cut "Dialing for Dollars" in New York. I liked our version better, but I guess he didn't like the track as much as I did.

Laid Back was out by then and quite successful; "Midnight Rider" was in the top ten and so was the album. Since the Brothers weren't touring at that time, there was an idea to have Gregg do a tour and re-create the album on stage. He hired a lot of the great musicians around Macon for the tour: Kenny Tibbetts, a really good bass player from Melting Pot; Tommy Talton and Scott Boyer, who both played guitar, acoustic and electric; and Ella Avery for backgrounds. Bill Stewart and Jaimoe played drums; sometimes they'd both be on drums and sometimes Jaimoe would play percussion. The band, with four or five horn players and about fifteen string players, had a huge sound. It was a family atmosphere and exciting to hear that band on stage.

The band played good-sized auditoriums on the tour, but my favorite was Carnegie Hall where we recorded part of the *Gregg Allman Tour* or, as we referred to it, *Laid Live*. I'd heard about the place all my life and always wanted to see it. It was everything I'd dreamed about. The room itself was incredible, the acoustics were amazing, and everyone was excited about playing there. The place had a great piano; it was so alive I felt I was hearing a real piano for the first time. A benefactor had loaned the piano to Carnegie Hall, and after he passed away less than a year later his family wanted to sell it. Capricorn was able to buy it for the studio.

Gregg performed the *Laid Back* album and some of the other songs we'd done in the HourGlass including "Are You Lonely for Me, Baby?" We recorded at Carnegie Hall in New York one night and at the Capital Theatre in Passaic, New Jersey, next. Between those two recordings we were able to get enough material for a double live album. It was a powerful band, and the recordings came out well.

I had a strange experience in Passaic when we were finished recording the second night of the gig. There'd been a good crowd, and at the end of the last set Gregg walked off stage and we went back to the dressing room to talk for a few minutes. When it was time to leave, he asked me to ride with him in the limo back to the hotel. I told him I would, so we walked out the side door. There were about fifty or sixty people outside waiting for Gregg to appear, and they started rushing him. The limo was on the other side of the street, so we had to hurry to get in and close the door as people tried to surround us. They were grabbing at Gregg's hair and his shirt, wanting whatever they could get—and half the time getting me instead because I was between them and Gregg. It seemed like they were willing to take out anyone else, like me, who was in their way. It was a heart-racing moment because I'd never been rushed before.

Another strange thing about the Passaic gig—whenever I'd do live recording, I'd get the Record Plant truck and always requested Tom Flye just about every time. He and I had worked together a lot out in Sausalito, and he was the engineer for the Passaic gig. The mic lines were coming back to the truck, which was parked outside the hall, and, when we turned up the mics, there was an incredibly loud buzz we fought all afternoon. Every once in a while it would go away, but then something else would be gone too and I didn't think we were going to get rid of it. The band came on stage and was about to count off the first song and it was still there.

Gregg started counting and on three the buzz went away and the recording was fine. I've never been that close to losing a performance due to technical problems, and this buzz was loud enough to have ruined the recording. Tom always had a little magic about him, and he came through on this one. I took the tapes back to Macon where we had to do editing between the two shows and, believe it or not, it worked. Tom got such consistent levels and sounds I was able to splice between parts of a performance done at Carnegie and parts of the same song done at Passaic.

Cowboy included Scott Boyer, Tommy Talton, and Bill Stewart. Randall Bramblett played horn, David Brown played bass, and Chuck and Jaimoe played drums and keyboard with the band. All of the musicians also played in Gregg's band. The shows started out with Gregg, then, an hour so into the set, Gregg would take a break and

Cowboy would play some songs. They'd play about forty-five minutes, and near the end of the set they'd play Tommy's song, "Where Can You Go." Gregg would come out in the middle of the song and play an organ solo.

Laid Back had been a big success, so there had been rumors Gregg was going to go out on his own and not be a part of the Brothers. Near the end of Gregg's tour, the rest of the band put those rumors to rest by surprising him; they came out and played part of the night with him. It was great to hear them play with the equipment Gregg was using rather than their much louder set-up.

The first Duane anthology had gone gold, and I had a meeting with Phil where the decision was made to release the second Duane anthology. When we'd finished putting the first album together, there was additional material Phil felt needed to be released, and he wanted me to put together the *Anthology II*. There were certain songs he and Frank thought should be on it, and there were songs I added to the selections. We got the rights to use the King Curtis instrumental "The Weight" on which Duane played a really nice slide part on the intro. Two of the songs were ones we cut over at Rick Hall's studio in Muscle Shoals, "Happily Married Man" and "No Money Down," which started out as recordings for Duane's solo album. We needed a lot of recordings from Atlantic, and I was able to get the tapes from there and from the other locations to compile the album.

In addition to the other projects going on, one of the oddest things I recorded while I was at Capricorn was an album with Kitty Wells. She was the queen of country music, and I'd heard her on the radio for a long time. Personally, though, I wasn't into country music; I was into blues, soul music, and the music we were doing in Macon with the Brothers. Phil told me he'd signed her and was really excited about it; I was shocked when he said he wanted me to produce the album. I kept telling him, "You know, Hornsby knows more about country music than I do, so why don't you get him to do it?" I asked for Paul to be brought in so we could both produce it, and that's how Paul and I ended up co-producing the album. It was our first co-production and I think it was our last. I love Paul—he's a great guy and he has excellent ideas and produces good records, but he and I just see different sides of things and

175

have different approaches to production. However we got through the first tracking session without a problem and cut about five or six tunes.

We had a great band for the album. John Hughey, who's probably the best steel player alive, was there and he did some playing that just kind of scared everybody else. But it was an odd situation. I wanted to cut something with Miss Kitty that they wouldn't do in Nashville, so we had all these long-haired Southern boys cutting Otis Redding's "I've Been Lovin' You Too Long" with the "Queen of Country." Miss Kitty went along with it; however, I don't know that she ever cared for it, and I'm pretty sure her husband, Johnny Wright, didn't.

We made it through the sessions without too much trouble, but it was very formal. In Nashville they cut most of the tracks for a record in two or three hour sessions and then did limited overdubs afterwards. In Macon we didn't do that. We went in and learned the songs and might get two or three tracks a day or we might only get one—whatever we could get that felt good and made a statement. It was a whole different world for them, and I don't think they were either expecting or prepared for it.

Although we didn't start the session uptight, I was getting that way. We were doing background vocals with three girls who were in a little side room for isolation instead of being out in the studio. We couldn't see them, but I could usually tell who was singing what. One of the girls (who will remain anonymous) missed her part and said, "Oh fuck." I was sitting in the control room where I could have reached behind me and touched Johnny Wright with Kitty sitting next to him, and I didn't know what to say. I think I said something like, "Watch your language." It was an odd moment because we'd talked about the possibility of that happening beforehand and I had to tell all the guys, "No swearing around Miss Kitty. You shouldn't even say 'damn' or 'hell' if you can help it, but don't go any further, no 'motherfucker,' none of that." The guys got through it without any problems, but the female singer was the first to utter the worst of the offensive words. Miss Kitty was shocked. I don't think she heard that word very often and probably never from a female.

To be honest, halfway through the album, I bailed. I felt I wasn't needed and Paul could finish it up just fine without me. Kitty was very nice and polite, a very proper lady, but things were too strange. She and her husband would be in the control room, and I would walk in and say, "Hi, Miss Kitty." Her husband would reply, "She says hi." Maybe I wasn't supposed to ask her questions, but I wasn't supposed to greet her? He always answered questions for her, and I'd never seen that happen before.

Kitty, in her fifties at the time, was very reserved while we were a bunch of pot-smoking hippies. It was a culture clash, but on some levels I think it worked. The album, though, had a short life, and they bought the record back from Phil after it was released. I remember some people in Nashville talking about the album being unusual, and I thought they were talking about how good it was. Now I think they meant it as less of a compliment and more of a "What happened?" A few years ago, one of her grandsons called me about re-releasing the record. He told me the whole story about how Kitty and Johnny Wright hadn't liked the record, so they bought it back and tried to make sure no one ever heard it again. Now, more than thirty years later, the grandchildren have it, think it's great, and have re-released the album.

26

Highway Call

In 1974, around the same time I was working with Kitty Wells, the Hydra album project came up. Frank Hughes, who eventually became my manager, was managing the band and he asked me about producing their record. I was busy at the time and recommended Danny Turberville, an engineer I'd met and worked with at the Record Plant in New York. He did a good job of recording and mixing the album, but Frank Fenter came to me and said the band wasn't happy with the mixes and wanted to know if I'd remix it. At first I said I wouldn't; I hadn't been involved with the project from the beginning and thought they should get Danny to do it. He did remix a few things, but when they still weren't happy, Phil asked me again and I agreed. Sometimes I enjoy mixing a project I haven't been involved in because I have a different perspective when I work on songs I haven't already heard about a hundred times during the recording process.

The album was well recorded and Danny did a good job, but I had records on the charts with the *Brothers and Sisters* album and *Laid Back*. When you have records on the charts, your mixes automatically seem to sound better to other people. I believe it's possible that my success played more of a factor in their decision to have me work on the record rather than anything to do with Danny's mixes.

I'd heard about Elvin Bishop since my very first involvement with Gregg and Duane because Duane had been a big fan of the Paul Butterfield Blues Band and Elvin was one of the guitarists. Duane was a big fan of Mike Bloomfield and had the *East-West* album when we first got together as the HourGlass. He listened to it a lot and could play all of the songs on the record. Elvin was playing slide before Duane, so I don't know who influenced whom the most; Duane influenced everybody, even people who could already play slide. They respected him for the things he came up with and his passion, the feeling he played with.

Elvin had a good band from out in San Francisco with Phil Aaberg, a great piano player, and Johnny Vernazza, who played guitar. Elvin and Johnny used to play slide harmonies. Although I've never even tried to play slide, I can imagine how hard it would be not only to play slide in tune, but to harmonize while you're doing it. They were both quite good. Michael Brock was on bass, and Don Baldwin was the drummer who stayed with Elvin for a long time before eventually going on to play with the Jefferson Starship. Phil signed Elvin to the label and wanted me to produce an album with him, but the band already had the album worked up. When they came in, my job was pretty much just setting up, getting the sound, and starting to run down songs.

Elvin was a good guitar player and while not a great singer, he was good. When the band came in and started recording the album, Elvin did the singing. Later, he got Mickey Thomas in to sing background, and he and Elvin had good harmonies. We cut a single, "Travelin' Shoes," which ended up being a hit for him and was probably the biggest record Elvin had up to that time. I know the album was on the Billboard charts in the top twenty, and the single made its way up the charts too.

The *Brothers and Sisters* record was out, Gregg had done *Laid Back* and the *Gregg Allman Tour*, and Dickey wanted to do his own album. I couldn't blame him because Dickey and Gregg were the two main writers in the band; in fact, they were just about the only writers at the time, and Dickey had several songs that would work better for a solo album. The songs on the Allman Brothers records show that Dickey's songs lean more towards country in a major key with major harmonies, and I thought Dickey had great songs for his album.

Dickey came in and we started talking about doing a record together. He already had some musicians lined up who were friends he'd played with before the Brothers: Stray Straton, a bass player who was living in Atlanta, and David Walshaw on drums. He got Chuck Leavell in to play on the album, and for the first few sessions, it was just those three musicians and Dickey.

We learned several songs and recorded them one night; then Dickey wanted to record a really long instrumental, "Hand Picked," that was based around Western Swing rather than the bluesy harmonies of a lot of his other instrumentals. We got John Hughey in to play steel and Vassar

Clements to play fiddle, and along with Dickey, David, Stray, and Chuck, we cut the song that turned out to be most of the second side of *Highway Call*. It was an exciting session, and we did two or three takes of the song, which was about fifteen minutes long. When we still lacked one song to complete the album, Dickey asked Vassar if he had anything. Vassar had a song without a title, and they recorded it. Eventually, either Dickey or Vassar came up with the title "Kissimmee Kid" because Vassar was from Kissimmee, Florida.

The Rambos were incredible gospel singers who were friends of Dickey, and he got them to sing on a couple of songs, including "Let Nature Sing" and "Rain, Rain, Rain." I got to play bass on "Rain" and on "Long Time Gone."

When it came to selecting musicians for an album, usually Gregg and I or Dickey and I made the selections together. There were musicians we used a lot, and some of the time we chose the musicians individually. On Dickey's album, he was insistent on using Stray and David. I got John Hughey, and Dickey got Vassar. Usually it was something we agreed to although I wasn't completely sold on some of the choices. Gregg was always bringing someone in to play on his album; sometimes they were very good, but sometimes they weren't. He may have just met them at the 7-11 that night on his way to the studio when he went in to get cigarettes.

Dickey was great to work with. I know at various times everybody's heard strange stories (or horror stories) about Dickey, but I enjoyed working with him. When we finished recording at two in the morning, we'd go up to my office and we'd play guitars and listen to country songs. We listened to Waylon Jennings's *Honky Tonk Heroes* album a lot. I wasn't a huge country fan then, but I loved Waylon and was a fan of Billy Joe Shaver's writing. Dickey is the one who really introduced me to country music, and because of him I started getting into that genre of music. Everybody I've ever met has taught me something. I learned a lot from Gregg and Dickey, but I probably learned most of all from Duane.

I saw Bonnie Bramlett in 1970 when I was in New York working on an album, and I'd gotten an invitation one night to go to the A&M studios where Duane was playing with Delany and Bonnie for a live broadcast. I mainly went to see Duane, but I was already a fan of Bonnie's. I had the Delaney and Bonnie records and loved what they were doing, but I'd never heard her sing live. It was one of those nights I'll never forget because when I heard Bonnie sing I thought she was the best female singer I'd ever heard. I couldn't believe the power and subtlety she had in her voice, the way she could use it, the way she could belt out a song. Right away I wanted to do a record with her. I enjoyed her albums but, as a producer, I wanted to do something different with her.

I didn't get to meet her that night, but I'd met her some years earlier in St. Louis when I was with the HourGlass; it had been just a "Hey, how are you doing?" kind of thing when she was still Bonnie Lynn singing on the Gaslight Square. When I returned to Macon, I told Phil, "Please, please sign Bonnie Bramlett if she ever gets open from her contract." He said he really liked her too and thought she was great. Only a few days later, he told me he'd heard she was free from her contract. I asked if he was going to sign her. He said he thought so—and sure enough—he did. I was just blown away to have a shot at producing her.

It's Time was an exciting album overall. As with any project, there were occasional "moments" during the recording. I wasn't always the easiest person in the world to work with. I used to tell people who made me mad or wouldn't listen to what I had to say that I'd bury them so far in the mix that they'd need an affidavit to prove they played on the album. We were keeping ourselves well "medicated" during the sessions, and everyone was a little crazy back then. There are often problems with artists in the studio but, rightly or wrongly, female artists are notorious for freaking out during sessions. Bonnie still tells the story about her lying on the floor, freaking out, and when someone asked me what to do about it, I supposedly replied, "Put a mic on her and hit record." I don't remember saying it. Bonnie, though, was no worse than others, and her kindness far made up for anything that might have happened. I loved her singing and was very proud of the record. I believed I'd be proud of it for the rest of my life, and I was right.

The original band Cowboy had pretty much broken up by then, but Scott and Tommy had written some songs and put a really good new Cowboy line-up together. Along with Tommy and Scott, there was Bill Stewart on drums, Charlie Hayward on bass, and Randall Bramlett played keyboard. There couldn't have been better musicians. Cowboy was still signed to Capricorn. The thought was that we could record an album with the band in hopes they'd tour and sell more records, so we went in and cut what became the *Boyer-Talton* album. I think it was one of the best Cowboy albums.

The more success any of us had, the more problematic it became to work together. For a while, Tommy had more than his share of problems. Some people can abuse substances and not be drastically affected, but eventually the drugs get to them and they start screwing up...and screwing up badly. I went through it a few times, and Tommy's gone through it. There were occasions he was just difficult to work with.

After Cowboy, Tommy was playing with Bill, Scott, and Neil Larson, an amazing piano player, and I'd gone to hear the new band, 360, in Athens, Georgia. I was blown away and went back to Macon excited. I talked to everyone in the office, trying to get them excited too. However, from lack of any major success with Cowboy and from some of the attitudes at times, I couldn't get anyone nearly as enthused about the band as I was.

Finally the band got a gig in Atlanta opening for the Atlanta Rhythm Section at what used to be the Georgian Terrace ballroom. I asked everyone in the office to come see them or they would miss out on something great. After annoying people long enough, I guess they decided it would be easier to go hear the band rather than to keep telling me no. We had a roped off section in the balcony for Capricorn people in the back of the hall with good sightline to the stage, but when the band came out to play, Tommy was shit-faced. One of the first things he said was, "Well, I see a lot of record people out there. We'd just like to say 'fuck you' to all the record people."

These were people who'd taken time to travel from Macon to hear the band I'd been hyping, and he was in bad shape. It was as horrible a show as the one in Athens, Georgia, had been good. It was one of the worst nights of my life, and I feared it had damaged my credibility. I wondered if anyone would believe me again if I told them something was good? Tommy is a talented guitarist, singer, and writer—and when he's on, he plays great. The only limits to Tommy's success were ones he put on himself, and I'm glad he's very doing well now with the Tommy Talton Band.

27

Win, Lose or Draw

It had been two years since the release of *Brothers and Sisters*, and by 1975 it was time for another Allman Brothers album. Gregg had been coming into the studio between projects when he was in town, and we would record some of the songs he'd written, including "Win, Lose or Draw," which became the title of the new album. Dickey had a couple of new songs, and the band was starting to get excited about recording again. Getting everyone together to do another album was the hard part because there were a lot of distractions. They'd been touring a lot, and I think the guys were just tired. They'd made good money, and no one was going to miss a meal if they took some time off to enjoy their success. Plus, we all had been using drugs more heavily, and some had been in and out of rehab.

When we went in to record, the band set up in the studio as they had before. We usually started the sessions at nine or ten at night, except for whatever night *Kung Fu* was on, because Dickey couldn't make it until after the show was over. Usually Jaimoe, Chuck, and Lamar would be there on time. Often, Butch was there, but Gregg and Dickey started arriving later and later and we had to wait until they were there before we could work. Dickey would come in, and sometimes Gregg would come in, or sometimes we'd cut tracks without him. It was harder to cut tracks without Dickey than it was without Gregg because Dickey's guitar was such a central focus in the music.

The band spent several days working up "High Falls," which I always thought was a beautiful instrumental and in keeping with some of Dickey's best. The band would come in, say, ten o'clock at night, work two three hours, and when they could go through the whole song, we'd record it. They'd come in the control room to get a copy of the track, go home, and listen to the rough to get ideas. The next night they'd come in and improve on those ideas. I usually had a two-track running during the sessions in case something special happened while they were working on the song; as the song started coming together, I'd start running the multi-track and go for the final take. In the case of "High Falls," we worked on it about a week before we got the track that ended up on the record. In most cases, the guitar solos were live and, quite often, Chuck's solo was live. Sometimes Gregg's parts would be live and other times they'd be overdubbed, but when everyone was at their best, the band was all in there playing together. One night while they were working on the song, I started grooving on the congas while they were running it down. Dickey liked what I was doing and wanted me to play on the track.

I liked the title track, "Win, Lose or Draw." I thought that was a beautiful song and the way Gregg sang it could make you cry. It was really emotional and you felt like he was either telling his life story or about something that was near to his heart. The band also did a reworking of "Can't Lose What You Never Had," which I didn't remember having heard before. Even though I used to listen to Muddy Watters religiously, I somehow missed that song. They totally did a different arrangement from how Muddy played it, and I thought it was a great version. The words are very insightful—"you can't spend what you ain't got and you can't lose what you never had."

Two of songs on the album had a little bit of a different twist on the personnel. Butch and Jaimoe were out of town when Dickey had a couple of songs he wanted to record. Lamar was around town, as was Chuck, so Dickey got them and came down to the studio. Bill and I were there at the time and when Dickey asked me about recording the songs, I reminded him Jaimoe and Butch weren't available. He really wanted to get the songs down right then because they were ready to go, and he had other plans for later. I told him Bill and I could at least demo the songs, so he asked us to go out and work them up. Bill moved his drums to the middle of the room and I moved the set I had. Bill and I were side by side, facing Dickey with Lamar to my left and Chuck on my right.

We worked up "Louisiana Lou and Three Card Monty John" and "Just Another Love Song" and did a few takes. The tracks with us playing were the ones that ended up on the album. Bill and I decided it would look better if we didn't credit ourselves on the record, but later, after the album was released, we admitted it in interviews when asked about it. In some review, it might have been *Rolling Stone*, the writer specifically complimented the drumming on "Louisiana Lou." I swear, I had nothing to do with the review, but I got a kick out of it. Our drumming wasn't bad—it just wasn't Butch and Jaimoe. Evidently, the one reviewer liked it.

It got to be very strained and strange during the recording of the album because a lot of the drug stuff with Scooter Herring, Gregg's personal manager, was happening at that time. I went to the office one day and people were talking about how the district attorney was investigating drug use as a way to bring down the record company. The DA was looking to make a big name for himself in Macon and wanted someone with star power. Of course, the biggest star would have been Gregg and next would have been Phil. If he couldn't bring one of them down, he'd go after anyone he could who was involved with the record company.

A lot of us didn't want to admit it, but everybody knew drug use was a problem. One of the people at Capricorn who'd been in on some of the meetings about what was going on with the district attorney told me, "There's a good chance we'll be able to keep you out of jail." I hadn't been in on any of the briefings, and freaked me out and scared me worse than anything I can think of. I went home right away, flushed the drugs I had down the toilet, and got everything out of the house. I lived out in the country and wasn't expecting a major raid, but the guys would drop by...and we had various substances I needed to get rid of that weren't in accord with the local laws.

Macon hadn't like us from the beginning. First of all, Phil had managed a lot of black artists and was helping with their careers when they became successful and rich. Percy Sledge did well, as did Sam Moore and Dave Prater of Sam and Dave, and of course Otis Redding was the biggest star of all. Although Otis wasn't born in Macon, he lived there, and Phil managed him until he died. You can imagine what the local white establishment thought of a black person getting rich in their area; it just wasn't done in the South during the '60s and early '70s. It didn't happen very often anywhere, but especially in the South. There were plenty of artists from the South who did well, but they went to the bigger cities—New York, Los Angeles, Detroit, or Memphis.

After being told they were going to try to keep me out of jail, I don't remember hearing a lot more about what was going on. Thereafter, drugs were done on the down low. Fortunately for me, I was okay, but eventually Gregg was charged, and Scooter Herring ended up taking the fall. It was sad because Scooter was always as great a guy as you'd ever want to meet. He looked after Gregg and was good to all of us, especially me. He was initially sentenced to seventy-five years in prison; however, after his appeal was upheld, he pled guilty to one charge of distribution of drugs and served less than two years. There'd been pot busts before and some other low profile legal problems, but I don't think anyone needed to go to jail.

To be honest, almost everybody connected with the record company could have been busted because we were all doing drugs (mostly pot, but also cocaine or, in some cases, lots of cocaine). I'm not ashamed of the pot in the least, but cocaine was the biggest waste of time and money in my whole life. The stuff was expensive and hurt relationships; it made things ugly that could have been beautiful. People lower their standards when they start doing coke, and they end up having to hang around and be nice to drug dealers. Most of the hard core drug dealers weren't people you wanted to be associated with, and it made you feel cheap and tawdry just being around them. Then there was always the thought, "What am I going to do if I run out of cocaine?" It wasn't so much I was going to hurt and go into withdrawal, but more like all my energy was gone without it—energy I could've had in the first place if I'd never started using it.

The drug problems were a concern with everyone in the record company, and Gregg was so weirded out by everything that was happening that he left to go to California. He and Cher were together at the time, and since Gregg didn't want to go back to Macon, I went out to California. I booked time in studio B at the Record Plant in Los Angeles to record some of Gregg's vocals for the album. Gregg and I both were doing coke and drinking heavily, and it's hard in that situation to communicate with people without someone getting their feelings hurt or looking for a reason to get angry about something. But we finally got some good vocals with Gregg and I took the tape back to Macon. Dickey added some parts, and I played a couple of things, some percussion and maybe an acoustic guitar part or so. It wasn't that anyone else couldn't do that particular part, especially Dickey; it was just that he wasn't available.

That was the most difficult, time consuming, and just strange record I did with the Brothers. It was a bad experience for everyone because, by that time Gregg and the whole band were at odds. Feelings were strained because Gregg had testified against Scooter, sending him to prison for two years. Everyone blamed Gregg for what happened because Scooter had more or less been the go-between and had been looking after Gregg.

The band was disintegrating before our eyes and we knew it. There seemed to be hard feelings all the way around even though there were never any hard feelings among Chuck, Jaimoe, and Lamar. In fact, the three of them used to come into the studio at whatever time we'd set and start jamming. Those sessions were the beginning of Sea Level. I guess everyone was thinking about what they might do in the future if the Brothers broke up. For a long time I'd heard that, instead of naming the band Sea Level, they were going to call it Waiting for Gregg. It seemed like he and Dickey would compete to be the last one there—and sometimes neither one of them showed up.

The band treated me with indifference during much of that time. Sometimes they'd listen to what I had to say, and sometimes they didn't. As a producer on a major project, or any project for that matter, you want to feel your opinion is respected. They weren't being especially rude, there were just some things they wanted to hear and some things they didn't. However, working with the Brothers was always good because, when I finally got something finished, it was very satisfying. It was good music played by great musicians and worthy of being recorded, but it was like pulling teeth to get it done. I felt bruised and battered when I got through with the project.

Juke Joint Jump was the second album I did with Elvin Bishop. At the time, Elvin was living in the Sausalito bay area and wanted to record there, so I went out to the Record Plant. Sausalito was a beautiful place and I had a lot of fun there, but after two or three weeks I'd really miss the South. Elvin had some songs he and the band had worked up (and there were a few we added that the band hadn't worked on), so we rehearsed in the studio and then recorded them. Elvin is a good guy, and I loved him, but he was hard-headed. Of course I was too, so we'd get into some arguments on occasion about how things should be, but it would usually work out.

One of the songs we did cut was "Crawling King Snake," a John Lee Hooker song, with Elvin and Johnny Vernazza playing twin slide harmony parts. They'd twin the guitars like Dickey and Duane used to do, only they'd play it with the slide. At times it would sound almost cartoonish, especially the higher they went, but it was effective. I hadn't heard that done before in any other music.

During this time he sang "I Fooled Around and Fell in Love" for me, and I especially liked the song. Mickey Thomas from Valdosta was a great kid with an astounding voice who sang back up with Elvin. I tried to get Elvin to let Mickey sing the song, but he wanted to sing all the songs himself. I didn't want to do the song with Elvin, so I didn't record it. It came out on the very next record, which was produced by Bill Szymczyk and Alan Blazek. I guess Bill and Alan changed Elvin's mind because Mickey was singing the song, and they had a big hit with it. I heard it on the radio and thought it sounded good, but I just hated missing out on that one.

Since I'd mixed the first Hydra album they were really insistent about wanting me to produce the next one, *Land of Money*. I was working on another album at the same time, so I'd work with the first group part of the day and at night I'd work with Hydra. I was stretched pretty thin. That's the way it was most of the time during those years. I'd be working on two or three albums at once, so that they tend to run together in my mind as to when I did what on which album.

Hydra was a good band. They really wanted me to do the album, and when a good band really wants you to do their record, it's hard to turn them down. Plus, Frank Hughes was a good friend and by then he was my manager; still, I don't remember a lot about working on the record. It was another case where the band came in and had the songs already worked up; then I made a few changes, worked on the sound, and got it on tape. I'm credited with playing tambourine, but I used to insert myself on a lot of records. I'd do a tambourine hit and get credit on the album.

When it came time to release the compilation albums Capricorn began putting out, I had input on all of them. Phil would have various people in the office select songs, but it was usually my job to round up the tapes and see that the album was finished. When it came to acts I didn't produce, it depended on which act it was as to my involvement. There were records on the label I didn't have anything to do with because Phil was getting involved with country artists out of Nashville. After Kitty Wells, he and Frank knew I wasn't a country producer. The slogan for the country division of Capricorn was "Kickin' Country," and the logo was the rear end of a mule kicking, which I thought was kind of funny.

Our way of doing things in Macon was not to have a formal way of doing things. We'd go in the studio and, depending on the group, we might get four or five songs in a day or we might get one in two days. It depended on the song and the people working. When Capricorn got involved with country acts, it was a whole different way of recording. Nashville was very rigid at the time; they'd cut an album in three-hour sessions, or at least most of them would be done that way. Maybe they'd record on consecutive days, but they had a system that made for efficiency. However ours, I'd like to think, made for a different way of looking for something new and unusual whereas Nashville was traditionally "more of the same."

It wasn't too long before the Brothers' music was labeled Southern Rock, and then Lynyrd Skynyrd defined the sound. What I think of as Southern Rock is country-type songs with an edge to them done by a basic rock and roll band. Skynyrd is a perfect example, and they've really done well. They took country-redneck-Confederate-flag-waving and made it their thing. The Brothers came from a whole different school of music from Skynyrd. The Allman Brothers came from a blues and jazz base and combined the two to create their sound. It was only later, after Duane died and Dickey became the more prolific writer in the band, the country side of the Allman Brothers emerged. Southern Rock became the label, but as Gregg said, "Southern Rock is like saying Rock Rock." Of course the first guy who really popularized rock was Elvis, and he was definitely Southern.

28

Lady's Choice

The Talton, Sandlin, Stewart (TSS) *Happy to Be Alive* album came about in 1976 when Tommy and Bill were hanging around at the studio one night and we were all looking for something to do. Tommy came in with a song he'd written, "Never in My Life" that I'd always liked but had never gotten around to recording. Tommy was a prolific writer, and there were always things he'd written that hadn't made it on a Cowboy album but were still good songs. Since we all liked the song, we set up and recorded it on a lark.

The track came out well, and for several months I kept a copy of the two track mix I'd done that I'd listen to and play whenever someone wanted to hear it. We finally decided to put together a band with the three of us and record some of Tommy's extra songs. We talked to Phil; he thought it would be a good idea to do a whole album, so we got some of the other people around Macon to join us.

Tommy, Bill, and I were the foundation of the rhythm section. We got Bonnie Bramlett to come in to do some singing. Ricky Hirsch and Dru Lombar sat in and played guitar on a few songs, and Joe Walk, my old friend from Decatur, came over and played piano on a couple. After Chuck Leavell and Scott Boyer came in, we decided to use two drummers on some of the songs, so Joe English came in and played with Bill.

The album was more pop than blues, and during the recording, Joe hit the drums so hard that toward the end of enough takes for just one song, the drum heads were all ruined. I thought I couldn't afford to let him play my drums if I had to keep replacing the heads! Joe was a great drummer who played with Paul McCartney's band Wings, and he'd go out with McCartney two or three days at a time, then take the Concord back to the States. He told me all about the Concord, and I thought how great it would be to get on a plane in England and, in two or three hours, be back to New York. Joe's a good friend, and we had a lot of good times together.

Sam Whiteside was engineering the album and had a lot to do with the unusual sound on "It Might Be the Rain." After Tommy had done the original vocal, Sam had him do another spoken word vocal in a sinister voice that was about an octave lower. Then he ran Tommy's second vocal through a B-3 Leslie to give it that real dark, almost devilish voice on the song. This was before easy access to digital effects was available; the only digital effects at the studio were a harmonizer and an Eventide delay that cost about three thousand dollars each. There weren't little plug-ins like there are now. Thank you, Sam, for the idea; I've used that a lot on several records since then.

The only cover song on the album was Allen Toussaint's "Workin' in a Coal Mine" and after we recorded the song, I got a lot of 7 1/2 ips tapes of Allen's songs from his publishing company that were just amazing. The tapes also had demos of some of his hits, i.e., "Mother-in-Law" and "Workin' in a Coal Mine," and I still have them today. The rest of the songs on the album were Tommy's.

When it was time to do the cover, Diana Kaylan, the art director at Capricorn, wanted us to fly to California. When we showed up, she had make-up people on hand, a street scene set up, and everything ready for the shoot. The idea behind it was Tommy, Bill, and I were supposed to be in a funky night club that looked almost like a New Orleans street scene. I was proud of that album, but we never toured the record and I didn't particularly want to. Tommy and Bill hooked up with Neil Larson and Charlie Hayward to do some gigs as T.S.S. Eventually, they changed the name of the band to 360.

Since Bonnie Bramlett was one of my favorite artists to work with, I'd been after Phil for a while about doing another record. Finally, he and Frank wanted to talk about doing one; however, they were adamant about it being an album of duets and were really set on the idea. To be honest, neither Bonnie nor I particularly wanted to do a duets album. Phil and Frank were insistent, so we started putting together songs that would work for the concept.

I went over to the old Muscle Shoals sound studio on Jackson Highway to cut the album because I wanted to use Roger Hawkins,

David Hood. and Barry Beckett. Back then, if you didn't use them in their studio, you had to hire them to come to your place and *still* pay for their studio, which was more expensive. Along with Jimmy Johnson, they were all owners of the studio, and it was important for them to make money even when they were gone. I decided to go over there to record the tracks to Bonnie's album and then return to Macon for overdubs and mixing.

I think Bonnie already knew some of the guys in the Muscle Shoals Rhythm Section, but not all of them; she definitely didn't know Barry Beckett before we went over there. The way the studio was laid out, Bonnie was sitting on a stool facing the control room where we could all look at her, and she had a view of everyone with Beckett directly in her line of sight. Barry was a real sweet guy, but when he was playing the piano, he could look stern and intimidating to people who didn't know him. After a while, Bonnie asked me if he was mad at her. I pulled him aside when Bonnie wasn't around and told him he was scaring my artist. "She's afraid of you, Barry. Smile!" He did and everything was okay. Once Bonnie got to know him, she was fine, but it just one of those funny moments.

There's a really strange story involving Joe Cocker and *Lady's Choice*. After she was signed to Capricorn, Bonnie sang on a Joe Cocker album, and his record company had to get a release from Phil to put it out. Phil leveraged the release into getting Joe Cocker to come to Macon and sing on Bonnie's album. That's the only way Phil would agree to let Bonnie sing on Cocker's album. I'd always loved Joe Cocker's singing, but I was kind of apprehensive about him coming in because I'd heard the stories about his drinking—and all the stuff that goes along with it. And that's exactly the way it worked out.

Joe was okay when he first arrived. I told him I wanted him to sing "I Need Your Lovin' Every Day." We had the track and just needed vocals on the song, which I thought would be a great one for him to do with Bonnie. He didn't agree. We fooled around for twenty minutes or so, trying to get him interested in it, but that didn't work out too well. He and Bonnie were standing next to each other singing on the same mic, but I could tell he wasn't happy to be there. In the meantime, he was getting loaded. In a photo someone took of Bonnie, Joe, and me in the control room, it's easy to see that Joe was obviously pretty well looped.

Shortly after the picture was taken, Cocker passed out in the middle of the floor in the studio next to Bonnie. A couple of guys came in and one picked up Joe's legs, the other picked him up under the arms and they carried him into the control room and tried to wrestle him into a chair. When that didn't work, they just left him passed out on the floor behind me while we went on to something else. It was obvious he wasn't going to be on the record at that time. Eventually someone came and got him. Personally, I didn't want him back in that condition, and he never did make it on the album because we ended up not even using that song on the record.

While we were in Macon doing vocal overdubs, I got Gregg in to sing on "Two Steps from the Blues," a Bobby Bland song, and we'd set up with him and Bonnie in the side room that had good isolation and was less distracting. Phil had come by the studio that night to hear what we were doing. He wasn't there very often, but he was there that night. He'd gotten word Dickey was out roaming the town, probably drinking, and not in a good mood. Dickey could be a real troublemaker when he got loaded, so Phil told the new night manager, Stan, to not let Dickey in no matter what. Stan replied, "Yes, Mr. Walden, if that door will hold, he won't get through here." There was a buzzer at the door along with a television camera hooked up to monitors at the front desk and in the control room. If the person at the door had business there, you could see them and buzz the door open. Otherwise, they were locked out.

True to form, thirty or forty minutes into doing the overdubs with Gregg and Bonnie, Dickey showed up at the door. This was Stan's first night on the job, and he was going to make every effort to do what Phil had told him. He told Dickey, "I can't let you in, I'm sorry." Dickey just kept banging on the door. Dickey knew about the camera at the front door and had somehow knocked it down, so we lost that feed. He kept beating on the door until he got it open; he started down the hall and took out the hall camera, knocking out that feed, and we lost sight of Dickey. I thought, "Oh...shit." I didn't know what was going to happen next, and after all the effort it took for him to get into the studio he was going to be pissed.

Dickey walked into the control room and although he was calmer than I expected, he wasn't *calm* by any stretch of the imagination. He came in with a beer in his hand and sloshed it into the console, which pissed off Phil. He wanted to know what we were doing and we told him we were just doing some vocals. He and Phil exchanged a few heated word. Eventually Dickey left, but it was a tense and uncomfortable moment in every sense. It's kind of funny looking back on it, but at the time, it wasn't very funny at all. Dickey was mad and wanted everyone to know it. At that point, there was still a lot of tension between Gregg and Dickey because Gregg had rolled over on Scooter. Bonnie and Gregg wisely stayed in the side room out of sight and didn't come out until after he'd left.

There seemed to be tension in the band from the time Duane died, but wasn't as bad as it got to be later on. They hung together for a while until Berry died, but then it fell apart. Gregg and Dickey were the two logical successors as leader in the band, but like in any organization, little camps form and people go off one way or the other and tension builds up between them. Duane kept everyone in line because they'd all listen to him, but after he was gone, Gregg would assume the position of band leader at various times, but at other times, Dickey would assume the role. Ultimately, they seemed uncomfortable with each other.

29

Leaving Capricorn

Jimmy Carter had either just announced his candidacy for president or was considering doing so when Phil started working with him. Carter was governor of Georgia, and I think Phil always had political ambitions, but he knew, after all the stuff that had gone on in Macon by that time, politics wasn't a viable option for him. I don't know for sure where Phil first met Carter, but I think they might have met at a dinner at the governor's mansion. Phil backed Carter's run for the presidency and involved some of the Capricorn bands, especially the Allman Brothers and Marshall Tucker. The bands played gigs to raise money for his campaign, and in the beginning, the Brothers were instrumental in keeping Carter's candidacy afloat financially until it took off.

It was shortly after Carter began running for the party nomination that Phil called and told me he was bringing him by the studio for a photo op. Macon was just down the road from Atlanta, and I guess it showed Carter's musical credentials to go and visit the studio. He was a nice man and I liked him a lot, but there wasn't much to the meeting. I still have the picture taken that day with me, Dickey, Phil, and the governor.

Phil more or less took a leave from the company to work on Carter's campaign and hired Don Schmitzerle, who came in as vice-president of the business part of the record company. Ted Senters, who'd been the accountant at Capricorn, ended up with a large role in running the label, but Phil's leadership with the company was crucial in making it work. Phil was about the only one who could keep the various factions getting along and working together. Because Don was kind of new to us, working in Phil's absence wasn't always a comfortable situation.

It was Phil's label, and he made it work because of his personality. There was always a little give and take and he'd work with you, but Don came in with his own ways of doing things. I liked Phil's ideas about music more than anyone else's, and I wasn't comfortable working with

Don. Even with Phil still there things had been easing downhill, but without him, we were going downhill fast. The bands increasingly weren't getting along, and they didn't get along with Don very well either.

To make matters worse, there was a lack of sufficient royalty statements. Many people at the label believed the statements we'd received didn't accurately reflect how the records were selling and what was actually owed to them. The perception that the accounting was inaccurate was instrumental in leading to the initial lawsuits being filed against Capricorn. I felt I wasn't getting paid on a lot of the records, even though some of them probably hadn't recouped. "Recouping" is how you have to pay for the record through record sales before the artist and producer get paid, but I didn't knowing anything about recouping at the time. Some of us thought that we would be paid for each record that was sold. We weren't business people, and I never wanted to be one. I didn't know anything about contracts to begin with; my contract was only two or three pages, and the specifics about recoupment weren't spelled out.

I hired an attorney and an accountant to see what, if any, money was owed to me. Believe me—hiring an attorney wasn't cheap. What I learned much later, to my chagrin, is that what your *attorney* says you're owed and what your *accountant* says is due to you is a matter of opinion. It's not fact. I discovered it's all open to interpretation, and there are always two sides. According to my accounting, I was owed a million dollars, but when the case was presented to Ted, he said *I owed the company $75,000.* It was a combination of naiveté on my part in not realizing how those things work and not getting good advice. The attorneys I'd hired were from Nashville and weren't familiar with the pop side of the business. I don't even know any more what was correct.

I never could get direct answers to my questions, and once Phil was involved with Jimmy Carter, my only remedy was to go to Ted Senters, the accountant for the label. I thought money was owed to me, and it bothered me that I didn't get any answers from Ted or Don. Ted really didn't have any authority to do anything, but he had his hands on the purse strings. I'd always been handed off to him when I tried to talk with Don about the problem. The lawsuit I filed was my way of saying, "Let's work on this; let's come to an understanding."

With Phil, there was always the thought it would all be okay, even if things weren't exactly right at the time, but without him, Capricorn was like a ship without its captain. It's been written that I filed the first lawsuit against Capricorn, but Dickey filed right before I did. Everyone was unhappy. Dickey sued Phil for lack of royalties paid, or his assumption they weren't being paid, and I did the same thing. I'm not very happy about what I did or what followed, and I wish it could have worked out differently.

I can think of a thousand reasons Capricorn was in financial trouble, but it would all be in hindsight. I do have some ideas though. After Phil and Frank decided they wanted to branch out with a country division for Capricorn, they signed five or six artists from Nashville. A lot of them were good, but they didn't fit in with the kind of renegade thing we had going in Macon. Nashville was the "closed shop" with production line studios that did perfect records with great musicians, but it was not the raw music we were going after. However, they signed the artists anyway, and with a few exceptions, didn't have any luck with them. Our audience was more into rock and what you'd now call jam bands. I guess Marshall Tucker was the closest artist that had any country appeal, and that came long after the fact of Capricorn.

I don't know for certain what effect the country part of Capricorn had on the financial difficulties at the label, but it certainly didn't help. A lot of money was spent signing those artists, and most of their recording, as I remember, was done in Nashville. At Capricorn, we had our own studio and people already on payroll to work on the records, but in Nashville they had to pay for studio rental, hire an outside producer, and pay for musicians. Even though Capricorn was doing extremely well with our major acts, when you sign a bunch of new people who have needs and demands, it takes a lot of money—especially back then when records had big budgets. It's not like now. Anyone with a few hundred dollars can make a record at home, but in the '70s it took big money and well equipped studios. It was a whole different ballgame.

I never talked about the lawsuit with Phil. He was out of the country when they delivered the papers, and I'd never filed a lawsuit before so I didn't know what to expect. I just thought they'd take me seriously and say, "Well, let's talk." Instead I was immediately told to clear out my desk. I didn't actually have a desk, but I knew what they meant.

I didn't work for Capricorn again right away even though they asked me because they wanted to put out *Wipe the Windows, Check the Oil, Dollar Gas.* I was the producer of record for that album, (although Phil was angry about the lawsuit and wouldn't give me the credit) and they wanted me to come and mix it. They said they'd pay me, but they wouldn't pay me near what I thought it was worth. I knew where the tapes were and had notes about the best takes. We talked about it, but they ultimately got Sam Whiteside to mix it. At the time it really pissed me off, but I have no hard feelings about anyone now. Sam wanted to make a career for himself, and I don't blame him. He'd had been working for me most of the time and didn't know where my career was going; at the time, neither did I.

I was still friends with the Brothers after I left, but the band was in disarray and I had no idea what was going to happen with them. Gregg was in California, I don't know where Dickey was, and everyone else had scattered. It didn't look like there was even going to be a band much longer. I still wanted to produce the band, but it they decided to stay with the record label and did one more album for Capricorn, *Enlightened Rogues.* I had nothing to do with it.

I was friends with Phil and his wife, Peggy, and thought the world of both of them. It was never personal; I just thought I deserved to get my questions answered about the accounting, but Phil was really pissed. We parted on bad terms, and it was three or four months before I talked to him again. It wasn't a good time, and I didn't know which way to jump. I think I got some bad advice from a lot of people, but it was my responsibility to make the decisions. I'm not saying that I was totally wrong; I just think it could have been worked out.

Lawsuits bring so much pain and suffering to both sides that they're almost not worth it. I wouldn't want to go through that again or put anyone else through it. It was like your family and you'd sued them for this and they'd accused you of that. It was just ugly.

30

Going Independent

After leaving Capricorn, I became an independent producer and for a while I was really busy. In the summer of '76, about the time I left, Phil had been working on a deal with Corky Lang, the former drummer with the group Mountain. He was going to rent me out to the record company who'd signed Corky, but when Phil and I parted on unpleasant terms I didn't want him brokering the deal. I'd already been talking with Corky's people, and as far as I know, I got the gig on my own. Although I was no longer employed by Capricorn, I could still rent the studio at a good rate, so Corky came to Macon. We did demos then cut the album *Makin' It on the Streets*.

It was while I was working on the album I got to meet Eric Clapton. He was performing in Atlanta, and Corky and his wife, who were both friends with Clapton, convinced him to come back and play on the record. I was kind of uptight because I could tell he didn't especially want to be there to begin with. Clapton was only going to do a couple of over dubs, but we ended up cutting a whole track. He didn't do any solos, just played, and because he hadn't even brought a guitar with him to Macon, he played my '62 Strat. He didn't have a work visa and wasn't supposed to be recording while in the states, so we couldn't credit him on the album. He's listed as "Old Slow Hand."

We cut several songs with a great band; then I got Pete Carr in from Muscle Shoals to do most of the lead guitar tracks, and I enjoyed working with him again. I finished mixing the album at Westlake in Los Angeles, one of the few times I didn't work at the Record Plant.

I also got a gig producing an album with Katy Moffett. I thought the world of Katy, and when I think about her now, I just smile because she was such a sweet person and a great songwriter and singer. That was a Columbia project that came to me through her manager, Doug Morris, who lived in Colorado. I went out and met with Doug and Barry Faye, and we worked up a deal to do the record in Macon. We had a super band and cut tracks that had a good feeling about them. I loved what we were doing, but the guy in New York who'd signed Katy to Columbia didn't like what we'd done at all. I talked with him on the phone, and all he could do was tell me what he didn't like about the record. Katy and I flew to New York. As we rode to the label, I remember looking over at Katy, and she was so angry her red hair seemed like it was on fire. When we met with the guy, he reiterated what he'd already said.

He came in and started playing a James Taylor record and told us he wanted her album to be like a James Taylor album. I thought, "Damn, then get Peter Asher or someone like that to do it." I was genuinely upset about it, and so was Katy. He decided to re-do the album with another producer and only used two cuts I'd recorded. He then did versions of the other songs, which were worse than what we had done. Of course, that's just my opinion. I don't see her very often, but I still consider Katy a friend.

I knew Gregg was out in Los Angeles cutting an album and that he was still hooked up with Cher and not coming to Macon much. I was home one day when he called and asked if I wanted to go to California to work with them. They'd been cutting tracks with a producer who'd done some work with Cher in the past; for whatever reason, he wasn't going to finish the recording, so Gregg asked me to fly out there to help with the album. I loved working with Gregg (and Cher was a celebrity who'd had giant radio hits), so I was happy to go.

When I walked into the Record Plant, Gregg came up with this dark haired lady and, although I'd met her before, at first I didn't recognize who it was. I said, "Hi," and Gregg said, "Well, you know who Cher is, don't you?" Then I realized who was with him.

The album, aptly named *Two the Hard Way*, turned out to be a real adventure. Only two or three tracks had been finished, or mostly finished, with the other producer by the time I arrived. We went over some additional material they wanted to cut. Gregg and Cher each had a solo song they wanted to record, so I thought it would be nice for each of them to have a solo cut with the rest of the songs being duets. I caught up with what was going on with the album to that point and then recorded the rest of it in studio A at the Record Plant.

Bill Stewart was the drummer in Gregg's band at that time and was out there playing with him. Since I'd used Bill for the majority of recordings I'd done in Macon, I was quite comfortable working with him again. I met Willie Weeks out there and was excited about getting him to play bass on the album because he's not only an amazing musician, he's an amazing guy and a good human being. Someone else started out playing bass, but he was kind of young and he overplayed some of the time, so Willie came in to finish the tracking. Neil Larson, whom I'd also worked with on several sessions in Macon, played piano, and Stevie Beckmeier played guitar.

It was an incredible band! All we had to do was come up with songs for them to play and we'd cut great tracks. Some of the time, either Gregg or Cher would sing the guide vocal, but on one of them, I "sang" the guide vocal. Cher wanted to cut the Elvis song, "Love Me" and planned to come in and sing the guide vocal while the musicians laid down the track, but for some reason, she didn't make it. I already had the musicians in the studio, so at the last minute, I had to step in. I don't sing, so I sort of talked my way through it to let everyone know where they were in the song, and we cut a decent version. When I set up the session, Willie wasn't available. I was looking for bass players when I read Klaus Voorman was in Los Angeles. He'd played with John Lennon and the Beatles. I only knew him by reputation, but I got him to come in and play bass on "Love Me."

It seemed to take forever to finish the album, and there was a lot of drama during the recording. Gregg and Cher were fighting, and one or the other wouldn't show up. More than likely, neither one of them would show up. One day we were doing tracks, and everything seemed to be on an even keel when something else happened. I walked out of the control room into the studio and was talking to Gregg about songs and ideas when he said, "I've got a tape out in the car I want you to hear. I'll be right back." He left. I waited around for a while, but he didn't ever come back in. I went outside to look for him, but his car was gone. I didn't hear from him again for two weeks, and when I did, he was in Florida. It was things like that.

Another instance was when I booked a string session in Los Angeles with about seventeen strings. I got Ed Freeman to do the arrangements since he'd worked with me on the *Laid Back* album. We cut three songs without a hitch and started on the fourth with enough time to finish, but it was going to be tight. It was a three-hour union session, and, believe me, string players start a stop watch when they come in. If you go past three hours, you begin what's called "golden time"—that's double pay or at least time-and-a-half. Seventeen strings makes for a lot of expensive people.

We were on the last song, and I was out on the floor with the players when the audio went dead in the control room. From what I was hearing in the studio, everything was going fine. The strings kept playing, but I saw someone frantically waving at me through the window. The engineer said, "Hold it, we've got a problem. I think I know what it is and it will only take two or three minutes to fix." It turned out the power supply had blown.

The Record Plant had the greatest tech people around, and it seemed like all the top guys worked there. They had a spare power supply on hand, so they got the power back on. We got about two bars into the song when the power supply blew again. We had a budget and knew we were going to go over, but we were trying to keep it under control. By then we'd gone into golden time, so everyone was uptight and nervous. Finally we were told that the problem couldn't be fixed in a timely fashion and we'd have to do the strings later.

I went back home to Macon for a while before we reconvened at the Record Plant in New York to do some overdubs. The strings were set up to be recorded there. We had to book them for a whole session, so I used them on another song and it worked out to our benefit. It wasn't to Chris Stone, the owner of the studio, though. When something goes wrong in the studio, especially with that many people, they're responsible for making it right. With Chris, you knew he'd take care of any problems.

There was another thing that was technologically interesting when we were recording. Gregg might come in and sing a verse and then we'd sit there and want to do something else, but we were limited with only twenty-four tracks. That was all we had unless we wanted to stripe the tape with time code and sync it up with another twenty-four track machine, which would give us forty-eight tracks. I'd never done that before, and it wasn't being done frequently back in those days; however, that's what we decided to do so we'd have extra room if we needed it. Instead of erasing the take, if either Gregg or Cher sang a few words, we could try to piece several takes together for the vocals. However, that proved to be a major pain in the tail and not something I've done since or will ever need to do again.

The whole endeavor was fraught with disaster. The manufacturers were sending the first production model of their time code generators to Sausalito from Los Angeles, and the thing was dropped getting it off the airplane, so they ended up sending the prototype. It was just a bitch because it was in the early days of syncing machines, and no one I knew of was doing that at the time. Of course now, with computers, you don't need to resort to those measures.

I met Ron Goldstein, who was with Warners, while I was working on the Gregg and Cher album, and we became friends. Although everyone knew there were difficulties in getting the record finished with something halfway decent, the record company really wanted to get the album out and put a lot of pressure on me to get it done. During that time, Ron was always someone I could talk to, and later he asked me about doing an album with Doug Kershaw. I thought about it and decided it might be interesting. Kershaw was from Louisiana, and I figured there had to be a lot of Louisiana music in him, but I didn't know anything about him other than the few things I'd heard on the radio.

I listened to some of his records and devised a plan to do the album in Muscle Shoals. I thought it would be the perfect place for him: in the South, in an intimate little studio where we could get a great sound with fantastic players. I called Jimmy Johnson about renting the studio and he said, "You know, I gotta tell you. There are only two people we won't let back in the studio here and one of them is Doug Kershaw." I asked him why and he told me a story that sounded like one of those things that happen when people drink too much, get loaded, and act up. I thought the story put a new light on the situation, but unfortunately, it wasn't anything I wasn't used to. I decided to go ahead and do the album and booked the Record Plant in Sausalito.

Doug had heard Gregg's solo band and really liked them, so I used most of those players. Bill Stewart played drums, Neil Larson played keys, and Calvin Arline played bass. I also got Mac, Dr. John, to play on it. I only had him for a day or two, but having him around always makes a project better. He's *the* gris gris man, and he can do anything. Neil Larson and Dr. John were a great combination, and with those two you've got anything—and I mean *anything*—covered keyboard-wise.

We cut a version of the Fats Domino song, "I'm Walkin'" and tried to get a little bit of a New Orleans vibe. We also did a version of the Band song, "Rag Mama Rag." Mac was playing piano on that one and just tore it up. It had a New Orleans flavor to it with a second line beat going on.

From what I understood, Doug had had some kind of substance problems in the past, but he was very straight and very business-like when I worked with him. We went out to eat together a few times. He was pleasant but very reserved. I never got to know him well, but I liked him. The record came out and did okay in certain areas, but in most areas it didn't.

Dickey had recorded and produced the *Great Southern* album in Miami, but after it was mixed, he wasn't happy with the mixes. He'd done the album at Criteria, and he asked if I'd mix it for him and, if so, where I wanted to do it. I wanted to go to Bill Szymczyk's place in Miami, so they moved from Criteria over to Bill's in Coconut Grove where my friend Buddy Thornton was doing technical work for Bill. Although Buddy had stopped doing front-of-house sound for the Brothers a while back, I knew Dickey would be comfortable in the surroundings. Buddy's been one of my dearest and most trusted friends since high school. He's a super-talented musician and technical engineer and, as I mentioned before, he ended up working in a government job so secret he couldn't even tell me what he did.

The engineer from Criteria went over with us, but he was kind of pissed Dickey wanted someone else to mix the album. It made me uncomfortable, and I think made Dickey uncomfortable too, because he finally just told the guy to leave. There were some really good songs on the album, and I thought Dickey had done an excellent job of producing it.

I was hired to do an instrumental album with Tim Weisberg, the flautist, and that was a really different experience. They were trying to capture something like Dickey's instrumentals—only featuring a flute. Tim was an Los Angeles guy and didn't want to go to Macon, so I ended up going back to the Record Plant in Sausalito to record the album. He had a great drummer with him and a really good band, and since they kept talking about the Allman Brothers, I decided to put two drummers in. We got Bill Stewart to play the Butch or Jaimoe parts and Rick Jaeger, Tim's drummer, to play the other parts. We cut some neat instrumentals, but it was really hard to distinguish the songs! We had an album with all instrumentals featuring a flute so the standard joke was, "Which song do you want to do next?" "Oh, it's the one with the flute."

It seems like we all got to name one of the songs. Tim had names for some of them, and if I didn't like one of the names, we negotiated. He let me change one or two of them. I don't say we necessarily improved on the titles, but what do you do with an instrumental without any memorable lyrics?

I always liked working at Sausalito and did several albums out there. Thank God for Chris Stone. He and Gary Kellgren did a lot for me. Chris took care of me and made me feel like a king from the first time I met him when the Johnny Jenkins record was the only album I had out. They even knew about *Ton Ton Macoute* at the Record Plant in New York the first time I went there. Gary Kellgren was a gifted engineer who always encouraged me. I'd go to him and ask how to do something or get his opinion about this or that. He always gave me something that made my day go better and gave me enough confidence to go on.

I got a call from Gary Lazar about a group he was representing from Detroit called The Rockets. They were looking for a producer and sent me some demos. Gary was associated with "Punch" Andrews, the man who managed Bob Seger, whom I, in a fit of madness, had passed on the doing a record with previously. In all fairness, I'd been incredibly busy and had a lot of other things going on, but I probably did an album that never saw the light of day rather than doing a Bob Seger record. Anyway, I liked the guys in the Rockets. They came in with a good attitude and good songs, and we started recording tracks.

One of the members was Johnny Badanjek, a fantastic drummer who had played on the early Mitch Ryder and the Detroit Wheels records, "Devil in a Blue Dress" and "Jenny Take a Ride." If you were a drummer in a band during that time, you had to learn to play "Jenny Take a Ride" because it was such a great drum part. I'd played all Mitch

Ryder's hits when I was drumming. Dennis Robbins was on guitar along with Jim McCarty, a guitar player who had played with the band Cactus, and the rest of the band was solid. David Gilbert was a quite a character who maybe imbibed a little too much during the sessions, but he could sing. He was a shouter, and they played very energetic rock. It wasn't Southern Rock, it was Northern Industrial hard-edged rock compared to what I was used to doing, but I liked it.

We had a problem with their first bass player who was a nice guy, but wasn't as good in the studio as the rest of them. He only played on one track before I got David Hood to come down and fill in the rest of the time. It was an exciting record, and the one song I was kind of proud of was a version of my favorite Fleetwood Mac song, "Oh Well." I was late coming to that song, but I'd fallen in love with it and played it over and over in my office thinking what a great record it was. Fleetwood Mac had some radio play with the song, and we re-cut the song and had a top-twenty single. The band had a song Johnny Badanjek had written called "Can't Sleep" that was also a top-twenty single. We did the recording at Capricorn Studios for a relatively modest budget. It had decent success for a first album, so I actually ended up making some money off the record.

31

Saturday Night Live

After a while, Phil, Frank and I kind of patched things up, and they still wanted me to do some work with them. While I wasn't a hired employee, I wanted to work, and they had the artists I loved to work with. Shortly after I left Capricorn, they'd sent me a demo tape of Delbert McClinton's new stuff. I liked it, but they'd sent me a slow ballad that sounded very country, and I didn't especially want to do a country project. Then they sent me the Delbert and Glen album, and I loved what I heard. Delbert's an incredible singer, musician, and writer; in fact he's one of my favorite writers. When I realized the history, I went back and researched all of Delbert's albums, the Delbert and Glenn albums, and everything else I could find that he'd recorded. Phil and I worked out the details, and I produced *Second Wind*, Delbert's first record for Capricorn.

For the album I wanted to do something different, so I hired the Muscle Shoals Rhythm Section to come down to Macon to record tracks for the record. Jimmy Johnson played on it as well as Roger Hawkins, David Hood, and Beckett Berry. I got the Muscle Shoals horns with Harrison Calloway, who played trumpet and arranged the horn section. Delbert brought in a couple of the players—Lewis Stephens, the organ player; and Billy Sanders, who played guitar on some of the tracks.

We recorded some great songs and the album got critical acclaim and sold a few. We cut one of the songs Delbert had written, "Take it Easy," that got airplay. It later became a big hit for Emmylou Harris. I had fun doing the album and hanging out with him.

The second album I cut with Delbert was *Keeper of the Flame*, and again I wanted something different. On one of my favorite records there was a song by David Bowie, "Fame," and I listened to it a lot and loved the production. I thought Andy Newmark played drums on the track, so I got a number to contact him. I was using John Hug a lot then; he'd played on Gregg and Cher's album. I really liked his guitar playing, so I hired him for the sessions. Delbert got Billy Sanders from his band, and

Hug convinced me to use John Jarvis, a piano player I didn't know. John almost had to promise he'd pay for Jarvis if I didn't like him, but he turned into one of my favorite piano players in the course of two or three tracks. I couldn't believe someone I'd never heard of before was that good and played so effortlessly.

When we started cutting Delbert's tracks, I didn't know Andy Newmark and he didn't know me. He seemed to think I was some hillbilly from the South. I was trying to get him to play a pattern I wanted and he told me, "Man, I'm not one of those Southern drummers. Maybe you ought to get Roger Hawkins or somebody." I replied that I'd worked with Roger a lot and wanted something different. He started to play a pattern that was grooving, and I told him I thought it was great. From there on we seemed to get along fine.

Andy was fairly wealthy, and one night during tracking a waiter showed up at the door of the studio. He was from an upscale restaurant next door, dressed like a waiter from a fancy place, and carried a tray covered with napkins. Thinking it might be a joke, I asked, "Can we help you?" He replied, "I have Mr. Newmark's dinner." It turned out to be a nightly occurrence.

We cut all the tracks out there and went back to Macon to do overdubs and mix. I got my friend Joe Walk to come in and do some overdubs on the album.

Delbert booked a gig in Acapulco to play for a large corporation that took all their clients and employees to stay at the Acapulco Princess Hotel. He had a deal where he had to play the second night after he got there and one night before he left. He was unhappy with his bass player at the time, so I got to go on the trip with him. We only had to play two or three hours for the two weeks we were there, and we stayed at a fancy hotel with a lot of the stuff comp'ed, including the room service. That was the start of my road gig with Delbert that lasted about eight or nine months.

Shortly after we finished the album, someone with Capricorn booked a gig for Delbert on *Saturday Night Live,* a show that everyone in our crowd watched since it was about a lot of values we held dear (plus you could tell everyone on it was half stoned). We were going to take most of the band that played on the record—John Jarvis, Billy Sanders,

John Hug. Although I didn't play on the album, I'd produced it and knew all the songs, so I went. I called Bill Stewart to play drums at the gig. We wanted to rehearse for the show, and for some reason we thought the best place to do it was in Los Angeles. While we were there, I ran into Bill Murray, whom Delbert had met before. We were all staying at the Chateau Mau Mau, and he came over to Delbert's room and hung out for a while. It was a brief encounter, but I enjoyed meeting him because I always liked his work.

We were going to play two songs on the show, so we worked and got them really tight. We left for New York the next morning to get there for the rehearsal that night. The show had a rehearsal, then a dress rehearsal the next day (which was recorded), and the actual performance was that night. Of course, we were running late, and when we left the hotel and got in the car heading for LAX it was the beginning of a series of unbelievable misadventures. Right off, Billy, who was driving, looked at the gas gauge and said, "Hey, we're low on gas." I was thinking that was just great. Bill wasn't feeling well and rode with his head hanging out the window, throwing up most of the way to the airport.

We were on the freeways out in Los Angeles, which were notoriously clogged, and we ran into a complete traffic jam. After waiting for a few minutes and seeing the traffic wasn't going to move, Billy took off down the shoulder of the road. I figured we'd end up under the jail if we were caught. Sure enough, I looked to my left just as we passed a cop who was caught in the bumper to bumper traffic. I thought he was going to get out of the jam somehow and come after us, but he looked as surprised as we did and left us alone.

About that time, the engine started sputtering and we ran out of gas. Fortunately, we were close to an exit and were able to coast most of the way up the exit ramp before we had to get out of the car and push it to a gas station to get enough gas to make it to the airport. This was the first time I'd ever been this rushed for anything, but we were determined to make the flight. We were in a rent-a-car and, when we arrived at the airport, Billy decided we didn't have time to fool with returning it, so he pulled up in front of the airline of the flight we were catching, got out of the car and left it at the curb. He told the skycap it was a Hertz rental and the keys were in it. We figured they'd find it eventually. We managed to make it onboard the plane in time and thought everything was going to be okay from there on.

We were all in first class, and I was sitting next to Tom Flye, who was going to go out there with us to mix the sound going out over the air. John Jarvis was sitting in front of me; Delbert and Billy were sitting across the aisle from me, and Bill Stewart ended up sitting next to Norman Lear's wife and holding a barf bag. *All in the Family* had been a gigantic hit, and we knew it was a Norman Lear production. He'd had so many television series out at that time that it was kind of a big deal for us to be on the plane with her.

Everything was going fine until we were about forty-five minutes to an hour out when the pilot came on the intercom and said, "Ladies and gentlemen, I have an announcement. We've encountered something we've never experienced before in this aircraft and we're going to have to turn around and go back to Los Angeles. We'll try to get you all back there safe and sound."

The word "try" in there kind of stuck in everybody's mind, and we could hear crying and praying. We all thought we were going to crash. Flye and I looked at each other and one or the other of us said, "If we're going to die, you're a good person to go down with." I tried to not let it get to me, but I remembered there had been a loud thump right before the pilot made his announcement. About ten minutes later, John Jarvis turned around and cracked us up when he said, "I'm just sorry John Hug isn't with us." Fortunately for Hug, he'd booked a later flight.

Meanwhile, we were flying back to Los Angeles, and everyone was saying their goodbyes. As we got closer to the airport, the stewardess announced we should prepare for an emergency landing and gave the "take your shoes off, your glasses, whatever is in your pockets and put your head between your knees" speech and…we knew the rest of the saying…"kiss your ass goodbye." That's about what it looked like. An irony is the in-flight movie playing was *The Buddy Holly Story* in which John Jarvis had the part of Ritchie Valens's piano player. We figured that was gonna be it for us, but the pilot took it down. There wasn't anything extraordinary about the landing except that we made it. After we touched down and started rolling, the pilot said, "We're all clear and we have landed." All of the passengers applauded.

We returned to the gate, deplaned, and waited around for the airline to make arrangements for another flight. About an hour and a half later, they announced they'd found the problem with the plane, had it fixed, and were ready to go. I didn't want to get back on that particular plane. No one did, so eventually they found another one, and we finally made it to New York without further incident. We were late to our run-through for the show, but we made it.

As soon as we arrived in New York, we went to the theater at 30 Rock and did a rehearsal. There was nothing really odd about it except, after we did the rehearsal, I realized it was going out to probably millions of Americans who were our contemporaries. I was just hoping I didn't screw up. There was a real possibility I might, but I was hoping I wouldn't. The dress rehearsal was literally a dress rehearsal, and we went through everything in costume or whatever we were going to wear. The show itself was a fun evening, but it turns out our appearance was on the thirteenth show of the season. I'm not a fan of the number thirteen, and I'm glad I didn't know that at the time.

At the end of the show everyone stood on stage with all the cast members, musicians, and the featured band waving at the cameras. Afterward, while I was walking out, I had a brush with greatness. We'd met several people in the *SNL* band, and Jaco Pastorius walked up to me and said "Nice '57!" I was playing the old '57 precision bass Duane and Berry had given me from the band. I said, "Thank you. I really enjoy your playing. You're great." He said, "Yeah, I know" and walked on by. It kind of cracked me up, but I thought it was an appropriate response because he was great, if not *the* greatest.

While we were in New York, we played the Lone Star. Before it closed in 1989, it featured a lot of Southern acts. I think the reason Delbert got the *SNL* gig was because John Belushi and Dan Aykroyd were huge fans of Delbert's music. They'd covered one of Delbert's songs, "B Movie Boxcar Blues," which Delbert had recorded on the *Second Wind* album, and it was one of the songs we played on the show. We also played a Chuck Berry song, "Talkin' about You," that Delbert had recorded on his new album. Belushi sat in with us at both the college gig and the one at the Lone Star. I have a photograph from that time with Delbert, Belushi, and me on stage. Belushi was a character, but it was like

211

being around a lit firecracker; you didn't know what was going to happen next. You knew you were probably going to enjoy it, but even if you didn't, you had to stick around to see what was going to happen. He was an interesting, super-talented person.

Another of the gigs I played with Delbert was at a 4th of July blues festival in Milwaukee. I figured July 4th was going to be hot, but it was the coldest I've ever been playing music. I thought Bill was slowing everything down, and he thought I was rushing everything. It seemed as if we'd never get through a song. As cold as it was, I thought if either of us was going to be off tempo, rushing was preferable.

I had all kinds of fun on the bus with Delbert and the band. They were good folks, and we traveled all over the country having a good time. We played a lot of other good gigs and a few clubs in the middle of nowhere that, if they didn't have chicken wire up around the band stand, it was only because they hadn't gotten around to it.

Being on the road had its moments. Our bus driver, Madison "Red" Bradley, had a malfunctioning mental GPS, so we were frequently lost, and several times the bus broke down. I remember coming from Lubbock, Texas, heading toward Tennessee when the air-conditioning in the bus went out. It was hot so we had to roll down all the windows. I'd been asleep, and when I woke up there were flies all over me. Then I looked around and everyone else was covered with flies. I don't know why that happened, but it was really weird.

David Pinkston, an engineer who was still working at Capricorn, was on the road with us to do sound for the band. He is one funny guy. We'd go into a restaurant and when the waitress came to take our orders, he'd lean over and tell her, "Don't tell the papers we're in town." Immediately the waitress would ask who we were, and David would start telling a story that usually ended up getting us better service.

We were on the road promoting the album, and one day, riding through Texas on the way to our next gig, we were looking over the Billboard chart and saw the album was beginning to get some action on the charts. It seemed like the pick for a single from the album might be "Shot from the Saddle," a song I'd gotten from FAME publishing company. We were pretty happy, and I was starting to feel vindicated;

I'd cut a record with Delbert that was after my employment with Capricorn, and it looked like something might really happen with it.

Delbert called Capricorn to see what they were doing to promote the album, but the phone had been disconnected. We knew right then something was up. He tried to get in touch with his manager, Don Light, to see if he knew what was going on. Finally, he reached someone at the studio who told us the label had gone under. I thought, "What the hell?" I just couldn't believe it. The album and single had just started to get some chart action when the label went out of business, which meant the record was dead. There wasn't anything that could have been done at that point to salvage the album.

I was in shock. Not only was Delbert's record dead, but Capricorn was still my home. I had friends there. I liked to work in the studio, and all of a sudden Capricorn as we once knew it was over. I didn't know what was next. The label was finished, but I didn't know if the studio was still operating. Capricorn had been like the parent company, and I wasn't certain how it was going to affect everyone. Sadly, it turned out Delbert's album was the last record I ever recorded at Capricorn Studio.

The first Rockets album had been doing well with two top-forty singles when I got a call that the band was ready to do another record. I talked with Chris Stone and told him we needed some pre-production time, so he let me have a couple of days rehearsal time in what used to be the Sly Stone studio C in the back of the Record Plant. They called it the pit because in the middle of the room there'd been a hole about fifteen feet in diameter and about twelve feet deep. Gary Kellgren had thought it would be a good idea to put the console down at the bottom of the hole so the musicians could either stand or sit around and be able to look at each other. By the time we got there the hole had been covered over, but the name hung around.

I flew out to Sausalito, and the band rehearsed for two or three days to work out some arrangements in the pit. Then we went into studio B. Tom Flye was engineering on the record, and it was during this time Tom turned me on to new Meyer speakers that were supposed to be one of the best things ever. Tom brought some to the studio. They sounded incredible, and I fell in love with them.

On November 16, 1979, during the recording of the album, I was in the control room when Chris came in and said, "I've got some bad news for you." I asked him what was up and he told me Twiggs Lyndon had just died in a parachute accident in Duanesburg, New York. It cast a pall on everything.

Twiggs was one of the most interesting people I've ever known, and he had the intellect of two or three people combined. I met him when I first moved to Macon when he'd been the road manager for some of Phil's black acts. He was Duane's good friend and the first road manager for the Allman Brothers Band. He loved music, was a talented guitar player, and a true friend. It was another chapter in the Allman Brothers tragedy. I always saw Macon as having a bright light shining over it, but with each death, the light dimmed a little more: first Duane, then Berry, then Twiggs. It was just a sad, sad thing.

32

Decatur

By 1979, I'd moved from Macon and was living in Atlanta when Randy Richards called asking me to check out his studio, The Music Place, in hopes I'd consider doing a project there. His studio was in Birmingham, Alabama, so we worked out the details and I went over to look at the place. The studio was nice, and the control room had a Neve 8068 console and a brand new Studer 400, which was the first of that particular Studer model I'd seen. You could punch in almost instantly, and it seemed almost as quick as digital is today. There was also a decent selection of microphones and other top notch equipment, so what was not to like?

I got a call from Gary Lazar, one of the co-managers of the Rockets, about another band he wanted me to work with called the Look, and I went to Detroit to see them. They must have gotten a pretty good deal from a studio in Canada because that's where I ended up cutting some demos with them. That was a real trip. The studio itself was in a farm house in the middle of nowhere. It was the first studio I remember working in that had windows. When you looked outside, all you saw was a long cornfield. It certainly beat being locked up in a cave-like studio, but it was just odd. Looking back, they seemed to be on the leading edge of a coming trend because now, everyone who wants one has a studio in their house. Eventually I brought the Look to Birmingham to record them at the Music Place.

I never did get on well in Atlanta. I couldn't take the size of the place or the traffic, and I stayed lost for the year I lived there. Randy offered me more work at the studio, so I decided to move. The move meant I'd be closer to my parents in Decatur, which was a little over an hour away. Shortly after we relocated, I got a call from Warner Brothers about recording a band called Billy Karloff and the Extremes. It was a punk band from England with good musicians. I told him I was working at a studio in Birmingham and wanted to do the album there. He didn't like that idea because it would mean flying five people over to the states for the recording. He wanted me to go to England to do the record instead, but I was busy in the studio and didn't want to leave. Finally, after a price negotiation, they agreed to bring the band to Birmingham, Alabama, which, I'm certain, was a culture shock.

I really liked the guys and got on well with them. We made a pretty good record that never sold very many copies. John Osborne was the lead singer, and while he was there, he became another good friend. I stayed in touch with John and Dolphin Taylor, the drummer, every once in a while, but I never saw any of them again. A few years ago I heard John had passed away.

After I'd been working at the studio a while, Randy had an idea about doing an album with Eddie Kendricks, a Birmingham native who was the former singer with the Temptations. When the project was put to me, we were going to co-produce the album. I had my reservations, but because I'd always admired Eddie, I decided to do it anyway just to have the chance to work with him. I hadn't done a lot of co-producing, and it didn't work out so well.

That album turned into the weirdest thing I've ever been involved with, and I about lost my faith in humanity. Toward the end of the album, Randy tried to take over the whole project just when I was ready to start mixing. It ended in a lawsuit that was pretty ugly. I'd done all the engineering and most of the producing, and not only was he not going to pay me the money we'd agreed on, he was going to leave my name off the album and not give me production credit.

I found a lawyer from Atlanta and sued Randy and Atlantic Records in Federal court. There was a lot of testimony and a lot of stress surrounding the proceedings. When the verdict was issued, the judge found no immediate copyright infringement, but wrote in her opinion if the album was released without my name, she'd find the parties guilty at that time, which meant they had to settle with me. One of the craziest parts of the lawsuit was Randy's accusation that I had plotted to kidnap his children, whom I'd never even seen. By that time, I already had three children of my own and I didn't know why he'd think I wanted his. Since Randy and his family owned the studio, I stopped working there all together.

After I left the Music Place, I got a call from Rick Hall, who wanted me to do some engineering for him. For a while, I commuted between Birmingham and Muscle Shoals. Then, in 1981, my wife, Ann, and I moved back to Decatur and lived in the little house for about six months, which was kind of small for a family of five.

Aside from the long commute, the main reason we moved back was because my dad was sick. He'd had a few strokes and been diagnosed with Alzheimer's. When my mother wanted me to come back to Decatur to help take care of him, I knew I needed to go. In retrospect, I think my mother was already in the early stages of the disease. My dad lived until 1988 and my mother until 1997. They both ended up unable to communicate and by the end of their lives were totally paralyzed. It was a horrible existence.

While I was doing sessions at Rick's, Owen Brown, a good friend and a bass player who lives in Town Creek, introduced me to Ronnie Dunn, a friend of his from Oklahoma. Ronnie wanted to do an album, and he came to town to sing for me and play some of his songs. I thought he had an incredible voice, and I ended up cutting an album with him in Muscle Shoals.

At the time, there were a lot of studios over there running full tilt: FAME; Wishbone with Clayton Ivey and his partner, Terry Woodford; the new Muscle Shoals Sound on the river. A lot of hit records were coming out of Muscle Shoals. I took Ronnie over to the Shoals to listen to some songs from a few local writers. We ended up cutting some of the album at Wishbone Studio and some at the new Muscle Shoals Sound, which was the most technologically advanced in town.

Wishbone had cabins they rented out to people recording at their place, so we stayed in one while we were there. Later we stayed in a house near Muscle Shoals Sound they rented to the artists who were recording in their studio. It was like a band house with your friends staying there. It had a community kitchen and a television room. I really liked Ronnie; he and I got along well. We had a good time and cut some good music.

To be honest, I thought I had a hit record on my hands. I took it to Jimmy Bowen, who seemed to run Nashville during that time, but he said, "Nope, Ronnie doesn't have a radio voice." When he said that, I couldn't believe it. In fact, it distressed me in all kinds of ways, and I thought, "Damn, I must not know what I'm doing if Ronnie Dunn can't sing." Deep inside I knew better, and of course a few years later my instincts proved to be right.

I really poured my heart into what we were doing, but it turned out to be a limited release of only a few songs through Churchill Records. Even though the material and production were good, the whole album never came out. But I damn sure knew Ronnie could sing, and I couldn't believe anyone in Nashville could think he didn't have a "radio voice." I thought if that's how it was up there, I didn't want to have anything to do with the place.

I've always had a love/hate relationship with Nashville. I have a lot of close friends living there, and many of my favorite players are up there. Still, I've never had any luck with the music industry in Nashville. I'm either too rock and roll, not country enough, or I just don't fit with what they're doing. I guess I've resolved myself to the fact I don't look at things the same way they do.

Delbert and I stayed in touch. I kept talking to him about doing some more recording. I'd done the two records with him when we were in Macon, and I thought we could do some demos and get something going. He said he wasn't writing anything, so I told him I'd find some songs. He asked me to send him something and if he liked it, we'd talk. I found some songs from Rick's catalog written by Walt Aldridge and Tommy Brasfield and a couple by some other writers and sent them to Delbert. After he listened to them he called and said "Let's do it."

I'd just gotten a royalty check and had the money to front for the musicians. Because I was cutting a bunch of his catalog songs, Rick gave me a good deal on the studio. Delbert came in and we cut "Sure Got Away with My Heart," "Thin Ice," "Never Say Never," "Married Man" and "None of That Like Before." Owen Hale played drums, Ralph Ezell was on bass, Walt played guitar, and Clayton Ivey played on one or two songs. Mac McAnally, my favorite acoustic guitar player, was there as was Kenny Mims, my favorite electric guitar player at the time. John Jarvis, who'd moved to Nashville by then, came down to play keys on the sessions.

We cut tracks only for a day or two. The first day we were in the studio, rain poured hard, and more was in the forecast. There'd been one other situation over at FAME when rain came like that. They'd had to put the piano up on concrete blocks because it looked like the whole place was going to flood when the water started backing up to the studio. I watched the weather and thought for sure it was going to happen again.

I talked to Ann in Decatur and one of the toilets at the house had overflowed. Water was starting to flood the yard from a creek behind the house, and it was almost to the back door. John, his wife, and their baby were staying with us, so she booked some rooms and got everyone moved into the hotel while we finished the session as fast as we could. We then drove through flooding roads to get home.

When we were in the studio the next day, it seemed for a while as if nothing was going to go right on the session. Every idea I'd come up with had bombed, and it took a while to come up with something that worked. In the end it turned out to be a great session, and Delbert did most of the keeper vocals live with the band.

Every once in a while I'd hear about Phil or I'd talk to him. He was still in Macon, trying to get a record company or at least a production company back together. Delbert and I decided Nashville probably wasn't going to like what we'd done, so we called Phil to see if he might be interested or maybe have an idea of how we could get it to a label. He invited us to Macon and sent tickets for both Delbert and me to fly out of Huntsville.

When we went in to see him, Frank was there with him at the office. I thought for sure they would be knocked out by what we'd done and say, "Yes, tell us what you want. We'll give you anything. We've *got* to have this." It didn't quite work out that way. We had songs on it that turned out to be hits for other artists, so I think Phil and Frank made a mistake. Phil was just lukewarm, and I think he wanted to play it for some other people to see what kind of deal he could work out. In retrospect, I think Phil was having a hard time trying to put Capricorn back together, and there wasn't anything he could do for us.

It was the first time I'd seen Phil since the bankruptcy. I was a little uneasy at first, but he was nice to me and I couldn't be mad at him. After all, I've had a really good life, and without him and his magnetic personality, my life would have been totally different. Sadly, that turned out to be the last time I saw Frank. It was a good while after it happened that I heard about he'd had a heart attack and collapsed at the Capricorn office. I was shocked that no one from there called me. I guess they forgot to let me know, but I'm certain Carolyn Brown would have called if she'd had my number.

33

The Decoys

After producing what I thought were good commercial records and not getting any interest in them, I just wanted to engineer for a while. So, I went from being a full time producer who engineered some to being a full time engineer for Rick Hall. I engineered a couple of Mac Davis albums, one with the Gatlin Brothers, and I worked on a couple of Jerry Reed albums that produced several hit singles including, "She Got the Goldmine and I Got the Shaft." Jerry was a nice guy and one of my favorite guitar players, and I really enjoyed working with him. I also engineered a single with Marie Osmond that's caused some confusion over the years. Some writers have had a disconnect when looking at my discography and written that I was producer of the Osmond Brothers, rather than the Allman Brothers.

On a personal level I love and admire Rick, but working for him is hard in every way. After a year or so of working at FAME, I needed to leave. I got to where I didn't enjoy music anymore. I had reached a point where I wouldn't even listen to music other than in the studio. I've always loved everything about music, even the bad bars I had to play in sometimes, but working for Rick was worse than playing in the bad bars. It was hard because he expected a lot, and sometimes I didn't know exactly where he was coming from. He's a real talent, has a lot of hit records, and knows what he's doing—but I just couldn't work for him. I was just miserable, so Ann told me I needed to quit. I didn't know what we'd do, but she said we'd figure out something. So in 1984, I quit and started my own studio and publishing company.

They've written many books on what I didn't know about music publishing at the time, but I learned the hard way. Joe Walk, Ann, and I were partners, and when we first started trying to do demos of some of the songs for the publishing company, it was really a mess. We set up to record in the living room with a drum machine and a couple of microphones, just minimal equipment, and I was using my hi-fi speakers for monitors. We were living in town in an older house, and it about drove Ann crazy because the studio was adjacent to our bedroom. Where we worked was wide open to the rest of the house. When it was bedtime, if anyone was making noise, it messed me up—and if I wasn't making noise, nothing was happening.

I'd met Mike Higdon over at Owen Brown's house and he talked about wanting to put together a studio. I told him I was interested in doing something too and talked with my mother about using the little house, which was originally built for me back in the HourGlass days. She let me have the place, and we started the studio out where it is now.

After the studio was relocated to the little house in '85, I tried to get something going and started doing demos. I recorded on an 8-track, mainly using drum machine parts I'd programmed. I'd play bass and sometimes guitar, or I'd get a guitar player, and Joe would play piano. I did publishing company demos and demos for people wanting me to record them who were nice folks but just weren't ready to make a record. I even did some commercials for a car dealership in town.

My dad was sick all this time and getting worse. I was helping take care of him, which naturally took precedence over anything else I was doing. Of course, such care giving isn't easy, and usually I was needed at some inopportune times. I hadn't been away from the studio in the several years leading up to my dad's death because I'd needed to stay close in case of an emergency. After he died in '88, I wanted to get out and back to where it all started, making music, and I wanted to play again.

I thought I'd go back to the early part of my career when I was playing drums, so I started a band, the Decoys. The band consisted of two writers I was working with, one the singer, and the other writer on guitar, Joe Walk on piano, me on drums, and a bass player to be named as soon as we could find him. In fact, one night we played without a bass player which was pretty odd, but we made a valiant effort. We played a few gigs in Gadsden at the Chestnut Station, and that's where I first met Carl Weaver.

I was at the bar having a beer, something I don't usually do because I don't drink beer, and Carl was sitting at the bar there with me. He said, "Man, did you produce that Gregg and Cher record?" I looked at him kind of funny and said, "You're kidding. You know about that record?" He said, "Yeah, I love it." I told him I thought we might have been the only ones who did; the record came out just as Gregg and Cher split up, and there was no promotion put behind it.

He said, "Yeah, I listen to that all the time. In fact my copy is scratched up from listening to it." I told him I just happened to have a couple of boxes of the album at the house and I'd bring him one the next time we were down there. I took him a new copy of the album. It was so odd to have someone come up and mention Gregg and Cher to me that I remembered him when we met again about fifteen years later.

I'd been talking with Scott Boyer on and off for a while, and after the Decoys had been playing for a couple of months, I gave him a call. He was living in Mobile and told me he might be moving up my way to Muscle Shoals. He and his wife had just split up, and he was leaving town. I think Scott had been living in Mobile ever since Capricorn folded, or maybe even before the final gasp, and he'd been gigging all that time in the Convertibles with drummer Bryan Wheeler (B. W.), Tommy Talton, Topper Price, and Art Schilling—all of whom I knew from Macon.

Since Scott and B. W. were heading my way, I told him to come and we'd play some music. I thought we could have two drummers in the band, but first I wanted to hear B. W. since I'd never heard him play. I'm very particular about drummers, but when I heard him, he was wonderful. He would have answered the prayers of anyone looking for a great drummer. He played great fills, was easy to get along with, and was usually in a good humor. Of course, I'd known Scott since we were young and living in Miami.

Once I heard B. W. play, I figured I didn't have any business behind the drums. Since we didn't have a bass player, I changed over to bass, which was certainly more my instrument. We had a good band with Joe on piano; Scott playing guitar and singing; me on bass, and B. W., the anchor keeping things together and solid, on drums. We had a number of guest guitarists who joined us off and on: John Willis from Nashville; Duncan Cameron, who played with Glenn Frey and went on to play with Sawyer Brown; and finally Kelvin Holly who played with the Amazing Rhythm Aces and tours now with Little Richard. Kelvin is the reigning guitar champ, and he and Scott are the only original members of the Decoys still playing with the band. The current line-up is Scott, Kelvin, David Hood, N. C. Thurman, and Mike Dillon. I had no idea the band would last more than twenty years.

We played at lot at B. J.'s Deli, a small place, but if there was any art scene in Decatur, B. J.'s was at the center of it in the 80s. He had live entertainment at his old deli and, before he even got his new place opened, he would let us rehearse there. We played some other small clubs around Alabama and called it the Decoys Deli Tour. Then David Johnson, director at the time of the Alabama Music Hall of Fame, called and asked the Decoys to play for the opening of the museum. We had a good band and I thought it would be a way to get the folks in Muscle Shoals out to hear us.

There was a stage set up outside the Hall of Fame and for the gig the band included Scott, Kelvin, two drummers, Brian Owings (B. O.), who occasionally sat in with the band, and Bryan Wheeler (B. W.). B. W. was one of the best when you needed shuffles or the New Orleans feel. Joe Walk was playing piano, N. C. Thurman was playing piano, and I was on bass. We had a good time playing some of our regular set list. There was a ribbon cutting to officially open the museum, and it was a beautiful day.

A while later David Johnson called and asked, "How would you like to play with your original band, Dan Penn and the Pallbearers?" I couldn't think of anything I'd rather do than to play with them, but I told him I didn't think I could do it because I didn't play guitar any more. I still had a couple of guitars that were used in the studio a lot, but I hardly ever picked one up. He told me it was going to be Norbert Putman, David Briggs, Jerry Carrigan, Dan Havely, me and Dan Penn. I told David, "Man, I didn't do a lot of sessions and I wasn't a great guitar player, but I was there." Originally, I'd kind of fallen into a neat spot because back in the early days, when there weren't very many guitar players around, I had an electric guitar and a decent amp. Norbert reminded me of that recently.

I wasn't very good, but I practiced for the gig with dedication because the worst thing I could imagine was embarrassing those guys, or embarrassing myself by looking bad in their eyes. Although the line-up was the same, I wasn't ever actually a member of the Pallbearers, but I'd played with Dan in the Mark V. I loved all those guys; they were my heroes. We played mostly the same songs we'd played when we were in the Mark V, and I can't begin to describe how proud I was to play with all them again. The whole gig with all the bands was recorded, and the CD, *Muscle Shoals Bands of the 60s Reunion,* was released for sale as a fundraiser by the Alabama Music Hall of Fame.

On July 4, 1990, the Decoys was the opening band for the opening band at the Allman Brothers concert at Oak Mountain in Birmingham. I think Scott had talked with Butch and gotten us the gig. I hadn't seen the Brothers in a long time, and some of the guys walked out front to listen to us play. Afterward, I went back to talk to them. It was the first time I'd seen Gregg in several years. It was kind of funny because Gregg had recently gotten married again; when he went to introduce me to his new wife, he forgot her name. It was a short-lived marriage.

I continued to play with the band and work on demos in the studio until a few months later when I got a call from Phil that turned me in another direction.

34

Mom's Kitchen

I was in my studio early in 1990, working on some demos when, out of the blue, I got a call from Phil. I'd talked with him occasionally over the years and gone to see him at his office in Nashville a couple of times. It was good to hear from him again. Phil told me he had a group, Allgood, he was interested in and asked me to come to Nashville to hear them play. He thought they were a good band and something people needed to hear, so I told him Ann and I would be up there on whatever night they were playing.

They had a great guitar player, John Carter, and an interesting singer, Corky Jones. Charlie Pruet, on drums, and Mike Sain, on bass, were solid players; Alberto Salazarte, on percussion, locked in as needed with the bass and drums. Clay Fuller wrote most of the songs and played lead guitar. You could tell they were young and just getting started, but they were a good band. Phil wanted to watch them for a little while and then, when they were ready, wanted me to record an album with them.

He was in the process of putting Capricorn Records back together and basing it in Nashville, which was a lot closer than Macon and perfect for me. I was glad to hear about the revival of the label. Phil said he was going to get a deal for Allgood and told me about another band from Athens, Georgia, named Widespread Panic. Although the band had been playing around the South, I wasn't familiar with them at that time.

Next thing I know, Phil asked me to go to Athens to listen to Panic. I agreed, and although Phil couldn't make it, Don Schmitzerle would meet me there. I drove to Athens and met up with Don and the band's manager, Sam Lanier. After dinner together, we went to the Georgia Theatre to hear the band. We sat in the balcony, which reminded me of the Fillmore and the time I spent with the HourGlass when we used to go up to the balcony where they did the light shows to watch the bands. Of course the theatre wasn't as large as the Fillmore, but it had the same vibe.

Panic was impressive. There was no doubt about it; the guys were going somewhere. You could tell this band had been playing together for a while because they were both tight and spontaneous, which is hard to pull off. The music reminded me of the way jazz musicians might approach a song, but with a rock edge. I could tell they really connected with each other.

I loved John Bell's unique, big, gruff voice; if you ever heard it once you'd always recognize it. He played rhythm on electric and acoustic guitar and was the most prolific writer in the band. Sometimes, when I record bands, I solo the drums, bass, and percussion. I was blown away with how Dave Schools, on bass, Todd Nance, on drums, and Sonny Ortiz, on percussion, locked in together. It took me a while to appreciate Mikey Houser's original abilities on the guitar. He had a lot of technique and a different style, but it fit the band perfectly. The more I heard it, the more I liked it. Although he didn't sing much, Mikey had a good, deep voice. The band had talented people all through the line-up; I liked how they sounded and how they played, and I grew to admire and love every one of them.

The next time I remember seeing the Widespread Panic was when they played the Cotton Club in Atlanta for two or three nights leading into New Years. I remember most of the show on New Year's, but I'd had two or three drinks of whiskey leading up to the stroke of midnight. When they brought out the champagne, it made me sick, and I told Ann we had to leave...*now*. I wasn't obnoxious or anything, I just went down in a hurry and had to get back to the room.

I saw a lot of people I knew at the New Year's show, and I met a lot of folks from Athens I later worked with. I'd run into Bruce Hampton earlier in the day. He was at the gig, and Danny Hutchens's band, Bloodkin, was on the bill. John Bell was a big fan of Bloodkin and had talked to me about them before. Phil and Don were there that night, and I saw Dick Wooley, which was a kind of strange situation because Dick was with Bill Hamm, who managed ZZ Top.

Phil had a basic agreement with Panic, but they hadn't signed papers yet and it seemed Dick and Bill wanted to sign them too. Dick had called and asked if I'd leave his name at the door, so I did. While Phil was talking with the band about the contract, Dick and Bill walked up, making for a very uncomfortable moment. I hadn't realized Phil and Dick were on bad terms at the time or that they were vying for Panic, and I was really embarrassed. All I wanted to do was extricate myself from the situation, and I don't remember what all happened after that.

When all the details were worked out and it was time to record Panic, I listened to songs and had the guys come in for pre-production at my studio. I'd heard the band live, and I wanted to hear them in the studio and maybe work on arrangements of songs. I'd told Phil I thought the band would sound good with a keyboard player, so he hired T Lavitz to play on the album. T had played keys with the Dixie Dregs, another Capricorn band from the old days in Macon, and he's a great player.

The band was very easy to work with. They were nice and listened to me, and we had a good rapport. We changed a few things and made the songs a little more concise to work better for an album, then selected the songs to record. We were pretty much ready by the time we got to Emerald Studio in Nashville, where we cut most of the basic tracks for the self-titled album, *Widespread Panic*, or as the band informally called it, *Mom's Kitchen*.

Once I knew we were getting ready to record with Panic, I began scouting studios for the sessions and made a couple of trips to Nashville to check out the various ones before settling on Emerald Studio. Emerald had a great live room, and it was where I had my first experience with digital versus analog multi-track recording. At that time, my studio was still 24-track analog. Emerald had a Studer 24-track analog tape machine and a digital Mitsubishi 32-track. Right away you had eight more tracks that were digital, so there was no noise. With digital, I wouldn't have to deal with noise reduction. Digital tape was also cheaper than analog, which was a big consideration then because analog tape was a $130 to $150 a reel. In the past, I'd used approximately twenty to thirty reels of tape on an album.

Kerry Kopp, the tech guy at Emerald, set it up for me so we could record something on both machines at the same time through their SSL console, line them up, match the volumes and switch between them. It was a pretty big deal to get it set up, but I wanted to hear the difference.

I was open to digital because it had more tracks, but when I listened to it, I was surprised. There was very little contest as to which one had the better sound. Although digital had a bigger bass end, nothing sounded better on the digital machine. The piano didn't even sound real compared to what I was used to. Analog was much more realistic and better sounding to me.

That was my first experience with digital multi-track. However, given the fact digital tape was cheap, I got them to keep a reel of digital multi-track tape on the machine in case there was any kind of jamming we wanted to capture. Sometimes Panic's jams could go on for a while. We were cutting at 30 ips, which means there were only sixteen minutes on a 2-inch analog reel of tape. With the digital machine, they could play for an hour or so. John Keene had produced Panic's first album, *Space Wrangler*. For the reissue we added a song I recorded, "Me and the Devil," a Robert Johnson tune, that was cut on the digital machine.

At that time Nashville was booming, and I had to plan ahead and make advance arrangements if I wanted time in a studio. It's the antithesis of what it is now; today, you can get about any studio in Nashville at a reasonable price and most likely it's available. We paid close to $2000 a day for Emerald, and it was hard to book. We only had a few days at a time at Emerald, and I didn't want to be held up by a studio when the band was ready to record again. Since I liked the good vibe in Memphis, I booked Kiva Studio, which had an SSL console and Studer 800 tape machine like we were using at Emerald.

I'd worked with Alan Schulman on projects at Rick's, and he went to Kiva to engineer for me. At that time, I'd do engineering and most of the mixing at my place, but I preferred to have an engineer for a major label recording session, especially when I had a band in a place that was expensive. We got to Kiva, and it was a beautiful studio. The control room was a little small, but it was certainly big enough. The main room was incredible, all wood floors, nice size, and nice space for doing drums. I usually look for a good place to do drums since guitars and pianos are less sensitive to the environment.

Unfortunately, we encountered some problems and got off to a bad start when something went wrong with the tape machine. It just quit, and Kiva's tech guy was on vacation. It's really important to have a tech around who knows the equipment, but we had to get an outside tech who wasn't familiar with the machine and then have parts flown in overnight from Studer. After that was fixed, more problems arose. At Emerald we had an individual headphone system with a little mixer for each of the musicians so they could dial in whatever they wanted to hear. It was very useful and everyone loved it. The system worked flawlessly and we came to rely on it, but when we got to Kiva, their system didn't work very well.

We got it working about as good as it was going to, but we had five headphone boxes and six musicians. Plus, I like to have one to listen over headphones to make sure of what the band is hearing, so we were at least two short. Sonny Ortiz, the percussionist, said he didn't need one—he'd just listen closely. Sonny, though, was off in a booth, and there was no way he could hear what was going on or lock in other than by watching Todd play. I was trying to figure out what to do so there would at least be a stereo mix going to the players. Everyone would get the same mix, hopefully one they could live with, but Kiva didn't have a way we could hook up normal headphones. Even then, we still had only five headphone systems for six players.

I got on the phone with Gary Belz, the owner of Kiva, who was also off on vacation. He was nice, but he didn't understand the situation. It wasn't that we were hard to please; Kiva seemed to have everything we needed when I was checking out studios, so I'd expected an adequate headphone set-up. We thought we'd just be changing locations, not getting used to a new system. They had the same console, basically the same tape machine, but they just didn't have the type system that would allow each musician to set his own listening levels that we had in Nashville. We managed to cut three or four tracks we could use at Kiva, but the headphone situation became intolerable, and we needed to move on.

We had a day left in Memphis, so I booked a night for the band to go into Sun Studio. I'd always wanted to record there. It was about the time U2 released an album that was recorded, in part, at Sun. Of course, I was familiar with the records and music that came out of Sun with Jerry Lee, Carl Perkins, Johnny Cash, and Elvis; the band was probably familiar with Sun for the same reason, but if not, certainly from U2.

I had to book a night session because they gave guided tours of the studio during the day to let people see the room as it was when Elvis recorded there. They have the studio set up as it was originally, and I assume the control room is the same or about the same, although the equipment was different. They had a different console, a Soundcraft 24-track, but it sounded good. The studio is a great room with good acoustics, and there wasn't as much leakage as you might think, given that everyone was out in the room with no isolation. The drums were in the back of the room, the upright piano was over on the side wall, and a small Hammond organ was right next to it. There were a lot of old amps and fun gear to play through.

Everyone sat in the same room looking each other in the eye. It was like the old days when, if one person screwed up, the whole take was probably bad and un-useable. The band just played a lot of the stuff they did live, either cover tunes or album songs we'd decided not to record. We attempted to do a good recording of the Van Morrison song, "Send Your Mind." Mikey had played the song for me, and I thought it would be a good one to cut and something we could get played on the radio. We spent some time trying to cut it and got a decent version, but we cut a better one later at Emerald. That night was a lot of fun. The band enjoyed it, I enjoyed it, and recording at Sun was something I'd wanted to do my whole life.

When we rented Kiva, we got a great deal on rooms at the Peabody in downtown Memphis because the family of Kiva's owner, Gary Belz, owned it, and the rooms were part of the deal. Everybody had a nice room, and we watched the ducks walking through the lobby to the fountain each day. It was in a good area, had an upscale restaurant and all-around nice accommodations. Plus, it was next door to the Rendezvous barbeque restaurant. If there was any one particular thing Panic and I agreed on, it was ribs. However, if we left Kiva to go to another studio in town besides Sun, we'd lose the deal on the rooms. Since I was trying to stay within the budget for the record, going to another studio in Memphis wasn't an option. We left Kiva and went to Nashville where we managed to squeeze another day out at Emerald to re-cut "Send your Mind" and finish the album.

By the time I was ready to master the first Panic album, Glenn Meadows, whom I first met in the '70s when I was living in Macon, was one of the partners at Masterfonics in Nashville. I'd only been at

Capricorn about six months when I read a review about an Advent cassette deck, one of the early versions of cassette players that had a Dolby B system, and I wanted one. I called the hi-fi store in Atlanta where Glenn was working to ask about the cassette player. He had one in the store, so I asked if he could ship it to me. When I told him I was in Macon, he said he was going to be there that weekend and he'd drop it off. So he came by my house with the cassette player.

I thought of Masterfonics as the Nashville version of the Record Plant. One of the things I liked about the place was that Tom Hedley had designed the room. Tom had done the room at the original Capricorn and the rooms at the Record Plant as well as hundreds of others. I loved his designs and his speakers and his whole philosophy. Tom's a great man; I'll always think highly of him and be indebted to him for what I learned about speakers and room design.

I went to Nashville and talked with Glenn about mixing at Masterfonics and told him what I could afford. He gave me a deal that was within the budget, so I mixed that album there in studio 6. Steve Tillisch, another Capricorn alumnus, did a lot of the engineering at Masterfonics. He had done the first recording at Emerald for Panic's album along with Jeff Coppage, who'd been his assistant. Steve had commitments, so Jeff stayed with me to assist while I mixed the album and has helped on many of the records I've done since then.

Studio 6 had an SSL board and Otari tape machines, a plethora of outboard gear, and one of the first Fairchild compressors I'd ever used. It's a huge piece of equipment, but it sounded good on everything. It was a great place to work and I still master there now with Jonathan Russell.

Mikey Houser's wife, Barbette, who is an artist, designed a cover for the album that was a beautiful picture with soft earth colors. We all thought it was perfect, but the record company didn't like it. They kept asking the guys in the band if they had any other ideas until Mikey, in frustration, took a sheet of paper and some colors, traced around his hand and told them he thought *that* would make a good cover. Ultimately Capricorn hired a company to do a cover none of us liked, and we referred to it as "the chicken and the snake."

35

"All My Friends"

By 1990, Eddie Hinton had moved to Decatur. He was going through some hard times. I'd played in bands with Eddie from the time I was eighteen, and I loved him, but he'd changed some over the years. He was still playing music, though. He knew someone he could get a deal with at Rounder Records, so he wanted to come to my studio and cut some demos. At that time my studio wasn't set up to record a whole band. I told him about the only thing I could use for the drums was a machine, but he said that wasn't a problem, that we could add real drums later.

I loved working with Eddie, but this time it was strange. It wasn't a negative or bad thing, it was just strange. Some days he'd show up at the appointed time ready to play, and some days he'd come to the studio and tell me we would start "in a little while." He'd go sit in a chair and wouldn't say a word, so I'd go on about some other business. After a while, he'd tell me, "Okay, I'm ready now."

He'd get his guitar and play a little bit of the feel he wanted for the drums. I'd program them in the Linn 9000, and he'd ask me to change this or that. Not everyone knows it, but Eddie was a very good drummer as well as singer, guitar player, and writer. When Bill Stewart talks about drummers, he cites Eddie as one of his two biggest influences. When the drum track was finished, Eddie would put a guitar track down, double it, and then do a vocal. He'd get Owen Brown to come in and play bass, and on one song, "Well of Love," he added some live percussion and congas. Sometimes he'd add piano, then he'd get Joe Walk to come in and play organ. I had a B-3 and a Wurlitzer, and while Eddie would sometimes play the piano, he'd always get Joe to come over and play the organ.

We made slow progress with the recording, and then he sent some of the songs to Ron Levy, his contact at Rounder. The label wanted to make a deal for the album, so Ron came down to meet Eddie. While Ron was here, Eddie got Harvey Thompson to put horns on the album. He didn't want trumpets or other horns, just saxophone, so Harvey recorded four or five tracks of sax parts. A lot of the time Harvey would have an idea for the part, but more often, Eddie would have the ideas or would augment Harvey's.

At the time, I had a sixteen track Tascam recorder and matching Tascam board. Although they weren't considered top of the line equipment, the tape we recorded sounded good. Still, Ron didn't want to mix the album here. He was from the Boston area and wanted me to go mix on the equipment up there. I went to Boston and did a marathon mixing session to get the album finished. It was a good studio with a Neve console, but it lacked any effects and the only reverb I could find was a bottom line Lexicon, so I didn't use much reverb on the album. While we were up there, Ron either added or replaced some of the organ parts with some of his own. Eddie wasn't very happy about that and not being involved with the mixing.

Around this time, Scott Boyer came to me and wanted to do an album with all his friends and asked me to record it. Scott and I have worked together many times, and when we started out on this project, I was producing it with him. I really love Scott (and wanted to keep it that way), but since our ideas sometimes conflict, I eventually told him he should produce and I'd engineer.

We had an outstanding rhythm section; Brian Owings was on drums for most of record, and Butch Trucks came in and played on two or three tracks. Butch had been in the 31st of February with Scott and David Brown. Scott also got David to come in and play bass on the whole album, except for a couple of tunes that I played on. He brought in Chalmers Davis, who played keyboards with Scott a lot and had played with us in the Decoys. Joe Walk, who'd also been in the Decoys, came in one day and played keyboards.

The album was essentially Scott Boyer and the Decoys, given most of the players who were on it. The "Amazing" Kelvin Holly played lead guitar; Scott played guitar on all of it, and Chuck Leavell came in and played on quite a few songs. I'm so fortunate to know Chuck. He's played on many of the things I've done over the years, and he's always been my favorite piano player. When I work with Chuck, if I have an idea for a piano part, he knows exactly what I want by the time I say two words. He's easy to work with, has a good attitude, and always delivers a great performance. You can't ask for anyone better. We cut a couple of Scott's old songs, "All My Friends," and "Please Be with Me," some songs we played in the Decoys, and some of Scott's new songs. I enjoyed the project and had a good time.

Since Capricorn didn't seem ready to sign them at the time, Allgood decided to do an album on their own called *Ride the Bee*. When it was finished I took it to Phil. He still thought the band had potential, but he wasn't ready to sign them. Eventually they put it out on their own label, and I think it sold more than twenty thousand. The band continued playing, built up a good following, and were doing well. They'd been popular when they first came to me, but it was nothing like the popularity they had after the record was out; plus, I think they'd been playing some with Panic.

Phil had originally decided not to sign Allgood because Panic was going to be the first band on the label and he wanted to see what happened with them. As time passed and Allgood played a lot, their fan base began to grow and A&M started courting them. There was a guy from A&M records who was just crazy about the band and wanted to sign them, so their manager started negotiating. Phil decided to go hear them again, and at that point he wanted to sign them too. It came down between Phil, who had passed on the band, and A&M, who'd also originally passed on them.

I was there with Phil when he went to see them at the same time the A & R guy from A&M was there too. I'd recorded *Ride the Bee* when the band was running low on money, and I'd told them to come on in and finish the record anyway. I spent a lot of time working with them—a lot more than I was ever paid for—with only a very small royalty rate on album sales because I'd been assured I'd continue working with the band. I believed in them and thought they were going to happen. Phil bid on the band, and I think it was about the same offer made by A&M. I tried to talk with the guys about Capricorn, but they signed with A&M instead.

The band had been talking with other producers, and I thought, "Son of a bitch." I'd done the album for next to nothing, and it helped them get their deal. They'd had what I considered extremely good success for a self-released album, so I asked them why they were considering other producers. I reminded them that when their first album was finished, the band and their manager all promised me they'd definitely use me to produce their next one. Word to the wise: don't *ever* believe that, not even from your mother, because it rarely happens. Bands are notoriously fickle, and the only way you can be certain they're *not* going to use you to produce their next record is if they say they will.

When we were in the process of recording *Ride the Bee*, I asked them to draw up a one- or two-page agreement saying they'd use me to produce their next record. They didn't want to, saying that their lawyer wouldn't let them. It's been my experience that if a band says their lawyer won't let them sign a contract with you, it's a ploy to get out of making a commitment to you. You'll never do the next record because they're the ones who hire the lawyer and make the decisions as to what they will or won't do. What got me personally is that I'd been with them, had gone to see them whenever they were in the area, and I thought we were really tight.

They promised they'd talk with me before they signed to a label, and I tried to get them to go with Phil because it was kind of a home thing. A&M is a great company, but the executives come and go there, and you never know who's going to be running the label. Plus, they're in California and Phil was in Nashville. There was a personal connection with Phil; you knew if you signed with Capricorn that he was going to be there. He was the one to see and be held responsible if something went wrong. Still, they decided to listen to someone else. They ended up using someone out of Nashville to produce the record, but it didn't sell as well as the one I did with them. The guy who signed them left the company about the time their album came out, and the people who took over didn't do the same job of promoting them.

Allgood was just another disappointment in my long history of giving a good, young band my best advice and having them not pay a bit of attention to it. I shouldn't have let it bother me, but it did.

36

Aquarium Rescue Unit

The first time I went to hear Widespread Panic in Athens, Georgia, they were all raving about Col. Bruce Hampton and the Aquarium Rescue Unit (ARU). I'd met Bruce through Duane in 1969 and he was a unique guy, even back then. When I met up with him again in late 1990 he was living in Atlanta and hanging out with some of the guys in Panic. I really like Bruce. He's unique and one of the most likeable guys you'll ever meet, but back in the early years of Capricorn I was afraid to record with him because I didn't know what to expect. Bruce had a reputation somewhere between Groucho Marx and the Dalai Lama. There was really nothing strange about him, but everyone he'd ever met had a wild story to tell about him.

To give you an idea about Bruce, several years ago, he told me the story of the time he and his band had been hired to play at the University of Alabama during a tribute to the late Bear Bryant. It was a really big deal; the governor was there along with a lot of important alumni, and Bruce was supposed to open for Three Dog Night. Bruce said he and the band went out and played the Three Dog Night song "One is the Loneliest Number" over and over for the whole set. It made everyone angry, especially since the tribute was for Bear Bryant, and he and the band got a police escort to the Tuscaloosa city limits with a stern warning to never return or they'd be arrested for impersonating a rock band. Bruce maintains to this day he figured they could have beaten the rap on the technicality that Three Dog Night wasn't really a rock band. This story was later confirmed by one of the men promoting the show that night who told us it was every bit the fiasco Bruce described.

When I started working at Capricorn I got several of my friends a job with the label. Early on, I got my friend Tommy Compton to come to Macon. He hadn't been there long when Phil wanted someone at the studio to do demos with the Hampton Grease Band. Bruce had been signed to a management deal with Phil back in the early Capricorn years, and Phil introduced him to Columbia. On that label he released the Hampton Grease Band *Music to Eat,* which the Colonel brags about being either the worst- or the second-worst selling record in the history of Columbia. Hornsby and I had our reservations about doing the demos, and since Tommy was the new guy, we put the job off on him.

As Bruce tells the story, he was in the studio recording tracks, and between takes wanted to use the telephone in the control room. The first time he walked in, he saw Tommy sitting at the console with the phone receiver at his ear, so he went back out and recorded for maybe fifteen or twenty minutes more. Again, between takes, Bruce went into the control room, but Tommy was still sitting there with the receiver to his ear. The third time he walked in Tommy was still on the phone, so the Colonel asked if he could make a call. Tommy just stuck the receiver out and handed it to Bruce. There was no one on the other end; it was just a dial tone. Evidently Tommy had been afraid to talk to him, so he pretended to be on the phone when Bruce walked in. The Colonel still laughs about that whenever we get together today. I consider the him one of my closest friends.

I found out ARU was playing at the Tip Top club in Huntsville, and I went to see them. I couldn't believe it. Out of all the bands I'd ever heard, with maybe the exception of the original Allman Brothers Band, they were the best. Col. Bruce sang and played various stringed instruments—anything from a mandolin to a steel guitar. Oteil Burbridge was on bass, Jeff Sipe on drums, Jimmy Herring on guitar, and Matt Mundy played mandolin. It was like when I first saw the Mark V, every member in the band was one of the best musicians I'd ever heard.

The first time I got an up-close view of Oteil, I was amazed. He was awe-inspiring and the best bass player I'd ever seen—the taste with which he played, the groove he and Jeff Sipe laid down. It was so moving to hear music with such a good groove to it that it was hard not to smile and feel good. During a break I talked with Bruce for a while, and then I went over and started talking to Oteil. Bruce had told him who I was, and we hit it off right away. I mentioned I was doing some demos with Tommy Talton and some of the guys from Cowboy from the old Capricorn Records. I told him I'd been playing bass on some of the songs and that I'd really like for him to play on a couple of tracks. I'd taken the night off to listen to the band, but I had recordings scheduled for the next few days. He said, "Okay, I'll just go back with you." Next thing I knew, he was in the car with me and we were heading to Decatur.

I thought it was great. I'd just seen one of the best bass players ever, and he agreed to play on some of the things I was recording. On those sessions, we cut "All Roads Lead back Home," one of Tommy's songs, and a song Jim Bickerstaff had written, "Table of the Lord." The construction of "Table of the Lord" lends itself to a basic bass part, but Oteil made it groove like I never thought possible.

I'd expected Oteil to be great when I went over to see the band because everyone had been talking about him, but when I watched Sipe play, I was blown away. I couldn't think of a better drummer to play with Oteil. He was outstanding technically, and the groove he had was perfect. Jeff has a way of playing the right amount and not overplaying. As good a jazz and rock musician both of them are, they can play on a country song and sound just as relaxed with it. I got Jeff and Oteil to play on a country song I was demo'ing, and they sounded like everyone else—only better.

Until I heard Matt Mundy, I hadn't been a huge fan of the mandolin. I thought it was a different voice—a little more midrange than most guitars—but when it says something, it cuts through the mix and is a neat embellishment to the song. Matt was the best mandolin player I'd ever heard and probably ever will.

Jimmy Herring is such an amazing guitar player that, like Oteil, I kind of run out of adjectives to describe him. He has all the technique of Steve Morse but with more soul. That's what the Colonel did; he took these great jazz musicians and insisted they play with feeling, not just technique. He brings out the best in the musicians he plays with, and with him leading the band (or "de-leading" as he would say), they were all awesome. And there's not much more about the Col.'s playing that hasn't already been written all over the world.

I called Phil and told him I'd never heard anything like it and said, "Let's do some demos with them." He told me he had a demo they'd done in Atlanta, and I asked him to make a copy and send it to me. When I listened to the demo, though, it wasn't anything like how I remembered the band sounding live. I didn't know what was wrong, but I asked Phil to let me do demos of them. After a while, he relented and gave me a small budget to work with them at my place. The band came in, and it was what I heard live. I was more excited with the band than I'd been with anyone since the Brothers.

While we were recording the demos, Phil called and asked if we had any hits. I replied I didn't know if there were any hits, but it was the best band I'd ever heard. He asked me to send him the demos when we were finished, and after he heard the tape, he signed the band. He asked me what we were going to do with them. When he told me later he wanted me to record Widespread Panic in Athens at the Georgia Theatre, I suggested we get them to open for Panic and record ARU live. It wasn't going to cost much more, maybe just for tape and a few extra hours; it wouldn't be that long a show anyway. So Phil made arrangements for them to play the shows with Panic.

I used to go up to Phil's office in Nashville a lot, and we'd have meetings and talk about bands like we did in the old days. I don't think I knew about Billy Bob Thornton before then, but Phil was managing him and had been telling me some of the movies he was involved with. I was interested in meeting him. When I met Billy Bob, he was very nice to me and knew all about the records I'd done. I think he's one of the finest actors of our time, a great writer, the whole package, and I was surprised and pleased that he knew who I was. Phil wanted to film the ARU-Widespread Panic concert in Athens. I got to work with Billy Bob when Phil had asked him to direct a long form video with Panic, featuring four or five live songs interspersed with band interviews. It was the first film Billy Bob had directed.

Billy Bob was in Athens for three or four days filming Panic. During the day he did interviews with the band and filmed them out in public and talking among themselves, and then he filmed the shows while I recorded the audio. For the recording we brought in the New York Record Plant truck with Kooster McCallister and Paul Prestapino. Kooster was the recording engineer and Paul was the technical engineer; I'd done a lot of work with them over the years on mostly live recordings.

Both ARU and Panic were amazing the first two nights. The next day, Billy Bob wanted to film an interview with me about Capricorn in the old days and Capricorn in the new days. I thought at first he was kidding, but he seemed really interested. I agreed and talked about what we were doing with Panic and the new Capricorn. The interview seemed like it lasted for three hours, but it was probably only about ten minutes, and Billy Bob made it easy. I made my film debut that day with Billy Bob Thornton directing.

The last night of the show was open to the public and was unbelievably packed. At one point we had a problem with the mic cable and sent someone to see what was wrong. It took the guy longer to get to where the problem was than it should have. When he came back he told us, "I was sloshing through urine and other human excrement." I guess it was so crowded people couldn't get to where they needed to go—literally.

I brought the tapes back to my studio in Decatur to mix the audio for the video and the ARU album. We had plenty for a CD, and I ended up also using one of the demos we'd cut at my studio, "Planet Earth." I really liked the take of that song. In fact, there are three more great songs and great takes of ARU we recorded at my place that were never used.

Except for "Planet Earth," the album is all live. Jimmy Herring played very well and had as good a guitar tone as anyone could ask for, but at the end of the night he was so depressed about his performance he didn't even want to hear it. I don't think he heard the album until it came out, and then he was pleasantly surprised. Jimmy's an incredible guitar player, but he never thinks he's good enough. Sometimes that can be a good thing for a guitar player; some of the great ones can get very jaded or full of themselves. I've been fortunate not to have worked with the jaded or arrogant ones. Jimmy, like Duane and Dickey, was the nicest, sweetest guy in the world.

Phil thought the album was exciting. He wasn't a musician and didn't know how to play an instrument, but he could hear things that would surprise me. I've been accused of having excellent hearing, but back in Macon, I'd take things to Phil and he'd remark on some subtlety in the mix that personally I didn't think could be perceived by anyone who didn't mix records. I was blown away.

Phil got one of the local photographers to do the front cover of the album, and the photography couldn't have been better for a band named the "Aquarium Rescue Unit." We thought it was going to win a Grammy for best album cover and hoped it would for the music, but the album only sold modestly. Maybe people weren't ready for it. When the record was first released, it was sent out to reviewers in various publications; one of the reviewers in *Stereo Review* wrote, "This is the best live album ever made." I couldn't believe it. It was an amazing review, and the other reviews were good too. It's still an excellent album.

I met Steve Morse at the Capricorn office in Nashville when Phil signed him for an album with the Dixie Dregs, but I already knew who he was. I used to pick up an issue of *Guitar Player*, and he was the one voted Best Guitar Player in the World, or whatever, every year for so many years that they quit giving the award to him and barred him from winning to give the other guitar players a chance.

I talked to Steve about working on the album, but he already had it all planned out. He'd been involved in the production of most of the Dixie Dregs albums and had this one down pat as to what he wanted to do. He didn't want a producer, but it was finally decided I'd be the executive producer and would supervise the recording. It was a live album, and Steve wanted to do it in Atlanta; we got Kooster to come down with the truck and got everything set up. The band was Steve, Rod Morgenstein, Dave LaRue, Allen Sloan, and T Lavitz. When I worked with Panic on the first album, T Lavitz was the keyboard player. He'd been one of the early members of the Dixie Dregs and was back with them for the album.

I know Steve didn't want me involved—well, not necessarily me personally, but any producer—and the advance I got wasn't what I was used to getting. Still, I wanted to do it because I admired the band and wanted to work with them. Steve was concerned about the recording and came out to the truck worried about how much tape we were using. I had to order a large quantity of tape just to have enough for the recording because we'd gone from 15 ips with Dolby SR to 30 ips.

We recorded the show, and Jim Bickerstaff assisted me with the engineering. The Dixie Dregs played great, but I was used to getting sound levels on ARU and Steve's band was considerably louder. The louder things get, the more problematic it is to get the type sound you want. But we had everything mic'd up and a few safeties built in, and I think the album turned out well. The band hadn't played in Atlanta for a while, and the show was sold out to an enthusiastic crowd. Phil and Peggy were there, as was Don Schmitzerle, from the old Capricorn days.

Steve wanted me to go to his house in Florida to mix; he had a nice house in a community with its own landing strip. Steve was a pilot, and I thought it was pretty neat to live by his own landing strip. When I was there, he showed me his plane that was parked behind his house.

Steve had a studio set up in his garage with a 24-track Studer A-80 and an adequate console. I would have preferred a different console, but after we set up it worked better than I thought it would.

It was an interesting experience. He had about three or four sets of speakers, and he'd listen to a mix on each set before he made a decision. I took the KRK 703 speakers I bought in '91 that I really liked. Steve Tillisch, one of the engineers from Macon, was one of the hot shots in Nashville at that point, and he'd recommended them. I'd used his set when we were working on the first Panic album at Emerald, and Steve Morse hated them. He said they sounded like the bass was all screwed up. I admit they were a little tubby, but my mixes sound good on them.

When we were working, Steve would go into the house and do whatever he did during the day. I'd mix to a point where I almost got it finished or wanted to ask him a question, and he'd come out and help me. I went to Steve's house every day and mix until he was happy. Then we'd take breaks, I'd play stuff for him, and then go back to the hotel. It was a three- or four-day process, but I got the record mixed.

The album, *Bring 'Em Back Alive*, was nominated for a Grammy, but it didn't win. Still, I got to meet new people on the project and we'd taken a trip to Florida. How can you be unhappy in Florida?

37

Everyday

Widespread Panic's second album for Capricorn, *Everyday*, started at my studio in Decatur when the band did demos of most of the songs we ended up cutting on the album. At the time, I encouraged the band to write songs as a group because they were so good at jamming. I figured Todd could start a beat, and everyone would take it from there. The more a band does that, the easier it is to start a groove, have everyone join in with changes, and then write lyrics around it. That idea worked with mixed success for the band and the song "Better Off" came out of it, but it was more tedious than I expected and we only tried it once.

To fit with their road schedule, we had a certain time frame in January to start recording the album, so we started looking at studios again in Nashville. I'd been to Treasure Isle once before and knew they had a good sounding room with a Trident console and either Sony or MCI tape machines, so I booked time to record. The studio was nice, but the first thing I noticed when I walked in was the no smoking sign. I think just about everyone in the band smoked except for T Lavitz, and I should have seen it as an omen. The vibe at Treasure Isle wasn't as good as it had been at Emerald and Masterfonics, and we had several minor problems from the beginning.

T was still playing keyboards with the band, and there were a few musical differences between him and Mikey, who often had other opinions about things. Sometimes Mikey's idea was *technically* wrong but sounded *musically* right; therefore, I looked at it as right.

T and Wayne Sawyer, a member of Panic's road crew, were constantly picking at each other, most of it teasing. One night, though, T must have taken some of it seriously because after supper break, Wayne told us he and T had been having an argument in the car. T had told him to stop the car and let him out. Wayne said he'd been in the middle of an overpass, and since no one was behind him, he stopped and T got out. We'd been driving over that same overpass returning from dinner and had passed T walking along the road in the dark. I said something like, "that looks like T Lavitz," but because we didn't expect him to be out walking, we drove on by. Finally T made it back to the studio.

For various reasons, nothing seemed to happen right during those sessions. After a week of recording, we'd gotten enough for an album, and I figured we'd come to my place and do overdubs. It was considerably less expensive, and by then I had a Quad-8 console and a 24-track Otari MX-80 machine that was compatible with Treasure Isle.

We came back here and got in a couple days of overdubbing in before Phil called and said he wanted to meet with us, so John Bell, Mikey, Ann and I drove up to Nashville. Phil took us out to eat and came right out and said he didn't like the album and didn't want us to work on it any more. He wanted to re-think the project and return to it when the band came off the road. It shocked everyone, especially me, because things were going well with the overdubs, and the album was really shaping up.

The problem was that Phil had gotten some rough mixes before I was ready to send them to him. I was going to wait until we'd overdubbed for a week or so at my place before I sent him the roughs. After tracking is done I'll do roughs and gear them towards certain people. In this case, I'd geared them more for T because he wanted to work on his parts and re-do some of them. I'd kept the piano up in the mix so he could hear what he'd played and think about what he wanted to work on.

G. Scott Walden had come by Treasure Isle and insisted on getting a copy of what we were doing, so someone gave him a tape of the mixes. I had no intention of sending them to Phil and I never meant for him to hear them. I wanted to give him something he'd be impressed with when he heard it because there's no second chance for a first impression. I believed in what we were doing, and I knew some of the tracks were really good. Based on those mixes, though, Phil hadn't liked what he heard and wanted to stop the album, so we stopped. I was very surprised because this was one of the very few times that had ever happened with Phil. Since that was all the time Panic had for recording, they went on the road and we didn't get back to the album until November.

Phil wasn't certain T was a right fit for the band, and I think T was probably unhappy playing with them. All of the guys in Panic were living in the South, and even the ones who weren't born here had a Southern way of doing things. They took chances and did things that worked out for them; that's what makes them great. They weren't afraid to stretch their music, and they weren't afraid to do something people might not like. T is a fantastic player, but he was more regimented in the way he did things and needed more of a plan. Sometimes there wasn't a plan—things just *happened* with Panic. I loved it, but I don't think T was comfortable in that situation.

T was a strict vegetarian, and that caused problems for him in the South. One time when we'd all gone to Mom's Kitchen, a soul food restaurant in Athens, he wanted to know what they had that he could eat. Usually you'd think a salad would be vegetarian, but most of everything served was seasoned with pork, including the vegetables, so T ended up having a glass of iced tea while the rest of us ate lunch.

T was also used to a different way of doing things. Shortly before filming the live recording we did with Panic at the Georgia Theatre, T came in, looked around and asked J. B. and me where he'd find make up and wardrobe. We just looked at him—of course, there wasn't any make up or wardrobe. Then there was the time when we were mixing *Mom's Kitchen* at Masterfonics. We were taking a break sitting at one of the tables discussing the gig that evening when T looked over at John and said, "What are you going to wear tonight?" John was eating, and he looked down at his t-shirt and replied, "I haven't spilled anything on this shirt; I think I'll wear this one." T just threw his hands up in the air. He was a great guy, and I liked him a lot, but T really didn't fit in with the band.

Capricorn needed the album for the first of the next year, so we got ready to record again in November, which was the next time Panic was available. By then T had moved on and John (JoJo) Herman was playing with them. When the band and I first talked about possible keyboard players to replace T, I mentioned JoJo because I'd worked with him once or twice doing overdubs on the Allgood album. He was a good keyboard player and had the same mindset as Panic.

The question was where to cut the album. Their first album had been recorded at several different studios. Treasure Isle didn't work for us, so we didn't want to go back there. Plus, the studios in Nashville were still booked solid. The band wanted to look at Ardent in Memphis, but I suggested they also go look at Muscle Shoals Sound and see what they thought because it was an incredible place to record.

The studio was in an old armory building right on the river in Sheffield and had two back to back mirror image studios with Neve consoles and Studer machines and a very nice room for recording. There wasn't much more you could ask for if you were a recording engineer; it was the zenith of great things a studio could have—including a wonderful selection of mics, both new and old. There was a giant recreation room, a big kitchen, and was an all around comfortable place with a good vibe. Roger Hawkins and David Hood were the studio managers at the time, and they were both available if needed.

We went over and everyone loved the building and location. They looked around, and I showed them the room. They liked it but decided we'd go and look at some other studios before making a decision. It's funny how you remember certain things. The night after we looked at Muscle Shoals Sound, we were hungry and couldn't find any where to eat because J. B. was doing a vegetarian thing. We ended up at Wendy's. J. B. ordered a hamburger without the meat. Essentially, he ended up with a lettuce and tomato sandwich which, I thought was funny but proved you can get by if you need to.

After Muscle Shoals, we drove up to Memphis to look at Ardent. They had a nice selection of gear there, nice consoles and decent size recording rooms, but it was very busy and a little chaotic with things going on in each room and people moving fast. The band and I preferred Muscle Shoals Sound where Panic would be the only band recording and where we'd have a lot of privacy. The studio could be rented by the day, and we would have unlimited use of the place. It seemed like a better choice for us, so we went to Muscle Shoals, set up, and recorded.

By the time we started the second recording of the album, the budget was getting tighter. The songs we'd recorded at Treasure Isle were on 24-track 2-inch tape, which was expensive, and we'd spent two thousand dollars on tape. The record company didn't want to pay for any more tape and wanted me to go over what we'd recorded. I didn't want to do that without having a safety, so I backed it up to a Sony digital 48-track.

We went into studio A, the bigger of the recording rooms that was generally used for tracking, and everything went much better. We had a B-3, a great Wurlitzer piano, and a nine-foot grand piano. JoJo was quite content, and the room sounded good. Mikey and his amp were in one booth, and Todd and the drums were in the middle booth. I thought we got a pretty good drum sound and the guitars had a good tone to them. We rented a cue system like we'd had at Emerald in Nashville so each of the guys could dial it to have a stereo mix on one fader, and each player could turn his part up. The band had been playing all the songs live; when bands do that, the songs tighten up and the parts are refined. The guys took to the place and it was great.

As soon as we finished the tracking and overdubs, everyone took a few days off and went home while I started mixing in studio B. The room had the same basic console as studio A—an AD 88 Neve and a Studer machine with a very early version of flying faders on the console. I didn't use any of the later versions, but I understand they weren't a whole lot better than that one. They were often referred to as the "fighting faders" and kind of had a mind of their own as to where they wanted to go.

We'd been working over Thanksgiving, so Ann cooked dinner for everyone in Decatur and brought it over to the studio, and we all celebrated Thanksgiving together. I thought we might end up celebrating Christmas over there too, but I finished mixing on Christmas Eve day. I was really happy with the work and thought the mixes sounded good. Phil and all the folks at Capricorn seemed as excited about the second recording of the album as they'd been put off by the first.

38

Mirrors of Embarrassment

About a year and a half after the first album came out, Phil wanted to do another record with the Aquarium Rescue Unit. Even though the first one hadn't been a big seller, there'd been a lot of press and there was still excitement about the band. Phil liked the first album because of the publicity it generated, but he stressed the need for something the company could push to radio more easily for the next one. He wanted me to do some more demos with the band before we cut the second album, so I went over to Ricky Keller's studio in Atlanta and met up with the rest of the guys.

We got together to go over some songs, but they didn't have any with a hook that might get it on the radio. After really working at it, we ended up with one or two we thought might have some possibilities. We spent a day or so cutting some of the band's tunes, including "Too Many Guitars," which I really liked a lot and eventually recorded for the album. We cut the best demos we could at that time, and then I did mixes of the songs. That was the first time I ever used an ADAT recording system, which, at the time, was the big rage I'd been reading about in all the magazines.

ADAT recorders had just come out, and I'd borrowed one from the music store in Decatur to take over to Atlanta so I could decide if I wanted to go to that format. It was a single recorder with eight tracks that used SVHS tapes and sounded better to me than the digital machine I'd tried at Emerald on Panic's first album. It turned out I really liked the recorder and eventually went to the ADAT format and used it in my studio for several years.

Phil still wasn't totally sold on the project, but I kept telling him, "The band is so good, let's do the album." He finally gave the go ahead to record another album, and I went to Atlanta a second time to look at studios. Because Ricky's place was more of a smaller demo studio and I wanted to go high end for the recording, the band and I talked about some other places to record. Atlanta's known for having some great studios; I looked at a few of them, but the band wanted me to check out Bobby Brown's studio, conveniently located right next door to Ricky Keller's.

There were a lot of rap artists around when I went to look at the studio, and I was a little hesitant because I never liked rap music. They were nice enough, but the studio was set up more to record musicians in the control room with a lot of synths and drum machines. They had a huge room, but it wasn't used very much because there wasn't a lot of live music being played. I wasn't very comfortable.

The control room in studio A was almost too big. There are only a few control rooms I've ever seen I could say that about, but it was gigantic. About the only time the live room was used was maybe for some vocals or for musicians to record something to loop, but it really wasn't set up to record a band. Studio B was the smaller of the two and looked great. It had a medium size control room with an SSL console and was very opulent. What got me was the Neve 88 console over in a corner on its back they were selling for about $50,000, which was an unbelievably low price. Now it's a $200,000 or $300,000 console because they don't make them like that anymore. I didn't have the money to buy it at that time, but I've wished a thousand times I had.

I used studio B, and it took a couple of tries before we got the drums set up where they would work. The room was very large too, in fact it was so bright we found it impractical to record out there until we made walls for isolation out of the huge baffles they had around the place.

Everybody in the studio had headphones, and except for Jimmy, most of the musicians had eye contact with each other, which was what I wanted. Jimmy wanted to hear his amp directly, and even in that big room, the amp was so loud it was impractical to record without isolating it. To have any isolation on him at all someone suggested we put his amp in the attic, and I mean a real attic, so Jimmy went up there with his amp and everyone else was on the main floor where they could all see each other except for Jimmy. To be honest with you I never checked out the attic, but it couldn't have been comfortable. ARU is probably the best band I ever heard and they managed to pull it off in such strange quarters.

The really uncomfortable thing about the studio was the overall vibe. The first time I experienced a form of discrimination was when we drove through Texas in the HourGlass and were chased by some rednecks because we had long hair. At Bobby Brown's studio we seemed to experience a form of reverse racism. Bobby Brown and the whole staff were all black, which was cool, but all of us with the band would go out for supper. When we returned, the guy at the front door wouldn't let us in. We'd be standing out there knocking and trying to get in, and he'd just look at us, then look the other way and go back to reading his book. Eventually, we'd either keep knocking and he'd let us in, or we'd go around to another more inconvenient entrance. It really made me angry. Oteil is black, but he was with a bunch of white people, and he couldn't get in because he was with us. It was like they put up with us at the studio and took the money, but they'd just as soon the white boys would leave.

The opening track, "No Egos under Water," is my favorite one on the album. Matt Mundy's girlfriend, Missy, was incredibly smart, but she had a real country accent. It used to tickle us because she'd talk about these deep and profound ideas, and she did it with this heavy Southern twang. We'd been working late hours and, one morning after a long night, Bruce had this poem he wanted spoken on the album. It was just a short, one-line poem, but it seemed to have a lot of significance for him. We thought it would be a good idea for Missy to say it on the record. That's where Bruce came up with the title *Mirrors of Embarrassment* for the record. "A stained soul cringes at the small details in the mirrors of embarrassment" opens the album followed by "No Egos under Water."

It was inspiring every day to work with those guys. Everyone was such a master of their instruments that they didn't know how to sound bad. One of the secrets most of the great players know is that you have to listen to each other. You have to play off them and react to what they're doing and see that they listen to you when you do your stuff. That's what these guys did. I don't think there was a better group of musicians anywhere on earth at that time.

We recorded for about a week and got plenty of tracks for the album, as well as some good jams. We recorded one jam that was eventually named "The Disease." The whole band started out jamming together, but after a while, various ones would wander out and then return, or maybe not return at all. This went on for about thirty or forty minutes until it ended up with just Bruce sitting in a chair outside the control room playing his guitar and "singing" in his native language of Jupiter. It was amazing. The record company talked about doing a double album with one CD of the songs we'd recorded and this jam as the other disc. Eventually Phil decided against it, but I've still got the tape. It was insane and the words were just gibberish, but it was incredible.

Over all, the recording was a success. Chuck Leavell came in to overdub, and we sent a tape to New York for John Popper to play on "I Lost My Mule in Texas." I brought the tapes back to my studio and mixed them at my place.

When we were in Atlanta the first time doing the demos, Ann and I stayed at the Castlegate hotel. It seemed like a nice place, and we had reservations for the three nights we'd be staying there. Someone at the front desk screwed up the reservation, though, and they threw us out a day early. They wouldn't even try to find us another room, and Oteil ended up giving us his room at another hotel while he stayed with friends. When we went back to record the album, we stayed at the Castlegate again because it was close to the studio and we got a good deal on the rooms.

When we checked in, we were given a room on the ground floor way in the back. It was pretty deserted. The first night we were there someone tried to break into the room, but we didn't know it until the morning. When we woke up, the room was ice cold, and we discovered a broken window. We must have walked in right after the window was broken and scared them away. Immediately got a room on the second floor that no one could access. In fact, during the week, we had the floor completely to ourselves. It was like *The Shining*, Atlanta version. The hotel didn't have a large clientele on weekdays, so they turned off the hot water. On the weekends—because of football—the place was packed, and they turned it back on. I raised hell every day because I had to shave in cold water, but it never did any good.

Each day for lunch we ate at the Piccadilly, and then at night, after the session, we'd go to whatever restaurant Bruce picked out. Bruce says he used to have a job as a tour guide in Atlanta and knew all the places to go for good food. Usually, wherever we were, the waitress would walk up and Bruce would correctly guess her birthday. She'd freak out, and we'd get great service. It's pretty amazing how he can do that.

One night at the studio, Bruce came in and said he'd done an interview that was going to be on television. We turned on the T.V. and watched Bruce's interview. During the interview, the host announced that Carl Sagan, the astronomer, was going to be the next guest. Bruce then started describing how he and Carl had been in a Texas steel cage wrestling tag team death match. Bruce was going on and on like he usually does when a crawl started at the bottom of the screen. It read: "This man doesn't know what he's talking about" and "This never happened" and similar disclaimers. It was one of the best things I've ever seen on television.

Bruce always gave entertaining interviews. After the album was finished, a release party was held in Nashville. G. Scott Walden, Phil's nephew, had been taking Bruce around to do radio interviews to promote the party and the album. G. Scott walked up to us outside the club looking shocked, shaking his head, and saying Bruce had ruined the whole interview. Distraught, he explained how Bruce had told everyone to go to the release party and get the free patio furniture they were giving out to the first hundred people who showed up. G. Scott had no idea that was just a normal interview for Bruce.

39

Back Door Records

Phil was considering a number of artists, but there was only room for a finite number of them on Capricorn. A lot of times we'd do demos on some artist or band, and while it would be a close call as to whether they'd make it on the label, ultimately Phil would decide. There were times he'd turn down a band or artist I thought had potential. A couple of them were the band Bloodkin and artist Jerry Joseph. I met Jerry in Nashville when Ann and I had gone to meet with Phil. Phil was listening to some of Jerry's independently recorded records and suggested I do some demos with him. I listened to Jerry's voice and thought he was a great singer and talented songwriter.

I put together what I consider to be an ideal band including Brian Owings; Kelvin Holly, who played some outstanding guitar parts; Chalmers Davis; and Oteil Burbridge. Jerry came down to my studio for the recording and had some amazing songs that I listen to even now. He's is a little edgier than most I've worked with, but I thought those demos were some of the best things I'd ever cut. I also did demos for Phil with Danny Hutchins and his band Bloodkin. I liked the band and Danny's writing. Both Bloodkin and Jerry were really good, but they didn't fit into Phil's plans for Capricorn. I thought if I had my own label I'd want to sign them.

I called Sam Lanier, Widespread Panic's manager, to ask if he might be interested in starting a label with me, or if not, if he had any suggestions. He told me it wasn't anything he wanted to do, but John Bell might be interested in owning part of a record company. When I talked with J. B., he wanted to talk about it further, so he and his wife, Laura, rented a nice house at Orange Beach. Ann and I joined them down there to discuss the possibilities of a venture. I took them a brief prospectus of what we could do and how it would work. Shortly thereafter, they decided they wanted to do it, so John and Laura, Ann and I formed Back Door Records.

I think one of the reasons John wanted to start a label was to work with Bloodkin. John was a fan of the band, and Panic had recorded one of Danny Hutchens's songs, "Makes Sense to Me" on *Mom's Kitchen*. John was interested in giving the band a hand up, so Bloodkin was the first band signed to the Back Door Records label.

Danny came over to my studio with the rest of the band (Eric Carter, Chris Barrineau, and Jack Dawson), and we cut tracks for the album and did the overdubs. The guys in Panic played on some of the tracks, and it was a good album featuring Danny and Eric's songs. The album, *Good Luck Charm*, was the first release on the label, and John had CDs and cassettes of the album and posters and other merchandise for the band to sell at their gigs.

John hired Jen Bryant, a girl I'd met through contacts over in Muscle Shoals. She had gone through the music program at the University of North Alabama, to make calls and try to get the record placed. We got an 800 number and tried to hook up with the college kids because they were the ones who seemed to be buying Panic's records. We had moderate success in getting it played on college radio, but the album sales were modest.

Part of the problem was that Bloodkin could never quite get their live act together. The band would open for Panic when they played in the area; they could have ended up with an opening spot with them on their shows that would have broken the band wide open, but it never happened. When Bloodkin recorded the album they had a relatively new drummer who left the band after the album was finished. Then it was one thing after another that kept the band from going on the road to promote the album. When I record an album with someone now, I want to know if I invest my time in working with them that they're willing to go on the road, to leave their home town, their home state, and their comfort zone to build up a following.

The second release on Back Door records was *Love and Happiness* with Jerry Joseph. John already knew Jerry from some gigs they'd played together with Panic. I suggested doing a record with him, but I had trouble getting everyone lined up to do the album because all the musicians I wanted to use were busy. I ended up using a drum machine on some of the songs then had the musicians to come in and overdub on the tracks. It took a while to finish because in the middle of recording Jerry had to take some time off, but he came back afterward and we got the record finished.

Those two albums were the beginning and the end of Back Door Records. It was sad because I thought we had a couple of pretty good records, but we couldn't get distribution for the albums and couldn't figure out a way to sell them. I was always in the production side of records and knew how to do the recording, how to do the budgets, and come out with a good record, but when it came to selling them, I just didn't know that end of the business. So nothing happened with the company like we'd hoped. After a long period of inactivity, we got a letter from John and Laura wanting to dissolve the partnership.

I didn't give up on the idea of what I'd originally envisioned for a record company, and eventually Ann and I worked an indie deal with Microwave Dave Gallaher. I think it was Scott who'd first run into Dave and given him my number. I already knew of him and had listened to his blues show on the radio, so when Dave called and wanted to know if I'd talk to him I told him I said "sure." Dave is very knowledgeable about music and is an excellent guitar player, and he wanted to do a record. We talked about how to get the money to do it. He said he had some feelers out with Ice House Records, a blues label in Memphis, and they agreed to put up a pittance if we'd do an album. It wasn't enough to really even cover my costs, but I liked Dave and wanted to do it because he was playing all over the country and needed a record out.

We cut *Goodnight Dear*, and Dave ended up selling a good many copies of the record. It was played and sold well both here and in France. Dave even had a modest hit over there with a cover of Bo Diddley's "Roadrunner" when the French soccer team, the Soccer Princes, used it for their rally song. For a while, we were big in France.

When it came time to do a second album with Dave, he didn't especially want to do another one for Ice House. Despite the success of the first album, I don't think Ice House was interested in doing a second one with him. Even though Back Door Records hadn't worked out, I still believed the idea of a record company had merit, so Dave, Ann, and I struck a deal to cut the album and split the profits. We ended up doing Dave's second record on the Duck Tape Music label. At that time, if you didn't spend much making a record, you could sell a few and most of it would be profit. The way it was set up, Dave paid all the out of pocket expenses, and I furnished the studio and my services. Dave was on the road a lot and sold CDs from the stage. Once the manufacturing expense was recouped, we split the profits. It was a deal that worked out to be successful, giving me hope that my ideas for a partnership with an artist could actually work.

40

Rendezvous with the Blues

Around the end of August 1994 I got a call from Mark Harrelson, a friend of mine who's one of the owners of Boutwell studio in Birmingham, Alabama. He's connected with the local music community down there and told me about the Birmingham Jam. Birmingham Jam is a yearly event held at Sloss Furnace, an old steel mill that had been converted to an outdoor concert venue. Mark was responsible for putting together a tribute to Southern rock/soul, and he wanted to get Jimmy Hall and Dan Penn to play and Gregg to headline the show. I thought it sounded like a good idea, and when he asked me to help him get the band together and be the music director, I readily accepted. Mark knew how to contact Jimmy and Gregg, and I told him how to get in touch with Dan.

A few months earlier, Dan had called to tell me he was going to do an album and wanted me involved in the record. I told him to tell me what he wanted and I'd do it, that I'd be there even if he didn't want me, and he asked me to engineer. Dan had the very best of everybody I'd ever worked with—or even known—playing on the album: David Briggs, Roger Hawkins, David Hood, Jerry Carrigan, Reggie Young, Jimmy Johnson, Spooner Oldham, Bobby Emmons, Doug Moffet, Harvey Thompson, Wayne Jackson, Charles Rose, Carson Whitsett, Ava Aldridge, Cindy Richards-Walker, Lenny Leblanc, Buzz Cason, George Soule, and Gary Nicholson. Delbert McClinton blew in and played harp on "Memphis Women and Fried Chicken." That song just rocked. I could spend my life doing Dan's records, and I was looking forward to working with him again at the Birmingham Jam.

Mark was the hero of the whole thing because he put it together and got everyone lined up. He really had to jump through hoops to get Gregg to commit to the gig. He had to explain everything (what the Jam was going to be and who would be involved), first to Gregg and then to his people. Eventually Gregg agreed to do a ninety-minute set. Mark and

I decided to put together a southern R&B band with horns, percussion, the whole thing, to back up Gregg. We included Dan and Spooner as part of the band. My charge as music director was to put the band together. Gregg and I discussed various possibilities, and I told him I wanted to get some of the people for the gig who'd played on *Laid Back*.

I got Bill Stewart to play drums, Count M'Butu for percussion, Scott Boyer on electric and acoustic guitar, Kelvin Holly on lead guitar, and Jack Pearson, a player I'd heard of before who played with Gregg, also on lead guitar. David Hood played bass most of the time, and I played on some of the songs. Topper Price played harmonica, and we had five horns with Jim Horn as leader of the section. Clayton Ivey was there and for most of the night played Wurlitzer piano, and Spooner and Gregg played organ. At one point during the show, Gregg and Spooner were sitting on the stool together playing the same organ. We also had a Yamaha keyboard that simulated a grand piano.

We learned ten to fifteen of Dan and Spooner's songs and about twenty-five of Gregg's. Jimmy had his own four-piece band with him and also played with the band backing Gregg. The idea was to have Jimmy do a set with his band, then Dan and Spooner do a set with the band I put together, and then Gregg would come out for the rest of the show. We called ourselves the Alabama All-Stars, and it was an incredible band.

We rehearsed at the Black Arts Cultural Center in Birmingham, which was an excellent venue with a nice stage and p.a. Mark recorded some of the rehearsal, and some of it was filmed. Earl Hicks, an assistant who had worked with me in my studio, was there and helped with everything from mixing the p.a. to setting up mics. Whatever needed to be done, he did it. Earl was a hard worker and probably got more than he bargained for when he started working with me. It was a very busy time when he first came into the studio, and he didn't have a day off until about six weeks later. Earl later went on to work with the Drive-by Truckers.

At the rehearsals, it was my responsibility to call everyone to order and to get everything started, which was a big undertaking. It's like herding cats when you've got that many people. Some people are very responsible and at their positions when they're supposed to be, and some you have to chase down. Most of the musicians were there right on time, but Gregg came in late the first night, said hello to everyone, listened for a minute or two, and left. Fortunately Scott was there; he's the world's greatest stunt singer and was able to sing a guide vocal so we could rehearse Gregg's set. We worked up songs from *Laid Back*, songs we'd done in the HourGlass, plus a couple of Allman Brothers tunes. We rehearsed for three days, and overall everything went well. I think Gregg was there for one or two of the rehearsals, and when he was, it was exciting.

As director of the band I was onstage the night of the show, trying to keep things going even when I wasn't playing. I recall the monitors were the most screwed up of any place I'd ever been. The guy running the p.a. didn't want to turn them up because he was afraid he might blow the speakers, and they were down so low you couldn't hear them. People were putting their heads in the speakers to see if they were even working at all, but you make do with what you have.

The Jam was great. Gregg was a big draw in Birmingham, and there was a large crowd. The Alabama All-Stars was a band that had never played a gig together before, and that brought people in. Jimmy played, and then Dan's set went really well. I was onstage playing guitar for his performance, and it was one of the highlights of the whole show for me. It looked like everything was going smoothly; everyone was in a good mood, and Dan and Spooner's set was quite soulful.

When we got through with their part of the show, I announced there was going to be a short break and then Gregg's set would begin. I told everyone it would only be five or ten minutes and to stay close because when Gregg was ready to go on, we needed the musicians to be there. During the break Gregg was pacing. I could tell he was about ready, so the band went ahead up on stage. The set list started out with a song we used to do in the HourGlass, one of Otis's tunes, "Can't Turn You Loose." It is a dynamite horn song, but when Gregg walked on and started counting off the song, I looked over and Dennis Taylor was the only sax player on stage ready to go.

I just freaked. The stage was up high, and I hurried down the ladder and across the grounds into the trailer that was being used as the green room and asked where the horn players had gone. Someone told me they'd to get something to eat…and it flew all over me because I'd told everyone to stay close. The horn players had been on stage with everyone else when I made the announcement.

I walked out and saw the players sauntering back, carrying their food. Even after the song started, they were lollygagging around when they were supposed to be on stage. I was so pissed I screamed at them. I don't think very many people have seen me get really mad or curse at someone in public—because I just don't do that—but this was an exception. Dan said it kind of scared him, and he told me later he didn't know what to think. I normally don't behave that way, but I couldn't believe all this work had gone into the show and they'd just wandered off. Dennis played his part, but it was a big powerful horn song and sounded kind of silly with just the one horn. I'll always remember him and appreciate his being there and ready to play.

Jim Horn is a great bari sax and alto player. When I was doing an album with Gregg a year or so later, I hired him to go to Muscle Shoals to play horns. He'd kind of burned it with me the night of the Jam, but I hired him because Gregg wanted to use him on the album. He showed up late again.

Everyone played their set, and we did some jamming towards the end of the show when the crowd wanted us to keep going. Dan did some songs he'd written and some he and Spooner had written that had been made famous by other people, like Aretha. I wasn't originally planning to play for Gregg's set, but when the jam part came, I knew some of the songs David Hood hadn't played before and played bass on them. The Jam was a lot of work with a couple of mishaps, but it was a wonderful night overall.

While I was in Birmingham for the Jam I met Bunky Anderson. Bunky is a drummer and at one time had one of the largest booking agencies in the South. He's also a vintage guitar dealer. I'd wanted to play guitar on Dan's set and was talking about guitars with him when he told me he had something I needed to hear. He brought me a cherry Gibson 335 ("cherry" meaning both like new and cherry colored), which is my favorite guitar. I asked if he had an amp to go with the guitar, and he brought a black face Fender Vibrolux with two 10-inch speakers, which was the best sounding amp I ever heard. I was in heaven playing it, and later we used it on some recordings in my studio.

One day after I returned home, I spoke with Bunky, and he asked what I thought about doing an album with Jimmy Hall. I'd worked with Jimmy in Macon when he was with Wet Willie. I told Bunky it sounded like a good idea. I called Jimmy several times, but on the one occasion we spoke about doing an album, he was non-committal. I called a few more times, but he rarely returns phone calls. Even though I gave up trying to reach him, I told Bunky I wanted to do the album, but he had to corral Jimmy and get him to agree to it. Bunky made an issue of calling him often enough that Jimmy realized it would be easier to talk than keep getting the calls.

When Bunky finally got in touch with him, he told Jimmy we were coming to Nashville and wanted to meet with him. We drove up, met him at a little diner near his house, and told him we wanted to do a blues album with him because at the time blues was making one of its cyclical resurgences. A straight-ahead blues album would be fun and easy to do. With Jimmy's voice you can't go wrong with any kind of music, but I felt he had a natural affinity with the blues, and it would represent him well. I guess our driving up there that afternoon impressed him enough that he decided to do the record. Ann and I went into the project with Bunky; the deal was Bunky would pay the out-of-pocket expenses for the musicians and engineer, and I would put up my time and the studio.

I set everything up, and the recording was scheduled for late January 1995. Musicians for the first sessions were Bill Stewart, David Hood, Clayton Ivey, Jack Pearson, and Jimmy. We cut four or five songs the first day. The second day Clayton wasn't there, but Kelvin Holly came in to play. We had a strong rhythm section, and everything just worked. We did all blues except for a couple of Jack Pearson songs and a newer song Jimmy had written called "Money Doesn't Matter." When we recorded that song, Bill was set up in the kitchen of the studio instead of the drum booth; the kitchen has a tile floor. Bill was stomping the floor with his foot and drumming on a cardboard box. When I started doing the roughs, I got Jimmy to come back in to re-sing a couple of things and put background vocals on "Too Tall to Mambo." I mixed three or four of the songs and started to shop the album.

This was when you could still send a record around to the record companies for consideration, so I sent one to Capricorn and to several of the blues labels around the South. Bunky got on the phone, and I called a few people. Everyone seemed to like the album, but no one made an offer, and I never got an answer from Capricorn. I thought for sure they'd be interested since Jimmy had been one of their artists from the old days.

I had wondered why I hadn't gotten a response from Phil, so one day when I was in Nashville, I took a copy by the Capricorn office. I asked Phillip Walden to play it for Phil and try to find out why he didn't like it. Someone stuck their head in the office and told me he'd never gotten a copy. I asked if they would make certain he listened to the four or five songs on the CD. Evidently Phil listened to it because he called and said he wanted to release the album on Capricorn. We ironed out a deal on the phone, and Bunky and I went up to talk with him. Phil wanted to know how much money we had in the album and what we wanted to get for it. We'd done the album for as little as we could, so it wasn't a big money record. In the end, we got our expenses back, and I made a few dollars on the studio. I took the album to Denny Purcell at Georgetown Masters for mastering, and it was ready to go. All of Denny's work on my projects was good, but I think this record, *Rendezvous with the Blues*, was the best work he ever did for me.

This was at a time when record companies were still record companies, and Phil did the album release right. He had a party in Nashville with posters and souvenir harmonicas, and the record got a lot of press. The album cover was painted on one of the outside walls at Tower Records in Nashville and the song "Rendezvous with the Blues" got a lot of local airplay in the area. It reminded me of the old days in Macon; it had the same vibe and everything was first rate. The album was only a modest success with sales; however, it won a Nammy for best Nashville blues album of the year.

41

Searching for Simplicity

Since Mark Harrelson had been involved in the Birmingham Jam and was instrumental in getting Gregg and me back together, Mark talked about helping me do an album with Gregg. In the back of my mind I'd always wanted to do a follow-up album to *Laid Back*—a modern album, but one that had the vibe and uniqueness of the original, essentially a *Laid Back* two. This is what became *Searching for Simplicity*.

After talking with Mark, I'd gotten word that Gregg's drinking was getting away from him and screwing up his health. I called him, but I couldn't get in touch with him right away. He called me one morning and sounded really down. He wasn't doing very well and wondered what he was going to do. I told him we should get together and make some music because that always made things better. When drugs didn't work, when nothing else worked, music worked. I told him if we could get him focused on making a record, maybe things would straighten out. I also told him I had a studio and there were great players in the area; we could pretty much get anyone he wanted.

He wanted to think about it, and after we talked a few more times, he decided he wanted to do a record with me. I said I'd talk with the various people who represented him, set up a date, and schedule the players. Jack Pearson was on the Birmingham Jam and an incredible guitar player, so I told Gregg I'd see if Jack would do it. For the first session in February '95, I lined up Scott Boyer to play rhythm and acoustic and do guide vocals for Gregg, Jack Pearson on guitar, Bill Stewart on drums, David Hood on bass, and Jimmy Hall on harmonica.

In March, Gregg was scheduled to come back in to work on some demos, which I would send to the record company to get approval for the project. At the time, I had an apartment for people coming in from out of town to record, and he stayed there while we tried to work that week. We were able to cut a few songs, but everyone had told me doing an album with Gregg wouldn't work because of his condition. Maybe, in retrospect, we shouldn't have tried, but we got some good things cut. I sent what we'd recorded to Michael Caplan at Sony, and he got excited about doing the project.

Gregg was supposed to return to the studio to do some more recording for a couple of days in April before the Brothers played Oak Mountain in Birmingham. He was sick when he arrived and only got as far as the airport before Bunky Anderson picked him up and took him to the hospital where he spent a few days. The next scheduled trip to Decatur was in June, and when Gregg arrived, he wasn't in much better shape than he'd been on the previous trips.

When he had come in before, it was always touch-and-go, and the first day or two would be spent getting him straight enough to be able to record. This time I finally told him I couldn't work with him when he wasn't sober. We'd been friends for too many years and been through too much together for me to let him do something that wasn't his best work. He had a gift and was one of the best singers ever, but because of his drinking, *Searching for Simplicity* had come to a complete standstill. I asked him to help me finish something he would be proud of. After our conversation, Gregg decided to quit drinking cold turkey. We finally got a few more songs cut before he flew back out to meet up with the Brothers and do the *Jay Leno Show*.

Since Gregg had recorded "Between Now and Then" and "Please Be with Me" and both were Scott's songs, Scott wanted to thank Gregg with a surprise limo ride to the airport. The experience was memorable, but not necessarily in a good way. Things were running late, and before we'd gone five miles, the driver had to stop and get gas. In the meantime, it was incredibly hot, there wasn't air-conditioning back where we were sitting, and there was a suspicious smell emanating from the carpet. The twenty-minute ride to the airport was made without any cool air, the windows rolled down, and the sun roof open. Gregg barely made it to his flight, but he made it.

Several people had sent me versions of "Whipping Post," and I thought it was a good idea to re-cut it. On *Laid Back*, we'd cut "Midnight Rider" and had come up with a different way of doing it that worked well. I wanted to come up with something unique for "Whipping Post" as well. On the *Ton Ton Macoute* album, we did a version of "I Walk on

Gilded Splinters" that had an interesting groove, so I thought I'd try something similar for "Whipping Post." We recorded the track; Scott put a guide vocal on it, and when I played it for Gregg, he seemed to like what we'd done.

When I was in the shower one morning, I got an idea for a song, one of the few songs I've ever written or had a hand in writing, called "Wolf's Howlin'." The song was written around the time Scott Freeman's book *Midnight Riders: The Story of the Allman Brothers Band* came out, and Gregg hated the book. To be honest, I've never read it because I find it very hard to read books about that time in my life. I don't know why, but books like that make me uncomfortable—and a lot of times make me sad—so I don't read them. Ultimately, like the line from the song says, it's hard to live your life in color and tell the truth in black and white.

I told Ann about the idea for the song, and she helped come up with lyrics for it. I got with Scott and worked on the music and melody. Gregg heard the song, made a couple of chord changes, and then recorded it.

One of the few high points of the album was when I got to work with Hank Crawford. When we were in the HourGlass, we used to do some Ray Charles music. Gregg had the same kind of emotion and tone and could deliver a song like Ray, or as close as anyone I knew. Ray was one of our all time favorite singers, so Gregg covered Ray's song "I've Got News for You" for the album.

From the time I was a kid, I had the Ray Charles album *Ray Charles in Person*. It had a yellow cover and recording notes on the back. That used to be done with albums, especially those from Atlantic, and all the information about the album would be listed, including the kind of microphones used. This particular Ray Charles album indicated it had been done at a live gig with one microphone hanging somewhere in the audience to record the album. It really captured the band, and Ray was really on.

One of the songs on the album was, "Nighttime Is the Right Time." I'd sit and listen to the saxophone intro to the song, which I mistakenly thought was Hank Crawford playing tenor sax until I looked at the credits and saw that David "Fathead" Newman was the tenor sax player. Hank Crawford played alto sax. I used "Fathead" on the *Laid Back* album to play on "Queen of Hearts," so on this one I thought I'd get it right and called Hank to come in and play on "I've Got News for You" and a couple of others.

When Hank Crawford came in, I had a million questions for him about Ray and the recording of the original version of the song. It was probably just one thing he'd done out of all his other work over the years, but to me it was like a quintessential, all-time great live recording and some of my favorite music. He was a pleasure to be around; I enjoyed talking to him, and he played an intro to "I've Got News for You" that still gives me chills. It was one of the best days I had working on Gregg's album, and now I can say Hank Crawford was actually in my studio and played sax on the record.

I got most of an album recorded over the course of the summer without Gregg's being here. I got the band in to cut tracks and then waited for Gregg to come in to sing and play organ. He'd be on the road and then come in to the studio for a while and we'd try to get vocals, but he was having trouble singing. We got some vocals that were okay, but for Gregg they weren't great. It led to my pushing him at a time when he wasn't able to perform. As a result, in October 1995, we had a blow up that ended with Gregg leaving.

It was a huge disappointment because several months of my life had evolved around nothing but that album. I wanted to finish the work and make a great record with Gregg. I felt much of the time we were on the verge of it, but we never could quite push it over the threshold. It was sad because Gregg is one of the best singers around. He's a great writer and a great keyboard player; he can do anything he wants to do, but he wasn't on his game while we were working on the album.

After Gregg left, the record company contacted Tom Dowd to finish the album. Since I'd cut the tracks, I talked with him about it, and he said Gregg wanted him to do the vocals and asked me to send him the masters. He eventually went on to get Gregg's final vocals and added a couple of extra tracks to the album.

Part of the deal with my sending the tapes to Tom was the promise made by the record company and Gregg's lawyer that they'd be returned to me to finish the mixes. They never intended to honor that agreement, though. As it turned out, not only did I *not* get to mix the record, I wasn't even consulted or given a chance to voice an opinion about the mix. It was just mixed and put out. Those things happen, but it's like a knife in the back when it does.

The album was a huge disappointment because having started the record, I had it in my head how it should sound when it was finished. Of course, Tom came in at the end and did what he thought was right, but it wasn't what I'd envisioned had I mixed it.

When the album was released, I was supposed to get the rest of my advance, but two years later, I still hadn't received the rest of the money. Although they eventually paid me, Gregg's representatives caused unnecessary grief along the way. Jay Rosenthal, Gregg's manager at the time, is an asshole in every way humanly possible. He went out of his way to cause trouble and incite mistrust throughout the project. He's the personification of everything that was wrong about Gregg's situation at that time.

A few years later there, Dickey called and said the Brothers had fired him. He was upset, trying to collect money owed him, and asked if I'd testify on his behalf if he had to go to court. He wanted me to testify because the band was trying to say he was just a side man. That was kind of silly, at best; Dickey was one of the original members of the band. He and Gregg wrote nearly all of their original songs. I told him that wasn't right.

I'd worked with the Brothers in the studio for several albums, Gregg's solo album, and at least two of Dickey's. I knew Dickey was as big a part of the band as anybody. It seemed like the responsibilities were evenly divided among the members of the band with Dickey and Gregg writing most of the songs, and between the two of them, singing all the vocals. I told him, "Look, I'm not going to shade anything, but if they ask me a question, I'll give them a truthful answer. I'm not going to tell them you were a side man. There's no way on earth I'd even think that if that's what they're trying to say."

Rosenthal called me a few weeks later and asked, "Hey, how would you like to do another album with Gregg?" I told him he had to be kidding, that I wasn't interested in doing another one and to get someone else. He replied, "You really ought to do this. Gregg wants you to do it." I told him that if Gregg called me, I'd talk to him. He agreed. A few minutes later he called back and said, "You ought to think about this; you need to do it." I told Rosenthal again that I would talk only to Gregg —not to him—about it. He hung up, and that's the last I ever heard about it. Later I discovered there wasn't even any talk of Gregg even doing another album, and I thought the timing of the call in conjunction with Dickey's lawsuit was interesting.

It ended up that Dickey and the Brothers settled their differences without my needing to be involved.

42

Hard Luck Guy

Eddie Hinton died in July '95 while I was in the middle of working with Gregg. I don't recall who gave me the news—Mark Harrelson, Donnie Fritts, Spooner, or Paul Ballenger—but I remember it was in late July and hotter than hell when I got the call. Eddie was in his fifties, which isn't that old, but I heard he'd been in bad health for a while and didn't seem happy the last part of his life. Sometimes he'd be really up and then others he'd be real down. He would go from looking like a healthy person to being swollen and overweight, and then he'd go back down to normal size.

When Decatur was dry and you wanted a beer or something else to drink, you had to drive about fifteen miles to Madison to the beer store just across the county line. Eddie didn't have a car when he was living in Decatur, and it wasn't unusual for him to jog or walk to Madison, get some beer and jog or walk back home. He lived in town about six or seven miles from my place and would come out and do yard work for my mother while I was working in the studio. It was amazing all the stuff Eddie could get done. We'd offer to pick him up or take him back home, but a lot of the times he'd walk here, work, and then walk back.

The day of Eddie's funeral, Ann and I drove to Birmingham to pick up Mark Harrelson. The three of us went on to Tuscaloosa to the funeral home where the service was being held. It was the first time I'd met Eddie's mother, Deanie Perkins, and his step-father, Paul Perkins. They're good people and I grew to love them like my own parents. I know my mother always loved Eddie and would talk with him and help him any way she could. I felt Deanie and Paul would have done the same for me if I needed it. Sadly, Paul passed away recently.

A lot of Eddie's friends were there: Paul Ballenger, David Hood, Fred Stiles, Jimmy Johnson, and several others. It was a nice service, and some of Eddie's music was played, including one of my favorite songs he'd written, "Everybody Needs Love." That song was a fitting tribute to

Eddie's life. That song said it all, what the world, and what everybody in it needs. It's my philosophy of life.

That was the last song Eddie played on for me in the studio when I cut a version of it with Jerry Joseph. In fact I've cut it several times with different people, and I'll probably cut it again one of these days. When I was recording Jerry's album, I got Eddie to come out and play on it, but there was a part that kept bothering me because of the spoken verse about meeting a man while "I was out looking for cans." It was a great verse for Eddie, but I didn't think just anyone could sing it where it would make sense, so I asked him to write an alternate verse for Jerry. That's the only time that new verse was recorded, and Eddie played some beautiful guitar parts on it, as well as a great solo. The demo has never been released.

When Eddie died he'd been working on an album with Owen Brown and Jeff Simpson and had cut maybe a dozen or so tracks at Birdland Studio in Town Creek. Eddie worked with Owen and Jeff a lot, and they got along well and did some great records together. After Eddie was gone, his mother, Deanie, and Paul came up and talked with me about finishing the album. She told me Spooner and Donnie had recommended that I finish the record Eddie had started at Birdland. It felt good that they would put their trust in me. I told her everyone loved and admired Eddie and of course I'd be honored to do it. The idea was to take what Eddie had done at Birdland, and along with some of the older demos that were found, complete the album.

Jeff and Owen turned me on to some things they knew about in addition to the album tracks they'd recorded with Eddie. There were some demos my friend David Pinkston had recorded in Macon at Capricorn. When Eddie was there in the seventies, he'd go into the studio late some nights and want to put something down with David. Usually it would be an acoustic demo with just Eddie and a guitar playing and singing. He might be stomping his foot on a board or he might be playing piano instead of guitar, but it was mostly unfinished acoustic demos of songs Eddie had in mind. I had some demos of Eddie that were found along with the HourGlass tapes when we cleaned out the garage, and Peter Thompson had some ideas about songs to include. Peter owns Zane Records in Europe, an excellent esoteric blues label, and

I first met him when he came out to my studio after Eddie had passed. He's a great guy, and I consider him and his wife, Diana, two of my best friends.

I talked with Owen, Jeff, and Peter about songs to include, and of course, Deanie had some songs she's found for the album. We began recording. I wanted to fill out some of the acoustic songs with a band like I thought Eddie would have done and do something he would have been proud of.

It became a labor of love and was satisfying to be able to do it. I took a guitar vocal demo, for example, put it on my digital machine, and began overdubbing. The concept I had was to get people who had played with Eddie, either in bands or on sessions. All the people on the finished album, except for one of the horn players, had been involved with Eddie over the years. I was fortunate to get Roger Hawkins, David Hood, and Jimmy Johnson. I tried to get Barry Beckett, but he wasn't available. I got Spooner to play on several things along with Donnie Fritts and Bill Stewart, Charles Rose, Harvey Thompson and the Muscle Shoals horns, Clayton Ivey, and a lot of other people. Dan Penn came in to do backing vocals and my old friend Joe Walk played on the album. Joe usually played organ, sometimes piano, but mostly organ, on Eddie's records, and Eddie loved his playing. I played drums on one or two of the songs; in fact, Eddie's album was the last time I played drums on a record, and I played bass on a couple of other songs. I was playing a lot then and it was a true joy to play on that album.

It was great having all those people in the studio along with the good energy they brought. One of the songs we were overdubbing on was one of just Eddie and a guitar without a click track. I played it for Roger and David; they were so used to playing with Eddie that they locked up the first take and nailed it. It may sound corny, but you could feel Eddie's presence in the studio; everybody that was in there was talking about it too. It was a real feeling only Eddie could bring.

When the album was finished, Deanie, Paul, and Peter went to talk with Phil at Capricorn in Atlanta, and Phil decided to release the album on Capricorn Records. Eddie had been on Capricorn in Macon when he'd done the *Very Extremely Dangerous* album, so it seemed right *Hard Luck Guy* should be released on that label. Peter had been involved with

Eddie before he died and had long believed in Eddie's music, so *Hard Luck Guy* was also released on the Zane label in Europe. Working with Deanie, Peter has been mining some of Eddie's demos and has subsequently released albums in Europe with everything he's been able to find. In fact, *Hard Luck Guy* is still available through Zane at http://www.zanerecords.com. The album was a true labor of love, and when it came out it got good reviews. Many people dearly love that album; I'm one of them, and I'm proud of my work on the record.

I'd worked with Eddie since we were kids; we had been in bands and on the road together and had done sessions together. I'd played on sessions that Eddie had produced, and he'd played on ones I'd produced. Sometimes he would do arrangements for me. He played a key role in helping me getting my first regular session job in Miami and played a primary role in my desire to produce records. Everyone has demons to deal with and Eddie was no different, but he was a good human being and was always good to me.

Eddie is mainly known as a singer/songwriter, but he was also a great drummer. He could play drums better than I could and he used to play on some of the old stuff. He was always showing me licks. Everyone stole every lick they could from Roger Hawkins because he was "the man" around here back in the early days. Eddie would get a lick he'd gotten from Roger and show it to me, and Eddie or I would come up with a lick and it would go back to Roger.

Eddie was very in the moment, and I think if other things hadn't gotten in the way, he would have been one of the best record producers ever, not only for his own records, but for other people too. He had good ideas and knew how to explain them and how to challenge the musicians. When I played on a session when Eddie was the producer, I was twice as good as I was normally because of his directing and challenging me to do certain things. Duane respected Eddie…everybody did. I wish Eddie was still here and we were all about twenty again. We had some fun times playing together and they're great memories. I really miss him.

43

Blessed Blues

I first met Oteil Burbridge in 1991 when he was with Col. Bruce. We'd become friends, and he'd been playing sessions for me off and on since then. I'd use David Hood for bass most of the time, but on certain things, when I needed a hot bass part, it was nice to have Oteil available. One day he and I got to talking about doing a solo album together. The more we talked, the more it seemed like a good idea. I'd finished working with Gregg a couple of months before and wasn't doing anything at the time. Oteil wasn't really busy, so we put the project together. He drew on a number of good musicians, and I called on some of my friends. The album had an amazing group of players that included Oteil's brother, Kofi Burbridge; David Hood; Randall Bramblett; Roger Hawkins; Clayton Ivey; Derek Trucks; Jeff Sipe; Count M'Butu; Jimmy Herring; Yon Rico; Regi Wooten; Marcus Williams; Kenyatta Westfield; Woody Williams; and Sean O'Rourke.

We had a great time making the album; the vibe and the music were incredible. In fact, it was one of the most fun records I've worked on. We recorded a few things and sent it out, trying to find a deal, but because it was all instrumentals, we didn't have much luck. Oteil sent the record to Randy Jackson, who as another bass player, was naturally inclined to like it. Of course I can't imagine anyone not enjoying hearing Oteil play. Still, after the album was finished, nothing ever happened with it.

Although I hadn't worked with Johnny Jenkins since we'd done the *Ton Ton Macoute* album in '69, I'd talk with him every once in a while. I really liked him; he was a good guy, a great guitar player, and a truly good person. One day in late 1995, Phil called from Nashville to ask if I'd like to do another album with Johnny. I told him I'd definitely do it.

I got a band together and started selecting some songs for the recording. Then I'd call and talk about them with Phil because he loved blues songs and had a lot of old ones for me to consider. Since Johnny wasn't doing a whole lot of writing, we ended up doing mostly cover songs. I had the sessions set up in December with Derek Trucks and Jack Pearson, but about the time we were supposed to start the first track, I got a call that my brother, Howard Johnson, who'd been sick for a while, had passed away. I had to put the album off for a month or so after that.

We got back together in '96 and cut some good songs. Johnny was playing great, and we recorded all the tracks while he was here. Later, he came back in and did a few overdubs and maybe sang on one or two tracks, but he did a lot of the vocals live. One of his early 45s was an instrumental, "Love Twist," and we re-cut the song and named it "Miss Thing." Sometimes when you're recording, it seems like the sky opens up and the stars align and everything works in complete harmony—the sound of the guitars, the tightness of the playing, the arrangement. That's the way it was with that song, and for those three or four minutes, everything worked perfectly. Even though we had some other really neat songs, that instrumental is one song I'm especially proud of and my favorite thing on the album over all.

One thing you don't want to do is record with hungry musicians, so I try to keep snacks around the studio. I had a big box of banana-flavored Moon Pies out there at the time. After a few hours, everyone's blood sugar starts dipping and you need Moon Pies, chips, or some other food to snack on. It makes for better attitudes and a happier band. My advice: you don't want to play or record with a hungry drummer.

Johnny loved Moon Pies, and after he left he'd call and say, "Hey, Blessed, I'm sure wishing I had some of those Moon Pies." Ann bought them over in Huntsville at Sam's, and we'd send Johnny a case of Moon Pies. He'd call to say thank you; then a couple of months later he'd call again to let me know he was about out of Moon Pies. We'd send him some more. I felt something special for Johnny, and I was glad I could send him something that made him happy. He was always good to me when I'd go to his house to pick him up and take him down to the studio in Macon.

By 2006, Johnny had been sick for a while. From what everyone had been telling me, he didn't have long left. At the end of June, I got word he'd passed on, so Ann and I drove to Macon and met up with Paul Hornsby, and the three of us, along with Ronnie Knight, all went to the viewing at the funeral home the night before the funeral. I know Ronnie from Muscle Shoals; he's a great guitar maker and musician. He built guitars for Johnny and had gotten to be friends with him, so Ronnie got up at the viewing and started sharing a moving story about Johnny and the Pinetoppers. The four of us were the only white people in the place, and when Ronnie walked up to the microphone, someone turned the p.a. way down. Ronnie kept on telling the story and, as people realized what he was saying, the p.a. got turned back up. The next day we all went to the funeral.

It was July in Macon with a temperature of over a hundred degrees, and the air conditioning in the church wasn't working. We used the hand fans that had been given out at the funeral home the night before, but they basically just moved the hot air around. The small church was packed, and there were pictures of Johnny around the coffin along with records he'd recorded. A band with guitar, bass, drums, and piano was playing, and it was just great. The singing and response from the congregation during the service were in sync and filled with the spirit of the music, and the minister gave an incredibly moving sermon. It was the first funeral I'd ever been to in a black church, and it was amazingly uplifting. When we left, I was sad Johnny was gone, but there was also joy in the hopes of redemption.

44

Second Street

In the late 1990s, Ken Watters called to say he and his brother had recorded a jazz album featuring trumpet and trombone. They wanted me to mix it. Ken is an incredible trumpet player, and his brother, Harry, is as equally talented on the trombone. I thought the project would be great because it was something different from what I'd been doing. I told him I was definitely interested, so he came to talk with me about the project and let me hear what they'd done. It was all instrumental with excellent players. I really liked it, so I mixed the album, which was titled *The Watters Brothers*.

That record led to two more Watters Brothers albums and one with Ken as a solo artist that were all recorded at my place in Decatur. I thought each album was better than the last with superb players on the bass, drums, and piano. On Ken's solo album, he did a version of "Jessica," and on the last Watters Brothers album they recorded a short version of "Freebird." It was always great working with them.

One afternoon Ken called and told me about Carl Weaver in Gadsden, Alabama, who wanted to put a studio in his club and wanted to talk with me about it. To be honest, I'd had a lot of people calling and asking what it would cost to put a studio together. As it ended up, all of them had wasted my time. They talked like they were serious, but it never worked out. I figured this fellow was just another one of them. But Ken told me this guy knew what he was doing and knew what he wanted. He also said Carl had mentioned he'd met me at the Chestnut Station several years earlier when I was playing there with the Decoys. He mentioned that we'd talked about the Gregg and Cher album, but I might not remember him. I told him I'd remember anyone who'd asked me for a Gregg and Cher album and gave Carl a call.

When I talked to Carl, he told me he wanted to put a recording facility in the back of his club, Second Street Music Hall, in Gadsden. When he described the place, it sounded interesting: the club started out mainly as a blues club, and outside in front of the club there's a big neon blues sign that's visible from just about any place on 2nd Street. Carl asked me to get him a list of equipment to buy. From previous inquiries, I had a ready-made list of what would be needed, or at least I knew what I'd get if I was on a limited budget and wanted to make a facility for recording, especially in a live venue. I modified one of my lists and sent it to him. I thought it would be more than he wanted to spend.

After I sent him the list, he called and asked me to go down to check out his place to see what I thought, so I got Jeremy Stephens, an engineer I've been working with for the past fifteen years, to go with me for the afternoon. We met up with Carl, and I was impressed with the club he was putting together. It is still one of the nicest clubs I've ever seen. It was a beautiful place, well laid out and with a New Orleans look. Down one side of the room Carl had some iron work installed to replicate a small balcony looking out over the club with "windows" that made you feel you were looking into the second story of a French Quarter house. Down the other side of the room are large Mardi-Gras-themed paintings by Andrew Sharpe, who also plays with the band Toy Shop in Huntsville. There's a big stage with a set of drums, guitars, and a Hammond B-3. As a rule, you just don't see that nice a stage in a club. In most clubs you're lucky if you get a spot in the corner.

When Carl mentioned the list, I asked him what he thought about it. He told me he'd gone ahead and ordered most of the stuff on the list. I told him that had I known he was serious, I would have revised it a bit. Most of it was on the way, he said, but if I needed to add or take away something, he'd modify it.

We talked most of the afternoon, and he showed me where he was going to build the studio in the back of the room. The club seats a little more than a hundred, and in the very back was a space big enough for a small control room. Carl reads a lot and had some books on rooms design with information like avoiding the parallel surfaces in the control room—everything where you wouldn't have sound bouncing back and forth. I asked Adam Nichols, a true genius in building and keeping a studio running, to go down to look at the place.

In ninety-two days from the time work started on the room, the studio was up and running. It was a small control room, but had good isolation from where the bands were playing. Originally, the list I'd given Carl included a Macke console and generic mics, but we ended up getting an Otari console. I wanted something that would match up with the equipment in my studio in Decatur, so we got the Nuendo software and the Sonica Labs computer like what I was using. The computer had three hard drives; one internal hard drive for programs and two external ones for music and data. The music files were on a separate drive on caddies, so at the end of the night I could back up the music, take the caddy out of the computer in Gadsden, bring it back to Decatur, put it in the computer at my studio, and a couple of minutes later be listening to what had been recorded in the club.

On February 8, 2005, the first group I recorded at Second Street was Col. Bruce Hampton and the Codetalkers. Since I'd worked with Bruce a lot and had some great times with him, it was a perfect beginning. I was hoping everything in the new studio was going to work. I didn't know for sure until we got through the first performance, but we recorded and it sounded as good as I would have expected anything to sound. As the band played, I did rough mixes to CD and they sounded great. Carl was happy, I was happy, and the band was pleased.

Over the course of talking with him about the studio, I grew to really like Carl. Today I consider him one of my best friends, and Ann and I started going down to Gadsden frequently. Carl has other businesses, and he throws a yearly Christmas party for the employees of his company there in Gadsden. In 2004, he invited us to the Christmas party at the club. Jerry "Boogie" McCain was one of the acts playing that night. In fact, originally the club was named Boogie McCain's before it became Second Street Music Hall.

We went to the party and were enjoying the music when a lot of strange things started to happen. First, Carl's date called him to say she'd been in a car accident that had totaled the car but hadn't injured her. However, the driver of the other car had gotten out after the wreck and beat her up. The cops were involved, so Carl left to go check on her and take care of the situation. Meanwhile, everyone was continuing to have a good time when all of a sudden there was something happening in the front of the club.

I've been in a lot of clubs and thought this had the makings of a fight, but it turns out one of the guests had passed out. The people gathered around were worried he may have had a stroke or heart attack. Next thing I know, the lights went on in the club, paramedics came through the door, and a man from the audience got up on stage and announced, "We need to have a prayer for our brother here that's fallen." So, we all said a prayer as the paramedics put the man on the stretcher and took him out of the club to the ambulance. Then the lights went back off and the music resumed.

Carl hadn't yet returned when this happened, and I was thinking the evening was turning into quite an adventure. It wasn't over yet; a bit later, after Carl had returned, a couple of police officers came into the club and looked around. There were two groups of tables along each side, and down the center was a walkway where the officers were walking toward our table in the back. We didn't know what was going on and asked them if something was wrong. It turns out they were looking for Carl. Jerry McCain's daughter was missing, and they wanted to know if she was at the club or if Carl had seen her. Carl told them he hadn't seen her and they left.

A couple of hours later, Carl was sitting with us at the table listening to Jerry's show when the police returned to the club and asked him to step into the back with them. A few minutes later, Carl came back out. He looked shocked. Apparently they'd just found Jerry's daughter stabbed to death in her home. Carl would have to break the news to Jerry when his set was finished. It was a sad, sad thing, and by that time Ann and I had no idea what was going to happen next. The whole evening had been unbelievable. In the meantime, Jerry had finished his last song and was packing up his gear when Carl went up and asked him to step outside so they could talk. As soon as Ann and I could make our exit, we went back to the hotel. I got into the Jacuzzi and just melted.

Carl invited us to come back a couple of weeks later for the New Year's party at the club. I have to admit we had a few misgivings after the Christmas party, but we went and it turned out to be an uneventful, great time. Never have I experienced as much drama in one night as the night of the Christmas party; it's a night anyone who was there will always remember.

After the studio was finished, Carl and I had agreed I would do live recordings on the weekends at the club for a while to see what happened. I was essentially going down there just about every weekend and recording bands either Friday or Saturday, or both, in hopes that some of the artists would eventually do a record with us. We did a lot of recordings and a few made it all the way to CD as the Second Street Live Series on the Rockin' Camel label we eventually started together.

After Col. Bruce, it seemed like every week we had another act in the club to record, and Bill Perry was one of my favorites. I'd seen his name in blues magazines, and he blew me away with his playing. I talked to him about coming down to do a record, but he was from up north and I'm from down here, so it was geographically unfeasible.

I recorded shows with the Nighthawks, DeWayne Burnside, Jimbo Mathis, E. G. Kight, the Skeeters (a group I'd recorded a couple of really good albums with), and Bob Margolin came in with Nappy Brown. Bob would do a set and Nappy would sit in and sing, and then Bob would finish. The next set, Nappy would come in and sing a few more. The Amazing Rhythm Aces played the club; Microwave Dave was in for a couple of shows, and my old band, the Decoys, played there with Donnie Fritts. I recorded T. Graham Brown and Highly Kind, and I got recordings on another artist I'd worked with over the years, Walter Pousson Jr.

On May 14, 2005, Dru Lombar, whom I'd known in Macon and who had played on the TSS album, came in with a good band. I'm glad I got to see him and visit with him after the show because he passed away less than four months later. I guess the recording we did the night he played Second Street was one of the last recordings he made.

Jimmy Hall played the club three or four times, and he was always a big draw. He, along with Jack Pearson, always put on amazing shows. I especially remember the incredible solo Jack played on "Cross Cut Saw." In fact, I recorded a lot of really good music and we compiled a Second Street Live sampler with some of the recordings; however, the licensing got so complicated, in the end it wasn't worth trying to put out. Eventually we did release a CD on Toy Shop. The musicians were superb; Andrew Sharpe played piano, sang, and wrote most of the songs; and his brother, Antony Sharpe, played guitar and sang. We cut an album with them, and they were the first release on the Second Street Live series.

One band in particular I didn't record stands out in my memory; in fact, the band ended up not playing a note. Carl booked Leon Russell in the club; he told me the rider for Leon was specific as to what they wanted almost to the point where the club would have to remove the green M&Ms. The club is fairly small, and Leon's rider called for him to be able to have a stage volume of 120 decibels, which is like a jet plane. It was a ridiculous level for a room that only seats a little over a hundred people, and Carl told him he couldn't do that because it would just kill everyone. There were several other things in the contract that weren't going to work, and Carl offered to let him out of the deal. An agent for Leon worked it out, and it was decided the gig would go on. Leon Russell showed up and parked his bus in the club parking lot the morning of his show. I guess they'd driven there from the previous night's gig.

Jeremy and I got to Gadsden around noon or so and began to set up for the show. Carl had mentioned to Leon we recorded most of the shows, but we hadn't gotten a clearance to record his yet. We went ahead and set up to record just in case since there wasn't that much difference in setting up to do sound; the same microphones fed the front of house console and the one in the control room. After we finished setting up, there was a sound check in the afternoon, but before anyone ever hit a note, the road manager came in and got about ninety percent of their fee for playing.

We did a sound check, and the drummer was the most difficult musician I've ever met in my career in music. Usually I get along well with drummers, but not this one. He kept coming up asking me things like where all the eqs for the monitors were. In a little room you need a couple of monitors for the mixes, and it's just ridiculous to expect a complete monitoring system. Ours had a third octave eq, which is adequate for anything in my opinion. We didn't have the sixth octave he wanted, which would be twice as many knobs. He started making a fuss about it and showing his ignorance. The road manager tried to smooth it out, but ultimately the deal blew up over the fact that the meals Leon and the band ordered hadn't arrived on time. Carl told everyone he'd help them order from a place in town, but Gadsden doesn't have some of the services you'd find in a larger city. The band was unhappy because their meals were late and weren't hot on arrival.

It got so bad that Carl told them to get out, which was a mess because they'd already set up all their stuff—and there was a lot of it. It was hard to believe how much stuff they'd brought into the club. They packed up and got out of there. I guess they must have been afraid the villagers were going to go after them with torches and set their bus on fire because they called the police to be escorted out of town. Tickets had been sold, and Carl had to refund everyone's money; plus, he was out the money Leon had been paid in advance.

Overall I enjoyed doing the live recordings, but there wasn't much for me to do as a record producer. I like to do studio recordings where I have more input on the direction of the album rather than have a band show up with everything worked out. In those instances you pretty much have what they have. It may or may not be good, but you're stuck with it either way. So I talked with Carl about doing records and putting together some kind of record company and he liked the idea, so we jumped full bore into Rockin' Camel Records.

45

The Party

I was fifty-nine in early 2005 when I first started working with Carl, and I would turn sixty in April. The previous year, Ann and I had been invited to David Hood's surprise birthday party on his sixtieth birthday. It had been a big event at Doubletree Lodge in Town Creek with great music, great food, and a lot of friends celebrating the occasion. I hadn't wanted to tell anyone I was going to be sixty, but after having such a good time at David's birthday bash, I decided to embrace it. When Jim Hawkins started talking about everyone getting together for a party on my birthday, I told him it would be nice, but I didn't know of a place to have it. Ann and I started thinking about how much fun it might be. Mickey Buckins, a percussionist, songwriter, and good friend, has the same birth date as I do. We usually call each other on our birthdays, so I thought it would be a good idea to include him if we did anything. I have a number of friends born on that same date: Marlin Greene, whom I worked with when I first began doing sessions in Muscle Shoals years ago, and the late T Lavitz are two of them.

I mentioned to Carl that Jim had been talking about the possibility of throwing a party. He thought it was a great idea and said we could have it in Gadsden; it would help publicize the club, and my friends could see what we were doing there. It was decided the party was going to be at Second Street Music Hall, and Ann took on the massive preparations. I had a large guest list, and she designed the invitations and sent them out with the R.S.V.P cards. She cooked all the food and decorated the club the day of the party. Carl went all out and hired the Decoys to play and had t-shirts made for the occasion.

Percy Sledge was booked to play at the club on Friday; the party was scheduled for Saturday. A number of folks attending the party, including Ann and me, Galadrielle Allman, Tommy and Patti Talton, and a few others, arrived on Friday in time to hear Percy. Jeremy

Stephens and Adam Nichols were with me to help record Percy's show and they stayed over. Jeremy's wife, Gretchen, came down the next day.

Everyone was staying at the Gadsden Inn, a couple of blocks from the club, and I remember pulling into the motel parking lot Saturday afternoon and seeing several people gathered outside. Someone had a guitar and was playing, so the music started early. It was an exciting day, and I got to see a lot of people I hadn't seen in years. Eddie Hinton's parents, Deanie and Paul Perkins were there, as were our daughter Leigh Cauthen and granddaughter, Sandlin Graham. My cousin, Marsha Gunter, even managed to make it. Marsha, who lives in Birmingham, plays the harp and is the "real" musician in the family.

Several of my friends in Alabama came in; Tommy Compton, owner of the guitar Duane wouldn't give back when we were in the HourGlass, and his wife, Barbara; Mark Harrelson, owner of Boutwell Studios in Birmingham, and his wife, Allison; Mike Keith, a technical repair genius and designer of mic pres and compressors, and his wife, Patrice. Buddy Thornton, my old band mate in the Impacts, who also had worked at Capricorn, and his wife, Maureen made it from Florida; Ronnie Knight drove over from Cullman; and, of course, Mickey Buckins and his wife, Beverly came in from Muscle Shoals with some of their friends.

There were several people there from the Macon years. We'd invited Phil, but he was too ill to make it. Carolyn Brown-Killen, who had worked with Phil throughout all the Capricorn incarnations and beyond, was able to come. Paul Hornsby was there with Fred Stiles, one of the original members of the Five Men-Its, who'd flown down from New York. In fact, Fred wrote a song for the occasion, recorded it over at Paul's studio in Macon, and performed it at the party.

Jackie Avery, from my early days at Capricorn, was there and performed with Robert "Pops" Popwell who'd come down from Nashville. While they were playing, Jackie started telling stories on me. Popwell is a great bass player, but on some songs we recorded in the early days of Capricorn it was kind of hard to get him to settle down and play the song. Everyone had been kind of sniping at him during one session, and Jackie recalled how I finally just told him, "Play on the one and the three, I'll take care of the two and the four!"

Donnie Fritts was there and read a telegram from Billy Bob Thornton, who hadn't been able to make the party. Chuck Leavell was also invited, but since he wasn't able to make it either, he sent a nice letter that Fred read.

Jerry Wasley, a friend who works in the Birmingham school system, is a great bass player and came to the party. I met Jerry when he called me one day to tell me a Japanese friend he plays with, Kunio Kashida, wanted to do an album. We had some pretty extensive talks about where Kunio wanted to cut the record because he was interested in cutting to tape. Since everyone had heard about Muscle Shoals Sound Studios, they decided that's where they wanted to record. That was how I first met Kunio. He's a super nice man and has a dealership in Tokyo, Japan, that sells vintage guitars. Kunio is also an excellent guitar player and a huge fan of Duane and Clapton. He likes to work with people who've somehow been involved with them.

Since I'd worked with the Brothers a lot, he asked me to produce and engineer the album. I ended up doing two records with him over in the Shoals with incredible bands. Pete Carr came in to play on the second album, and it was good to work with him again. He was like a little brother to me and Hornsby, who also came in to play on the record. Chuck Leavell was there, Bobby Whitlock played on a couple of songs and sang some, and Bonnie Bramlett sang back up. Jamie Oldaker played drums on the album, and although I'd met him with Ronnie Dunn years earlier, I'd never had the chance to work with him.

We sent an invitation to Kunio, never expecting that he would come to the party; we just wanted to let him know we were thinking of him and wished he could be there. You could have knocked me over with a feather when Jerry called and said Kunio was going to fly over from Japan with his son, Masao, and that they'd both be there. When they arrived at the club, Masao presented me with a special gift he and Kunio had brought from Japan. Over there, Kunio explained, a man's sixtieth birthday is an occasion for celebration. On that day, a man receives a beautiful ceremonial vest and hat like the ones they were giving me. It was a gift of honor and respect that touched me deeply, and I wore them the whole night.

Kunio wasn't the only international surprise that day. We'd sent an invitation to Peter and Diana Thompson. We never expected them to come either, but we wanted them to know we'd be thinking of them. To my surprise and joy, they flew over from England to attend the party and stayed to visit with us for a couple of weeks afterward.

Jim Hawkins was there from Athens, Georgia, and David Pinkston and his wife, Carol, came down from Nashville. David was with us on the road when I was out with Delbert, and he worked as an engineer at Capricorn in the mid seventies. He's one of the funniest people you'll ever meet, and he lived with us for a while in Birmingham when he and I worked at the Music Place in the early eighties.

I've always admired Lee Roy Parnell, and in 2001 he called me and asked if I wanted to work on an album with him. I wasn't going to produce the record, but he asked if I'd engineer it. We went over to Muscle Shoals Sound and recorded ten or twelve tracks that were used on one my favorite albums of his, *Tell the Truth*. The song "South by South West" is just about as good as it gets for Southern rock. It was a really good band playing on the album. Lee Roy also came down from Nashville for the party.

As I mentioned earlier, Carl hired the Decoys to play at the party, so Scott Boyer, David Hood and his wife, Judy, were there along with Kelvin Holly, Mike Dillon, and N. C. Thurman. I always enjoyed listening to the band and sitting in on occasion. In fact, in 2000, during a slow period, I was talking with Scott and Kelvin about us making up a name and doing a fictitious record with a fictitious biography to do something fun and make some good music. I think the idea came from the Nashville country album *Run C&W*, and that kind of inspired me. They had Dad Burns, Rug Burns, Side Burns, etc. I enjoyed the album and the concept, so we did one of our own that was slightly swampier. It was Scott, Kelvin, Joe Walk, N. C. Thurman and Bryan Wheeler (pretty much the Decoys), and we recorded some brackish country music as the Scalded Dogs. The name comes from an old Southern expression for speed, as in "this car will run like a scalded dog."

We were Big Dog, Little Dog, Slaw Dog, Hot Dog, Chili Dog, etc. It was a fun album but another one that went nowhere. I have good memories from recording it, and it turned out to be the last thing B. W.

ever played on for me. Sadly, B.W. passed away a few years ago. He was an incredible drummer and such a great friend. I think it was the last album Joe played on for me too.

At the party there was music all day long and into the night. After the Decoys played, other people started getting up and sitting in with the band. Oscar Tony Jr. from in Macon was there. Back in the early days of Capricorn, Tom Dowd cut some tracks for Oscar, and the rhythm section played on them. One of the songs we played made the charts and did okay, but he never had the success he deserved. Oscar got up and sang with the Decoys as did Carla Russell. Carla is in the band Kozmic Mama from Huntsville, and she's one of the really great singers from around here. She has an amazing voice and can sing about anything. Avery and Pops sat in, and I got up and played bass on and off with some of the people throughout the night.

Microwave Dave and his band were passing through Gadsden on their way to another gig and they stopped in and played a few songs. The Skeeters played a set, too. The Skeeters were a band out of Fort Payne I'd recorded albums with in 2001 and 2003.

Matt Martin had called me about this band he was with called Chigger and the Skeeters (eventually shortened to the Skeeters). He wanted to talk with me about doing a record with them, so I told him to come over and bring me some of the stuff they'd been doing. He and Chigger (Bert Newton) came by, and I really liked their songs. After we finished the first album I thought for sure something was going to happen with them, but although there was some interest, nothing ever did. They had a big following and even started Skeeterfest, a yearly event that was held out in the country with some great music. I'd asked them to come to the party and play some if they wanted to.

Another friend, Walter Jr. from Lafayette, Louisiana, flew in for a few hours and played three or four songs. I first met Walter in the early '90s through Kathy Martin, a friend from Macon who was living with Walter at the time. Although I'd known her for years, I never knew Kathy sang until she asked if I'd help her and Walter Jr. do record with them in Lafayette. She started telling me about Dockside Studio owned by Steve and Wishy Nails. From her description, the studio sounded incredible and seemed very similar in equipment and size to Muscle Shoals Sound except it's built in a large, fenced estate.

Originally the main house belonged to a professional football player who fell on troubled times. In addition to the plantation style house, there was a walkway with a lake and small island in the middle, a swimming pool, and a long two-story building with the studio on the first floor and living quarters on the second floor. We cut three or four songs there. Kathy and Walter were both friends with Sonny Landreth, so I got to meet him. In fact, I ended up borrowing one of his ADATs to copy the songs we'd recorded so I could take them back to my studio to work on. I think Lafayette has the best food in the world, and we had incredible meals every night. Bill Stewart came down and played drums on the session.

On the way home from Lafayette, a really strange thing happened. Ann and I were taking Bill to the airport so he could catch a plane back to Atlanta. We'd stopped for lunch at a sandwich shop. After eating, we got back on the road to head toward the airport when we came to an intersection. The light was green as we went through it, but a car came barreling through on my left and ran the red light. We all braced for what looked like a certain collision, but the next thing we knew, the car was on the other side of us, speeding away. Even now, we can't figure out how we managed to avoid a certain crash, but I guess someone was looking out for us that day.

I've working a lot with Walter over the years since then. He was the one who had suggested to John Schneider that I be involved in mixing one of Derek Trucks's albums in February 1997. Tony Daigle was the engineer at Dockside, but for some reason he wasn't going to be able to do this album. I've only worked at Dockside two or three times, but I love working there. It's as nice a place as you could ask for anywhere with all the best equipment; Neve console and Studer tape machine and great-sounding rooms. If you can't make a great sounding record there, you can't make a record.

It was a good feeling to be playing with all my friends again at the party. Lee Roy knew everyone, and at one point when I was playing, it was Bill Stewart, Tommy Talton, Scott Boyer, Paul Hornsby and Lee Roy Parnell, who came up and joined in. We all just seem to groove together,

and that was the unofficial beginning of CRS, the Capricorn Rhythm
Section.

46

Capricorn Rhythm Section

We'd all had a great time at my party, and the next day Carl took a bunch of us out to eat at Top of the River, a great seafood restaurant in Gadsden. Lee Roy and I were talking about how hard it is to get the feeling we'd had playing the night before—as Willie Nelson said, the magic of "making music with my friends." There's a real thrill to that, and I told him I wish we could keep it going. Lee Roy told me how much he enjoyed the night before; in fact, he was the last one to leave when it was over, and we talked about getting something together to keep playing. I told him I'd talk with the rest of the guys and see what they thought about forming a band.

In the next few days I called Scott, Tommy, and Bill to ask them about it. Everyone seemed to have enjoyed the evening, and each was interested. After a lot of talking and cajoling, Paul finally agreed, and we put the band together. I talked with Carl about it, and he was very supportive. We rehearsed for a couple of days at a time. If it hadn't been for Carl, the band never would have worked because he let us use the club for rehearsals and got us all nice rooms to stay in at the Gadsden Inn.

We put a lot of thought put into the concept of the band and the criteria for a song to be included in our set list. For a song to be considered, there had to there had to be direct involvement by one of the group: one of us had to have produced the record, played on the record, or written the song. Naturally we did some Cowboy songs and some from Gregg's *Laid Back* album because everyone in the group except Lee Roy had played on that record. We did a couple of Marshall Tucker songs and played two or three of Lee Roy's from his records. It was a nice set list of good music that could be associated mainly with Capricorn and the music that had been made there. When it came time to name the band, we didn't know what to call it. I came up with "Cowboy and Lee Roy" since Scott, Tommy, and Bill had played in Cowboy, but

Bill came up with the Capricorn Rhythm Section (CRS). Because of our history playing together at Capricorn, the named seemed appropriate.

The first night the band got together to rehearse was August 29, and the remnants of Katrina swept through Gadsden knocking out the power on that side of town. Perhaps it was a warning of things to come; less than a month later, the second time the band got together to rehearse, Hurricane Rita blew through. It was as if the last one didn't get our attention, maybe that one would. Still, we decided to defy the warnings and go ahead with the band anyway.

The Jam for Duane, a yearly event hosted by Brent Sibley in Gadsden honoring Duane and his music, was coming up at the end of October 2005, and we wanted to play our first gig together for that event. We talked with Carl and decided to make our gig a three-day thing, with shows Thursday and Friday nights at Second Street before the Jam for Duane on Saturday. Thursday night we opened for the Blueground Undergrass, which gave us a chance to work out any glitches with the set list. The next night we headlined the show and played a couple of sets to a good crowd. The day of the Jam, Saturday, we played to a packed house.

While we were first putting the band together, Paul booked us for a gig in Macon at the Georgia Music Hall of Fame. They'd asked him to play, and he invited us all over to perform as CRS. The day after the Jam, we headed over to Macon for what turned out to be one of the best gigs I've played in my life. From where I was sitting, it looked like the place was wall to wall people. The band sounded good, the room sounded good, and everyone seemed to like us. It gave me even more enthusiasm to keep playing, and I figured why quit when I was having that much fun?

Gregg drove over from Savannah and played two or three songs with us. It was the first time I'd seen him since he'd left my house on such bad terms in 1995. He came in while we were playing and left right after he finished, so I didn't get a chance to talk with him. I was glad he came to play, though, and he seemed glad to see me. It was good to be back in Macon with the band making good music like we used to.

We played Second Street December 30th and New Year's Eve. By then everything was hitting on all cylinders; the band was tight and the crowd was enthusiastic. In my career of being involved with music, playing live is the best part. When you're onstage there's not a much better feeling than when the audience is into it and there's energy between the players and the crowd. I haven't been able to find anything else that wonderful. It was even good when I was playing bars—not as good as playing before a reasonably sober crowd who came just to hear you—but I still enjoyed doing it.

Along the way we lost Lee Roy. He still had his own solo career to take care of, so he quietly quit the band by not showing up for rehearsals. We decided to get Bonnie Bramlett or Jimmy Hall to sit in with us at some of the gigs. I hated that Lee Roy left. I hadn't played with him in the old days, but he has a great personality and I enjoyed his company, singing, and playing. I missed him.

We played a club gig in Macon with Bonnie in March 2006 and a biker rally with her in Huntsville in May that was held at a big field with a nice stage and a big p.a. set up, but there were only about fifty people at most. There'd been heavy storms predicted for that night, so not many people other than the staff were there. Halfway through the set, we had to get off stage because of the rain.

A couple of weeks later, rain almost ruined another show. Carl had booked several bands into the Gadsden amphitheatre, and it rained all the day before and the morning of the show. Percy Sledge was there, as were the Decoys, Donnie Fritts, and CRS. The thing about the outdoor stone amphitheatre is it was so well built there was no drainage; several inches of rain water had to be pumped out of the place before the audience could be let in and the bands were able to play.

We did a couple of shows with Jimmy, including one in Waycross, Georgia, for the Graham Parson festival where we were the headliners. There were a number of acts scheduled before we were supposed to go on, so we started playing two or three hours late. It was also colder than we'd anticipated for July, and most of the crowd had gone home so they could get up for church the next morning.

John Carter (from Allgood) was there and stopped by to say hello, and Bill and Patti Thames drove up from Florida to see the show. I'd met Bill several years earlier when he came to the studio to play a recording of the HourGlass he had and we've been friends since. Ann had designed a logo for the band based around a Capricorn astrological symbol, and Bill had made gold pendants of the design for Ann, me, and other members of the band. He does great work, and they're beautiful pieces of jewelry.

The band was booked in July to play at Mama Louise's birthday party, and it was a good trip back to Macon. I got to see a lot of people I hadn't seen since the '70s, and Gregg sat in and played. We'd had a chance to rehearse for the show, and it was even better than when we'd played the Hall of Fame. Gregg sang well and seemed to enjoy the set. We were all staying in the same hotel, and the night before the show, Gregg came down to my room. It was the first time I'd had a chance to talk with him since '95; he was very together and I was happy for him. It had been a long time since I'd seen him in such good shape, and we talked like we did when we first met.

The next show we did was the Jam for Duane in '06, and then, other than another show in Macon, where Charlie Hayward filled in for me, our next gig was in April 2007 at a benefit for Scott. He'd had an operation on his foot, and as is the case with most musicians, he had no medical insurance. No matter what a doctor does in the hospital now, it's expensive. The way musicians take care of each other is to have a benefit. The first one was in Florence at the Shoals Theatre, and a lot of Scott's friends came in to play, including Bonnie. It was a good night of music. The Amazing Rhythm Aces played; Dan Penn and Spooner Oldham performed, as did Donnie Fritts, Jerry Carrigan, Rick Kurtz, Charlie Hayward, Microwave Dave, the Decoys, and CRS. People who came to the event really got their money's worth with the talent on the show that night.

The second benefit was in Birmingham at the Alabama Theatre, and Scott had arranged for Gregg to come in from Georgia and play. Most of the same people who had played in Florence were there to perform, as were Paul Thorn and Topper Price. Topper was a great harmonica player and singer, and I'd worked with him over the years using him as a session player and producing some of his songs for an EP release on him. Scott's benefit was the last time I saw Topper because less than a month later, Topper passed away unexpectedly.

When CRS played at Second Street in Gadsden, the shows were recorded, and I put together a compilation of some of the performances for a CD that was released on Rockin' Camel. We got some nice reviews of the record in a lot of magazines. Mark Pucci, from the Capricorn days, was working with the label handing publicity. He's the best there is at the job, but by the time it was released, we really weren't a functioning band.

We tried our best to get an agent, but no one was interested and booking gigs on our own was difficult. We had a price that had to be met to make it worthwhile for us to keep playing, and the money wasn't there. Getting equipment the band needed was expensive because there was no way we could carry around a B-3, the piano, and all the amps. I hate when music gets compromised over money. A lot of places would have been nice to play, but it would have cost us to play at them. A club in Wyoming contacted me about playing out there, but the job paid only five hundred dollars. It was an interesting offer, but we couldn't have driven out there and back in one car for that kind of money.

The gigs got further and further apart. Since there wasn't a big demand for the band, the benefits for Scott were my last gigs with CRS. They played one last Jam for Duane with David Hood on bass, and that was the end of the Capricorn Rhythm Section.

I love everyone in the band, but after a while the joy went out of it. There weren't any hard feelings. Tommy had started his own band while we were playing in CRS, and it began to take more of his time. Paul was working in his studio, and I was busy in mine working on Rockin' Camel projects. Bill was doing a lot of gigging and session work in Atlanta, and Scott was playing with the Decoys, so everyone had other things going on. It didn't feel exactly like the old days, but it was reminiscent of going back to that time, and it was fun. It's probably my last time playing in a band, and I'm thankful for the chance to have done it.

47

Phil

April 26, 2006, a light, steady rain began to fall as the white Cadillac pulled into the church parking lot. Even from a distance, the Cathedral of St. Phillip dominated the Atlanta skyline; up close it was almost overwhelming. But then, if you thought about it, so was Phil Walden.

Since 2001, when he was first diagnosed with lung cancer, Phil had refused to sit quietly on the sideline of life. For the next five years, through additional surgeries and rounds of chemotherapy, he had greeted each day as a chance to make another dream come true, and as everyone knew, Phil always had a dream.

When the second incarnation of Capricorn Records ended, Phil kept his office in Atlanta with Velocette Records, and he began calling me about putting Capricorn Studio back together in Macon. He had some good ideas, and along with the studio, he wanted to include a record company and a performance venue out back with a sound stage—kind of a whole block of a record company and entertainment-related facilities. He wanted to hold auditions, offer studio time, and cut demos on any bands that showed potential. If they had something interesting, we'd cut a record with them and give them a super deal.

The plan involved my going back down to Macon to take a look at the old studio. Mike Keith, from Birmingham, had been doing a lot of tech work for me, so I asked him to meet me there to have a look at the place to see what the possibilities might be and let me know if my ideas for putting the studio back together seemed feasible. When we arrived at the old building, there was no electricity, but we had lights with us we used to check out the place as we walked back to the control room.

Tom Hedley had originally designed the room and overseen construction, and it was still in wonderful condition. It needed a little decorating—the original curtains were still hanging—but it had been built well and was still solid. Even the Hedley speaker cabinets were still in place. They were all soffit-mounted around the walls, and there was a quad set-up, so turning it into the more common surround format, 5-1, would have involved mounting a middle speaker up front and sub wolfer.

The studio wasn't in quite as good a shape. The drum booth was in the corner at the far end of the studio, and at the other end was about ten to fifteen feet of wood floor. The original orange and yellow shag carpeting was still on the floor and walls, and the wood part of the floor in the studio, never especially solid to begin with, creaked as we walked along. Though it looked like it would take some work, with the control room intact and a good studio, I didn't think it wouldn't be all that hard to put everything back in working order.

Next we went down into the basement. Originally there was only a bathroom, but later, echo chambers had been built. It had always been creepy down there and it still was. It was damp, likely moldy, but the problems didn't seem insurmountable. The floor would probably need some bracing, but that was doable.

We went back upstairs and into places I'd never been when I was working there in the 1970s. When you first walk in the front door, off to the right, there used to be a nice-sized room we used for rehearsals. Someone had turned the area into what looked like a little demo room, which wasn't a bad idea. It would be great to have two studios, especially if they had compatible equipment that could be used for overdubbing. I thought we could track in the big studio and overdub in the smaller one. It would take a good bit of money to put it all together, but it was possible to get the place back up and running.

Phil was very serious about restoring the studio, and we were excited about the prospect. He'd secured about half the financing he was going to need, and we talked about personnel to hire and equipment to buy. In fact I'd already prepared a list of my preferred equipment. There was a friend of Phil's from Atlanta who had a studio with some equipment that Phil thought might work, and he could help us with getting great prices on whatever else we might need.

Everything was in the works, and we talked about my moving back to Macon. Ann and I looked around town for an area where we might like to live. We looked at some of the beautiful old historic houses downtown while making plans to relocate, and I was excited about it. I always loved Macon and figured it would be a chance to go back "home." We tried, but it didn't come to be at that time.

Meanwhile, Phil continued to call and we'd talk about it. He was a very enthusiastic person and would get you excited about whatever he was doing. He'd call frequently to discuss in more detail what we could do and how we could make it work, and this went on for a couple of years. Then, one day he called and wanted us to meet again back in Macon. I told him I'd be there.

This visit Phil had some people with him who were interested in investing, and some people from Mercer were also there. It was my understanding Mercer owned the building and was in the process of working out a deal with Phil for him to buy back the studio. We did another tour of the building, and although the studio and control room seemed about the same, the basement had standing water and mold was growing up the walls. Time had done a number on the place, and it was obvious restoring the studio was going to take a lot more work than before. Then we went to look around the Hamlin building next door to the studio where the Brothers used to rehearse. It was still possible to do what we wanted, but it was going to cost substantially more than originally estimated when we were there previously.

Phil and I continued to make plans, but about the time it looked as if he had the money lined up, his health started failing. All fired up, he still called frequently, and we'd talk for a couple of hours about the things we wanted to do. Phil was involved with some film projects during that time, and he always had really big ideas. Doing something like everyone else was doing wasn't enough; he wanted it big and over the top. He was an exciting person to be around or to talk with.

The last time I talked with Phil, I could tell he was really ill, but he never gave up on the idea of the Capricorn re-birth. His enthusiasm inspired me. At that point, I knew it wouldn't happen, but I *wanted* to believe in it—and I think he did, too.

I'd gotten several calls from people who told me he was really sick and wasn't expected to last much longer. I heard his family was with him, and knowing the end was near made me sad. It wasn't long before I got the call that he was gone.

The funeral was in April. I'd talked with Galadrielle Allman, who was going to Atlanta for the funeral and then on to Macon for the interment. The Cathedral of St. Phillip in Atlanta was the fanciest church I'd ever seen. I couldn't believe how large it was; it looked more like a domed stadium. There were people there from all over and several from the old Capricorn days. I saw a lot of folks I hadn't seen in thirty years or more, and I got to talk with Dickey for a couple of minutes. Gregg sent a note that Galadrielle read, and the Brothers sent a huge floral arrangement, but Dickey was the only one who attended the service. I was happy he was there because he and Phil had had a lot of problems, and I wasn't certain they'd straightened them out before Phil's death. He may not have been completely comfortable, but everybody loved Dickey—and I respected him for being there.

The church was beautiful. I've never seen that much stained glass, and I doubt there's that much stained glass in heaven. It was an Episcopal service and the longest funeral I've ever attended. It lasted at least two hours, and I didn't think we were ever going to get to leave. Bruce Hampton was there, and I was talking with him about it afterward. He observed, "Yeah, that's just the way Phil would want it."

Many people eulogized Phil. His close friends told stories about him, a lot of them I'd never heard or some I'd heard and forgotten, and it was refreshing hearing them again. Little Richard spoke, and we almost got a sermon from him. Jimmy Carter sent a representative to read a letter on his behalf, and Carolyn Brown was there. I love Carolyn. I've known her since 1969 when I first walked into the building to see Phil, and I liked her right away. There's something about just looking at her that makes you feel good.

Before I even met Phil, I knew about him from the R&B artists he managed; I had all their records, and sometimes I'd see a mention of him on the album covers. I'd heard his name knew he had to be a good guy because he managed Otis Redding. Then I met him in Muscle Shoals when we were doing tracks for what we thought was going to be a Duane Allman project, and I liked him right away. He was magic. Without Phil, Duane, and Jerry Wexler, I don't think the whole Southern music scene would have happened. It certainly wouldn't have happened the way it did with Capricorn, which was the flagship for Southern music.

Phil and I always had fun conversations, and he was pretty opinionated. He was the life of the party and could tell one story after the other, each funnier than the last, and he could be inspiring. He expected good things and made you want to do the very best you could and push yourself a little harder. He worked hard for the artists too, busting his tail making calls and being the guy who could bullshit with people and make the deals.

I think about Phil every day. I'll remember something he said or did, or I'll wish I could ask him about something: "What do you know about that?" or "What do you think about this guy?" or "How'd you like that movie?" I miss him beyond words.

48

Rockin' Camel

I'd been going down to Gadsden about every weekend to do recording at the club, and from the beginning, Carl had talked about making some of the live shows into CDs. I wanted to do something in the studio where I had more of a hand in production. For several weeks I talked to Carl and really lobbied for us to start putting out records that were recorded in the studio with artists we signed to the label. He thought it over for a while and finally decided he wanted to do it.

Carl owns the top of an incredibly beautiful mountain outside of Gadsden. He calls "Disgraceland" and has miniature sheep, miniature horses, horses, a longhorn steer, fainting goats, and other interesting animals. Around the time we were talking about starting a record company, he bought himself a camel he named Akbar. I never thought I'd like a camel, but Akbar was unique. He was friendly and inquisitive, and he'd check us out for any treats we might have brought for him. He was also incredibly quiet for such a large animal. You could be standing several yards away from him, and next thing you know he'd stick his head over your shoulder. He was just a fun creature, and Akbar became the inspiration for and namesake of the label...Rockin' Camel Records.

The first release on the Rockin' Camel label was the Second Street Live series. *Toy Shop* was the first album in the series, followed by the *Capricorn Rhythm Section* album. Next there was a CD with Microwave Dave and one with Kenny Acosta. All of the album covers for the series featured original artwork by Andrew Sharpe from Toy Shop, and they were incredible.

The studio albums were recorded at my place in Decatur, and our first studio album, *No Easy Way Out,* was recorded with Danny Brooks, a Canadian artist Mitch Lopate introduced me to. Danny was a good player, singer, and writer; I got David Hood, Kelvin Holly, Bill Stewart, and Kevin McKendree in to cut ten of Danny's original songs and a song, "Carry Me Jesus," written by Ann, Carla Russell, and me. I felt good about the album; it got some publicity, sold a few, and was nominated for several awards in Canada.

The first person I talked with Carl about signing to Rockin' Camel was Bonnie Bramlett. When we first started the company, she was recording for another label, but after she was free from them, she called and let me know. She and Carl began talking, and it wasn't long afterward that Carl signed her and we started recording an album. Working with Bonnie has been one of the personal highlights in my career of producing; she's one of the best singers around and one of my favorites to work with.

Bonnie and I talked a lot about the record before we started the album, and we'd both come to the same realization that we needed to do something age appropriate. Some of the songs are really heavy and some are lighter, but there are poignant and relevant lyrics in all of them. The album was titled *Beautiful*, and Carl went all out for the record. He lined up photo shoots and ordered merchandise to promote the album; Mark Pucci got reviews in a number of important publications.

Mark had been at Capricorn in the early days and was one of the men responsible for all the promotions coming out of label in the '70s until Capricorn went under. Later, when Phil restarted Capricorn in Nashville, Mark handled promotions for the new label and stayed with the new Capricorn until it was sold. At my suggestion, Carl hired Mark to handle the publicity for the label and did an excellent job of promoting the records released on Rockin' Camel.

About the time we started the company Carl purchased the building beside the club and turned it into the offices for Rockin' Camel. He had vintage memorabilia and a jukebox in the reception area. His office was behind that, and there was a kitchen area, a stock room, and a workroom where they were able to make buttons and print posters and other items. He also purchased a nice older house four or five blocks from the club to renovate and turn into a band house for some of the artists recording at the club. CRS stayed there, and Ann and I were there almost every weekend when I was doing recording at the club. It was a wonderful old place and beautifully decorated, with two bedrooms and a bath upstairs, a living room, music room, kitchen, bath, and two bedrooms downstairs. In fact, we spent so much time there that Carl named the room we always stayed in the Sandlin Suite. Right outside the door of the bedroom was a nice wooden porch with a swing that was great to sit in during the summer. It was a good place to stay. It became our home away from home.

I still had the rights to the Jimmy Hall *Rendezvous with the Blues* album, and we released it with a couple of bonus tracks. When I originally recorded the album, I'd cut more songs than the eleven used on the first release, so we added two of the previously unreleased tracks for the record. Carl bought the rights to the artwork, and it went out like the original only on the Rockin' Camel label.

The next studio album I recorded was the group Highly Kind, headed by Albert Simpson, who lives in Gadsden. He and Carl are friends, and I'd previously recorded the group live at Second Street. Highly Kind had a good band with excellent players that included drummer Duane Trucks, Derek Trucks's brother. We spent some time looking for material and finally selected some of Albert's songs to record. I got three songs from Randall Bramblett and a couple by Walt Aldridge. We put out a good album that got good reviews and sold a few, but it's become difficult to sell records for new artists.

Today there exists the option of doing everything on the Internet. Even though Carl had a Rockin' Camel website, with so much music available online, it's difficult to get the music heard. I think these days a band has to go on the road and be a viable live act for something to happen. That's the way it was with Capricorn. Every act we had then was out on the road building their following all over the United States. Some of the older acts we signed to Rockin' Camel weren't able to get out and work on the road to make a go of it.

Distributing music is much different from what it was from the '70s through the '90s. As CDs are slowly being phased out, downloads have become the popular way to get music. You can buy songs easily on iTunes, which has a better selection than any of the brick-and-mortar record stores that still exist.

Things were changing in the whole industry, and none of the Rockin' Camel albums were making any money. We gave it a good long try, from 2005–2009, but it just wasn't feasible to continue. The record company was a lot of fun, and we made some really good music. I enjoyed working with Carl; we are still close friends, but, at least for now, the record company is on hold.

49

Final Thoughts

I've been working in music, playing, engineering or producing, for the past fifty years. When I look back over my career, I feel very blessed that I've gotten to work with some of the best musicians, singers, and songwriters in the world. I got to work closely with Duane—and it simply doesn't get any better than that—and with Gregg, Berry, Dickey, Jaimoe, and Butch of the Allman Brothers Band. People I've known since I was fifteen are still playing music and writing songs: Dan Penn, Spooner Oldham, Donnie Fritts, and David Hood, for example. They remain my friends to this day. I'm still working with Scott Boyer, Bill Stewart, Tommy Talton, and Paul Hornsby, and along the way I've found new people like Oteil Burbridge, Josh Gooch (an upcoming young guitar player), and Kelvin Holly, who played guitar with me in the Decoys and is my first call for sessions.

I've had some amazing experiences. I remember the first time I ever wanted to get an autograph from someone was when I met Al Jackson. I was a big fan of Stax music out of Memphis, and Booker T. and the MGs were playing at the first Atlanta Pop Festival. Roger Hawkins, Jerry Carrigan, and Al Jackson were my favorite drummers, and although I didn't get the autograph, I got to shake Al Jackson's hand. I'll never forget that or getting to see him play. And in 1965 I got to see James Brown in Huntsville when he was at his peak. There were four drummers on stage with horns, piano, organ, guitar, bass, and background singers. The show was outstanding.

One of the high points of my playing career was when I returned to Macon and played at the Georgia Music Hall of Fame with the Capricorn Rhythm Section. We were all treated like rock stars, and I loved it. And I loved playing the Fillmore with the HourGlass. Every show we played out there was wonderful.

I'm really proud of my work on Gregg's *Laid Back* album and on Dickey's *Highway Call*. I'm proud of the two albums I did with Bonnie in

Macon, *Lady's Choice* and *It's Time* and the *Beautiful* album we did together for Rockin' Camel. I'm proud of *Brothers and Sisters*, partly because it sold so well, but mainly because it was a great band that was able to do a great album after the death of Berry and while they still struggled with Duane's passing. I have immense respect for a band that can go through such hard times and still put out a hit record.

I've seen a lot of changes in the recording process over the years. The music industry is still changing. Sometimes we all wonder how we're ever going to make a living, but in some ways the changes might be good because people aren't going to get in it just for the money. Being a musician certainly isn't a way to get rich, and most of the time it's hard to figure out how to survive. With the popularity of downloads, my hope is that things will get worked out so the people who create the music can be fairly compensated, whether through subscription services, a surcharge for music on cable, or through legitimate purchases on iTunes or some of the other download services.

The things I really miss most about vinyl records are the album covers. I used to take the records and look at the covers and study who played on it, who produced it, the studio where it was recorded, the engineer, the writers, etc. That information isn't easy to find anymore. If you download an album from iTunes, it doesn't come with all that information. It's really a shame because that's how I developed my style. Some records would sound better compared to others, so I'd look for certain producers and players. For example, I listened to something Tom Dowd produced or engineered or other records from the Atlantic label and tried to figure out what made it work. I enjoyed listening to the different songs, and if it was something I liked, I'd listen and pick it apart to find out what made that particular feel happen. That's what I'd listen for mostly, the *feel* of the song—is it moving or not, how is it being delivered? I'd think about how I might have done the record. It was a big deal to have that information on albums readily available, and it's just not there anymore.

There are a lot of positives with digital. If the band is good, digital can help, and of course it's easier to make a bad band sound better. I loved the analog from the old days because it has a certain sound that digital hasn't been able to capture yet. On the other hand, digital is easier to work with and allows for more creativity. You can take a guitar lick and move it around if you need to. I've had a lot of guitar players come in and do an amazing lick and when I've asked them to do it again, but they can't remember it. With digital, you can physically move it yourself and put it at the intro or the end of the song and tie it together. I'd rather mix through an analog console, but even though I have one, it's not as convenient as doing it on the computer. Of course I wouldn't mind having a Neve or API console available.

If I were going to give advice to someone who wanted to get into engineering or production, I'd tell them to hang out in the studio. I'd tell them to spend a lot of time there and be the go-fer, to learn everything possible from start to finish; to learn how everyone works in the studio, how they handle the session, how they run a session, what's important to them, how they relate to the band or musicians. I read an article by someone who told their engineering students to go into the studio, watch everything that went on, and not say a word. At the end of three months, if they still had any questions, they could ask then. He's right. If you did that, by the end of three months I'm pretty sure about any question you had would've been answered just by paying attention.

And I'd tell someone wanting to get into the production side of the business to learn how to recognize a good song, one that has potential with good words and music. Then make sure you have a good arrangement and get a track that makes you feel good. I've noticed when I'm cutting tracks that I generally get the master track within the first five takes. Usually there's one in the first few takes with a feel that sets it apart from the others. Essentially it's the same song, but there's a different feel, a different lilt to it. There's some magic thing that happens that I can't explain, but I know it when I hear it. I'd suggest you learn to recognize it when you hear it too.

Listen to music. You can't go wrong with Ray Charles, Otis, the Stax, and Motown music, albums from Muscle Shoals, music where you get to hear great people playing on great songs. Go back and get the history of music, get the blues, country, everything you can, because there are bits of everything I've ever heard that play a part in what I come up with. Understand the music and be well versed in it.

I've thought about things I might have done differently over my career. I wish I had taken advantage of the opportunities I've had to work in England. I feel like I've missed out on a lot by not doing so. People in Europe and Japan, for instance, appear to appreciate and enjoy the music I've been involved with—more so, it seems, than people here. I don't know why that is, but I wish I'd recorded in England when I had the chance. I've also thought about what would have happened if I'd taken the gig with the Brothers when Duane was putting the band together. Part of me is glad I didn't, though, because I can't imagine it could have been any better than it's been with Butch and Jaimoe.

I think a lot about the people who aren't here any longer. All of them have a place in my heart. I've often wondered what would have happened if Duane and Berry had lived, what the Brothers would have been doing today. Would they have discovered another new genre of music? Probably, I don't know, but I think about them and miss them every day. I miss Phil and Eddie and B. W. and Joe Walk. Joe and I kind of grew up together; he was one of my oldest friends, and now he's gone too. When someone close to you dies, you have memories with them you can't share with anyone else in the world, and you feel the void they've left behind. Bonnie summed it up pretty well though when she was talking about Duane. She said, "I don't think of him as dead, I just think of him as my rude friend. He never drops by any more, never calls, and doesn't write." Bonnie has a way of putting things into a unique perspective. It's a perfect way of looking at it.

I still have my studio and work coming up, and I plan to make music until the day I die. And there's a new generation of musicians in the family coming along behind me. Our grandchildren have been involved in music to varying degrees: grandson Reid Cauthen plays drums, but he and our granddaughter Avonlea Spain aren't interested in pursuing a career in music. Our granddaughter Sandlin Graham plays guitar and bass as does her husband, Zach Graham. Our granddaughter Ella Cauthen is a singer with an amazing voice, and our youngest grandson, Noah Spain, has been taking guitar lessons and is learning to play the drums. Another grandson, Gray Cauthen, has been bitten by the bug and eats, drinks, and sleeps guitar and gigs every chance he gets. We fixed up the garage just down from the studio, and he and his band rehearse out there. It's nice to hear the music coming through the closed doors. As I get older, I see things coming full circle through them, and I guess you could say they're all part of the never-ending groove.

It's not how many people know our names when we die, but whether we've touched the lives of others.
—*The Outer Limits*

Discography

Any time you try to document work that spans most of a lifetime something will be missed. The following discography is as detailed as possible.

ALBUMS & 45S

1958

Hollis Champion, 45, guitar:
"That Old Red Devil," "Let Your Conscience Be Your Guide"
Players: Hollis Champion, Butch Owens, Johnny Sandlin, Billy Smith

1964

5 Men-Its, 45, drums:
"The Old Man," "I Don't Love You No More"
Band: Paul Ballenger, Charlie Campbell, Paul Hornsby, Johnny Sandlin, Fred
    Stiles

1967

HourGlass, *HourGlass*, drums:
"I've Been Trying," "Nothing but Tears," "Cast Off All My Fears," "Heartbeat,"
    "Love Makes the World Go Round," "So Much Love," "Silently," "Got to Get
    Away," "Out of the Night," "No Easy Way Down," "Bells"
Band: Duane Allman, Gregg Allman, Johnny Sandlin, Paul Hornsby, Mabron
    McKinney
Additional Players: Mack Rebennack, Mike Melvoin

Bobby Vee, *Come Back When You Grow Up*, drums:
"Come Back When You Grow Up, "A Rose Grew In The Ashes," "You're A Big
    Girl Now," "Get The Message," "Hold on to Him," "World Down on Your
    Knees," "Objects of Gold," "Before You Go," "Mission Accomplished," "I
    May Be Back," "Double Good Feeling"

1968

Nitty Gritty Dirt Band, *Rare Junk*, drums, upright bass on one song:
"Reason to Believe," "End of Your Line," "Willie the Weeper," "Hesitation
    Blues," "Sadie Green," "Collegiana," "Dr. Heckle and Mr. Jibe," "Cornbread
    and 'Lasses," "Number and a Name," "Mournin' Blues," "These Days"

HourGlass, *Power of Love*, drums, guitar, gong:
"Down In Texas," "Power of Love," "I'm Not Afraid," "Going Nowhere,"
    "Home for the Summer," "Changing of the Guard," "I Can't Stand Alone," "I
    Still Want Your Love," "Now Is the Time," "To Things Before," "Norwegian
    Wood," "I'm Hanging Up My Heart for You"
Band: Duane Allman, Gregg Allman, Pete Carr, Paul Hornsby, Johnny Sandlin

HourGlass, demos, drums:
"Ain't No Good to Cry," "B. B. King Medley: Sweet Little Angel—It's My Own
    Fault—How Blue Can You Get," "Been Gone Too Long"
Players: Duane Allman, Gregg Allman, Johnny Sandlin, Paul Hornsby, Pete Carr

1969
Duck & The Bear, 45, drums:
"Goin' Up Country," "Hand Jive"
Players: Eddie Hinton, Johnny Sandlin, Duane Allman, Berry Beckett, Roger
    Hawkins, Wayne Jackson, Andrew Love, James Mitchell

Clarence Reid, 45, drums:
"I'm Doin' My Thing with Nobody but You," "Send Me Back My Money"

Clarence Reid, *Dancin' With Nobody but You*, drums
"Nobody but You Babe," "Twenty-Five Miles," "Doggone It," "Get Back,"
    "Don't Look Too Hard," "I've Been Trying," "Tear You a New Heart," "Part-
    Time Lover," "Shop Around," "Fools Are Not Born," "Polk Salad Annie,"
    "Send Me Back My Money"

Betty Wright, *I Love How You Love Me*, drums:
"I Love the Way You Love," "I'll Love You Forever Heart and Soul," "I found
    that Guy," "All Your Kissin' Sho' Don't Make True Lovin'," "If You Love Me
    Like You Say You Love Me," "Clean Up Woman," "I'm Gettin' Tired Baby,"
    "Pure Love," "Ain't No Sunshine," "Don't Let It End This Way," "Let's Not
    Rush Down the Road of Love"

Johnny Jenkins, *Ton Ton Macoute*, producer, engineer, drums, remixing:
"I Walk on Gilded Splinters," "Leaving Trunk," "Blind Bats and Swamp Rats,"
    "Rolling Stone," "Sick and Tired," "Down along the Cove," "Bad News,"

"Dimples," "Voodoo in You," "I Don't Want No Woman," "My Love Will
    Never Die"
Johnny Jenkins Players: Duane Allman, Tippy Armstrong, Eddie Hinton, Paul
    Hornsby, Berry Oakley, Robert Popwell, Johnny Sandlin, Butch Trucks
Background Vocals: Ella Brown, Southern Comfort

Arthur Conley, 45, producer, drums:
"They Call the Wind Mariah," "God Bless," "Hurt," "Your Love Has Brought
    Me"

Doris Duke, *I'm a Loser*, drums:
"He's Gone," "I Can't Do Without You," "Ghost of Myself," "You're My Best
    Friend," "The Feeling is Right," "I Don't Care Anymore," "Congratulations
    Baby," "We're More Than Strangers," "Divorce Decree," "How Was I to
    Know You Cared," "To the Other Woman"

Eddie Floyd, (unknown album name), drums

Macon, 45, producer, drums:
"Ripple Rap," "Pulley Bone"
Band: Pete Carr, Paul Hornsby, Robert Popwell, Johnny Sandlin

Cowboy, *Reach for the Sky*, producer, engineer, remixing:
"Opening," "Livin' in the Country," "Song of Love and Peace," "Amelia's
    Earache," "Pick Your Nose," "Pretty Friend," "Everything Here," "Stick
    Together," "Use Your Situation," "It's Time," "Honey Ain't Nowhere," "Rip
    and Snort," "Josephine beyond Compare"
Band: Scott Boyer, Tommy Talton, George Clark, Pete Kowalke, Bill Pillmore,
    Tommy Wynn

1970
Allman Brothers Band, *Fillmore East*, supervised mastering:
"Statesboro Blues," "Done Somebody Wrong," "Stormy Monday," "Hot 'Lanta,"
    "In Memory of Elizabeth Reed," "You Don't Love Me," "Whipping Post"

Swamp Dogg, *Total Destruction of Your Mind*, drums:
"Total Destruction to Your Mind," "Synthetic World," "Dust Your Head Color
    Red," "Redneck," "If I Die Tomorrow," "I Was Born Blue," "Sal-A-Faster,"

"The World Beyond," "These Are Not My People," "Everything You'll Ever Need," "The Baby's Mine," "Mama's Baby, Daddy's Maybe"

Livingston Taylor, *Livingston Taylor*, drums, bass:
"Sit on Back," "Doctor Man," "Six Days on the Road," "Packet of Good Times," "Hush a Bye," "Carolina Day," "Can't Get Back Home," "In My Reply," "Lost in the Love of You," "Good Friends," "Thank You Song"

Raw Spitt, *Raw Spitt*, drums:
"Put a Little Love in Your Heart," "Raw Spitt," "Call Me Nigger," "Freedom under Certain Konditions Marching," "Midnight Rider," "Who Do They Think They Are?," "I Dig Black Girls," "This Old Town," "Sweet Bird of Success," "Excuses"

Whiskey Howl, *Whiskey Howl*, producer:
"Caldonia," "Early in the Morning," "Mother Earth," "Rock Island Line," "Down the Line," "Let the Good Times Roll," "One Hot Lady," "Pullin' the Midnight," "I'm Not Talking," "Jessie's Song"
Band: Richard Fruchtman, Dave Morrison, Michael Pickett, John Witmer, Wayne Wilson
Additional Musician: Chuck Leavell

1971
Cowboy, *5'll Getcha Ten*, producer, engineer:
"She Carries a Child," "Hey There Baby," "Five'll Getcha Ten," "The Wonder," "Shoestrings," "Lookin' For You," "Seven Four Tune," "Right on Friend," "All My Friends," "Innocent Song," "Please Be with Me," "What I Want Is You"
Band: Scott Boyer, Tommy Talton, George Clark, Peter Kowalke
Additional Musicians: Duane Allman, Chuck Leavell, Johnny Sandlin

Melting Pot, *Fire Burn, Cauldron Bubble*, producer, engineer:
"Fugue to Rosie," "Await the Coming Day," "As I Lay Dying," "Feelin' Alright," "Welcome to the Party," "Kool and the Gang," "Sunday Tree," "Tell the Truth"
Band: Dick Gentile, Paul Hmurovich, Howie McGurty, Steve Nichols, Mickey Smith, Kenny Tibbets, Jerry Thompson, Bill Witherspoon

Livingston Taylor, *Liv*, engineer, bass, remixing:
"Get Out of Bed," "May I Stay Around?," "Open Up Your Eyes," "Gentleman,"
  "Easy Prey," "Be That Way," "Truck Driving Man," "Mom, Dad," "On
  Broadway," "Caroline," "I Just Can't Be Lonesome No More"

Alex Taylor, *Friends & Neighbors*, producer, bass, remixing:
"Highway Song," "Southern Kids," "All in Line," "Night Owl," "C Song," "It's
  All Over Now," "Baby Ruth," "Take Out Some Insurance," "Southbound"
Alex Taylor Players: Scott Boyer, Willie Bridges, King Curtis, Ronnie Cyber, Paul
  Hornsby, P. Kowalke, Danny Moore, Joe Rudd, Johnny Sandlin, Bill Stewart,
  Tommy Talton, James Taylor, Frank Wess

Allman Brothers Band, *Eat a Peach*, mixing:
"Ain't Wastin' Time No More," "Les Brers in A Minor," "Melissa," "Mountain
  Jam," "Way Out," "Trouble No More," "Stand Back," "Blue Sky," "Little
  Martha"

1972

Captain Beyond, *Captain Beyond*, mixing:
"Dancing Madly Backwards," "Armworth," "Myopic Void," "Mesmerization
  Eclipse," "Raging River of Fear," "Thousand Days of Yesterdays (intro),"
  "Frozen Over," "Thousand Days of Yesterdays," "I Can't Feel Nothin' pt.1,"
  "As the Moon Speaks," "Astral lady," "As the Moon Speaks (return)," "I
  Can't Feel Nothin' pt. 2"

Alex Taylor, *Dinnertime*, producer, engineer, bass, Moog synthesizer, remixing:
"Change Your Sexy Ways," "Let's Burn Down the Cornfield," "Comin' Back to
  You," "Four Days Gone," "Pay Day," "Who's Been Talkin'," "Who Will the
  Next Fool Be?," "From a Buick 6"
Alex Taylor Players: Scott Boyer, Roger Hawkins, Charlie Hayward, Paul
  Hornsby, John Hughey, Jaimoe, Chuck Leavell, Lou Mollenix, Jim Nalls,
  Wayne Perkins, Johnny Sandlin, Earl "Speedo" Simms, Bill Stewart
Background Vocals: Charles Chalmers, Ginger Holliday, Mary Holliday, Donna
  Rhodes, Sandy Rhodes, Temple Riser, Steve Smith
Eric Quincy Tate, *Drinking Man's Friend*, percussion:
"Brown Sugar," "Things (I Think I'll Find)," "Whiskey Woman Blues," "Another

Sunshine Song," "Water to Wine," "Can't Get Home for Your Party," "Texas

Sand," "Suzie B. Dunn"

Allman Brothers Band, *Brothers & Sisters*, producer, engineer:
"Wasted Words," "Ramblin' Man," "Come and Go Blues," "Jelly, Jelly,"
    "Southbound," "Jessica," "Pony Boy"
Band: Gregg Allman, Richard Betts, Berry Oakley, Butch Trucks, Jaimoe, Chuck
    Leavell, Lamar Williams
Additional Players: Les Dudek, Tommy Talton

Wet Willie, *Wet Willie II*, producer, engineer, mixing:
"Keep a Knockin," "Grits Ain't Groceries"
Band: Jack Anthony, Jack Hall, Jimmy Hall, Ricky Hirsch, Wick Larsen, Lewis
    Ross,

White Witch, *Spiritual Greetings*, producer, engineer:
"Parabrahm Greeting/Dwellers of the Threshold," "Lord Help Me," "Don't
    Close Your Mind," "You're The One," "Sleepwalk," "Home Grown Girl,"
    "And I'm Leaving," "Illusion," "It's So Nice to Be Stoned," "Have You Ever
    Thought of Changing?," "The Gift"
Band: Beau Fisher, Ronn Goedert, Buddy Pendergrass, Buddy Richardson, Bobby
    Shea

Alex Taylor, "Lizzie & the Rainman," 45, producer, engineer, mixing

Duane Allman Dialogs, *Duane Allman*, editing, supervision:
Interview with Duane Allman by Ed Shane WPLO FM (1970); Ed Shane
    Interview with Jerry Wexler, Executive Vice President, Atlantic Records
    (1972); Duane Allman Radio Show WPLO FM (1970); Ed Shane interview
    with John Landau, Critic and New York Bureau Chief, *Rolling Stone* (1972)

Wet Willie, *Drippin' Wet*, producer, remixing:
"That's All Right," "She Caught the Katy," "No Good Woman Blues," "Red Hot
    Chicken," "Airport," "I'd Rather Be Blind," "Macon Hambone Blues," "Shout
    Bamalama"
Band: John Anthony, Jack Hall, Jimmy Hall, Ricky Hirsch, Lewis Ross
Additional Musician: Jaimoe

Gregg Allman, *Laid Back*, producer, engineer, bass, arranger:

"Midnight Rider," "Queen of Hearts," "Please Call Home," "Don't Mess Up a Good Thing," "These Days," "Multi-Colored Lady," "Will The Circle Be Unbroken?"

Players: Gregg Allman, Scott Boyer, David Brown, Buzzy Feiten, Charlie Hayward, Paul Hornsby, Jaimoe, Chuck Leavell, Jimmy Nalls, David Newman, Johnny Sandlin, Tommy Talton, Bill Stewart, Butch Trucks

Background Vocals: Eileen Gilbert, Carl Hall, Hilda Harris, Emily Houston, June McGruder, Helene Mills, Linda November, Albert Robinson, Maeretha Stewart

Martin Mull, *Normal*, producer, percussion, sound effects:

"Wood Shop," "Jesus Christ Football Star," "Ego Boogie"

Martin Mull Players: Scott Boyer, Randall Bramblett, David Brown, Earl Ford, Tony Humphreys, Todd Logan, Johnny Sandlin, Keith Spring, Bill Stewart, Tommy Talton, Harold Williams

1974

Gregg Allman, *The Gregg Allman Tour*, producer, bass, remixing:

"Don't Mess Up a Good Thing," "Queen of Hearts," "I Feel So Bad," "Stand Back," "Time Will Take Us," "Where Can You Go," "Double Cross," "Dreams," "Are You Lonely for Me Baby?," "Turn on Your Love Light," "Oncoming Traffic," "Will the Circle Be Unbroken?"

Gregg Allman Players: David Brown, Randall Bramblett, Scott Boyer, Erin Dickins, Peter Eklund, Johnny Lee Johnson, Chuck Leavell, Todd Logan, Lynn Rubin, Annie Sutton, Bill Stewart, Tommy Talton, Kenny Tibbetts, Harold Williams

Kitty Wells, *Forever Young*, producer, guitar:

"Too Much Love between Us," "Forever Young," "Too Stubborn," "I've Been Loving You Too Long," "What about You?," "My Love Never Changes," "Don't Stop the Honeymoon in My Heart," "Loving's Over," "Do Right Woman, Do Right Man," "'Til I Can Make It on My Own"

Kitty Wells Players: Richard Betts, Scott Boyer, David Brown, Toy Caldwell, Paul Hornsby, John Hughey, Chuck Leavell, Johnny Sandlin, Bill Stewart, Tommy Talton

Background Vocals: Ella Avery, Mary Dorsey, Donna Hall, Joyce Knight, Diane Pfeifer

Hydra, *Hydra*, remixing:
"Glitter Queen," "Keep You Around," "It's So Hard," "Going Down," "Feel a
    Pain," "Good Time Man," "Let Me Down Easy," "Warp 16," "If You Care to
    Survive," "Miriam"

Elvin Bishop, *Let It Flow*, producer, acoustic & electric guitar, percussion:
"Sunshine Special," "Ground Hog," "Honey Babe," "Stealin' Watermelons,"
    "Travelin' Shoes," "Let It Flow," "Hey Good Lookin'," "Fishin'," "Can't Go
    Back," "I Can't Hold Myself in Line"
Band: Elvin Bishop, Phil Aaberg, Don Baldwin, Michael Brooks, Johnny
    Vernazza
Additional Musicians: Richard Betts, Randall Bramblett, Toy Caldwell, Vassar
    Clements, Charlie Daniels, Paul Hornsby, Jerome Joseph, Bill Meeker, Steve
    Miller, Johnny Sandlin, Sly Stone, David Walshaw
Background Vocals: Jo Baker, Gideon Daniels, Annie Simpson, Mickey Thomas

Richard Betts, *Highway Call*, producer, engineer, bass, percussion, remixing:
"Long Time Gone," "Rain," "Highway Call," "Let Nature Sing," "Hand Picked,"
    "Kissimmee Kid"
Richard Betts Players: Vassar Clements, Jeff Hannah, John Hughey, Chuck
    Leavell, Frank Poindexter, Leon Poindexter, Walter Poindexter, Johnny
    Sandlin, Stray Strayton, Tommy Talton, Oscar Underwood, David Walshaw
Background Singers: Buck, Dottie & Reba Rambo

Bonnie Bramlett, *It's Time*, producer, guitar, percussion:
"Your Kind of Kindness," "Atlanta GA," "It's Time," "Cover Me," "Higher and
    Higher," "Where You Come From," "Cowboys and Indians," "Mighty Long
    Way," "Since I Met You," "Oncoming Traffic"
Bonnie Bramlett Players: Gregg Allman, Scott Boyer, Randall Bramblett, Earl
    Ford, Eddie Hinton, Paul Hornsby, Jaimoe, Leo LaBranche, Chuck Leavell,
    Tom Ridgeway, Johnny Sandlin, Bill Stewart, Tommy Talton, Jerry
    Thompson, Butch Trucks, Kenny Tibbetts

Cowboy, *Boyer-Talton*, producer, engineer, bass, congas:
"Patch and a Painkiller," "Coming Back to You," "Everyone Has a Chance to
    Feel," "Where Can You Go," "I Heard Some Man Talking," "Love 40," "Road
    Gravy Chase," "Something to Please," "Long Ride," "Message in the Wind,"
    "Houston," "Houston Vamp"

Band: Scott Boyer, Tommy Talton
Additional Players: Randall Bramblett, David Brown, Toy Caldwell, Charlie
    Hayward, Paul Hornsby, John Hughey, Jaimoe, Chuck Leavell, Drew
    Lombar, Jimmy Nalls, Johnny Sandlin, Bill Stewart
Background Vocals: Ella Brown, Donna Hall, Joyce Knight

Don McClean, *Playin' Favorites*, percussion:
"Sitting on Top of the World," "Living with the Blues," "Mountains O'Mourne,"
    "Fool's Paradise," "Love O Love," "Bill Cheetham—Old Joe Clark,"
    "Everyday," "Ancient History," "Over the Mountains," "Lovesick Blues,"
    "Mule Skinner Blues," "Happy Trails"

1975

Allman Brothers Band, *Win, Lose or Draw*, producer, engineer, guitar, drums,
    percussion:
"Can't Lose What You Never Had," "Just Another Love Song" (drums),
    "Nevertheless," "Win, Lose or Draw," "Louisiana Lou" (drums), "High Falls"
    (congas), "Sweet Mama"
Band: Gregg Allman, Richard Betts, Jaimoe, Butch Trucks, Chuck Leavell, Lamar
    Williams
Additional Players: Johnny Sandlin, Bill Stewart

Elvin Bishop, *Juke Joint Jump*, producer, acoustic & electric guitar, percussion,
    remixing:
"Juke Joint Jump," "Calling All Cows," "Rollin' Home," "Wide River," "Sure
    Feels Good," "Arkansas Line," "Hold On," "Crawling King Snake," "Do
    Nobody Wrong"
Elvin Bishop Players: Phil Aaberg, Don Baldwin, Michael Brooks, Johnny
    Vernazza
Additional Musicians: Rick Kellogg, Ross Mason, Johnny Sandlin, Stephen Stills

Sandlin, Stewart, Leavell, "One More Try" (single song), bass

Hydra, *Land of Money*, producer, percussion, executive supervision:
"Little Miss Rock & Roll," "The Pistol," "Makin' Plans," "Land of Money," "Get
    Back to the City," "Don't Let Time Pass You By," "Let the Show Go On,"
    "Slow and Easy," "Take Me for My Music"

Band: Will Boulware, Wayne Bruce, Orville Davis, Spencer Kirkpatrick, Steve
    Pace, Dan Turberville

Allman Brothers Band, *The Road Goes on Forever*, producer:
"Wasted Words," "Ramblin' Man," "Jessica"
Band: Gregg Allman, Dickey Betts, Jaimoe, Butch Trucks, Chuck Leavell, Lamar
    Williams

Bobby Whitlock, *One of a Kind*, tambourine:
"Goin' to California," "Have You Ever Felt Like Leavin'?"

1976
TSS, *Happy to Be Alive*, producer, artist/ bass, electric guitar:
"Don't Ride Away," "Never in My Life," "Stalemate Blues," "It Might Be the
    Rain," "Help Me Get It Out," "You Got a Friend," "Working in the Coal
    Mine," "Happy to Be Alive"
Band: Tommy Talton, Johnny Sandlin, Bill Stewart
Additional Musicians: Scott Boyer, Joe English, Ricky Hirsch, Dru Lombar

Bonnie Bramlett, *Lady's Choice*, producer, guitar:
"Think (about It)," "Hold On! I'm Comin'," "You Send Me," "Never Gonna Give
    You Up," "Let's Go Get Stoned," "Two Steps from the Blues," "If I Were Your
    Woman," "Ain't That Lovin' You Baby," "You've Really Got a Hold on Me,"
    "Thrill on the Hill," "Forever Young"
Bonnie Bramlett Players: Gregg Allman, Berry Beckett, Richard Betts, Randall
    Bramblett, Harrison Calloway, Roger Hawkins, Ricky Hirsch, David Hood,
    Paul Hornsby, Chuck Leavell, Charles Rose, Johnny Sandlin, Harvey
    Thompson
Background Vocals: Anita Ball, Dianne Davidson

Corky Lang, *Makin' It on the Street*, producer, engineer:
"On My Way," "Makin' It on the Street," "Two Places at One Time," "See Me
    Through," "Don't You Worry," "I Know, Somebody Told Me," "Growin' Old
    with Rock & Roll," "Heaven"
Corky Lang Players: Calvin Arline, Randall Bramblett, Harrison Calloway, Pete
    Carr, Ronnie Eades, Neal Larson, Old Slow Hand, Charles Rose, Tommy
    Talton, Harvey Thompson, Frank Vicari
Background Vocals: Vanetta Fields, Clydie King, Sherlie Matthews

Allman Brothers Band, *Wipe the Windows, Check the Oil, Dollar Gas*, producer, engineer:
"Wasted Words," "Southbound," "Ramblin' Man," "In Memory of Elizabeth Reed," "Ain't Wastin' Time No More," "Come & Go Blues," "Can't Lose What You Never Had," "Not My Cross to Bear," "Jessica"
Band: Gregg Allman, Richard Betts, Jaimoe, Butch Trucks, Chuck Leavell, Lamar Williams

1977

Doug Kershaw, *Flip, Flop & Fly*, producer, guitar, percussion:
"I'm Walkin'," "Bad News," "Black Rose," "I'm a Loser," "Kershaw's Two Step," "Roly Poly," "You Won't Let Me," "Rag Mama Rag," "Louisiana Blues," "Flip, Flop and Fly," "Twenty-three"
Additional Musicians: Calvin Arline, Elvin Bishop, Randall Bramblett, Harrison Calloway, Ronnie Eades, John Hughey, Al Kaatz, Neil Larson, Jimmy Nalls, Pete Pendras, Mac Rebennack, Charles Rose, Johnny Sandlin, Bill Stewart, Max Paul Schwennson, Harvey Thompson, Marty Valadabene
Background Vocals: Bonnie Bramlett, Annie Rose DeArmas

Richard Betts, *Great Southern*, remixing:
"Out to Get Me," "Run Gypsy Run," "Sweet Virginia," "The Way Love Goes," "Nothing You Can Do," "California Blues," "Bougainvillea"

Tim Weisberg, *TWB*, producer:
"Cascade," "Lord Vanity," "Mercy, Mercy, Mercy," "Gentle Storm," "Southern Lights," "Gene, Jean," "Aspen," "Shellie's Rainbow," "Blitz"
Band: Tim Weisberg, Doug Anderson, Tom Dougherty, Ty Grimes, Todd Robinson
Additional Musicians: John Hug, Rick Jaeger, Neil Larsen, Chuck Leavell Tower of Power Horns

Gregg Allman/Cher, *Allman & Woman, Two the Hard Way*, producer, remixing:
"Move Me," "I Found You, Love," "Can You Fool," "You've Really Got a Hold on Me," "We're Gonna Make It," "Do What You Gotta Do," "In for the Night," "Shadow Dream Song," "Island," "I Love Makin' Love to You," "Love Me"

Cher Allman, Gregg Allman Players: Steve Beckmeier, Scott Boyer, Randall
    Bramblett, Ben Cauley, Harrison Calloway, Ronnie Eades, Dennis Good,
    Bobbye Hall, Ricky Hirsch, Jim Horn, John Hug, Neil Larson, Mickey
    Raphael, Bill Stewart, Fred Tackett, Harvey Thompson, Willie Weeks
Background Vocals: Doug Haywood, Pat Henderson, Clydie King, Sherlie
    Matthews, Russell Morris, Tim Schmit

Tim Weisberg, *Rotations*, producer:
"All Tied Up," "So Good to Me," "Power Pocket," "Sudden Samba," "Every
    Time I See Your Smile," "There Is a Mountain," "Catch the Breeze," "Glide
    Away," "Just For You"
Tim Weisberg Players: Doug Anderson, Harrison Calloway, Ernie Carlson, Ben
    Cauley, Ronnie Eades, Bobbye Hall, John Hug, Rick Jaeger, Neil Larson,
    Chuck Leavell, Mickey Raphael, Todd Robinson, Muscle Shoals Horns, Fred
    Selden, Bill Stewart, Harvey Thompson

Delbert McClinton, *Second Wind*, producer, electric guitar, remixing:
"B Movie Boxcar Blues," "Isn't That So," "Corrina," "Take It Easy," "Spoonful,"
    "It Ain't Whatcha Eat but the Way How You Chew It," "Sick and Tired,"
    "Maybe Someday Baby," "Big River," "Lovinest Man"
Delbert McClinton Players: Berry Beckett, Harrison Calloway, Ronnie Eades,
    Dennis Good, Bobbye Hall, Robert Harwell, Roger Hawkins, David Hood,
    John Hug, Jimmy Johnson, Billy Sanders, Johnny Sandlin, Louis Stephens,
    Harvey Thompson

1978
Kingfish, *Trident*, producer, bass:
"Hard to Love Somebody," "Cheyenne," "Hurricane," "My Friend," "Magic
    Eyes," "Movin' Down the Highway," "Hawaii," "You and I," "Feels So
    Good," "Take It Too Hard"
Band: Bob Hogins, Matthew Kelly, Michael O'Neil, Dave Torbert, Joe English
Additional Musicians: John Hug, Johnny Sandlin
Background Vocals: David Perper

Rockets, *Turn up the Radio*, producer:
"Can't Sleep," "Turn Up the Radio," "Oh Well," "Lost Forever, Left for
    Dreaming," "Long Long Gone," "Something Ain't Right," "Lucille," "Feel
    Alright," "Love Me Once Again"

Band: Donnie Backus, John Badanjek, David Gilbert, Jim McCarty, Dennis
   Robbins
Additional Players: John Fraga, David Hood, Chuck Leavell

Delbert McClinton, *Keeper of the Flame*, producer:
"Plain Old Makin' Love," "Just a Little Bit," "Shot from the Saddle," "I Don't
   Want to Hear It Anymore," "Have Mercy," "I'm Talking about You," "Two
   More Bottles of Wine," "See Saw," "I Received a Letter," "A Mess of the
   Blues"

Delbert McClinton Players: Bobbye Hall, Robert Harwell, John Hug, John Jarvis,
   Andy Newmark, Billy Sanders, Joe Walk, Willie Weeks
Background Vocals: Paulette Brown, Vanetta Fields, Sherlie Matthews

1979

Outlaws, *Eye of the Storm*, producer:
"Lights Are on but Nobody's Home," "Miracle Man," "Blueswater," "Comin'
   Home," "I'll Be Leaving Soon," "Too Long Without Her," "It's All right,"
   "(Com' on) Dance With Me," "Long Gone"
Band: Harvey Dalton Arnold, David Dix, Bill Jones, Freddie Salem, Hughie
   Thomasson, Monte Yoho

Rockets, *No Ballads*, producer:
"Desire," "Don't Hold On," "Restless," "Sally Can't Dance," "Takin' It Back,"
   "Time after Time," "Sad Songs," "I Want You to Love Me," "It's True,"
   "Troublemaker"
Band: Donnie, Backus, John Badanjek, Dave Gilbert, Dan Keylon, Jim McCarty,
   Dennis Robbins
Additional Musician: Lee Michaels
Background Vocals: Anita Pointer, Ruth Pointer

1980

The Look, *The Look*, producer:
"Nothin's Gonna Stop Us," "We're Gonna Rock," "Dreamin'," "Be With Me,"
   "Don't Let Me Be Misunderstood," "Been Used," "Can't Think Right," "Do
   You Want Me Too," "Race Against Time," "Last Night"
Band: Rick Cochran, Dave Edwards, John Sarkisian, Randy Volin, Sam Warren

Billy Karloff & the Extremes, *Let Your Fingers Do the Talking*, producer:
"Let Your Fingers Do The Talkin'," "Encore," "Moanin'," "Sloppy Song," "Don't
  Keep Me Down," "Here," "Headbangers," "Picture of You," "It's Too Hot,"
  "Reader's Wives," "I'll Be There"
Billy Karloff Band: Glen Buglass, Neil Hay, Paul Jelliman, Dolphin Taylor
Additional Players: Rick Kurtz, Chuck Leavell, Steve Nathan

Eddie Kendricks, *Love Keys*, producer, engineer:
"Oh, I Need Your Loving," "I'm in Need of Love," "I Don't Need Nobody Else,"
  "The Old Home Town," "Bernadette," "You Can't Stop My Loving," "Never
  Alone," "Hot," "Looking for Love," "In Love We're One"
Eddie Kendricks Players: Ronnie Eades, Ken Bell, Harrison Calloway, Ben
  Cauley, Davis Causey, Owen Hale, John Hug, John Jarvis, Rick Kurtz, Steve
  Nathan, Michael Panepento, Charles Rose, Harvey Thompson, Joe Walk, Bob
  Wray

1981
Telluride, *Telluride*, producer, engineer, mixing:
"Fables and Stories," "Hollow Eyes," "Birmingham Tonight," "Sensimilla,"
  "Scratch My Guitar," "Never Too Late"
Band: Rick Carter, Robert Churchill, Kevin Derryberry, William Harrell, Scott
  Walker
Additional Players: Gordon Burt, Steve Nathan, Michael Panepento
Background Vocals: Louise Davis, Lolly Lee

Mac Davis, *Midnight Crazy*, engineer:
"Midnight Crazy," "Dammit Girl," "I've Got the Hots for You," "You're My
  Bestest Friend," "Comfortable," "Tell Me Your Fantasies," "You Are So
  Lovely," "Kiss It and Make It Better," "Something's Burning," "Float Away"

1982
Ronnie Dunn, 45, producer:
"Written All Over Your Face," "You Never Cross My Mind"

Jerry Reed, *The Bird*, engineer:
"Down on the Corner," "Hard Times," "I Want to Love You Right," "Good Time
  Saturday Night," "The Bird," "Red River," "I'm a Slave," "I'm in Love with
  Loving You," "I Get Off on It," "She Got the Goldmine (I Got the Shaft)"

Jerry Reed, *Man with a Golden Thumb*, engineer:
"Man With a Golden Thumb," "Love Is Muddy Water," "Love Being Your Fool,"
"Best I Ever Had," "Patches," "She Got the Goldmine (I Got the Shaft),"
"Hobo," "Forty-Four," "It Tears Me Up," "Stray Dogs and Stray Women"

Dennis Robbins, "'Til I get Over You," 45, producer, engineer, mixing

Ronnie Dunn, 45s, producer:
"She Put the Sad in All His Songs," "Change of Attitude," "Where Did He Go
Right?," "He Ain't Got a Way with Women"

1983
Terri Gibbs, *Over Easy*, engineer:
"Anybody Else's Heart but Mine," "Steal Away," "I Can't Resist," "Tell Mama,"
"Bells," "Over Easy," "I Just Don't Love You, That's All," "Every Home
Should Have One," "You're Going out of My Mind," "What a Night"

Gus Hardin, *Gus Hardin*, engineer:
"Loving You Hurts," "If I Didn't Love You," "Since I Don't Have You," "After
the Last Goodbye," "You Can Call Me Blue," "I've Been Loving You Too
Long"

Mac Davis, *40-82*, engineer:
"Lying Here Lying," "It's Written All over Your Face," "Late at Night," "Love
You Ain't Seen the Last of Me," "Beer Drinkin' Song," "She's Steppin' Out,"
"Good Ol' Boys," "Shame on the Moon," "Spending Time Making Love and
Going Crazy," "Quiet Times"

Marie Osmond, "I've Got a Bad Case of You" (single), engineer

Gatlin Brothers, *Houston to Denver*, engineer:
"Houston (Means I'm One Day Closer to You)," "Dream That Got a Little Out of
Hand," "Daylight Lovin' Time," "It Takes One to Know One," "When the
Night Closes In," "Denver," "Not Tonight I've Got a Heartache," "If You're
Ever Down and Out," "It's Me," "The Lady Takes the Cowboy Every Time"

1990

Allgood, *Ride the Bee*, producer, engineer:
"Funky House," "Chore Boy," "Semprini," "Spiney Norman," "Train Song,"
    "Can't Get Next to You," "Ole #7," "Strings," "Overload," "Ride the Bee,"
    "The Nights You're On," "Trilogy"
Band: John Carter, Clay Fuller, Corky Jones, Charlie Pruet, Mike Sain, Alberto
    Salazarte
Additional Musicians: Mickey Buckins, John Herman, Chuck Leavell, John Willis
Background Vocals: Jim Bickerstaff, Scott Boyer

1991
Scott Boyer, *All My Friends*, engineer, mixing:
"The Sooner that I'm Dead," "All My Friends," "My Love Will Follow You," "I
    Won't Give Up," "Born In the Country," "Fatten Me Up For the Kill,"
    "Remote Control," "Please Be with Me," "I've Got Nobody to Love,"
    "Woodchuck"

Eddie Hinton, *Cry & Moan*, engineer, mixing, arrangements, drums, bass,
    percussion:
"Come on Home Baby," "Cry and Moan," "I Found a True Love," "Testify,"
    "Cook with Me Mama," "Got to Have You," "Good Times," "Last Train to
    Loveland," "The Well of Love," "Bottom of the Well," "Make It Easy on Me,"
    "I Remember Justice"

Widespread Panic, *Widespread Panic*, producer, mixing:
"Send Your Mind," "Walkin'," "Pigeons," "Mercy," "Rock," "Makes Sense to
    Me," "C. Brown," "Love Tractor," "Weight of the World," "I'm Not Alone,"
    "Barstools and Dreamers," "Proving Ground," "The Last Straw"
Band: John Bell, Michael Houser, Todd Nance, Domingo Ortiz, Dave Schools, T
    Lavitz
Additional Musicians: David Blackmon, Wayne Jackson, Andrew Love

Aquarium Rescue Unit, *Aquarium Rescue Unit Live*, producer, engineer, mixing:
"Introduction," "Fixin' to Die," "Yield Not to Temptation," "Working on a
    Building," "Time Is Free," "Basically Frightened," "Compared to What,"
    "Time Flack," "Davy Crockett," "A Walk with Peltor," "Jazz Bank," "Quinius
    Thoth," "Planet Earth"
Band: Col. Bruce Hampton, Oteil Burbridge, Jimmy Herring, Matt Mundy, Jeff
    Sipes

Additional Musicians: Chuck Leavell, Count M'Butu

Widespread Panic, *Space Wrangler*, producer, mixing:
"Me and the Devil Blues / Heaven"
Band: John Bell, Michael Houser, Todd Nance, Domingo Ortiz, Dave Schools, T
    Lavitz

Jupiter Coyote, *Cemeteries & Junkyards*, producer, engineer:
"Family Tree," "Jot," "That's Happenin'," "Crazy Woman," "Rose Hill," "3:25
    (Tick Tock)," "Ship In the Bottle," "Willow"
Band: Gene Bass, John Felty, Ned Grubb, Matthew Mayes, Matt Trevitt
Additional Players: Jim Bickerstaff, Chalmers Davis, N. C. Thurman

1992

Dixie Dreggs, *Bring 'Em Back Alive*, executive producer, mixing:
"Road Expense," "Assembly Line," "Holiday," "Country House Shuffle,"
    "Kashmir," "Odyssey," "Kat Food," "Hereafter," "Medley: Take It off the
    Top," "Divided We Stand," "Cruise Control"

Widespread Panic, *Everyday*, producer, engineer, mixing:
"Pleas," "Hatfield," "Wondering," "Papa's Home," "Diner," "Better Off,"
    "Pickin' Up the Pieces," "Henry Parson's Died," "Pilgrims," "Postcard,"
    "Dream Song"
Band: John Bell, Michael Howser, Todd Nance, Domingo Ortiz, Dave Schools,
    John Herman
Additional Musician: Matt Mundy
Background Vocals: Hampton Dempster, Danny Hutchens

1993

Aquarium Rescue Unit, *Mirrors of Embarrassment*, producer, engineer, mixing:
"No Egos under Water," "Lost My Mule in Texas," "It's Not the Same Old
    Thing," "Too Many Guitars," "Gone Today, Here Tomorrow," "Shoeless Joe,"
    "Lives of Longevity," "Memory Is a Gimmick," "Dead Presidents,"
    "Trondossa," "Swing," "Payday"
Band: Col. Bruce Hampton, Oteil Burbridge, Jimmy Herring, Matt Mundy, Jeff
    Sipe
Additional Musicians: Chuck Leavell, Count M'Butu, John Popper

White Buffalo, *White Buffalo*, producer, engineer, mixing:
"Funk 50," "New 92," "Mama's Got a Funky New Boyfriend," "Free the Weed,"
   "Goin' Home," "Machine," "Corn Boy," "I've Been Working," "Dream,"
   "Funky Stew"
Band: Randy Durham, Paul Edwards, Britt West, Samantha Woods
Additional Musicians: Chalmers Davis, Rick Kurtz
Background Vocals: Scott Boyer, Hempton Dempster, Albert Salazarte, BarbyQ

50 Lb. Head, *50 Lb. Head*, producer, engineer, mixing:
"All Over Me," "Been There," "Deep Inside," "Handy Man," "Richard
   Cranium," "(Good Ones Gone) Alabama," "Indian Dream," "Yesterday's
   Man," "Old 29," "Listen"
Band: Vic Cunningham, Jimmy DuBois, Mark Hamilton, Craig Schoen

Jupiter Coyote, *Wade*, producer, engineer, mixing:
"Flight of the Lorax," "On Trial," "Ballad of Lucy Edenfield," "Hopkins County
   Stew," "Real Thing," "Narrow Line," "Cindi," "Lies," "Modern Creek," "Blue
   Agave"
Band: Gene Bass, Jr., Sanders Brightwell, John Felty, Matthew Mayes, David
   Stevens Jr.

Bloodkin, *Good Luck Charm*, producer, engineer, mixing:
"Preacherman," "#1 Good Luck Charm," "Take It Back," "Quarter Tank of
   Gasoline," "Privilege," "Swallow Fire," "Can't Get High," "Looking for
   Something to Steal," "Leave It Alone," "Success Yourself," "New Horse and
   Carriage," "End of the Show"
Band: Chris Barrineau, Eric Carter, Jack Dawson, Daniel Hutchens
Additional Musicians: John Bell, Mickey Buckins, Roger Hawkins, John
   Hermann David Hood, Michael Houser, Todd Nance, Dave Schools, Jay
   Wilson
Background Vocals: Cassandra Ayers, Scott Boyer, Karen Estill, Conny Jackson,
   Jennifer Knight

1994
Truffle, *Nervous Laughter*, mixing:
"Trouble," "I Can't Shake It," "Forty Winks Away," "St. Mary's Glacier,"
   "Wrong Side Dream," "Steerhorns," "Twisted Old Tree," "The Wind and
   Me," "Walkin' Time," "Archetype," "Storyman"

Blue Miracle, *Blue Miracle*, producer, engineer, mixing:
"The Jones," "Throw It Away," "Part-Time Blues," "Do It for Love," "Jenna,"
   "She's a Lady," "Good Thang," "Move On"
Band: John Arthur, Steve Cyphers, Jon Gillespie, Derek Leiniger, Kevin O'Brian,
   Ryan Wick
Additional Musicians: Vinnie Ciesielski, Jim Horn, Matt Mayes, Charles Rose,
   Harvey Thompson
Background Vocals: Carla Russell

Both Sides, *Both Sides*, producer:
"Open," "Freedom," "Green," "Days of Gold," "The Sounds," "I'm Just Singin',"
   "Inspiration," "Unlucky Seven," "Again"
Band: Noel Felty, Mark Millwood, Mark Mundy, Alan Wolf
Additional Musicians: Chuck Leavell, Matt Mundy, Count M'Butu, Jay Wilson

Brides of Jesus, *Cookies & Milk*, producer, engineer, mixing:
"Let Me Have it All," "What's Gonna Set Your Free?," "Gas Money," "Shattered
   Visions," "Perhaps Some Cookies & Milk," "Turn Around," "Jamama,"
   "Shine On," "Why Away"
Band: Jeff Goulhart, Billy Iuso, Ted Pickman
Additional Players: Vinny Ciesielski, Col. Bruce Hampton, Kelvin Holly, David
   Hood, Phred Parker, Charles Rose, Harvey Thompson, Steve Vendetouili, Jay
   Wilson
Background Vocals: Scott Boyer, Carla Russell

Dan Penn, *Do Right Man*, engineer, mixing:
"Dark End of the Street," "Cry Like a Man," "It Tears Me Up," "You Left the
   Water Running," "Do Right Woman, Do Right Man," "Memphis Women and
   Chicken," "Zero Willpower," "He'll Take Care of You," "I'm Your Puppet,"
   "Where There's a Will"

Jerry Joseph, *Love & Happiness*, producer, engineer, mixing:
"Two Balloons," "Criminals In My Closet," "Hold on to You," "Thistle," "New
   Psychology of Love," "War at the End of the World," "Yellow Ribbon,"
   "Glow," "Henry," "Ric and Rikki," "Election Day"
Jerry Joseph Players: Mickey Buckins, Oteil Burbridge, Kelvin Holly, David
   Hood, Rick Kurtz, Chuck Leavell, Rob O'Hearn, Bryan Owings, Jack Peck,

Topper Price, Charles Rose, Johnny Sandlin, Dave Schools, Harvey
Thompson
Background Vocals: Cassandra Ayers, Scott Boyer, Conny Jackson, Carla Russell,
George Soule'

The Bluedads, *Hands of Fate*, producer, engineer, mixing:
"Shine for Yourself," "Don't Feel Alone," "Take a Ride," "Like a Symphony,"
"Tear the House Down," "We'll Stay This Way," "What the Hell Is Goin'
On?," "That's the Way It Goes," "River Tune," "Dreamin' for a While," "I
Don't Mind," "Where We Gonna Go from Here?," "Like a Symphony,
reprise"
Band: Ben Elkins, Porter Landrum, Terry Powers, Doug Royale

1995

Law of Nature, *More*, producer, engineer, mixing:
"Easiest Thing," "Carolina," "Better on Our Own," "Sun," "What Is This," "Up,
Up & Away," "Train Song," "With You," "More," "As Dark As You"
Band: Karen Estill, Michael Freed, Jennifer Knight, David Strickland, Chapman
Welch
Additional Musicians: Jimmy Hall, Ernie Welch

Jupiter Coyote, *Lucky Day*, producer, engineer, mixing:
"By and By," "Confusionville," "Breckenridge," "Drew's Theme," "Catch 22,"
"Riddle," "Lucky Day," "Tying Things Together," "Amorous"
Band: Gene Bass, Sanders Brightwell, John Felty, Matthew Mayes, David
Stevens, Jr.
Additional Musicians: Catfish, Josh Rabinowitz

Microwave Dave & the Nukes, *Goodnight Dear*, producer, engineer, mixing:
"Last Call for Alcohol," "Pay Bo Diddley," "Born to Boogie Woogie," "Got My
Mind Made Up," "Roadrunner," "If the Four Winds Don't Change," "20%
Alcohol," "Nothin' but the Blues," "Body and Fender Man," "Start Me to
Drinkin'," "Atomic Powered," "Highway's Like a Woman," "Jesus Was
Smart," "Peace in the Alley"
Microwave Dave Gallaher Players: Mike Alexander, Scott Boyer, Artie Dean,
Rick Godfrey, Roger Hawkins, Kelvin Holly, David Hood, Jerry McCain,
Johnny Sandlin, Bill Stewart, N. C. Thurman, Joe Walk
Background Vocal: Ann Sandlin

Jimmy Hall, *Rendezvous with the Blues*, producer, engineer, mixing, remixing:
"That's The Truth," "Don't Hit Me No More," "Twenty-Nine Ways to My Baby's
Door," "Rendezvous with the Blues," "Long Distance Call," "Too Tall to
Mambo," "A Change Is Gonna Come," "The Hunter," "Weep and Moan,"
"Hold What You Got," "The Money Doesn't Matter"
Jimmy Hall Players: Kelvin Holly, David Hood, Clayton Ivey, Dan Matrazzo,
Jack Pearson, Bill Stewart
Background Vocals: Dave Gallaher, Jimmy Keith, Ric Seymour, Topper Price

Gregg Allman, *Searching for Simplicity*, producer, engineer, bass, percussion:
"Whipping Post," "House of Blues," "Come Back and Help Me," "Silence Ain't
Golden Anymore," "Rendezvous with the Blues," "Wolf's A-Howlin'," "Love
the Poison," "Don't Deny Me," "Dark End of the Street," "Neighbor
Neighbor," "I've Got News for You"
Gregg Allman Players: Scott Boyer, Vinnie Ciesielski, Chalmers Davis, Jimmy
Hall, Roger Hawkins, Kelvin Holly, David Hood, Jim Horn, Clayton Ivey,
Sam Levine, Jack Pearson, Topper Price, Charles Rose, Johnny Sandlin,
Harvey Thompson, Derek Trucks, Jay Wilson
Background Vocals: Ava Aldridge, Cindy Richardson, Carla Russell, George
Soule'

1996

Johnny Jenkins, *Blessed Blues*, producer, engineer, mixing, bass, maracas:
"Don't Start Me Talkin'," "It Ain't Nothin' but the Blues," "Statesboro Blues,"
"The Truth Is Gonna Stand," "You Can't Lose What You Ain't Never Had,"
"Don't Feel Like Talkin'," "Rock Bottom Blues," "'Til the Blues Go Home,"
"Mean Mistreatin' Woman," "The Pinetopper Theme," "I Think I'm
Drowning on Dry Land," "Miss Thing"
Johnny Jenkins Players: Randall Bramblett, Mickey Buckins, David Hood,
William Howse, Chuck Leavell, Jack Pearson, Johnny Sandlin, Bill Stewart, N.
C. Thurman
Background Vocals: Scott Boyer, Ann Sandlin

1997

Eddie Hinton, *Hard Luck Guy*, producer, engineer, mixing, bass, guitar, drums,
maracas, tambourine:

"Hard Luck Guy," "Can't Beat the Kid," "Here I Am," "Sad Song," "One Mo'
Time," "Watch Dog," "I Can't Be Me," "Lovin' Chain," "Three Hundred
Pounds of Hongry," "I Got My Thang Together," "Ol' Mr. Wind," "Ubangi
Stomp," "What Would I Do Without You?"
Eddie Hinton Players: Owen Brown, Mickey Buckins, Donnie Fritts, Dan Havely,
Roger Hawkins, David Hood, Paul Hornsby, Clayton Ivey, Jimmy Johnson,
Spooner Oldham, Dan Penn, Charles Rose, Johnny Sandlin, Jeff Simpson, Bill
Stewart, Harvey Thompson, Joe Walk

John McAndrew, *I'll Play All Night Long*, liner notes

Derek Trucks, *Derek Trucks*, mixing:
"Sarod," "Mr. P. C.," "D Minor Blues #6 Dance," "Footprints," "Out of
Madness," "Naima," "So What," "Evil Clown," "Egg 15," "Sarod Outro"

NASA, "A Time for Courage" (single), producer

Chuck Leavell, *What's in That Bag?*, producer, mixing:
"It's Just Not Christmas," "Merry Christmas Baby," "Bethlehem," "Joy Boogie,"
"Please Come Home for Christmas," "O Christmas Tree," "God Rest Ye
Merry Gentlemen," "We Three Kings," "Even Santa Gets the Blues," "Away
in a Manger," "Greensleeves," "O Holy Night"
Chuck Leavell Players: Jim Armstrong, Mickey Buckins, Mike Copeland, Roger
Hawkins, Kelvin Holly, David Hungate, Mark Hynes, Bobby Keys, Joe
McGlohon, Doug Moffatt, David Pomeroy, Topper Price, Charles Rose, Bill
Stewart
Background Vocals: Lisa Fischer, Carla Russell, Tina Swindell, Cindy Walker

Walter Jr., *Louisiana Soul*, producer, engineer, mixing, bass:
"Bad Whiskey," "Hole In My Soul," "Be by Me," "She Ain't My Neighbor,"
"Ain't What You Thank," "Some Kind of Way," "Purple, Gold and Green,"
"Mama's Kitchen," "What I Want," "The Whole Night," "Highway 90,"
"Love Starved Louann," "See You Later Alligator"
Walter Pousson Jr. Players: Randall Bramblett, Mickey Buckins, Oteil Burbridge,
Phil Chandler, Vinnie Ciesielski, David Hood, Paul Hornsby, Sonny
Landreth, Joe McGlohon, Doug Moffett, Charles Rose, Johnny Sandlin, Bill
Stewart, Harvey Thompson, Joe Walk, Jim Williamson, Jay Wilson
Background Vocals: Carla Russell, Tina Swindell

1998

Watters Brothers, *Watters Brothers*, producer, mixing:
"The Girls Back Home," "Moonlight in Vermont," "I'm Getting Sentimental over
    You," "Autumn Leaves," "Diversion," "What Is This Thing Called Love,"
    "Close to the Vest," "Trinidad," "Body and Soul," "In a Sentimental Mood,"
    "Over the Rainbow"
Harry Watters, Ken Watters Players: Scott Colley, Scott Newman, Kenny Werner

Fiji Mariners (featuring Col. Bruce Hampton), *Live*, mixing:
"Fiji," "The Mariner," "Turn on Your Love Light," "Spider," "Spoonful,"
    "Earth," "Whippoorwill," "Sgoda," "Nowhere Is Now Here"

1999

Hank Becker & the Boogie Chillin', *Chillin' at Play*, producer, engineer, mixing:
"Give Me the Blues," "Standing around in the Rain," "Hot Sauce," "I Can't Give
    Up," "Bull Bream Blues," "Long Time Coming," "Henry's Truck,"
    "Suburbia," "Dig," "Hot Sauce (pig meat)"
Hank Becker Players: Ricky Chancey, Rick Long, Bo Roberts, Jimmy Roebuck,
    Jay Wilson, Warren Wolf
Background Vocals: Donna Hall, Randy Landers, Lisa Mills

Topper Price, *Topper Price*, producer, engineer, mixing:
"Nature," "All of You Baby," "Got Love If You Want It," "Be Careful,"
    "Nicotine," "Can't Hold Out"
Topper Price Players: Warren Anderson, Jim Boykin, Don Tinsley, Joe Walk

2000

Microwave Dave, *Wouldn't Lay My Guitar Down*, producer, engineer, mixing:
"Sugar Bee," "Hey Little Girl," "I Wouldn't Lay My Guitar Down," "Hat," "Soon
    as the Weather Breaks," "I Want My Rib Back," "Don't Care Blues," "King of
    the Blues," "Don't Throw My Baby Away," "Dynaflow Blues," "Sentimental
    Journey," "Stumblin' Home"
Microwave Dave Gallaher Players: Rick Godfrey, Skip Skipworth
Additional Musicians: Roger Hawkins, Kelvin Holly, David Hood, Brian
    Owings, Bill Stewart

Watters Brothers, *Watters Brothers II*, producer, engineer, mixing:

"Everything's Alright," "Somerset Road," "Days of Wine and Roses," "Judy
Rebecca," "There is No Greater Love," "Vessel," "Trainer on the Beach," "Out
of Nowhere," "Mrs. Howell," "Pure Imagination," "Port-au-Prince"
Harry Watters, Ken Watters Players: Jay Frederick, David Marlow, Roy
Yarbrough
Additional Musicians: John Miller, Tom Wolfe

Scalded Dogs, *Call off the Dogs*, producer, engineer, mixing, artist/ bass:
"She Cranks My Tractor," "Loser's Convention," "Sometimes It Sucks Being
Me," "Lovesick Blues," "The Blues Are Flowing Freely," "She Still Does,"
"Short End of the Stick," "The Mouth of Music Row," "Too Much Monkey
Business," "You Win Again," "Cats and Dogs"
Band: Scott Boyer, Kelvin Holly, Johnny Sandlin, N. C. Thurman, Joe Walk,
Bryan Wheeler
Additional Musicians: Rick Kurtz, Spooner Oldham. Brian Owings

Mike Roberts, producer, engineer, mixing:
"Don't Wanna See You Cry," "June," "July Rain," "One More Chance Again,"
"Monkey," "Squeeze Me," "Just Let Me Know," "Look Out My Window,"
"Insane/Country Medley"

Chuck Leavell, *Forever Blue*, remixing, sequencing:
"Forever Blue," "Song for Amy," "Blue Rose," "Comin' Home," "Ashokan
Farewell," "A Lotta Colada," "Just Before Dawn," "Walk a Little Closer,"
"Higher Ground," "Georgia on My Mind"

Kathy Martin, *Catahoula*, producer, mixing, bass:
"Grandma's Hands," "If You Get Down," "Witness For Love," "Reunion," "Here
Comes the Rain," "Love Me," "Gumbo Man," "Out of Left Field," "T-Yeux
Noir," "Blue Bayou," "Me and Bobby McGee," "Look but Don't Touch"
Kathy Martin Players: Al Berard, Randall Bramblett, Oteil Burbridge, Scott
Boyer, Phil Chandler, Mickey Buckins, Phil Chandler, Vinny Ciesielski, David
Hood, Danny Kimball, Sonny Landreth, Doug Moffatt, George Perilli, Walter
Pousson, Jr., Charles Rose, Harvey Thompson, N. C. Thurman, Bill Stewart,
Errol Verett

Spoonful James, *Seven Mile Breakdown*, producer, engineer, mixing:

"Seven Mile Breakdown," "It's All Gonna Pass," "Take It off Him, Put It on Me,"
   "Too Many Things," "Too Late," "Closing In," "Ain't No Way," "Big Legged
   Woman," "That's It For Now," "On the Ground," "Nothing on My Baby"
Band: Quinn Borland, Wynn Christian, Patrick Lunceford
Additional Musician: Mickey Buckins, Brad Guin, John Hughey, Clayton Ivey,
   Buddy Miles, Charles Rose, Harvey Thompson, Ken Watters, Jay Wilson
Background Vocals: Bonnie Bramlett

2001

Lee Roy Parnell, *To Tell the Truth*, engineer basic tracks:
"Right Where It Hurts," "Crossin' Over," "Breaking Down Slow," "South by
   Southwest," "Tell the Truth," "I Declare," "Brand New Feeling," "Guardian
   Angel," "Takes What It Takes," "Love's Been Rough on Me"

Ken Watters Group, *Southern Exposure*, producer, mixing:
"Jessica," "Cooler on the Horizon," "Both Sides Now," "Stella by Starlight,"
   "We'll Be Together Again"
Ken Watters Players: Jay Frederick, David Marlow, Roy Yarbrough
Additional Musician: Joel Frahm

The Skeeters, *The Skeeters*, producer, engineer, mixing:
"Rhythm of the World," "Clydesdales," "Country Pop," "God Bless 'Em All,"
   "Can't Get No Lovin,'" "Honey Chile," "Blues Are Flowing Freely,"
   "Backwoods," "Late Again," "High Gear," "Texas Day"
Band: Dan Barker, Rick Eller, Flash, Bert Newton, Matt Martin
Additional Musicians: Scott Boyer, Mickey Buckins, Donnie Fritts, James
   Pennebaker, Topper Price
Background Vocals: Bonnie Bramlett, Carla Russell

Walter Jr., *Back on the Bayou Road*, producer, engineer, mixing, bass:
"Hot Louisiana Rock," "Done Did Dat," "Back on the Bayou Road," "Gator Bait,"
   "I Gotta Moan," "Surrender to Love," "A Woman Like You," "Mojo Man,"
   "Leave Well Enough Alone," "Delta Cat," "Karma Come," "Mathilda," "Who
   You Gonna Hoodoo," "Two Tone Baby," "I'm a Louisiana Man"
Walter Pousson Jr. Players: Randall Bramblett, Mickey Buckins, Oteil Burbridge,
   Wayne Burns, David Hood, Paul Hornsby, Clayton Ivey, Carmen Jacob,
   Sonny Landreth, Doug Moffitt, Robert Nash, Brian Owings, Topper Price,

George Perilli, Charles Rose, Johnny Sandlin, Bill Stewart, Harvey Thompson, Joe Walk, Ken Watters, Jim Williams, Jay Wilson
Background Vocals: Bonnie Bramlett, Scott Boyer, Carla Russell

2002
Kunio Kishida, *Swamp Waters*, producer, engineer, mixing:
"Witch Face," "Thanks Anyway," "What a Fool," "I Got Sick?," "Long Time No See," "It's You," "It's Only Your Smile," "Helpin' Hand," "Elvis-A-Go-Go Blues," "Elvis-A-Go-Go," "At Midnight," "Better Days"
Kunio Kishida Players: Mickey Buckins, Ed Greene, Paul Hornsby, Jimmy Johnson, Samurai Taylor, Jerry Wasley Jr.
Background Vocals: Bonnie Bramlett, Scott Boyer

5ive O'Clock Charlie, *'Til She Speaks*, producer, engineer, mixing:
"Just Goes to Show," "'Til She Speaks," "Sing For Me," "Freak from a Small Town," "Voodoo," "Looking For a Way Out," "Worthless," "Savior Wanna Be," "Breakthrough," "Felchy Goes to Hollywood," "Up One Day Down"
Band: Scott Kennedy, Mike Roberts, Matt Ross, Jeff Woods

The Decoys, *Shot from the Saddle*, producer:
"Nadine"
Band: Scott Boyer, Kelvin Holly, David Hood, George Perilli, N. C. Thurman

Jimmy Thackery, *We Got It*, liner notes

2003
Ken and Harry Watters, *Brothers Vol. 3*, producer, engineer, mixing:
"Overflow," "Whitesburg Bridge," "You're My Everything," "Harmon Field," "Fall Festival," "Our Eyes Are Watching," "The New Horizon," "Another Reply," "Sometimes a Shadow," "The Very Thought of You," "Press," "Free Bird"
Harry Watters, Ken Watters Players: Erik Applegate, Jay Frederick, Tom Wolfe
Additional Musician: Bill Anschell

The Skeeters, *Easy for the Takin'*, producer, engineer, mixing:
"Easy for the Takin'," "Tryin' to Get There," "The Road," "Jester of Life," "I Have Just Begun," "Johnny," "Cut Me Down (and Turn Me Loose)," "Alabama Love Song," "Mother Trucker," "Memory Lane," "Dodgin' the

Blue," "I Met a Cowboy," "After the Fact," "Honky Tonk Keep Honky Tonkin"

Band: Chase Armstrong, Rick Eller, Matt Martin, Bert Newton

Additional Musicians: Jim Bickerstaff, Mickey Buckins, Owen Hale, Kelvin Holly, Paul Hornsby, LaRue Larry, Brian Owings, James Pennebaker, Ryan Tillery, N. C. Thurman

Background Vocals: Scott Boyer, Billy Joe Shaver, Tina Swindell

2005

Greg Koch & the Tone Controllers, *4 Days in the South*, mixing:

"Bored to Tears," "When Were the Good Old Days?," "Can't Get There from Here," "Your Face," "Them's the Breaks," "Fool's Gold," "Keep on Singin'," "The Love Contractor," "Folsom Prison Blues," "Chicken from Hell," "J. S. K."

Kunio Kishida, *Alabama Boy*, producer, engineer, mixing:

"Alabama Boy," "Celebration/Sadness," "Miss Your Dimples," "Don't Leave Me Please," "I'll Leave My Home," "Live In Hope," "N. A. City Woman," "Right Place," "Don't Say Nothing," "Sendai," "What Will Be Will Be," "You Knock Me Out"

Kunio Kishida Players: Mickey Buckins, Pete Carr, Paul Hornsby, Chuck Leavell, Jamie Oldaker, Jerry Wasley Jr., Bobby Whitlock

Background Vocals: Scott Boyer, Bonnie Bramlett, Carla Russell

2006

Toy Shop, *Get up Now*, producer, engineer, mixing:

"Three Flies," "Bed Bugs," "Interrupted Dream," "Knock on the Door," "Parking Lot," "Long, Long Time," "Crack," "Emily," "Walking Spanish," "Cave Crickets," "Get Up Now," "Train," "Time Machine"

Band: Jim Kolacek, Matt Ross, Andrew Sharpe, Antony Sharpe

Capricorn Rhythm Section, *Alive at 2nd St. Music Hall*, artist, bass, mixing:

"Time Will Take Us," "Everybody Needs Love," "Ought to Be a Law," "She Cranks My Tractor," "Please Be with Me," "Watch Out Baby," "Don't Hit Me No More," "All My Friends," "300 Pounds," "Where You Come From," "Where Can You Go?," "Shout Bamalama"

Band: Scott Boyer, Paul Hornsby, Johnny Sandlin, Bill Stewart, Tommy Talton

Guest Musician: Lee Roy Parnell

Microwave Dave, *Nukin' Down South*, producer, mixing:
"Road Runner," "Hip Shakin'," "20% Alcohol," "Got No Automobile," "Can't Stop Lovin' My Baby," "Ray Brand," "Body and Fender Man," "From a Buick 6," "It Don't Happen No More," "Shot Gun Slim," "Let's Say Goodnight," "Hey Little Girl"
Band: Dave Gallaher, James Ervin, Rick Godfrey

2007

Danny Brooks, *No Easy Way Out*, producer, engineer, mixing:
"Ain't That the Truth," "All God's Children," "No Easy Way Out," "Keys to My Heart," "Bama Bound," "Miracles for Breakfast," "Lonesome Road," "Where Sinners and Saints Collide," "Memphis, Tennessee," "I Believe in Love," "Carry Me Jesus"
Danny Brooks Players: Vinnie Ciesielski, Roger Hawkins, Kelvin Holly, David Hood, Kevin McKendree, Spooner Oldham, James Pennebaker, Charles Rose, Johnny Sandlin, Bill Stewart, Harvey Thompson, N. C. Thurman, Ken Watters
Background Vocals: Scott Boyer, Bonnie Bramlett, Carla Russell, Tina Swindell, Jay Wilson

Kenny Acosta, *Full Moon on Blues Street*, producer, engineer, mixing:
"Nobody's Better than You," "Hard Times," "Mr. Charlie," "Still Have the Blues for You," "Just to Have the Blues," "Louisiana," "Polk Salad," "The Thrill Is Gone," "House of the Rising Sun"
Kenny Acosta Players: Miguel Hernandez, Shaun Manguno, Kevin McKendree, Bill Stewart, N. C. Thurman

Sister Grace, *God Is Calling*, producer, engineer, mixing:
"All Day," "Sweet Taste of Heaven," "God Is Calling," "Home Again," "Love Flows Free," "Don't Worry," "I Keep Calling Out Your Name," "Your Love Never Fails," "Sister Grace Medley," "I Bless Your Name," "Lay Your Burdens Down," "Reach Out"
Band: Stephanie Fenton, Carole Ford, Whitney Hubbs, Tina Swindell
Additional Musicians: David Hood, Kelvin Holly, Kevin McKendree, Bryan Owings, Lynn Williams

2008

Bonnie Bramlett, *Beautiful*, producer, engineer, mixing:

"Sure Got Away with My Heart," "It's Gonna Rain," "Witness for Love,"
  "Strongest Weakness," "Beautiful," "I Do Believe," "Some of My Best
  Friends," "Bless 'Em All," "Shake Something Loose," "For What It's Worth,"
  "He'll Take Care of You"
Bonnie Bramlett Players: Scott Boyer, Scott Boyer III, Jimmy Bowland, Randall
  Bramblett, Mickey Buckins, Vinnie Ciesielski, David Hood, Kelvin Holly,
  Clayton Ivey, Joe McGlohon, Kevin McKendree, Doug Moffatt, James
  Pennebaker, Walter Pousson Jr., Charles Rose, Bill Stewart, Harvey
  Thompson, Ken Watters, Lynn Williams
Background Vocals: Bekka Bramlett, Katie Jane

2009

Highly Kind, *Don't Wake Albert*, producer, engineer, mixing:
"Don't Wake Elvis," "Have a Little Faith," "You Think You Know Someone,"
  "Bury My Soul," "Bits & Pieces," "Home," "Table of the Lord," "Done My
  Time," "Somebody's Gotta Make a Move," "Looks Can Be Deceiving," "Fell
  Off the Wagon," "Fading"
Band: Trey Evans, Kevin Scott, Albert Simpson, Duane Tricks
Additional Musicians: Walt Aldridge, Randall Bramblett, Josh Gooch, Joe
  Karacher, James Pennebaker, Darryl Tibbs
Background Vocals: Amanda Quarles

Walter Jr., *Standing on the Word*, engineer, mixing:
"I Heard a Story," "Christ Is Calling," "Standing on the Word," "His
  Outstretched Arms," "The Weight of the Cross," "Day of our Victory,"
  "Halle-Hallelujah," "Wedding Wine," "At That Very Moment," "It's about
  Love," "Our King Is Coming," "Lamp of the Lord," "The Kingdom Within,"
  "Won't Be Long," "Dark as Death"
Walter Pousson, Jr. Players: Doug Belote, Oteil Burbridge, Randall Bramblett
Vocals: Bonnie Bramlett, Bekka Bramlett
Background Vocals: Ella Cauthen, Bonnie Bramlett, Randall Bramblett, Walter Jr.

Kenneth Brian Band, *Welcome to Alabama*, producer, engineer, mixing:
"Texas Tonight," "Holding On," "Prayer for Love," "Nothing but You," "Bring It
  on Home," "Last Call," "Cry to the Dark," "Ponderosa," "Welcome to
  Alabama," "Ain't Nothin' You Can Do"
Kenneth Brian Band: Dickey Pryor, Travis Stephens, Zach Graham

Additional Players: David Hood, Charlie Hayward, Jason Isbell, Randall
    Bramblett, James Pennebaker
Background Vocals: Bonnie Bramlett

Compilations and Re-Releases

1972

Duane Allman, *Duane Allman Anthology*, drums, producer, compilation producer:
"B. B. King Medley," "Goin' Down Slow," "Rollin' Stone," "Please Be With Me,"
    "Down along the Cove"

1973
HourGlass, *HourGlass* (re-release)

1974

Duane Allman, *Duane Allman Anthology II*, producer, engineer, mixing, drums,
    compilation producer:
"Happily Married Man," "No Money Down," "I Walk on Gilded Splinters,"
    "Goin' up the Country"

Cowboy, *Why Quit When You're Losing?*, re-release (first two albums)

1975

Peaches, *Pick of the Crop*, various artists, producer:
Bonnie Bramlett, "Since I Met You Baby"; Richard Betts, "Highway Call";
    Cowboy, "Where Can You Go?"; Elvin Bishop, "Sure Feels Good"; Gregg
    Allman, "Are You Lonely For Me Baby?"; Allman Brothers Band,
    "Nevertheless"; Hydra, "The Pistol"

1976

Nitty Gritty Dirt Band, *Dirt, Silver & Gold*, drums:
"Collegiana"

1977

South's Greatest Hits, various artists, producer:
Gregg Allman, "Midnight Rider"; Elvin Bishop, "Fooled Around and Fell In
    Love"; Allman Brothers Band, "Ramblin' Man"

1978

South's Greatest Hits, various artists, producer:
"Jessica"

Hotels, Motels and Road Shows, various artists, producer:
Elvin Bishop, "Travelin' Shoes"; Gregg Allman, "Are You Lonely For Me Baby"

1981

Allman Brothers Band, *Best of the Allman Brothers*, producer:
"Ramblin' Man," "Win, Lose or Draw"

Duane Allman, *Best of Duane Allman*, drums:
"B. B. King Medley," "No Money Down," "Been Gone Too Long," "Happily
   Married Man," "Goin' Down Slow"

Time Life, *Ultimate 70s*, producer:
Gregg Allman, "Midnight Rider"

1985

HourGlass, *The Soul of Time* (UK release of *HourGlass* and *Power of Love* combined
   albums), artist

In the Beginning—Early Recordings of the Superstars, various Artists, artist:
HourGlass, "I Can't Stand Alone"

1989

Allman Brothers Band, *Dreams*, bass, drums, percussion, producer:
"Down in Texas," "B. B. King Medley," "Goin' Down Slow," "Wasted Words,"
   "Ramblin' Man," "Southbound," "Jessica," "Can't Lose What You Never
   Had," "Come and Go Blues," "Rain"

Doug Kershaw, *The Best of Doug Kershaw*, producer:
"I'm Walkin'"

Duane Allman, *Anthology* (re-release)

1991

Allman Brothers Band, *Decade of Hits 1969–1979*, producer:
"Ramblin' Man," "Southbound," "Ain't Wastin' Time No More," "Wasted Words"

1992

Elvin Bishop, *Sure Feels Good: The Best of Elvin Bishop*, producer, acoustic & electric guitar, percussion, tambourine:
"Ground Hog," "Let It Flow," "Fishin'," "Stealin' Watermelons," "Juke Joint Jump," "Crawling King Snake," "Calling All Cows," "Sure Feels Good"

Rock of the 70s, Vol. 3, various artists, producer, engineer, mixing:
Allman Brothers Band, "Ramblin' Man"

Rock of the 70s, Vol. 4, various artists, producer, engineer:
Gregg Allman, "Midnight Rider"

HourGlass, *HourGlass* (re-release) with bonus tracks:
"In a Time," "I've Been Trying" (version 2), "Kind of a Man," "Divorce," "She Is My Woman," "Bad Dream," "Three Time Loser"

1993

Alabama Music Hall of Fame Presents Muscle Shoals Bands of the 60s, various artists, guitar:
The Mark V with Dan Penn, "Two Steps from the Blues," "Ain't Nothin' You Can Do," "I Got a Woman"

Cowboy, *The Best of Cowboy*, producer, engineer, bass, congas:
"Livin' In the Country," "Pick Your Nose," "Everything Here," "It's Time," "5'll Getcha Ten," "Shoestrings," "Seven Four Tune," "All My Friends," "Please Be with Me," "A Patch and a Painkiller," "Where Can You Go," "Love 40," "Road Gravy Chase," "Houston—Houston Vamp," "It Might Be the Rain"

Mac Davis, *Very Best and More*, engineer:
"You're My Bestest Friend," "Let's Keep It That Way," "Midnight Crazy," "Shame on the Moon"

1994

Hard Rock Essentials: The 70s, various artists, supervised mastering:
Allman Brothers Band, "Statesboro Blues"

Arthur Conley, *Sweet Soul Music, The Best of Arthur Conley,* producer:
"They Call the Wind Mariah," "God Bless"

Marshall Tucker Band, *Best of Capricorn Years,* unknown contributor role

1995

Allman Brothers Band, *Legendary Hits,* producer:
"Wasted Words," "Jessica," "Win, Lose or Draw"

Hard Rock Essentials: 60s, various artists, supervised mastering:
Allman Brothers Band, "Whipping Post"

Arthur Conley, *Sweet Soul Music, The Best of Arthur Conley,* producer:
"They Call the Wind Mariah," "God Bless"

1996

Swamp Dogg, *The Best 25 Years,* drums:
"Redneck"

Allman Brothers Band / Wet Willie, *Back to Back,* producer:
"Ramblin Man," "Ain't Wastin' Time No More," "Southbound," "Red Hot
    Chicken," "Macon Hambone Blues," "That's All Right"

Allman Brothers Band, *Ramblin' Man,* producer:
"Southbound," "Ramblin' Man," "Jessica"

Johnny Jenkins, *Ton Ton Macoute,* re-release with:
"Backside Blues"

1997

Allman Brothers Band, *Brothers & Sisters* (re-release)

Capricorn Classics, (promo), producer, mixing, drums:

Johnny Jenkins, "I Walk on Guilded Splinters"; Captain Beyond, "Thousand
 Days of Yesterday Come and Gone"; Bonnie Bramlett, "Never Gonna Give
 You Up"; Elvin Bishop, "Fooled Around and Fell In Love"

Jerry Reed, *Super Hits*, engineer:
"The Bird," "She Got the Goldmine and I Got the Shaft"

Gregg Allman, *One More Try: An Anthology*, producer, engineer, mixing, original
 recording producer:
"One More Try," "All My Friends," "Can't Lose what You Never Had,"
 "Midnight Rider," "God Rest His Soul," "Multi-Colored Lady," "I Feel So
 Bad," "Wasted Words," "Turn on Your Love Light," "Can You Fool," "Please
 Call Home," "Will the Circle Be Unbroken?," "Come and Go Blues," "These
 Days," "God Rest His Soul," "Queen of Hearts," "Win, Lose or Draw," "Will
 the Circle Be Unbroken," "Shadow Dream Song," "Multi-Colored Lady,"
 "Bad Dream," "Oncoming Traffic," "Melissa"

1998
Livingston Taylor, *Carolina Day, The Collection* 1970, 1980, drums:
"Get Out of Bed," "Carolina Day," "Good Friends," "Lost in the Love of You,"
 "Caroline," "On Broadway," "I Just Can't Be Lonesome No More"

Wet Willie, *Drippin' Wet* (re-release)

Martin Mull, *Mulling It Over*, producer:
"Jesus Christ Superstar"

Elvin Bishop, *Let It Flow* (re-release)

Her Place, various artists, producer, engineer, mixing:
Holly Allen, "Her Place"; Eddie Hinton, "Everybody Needs Love"; Delbert
 McClinton, "She Sure Got Away with My Heart"; Microwave Dave and the
 Nukes, "Pay Bo Diddley"; Dan Penn, "That's Me"; Kozmic Mama, "I Got
 Somethin'," Jimmy Hall, "Nighttime Is the Right Time"; Mr. Wilson, "Agatha
 Mae"; Walter Jr. & the Juice, "Mama's Kitchen"; Jupiter Coyote, "Ballad of
 Lucy Edenfield"; Scott Boyer, "All My Friends"; Oteil Burbridge, "A-2 Fay";
 Ken and Harry Watters, "Girls Back Home"; Carla Russell, "Won't You Carry
 Me Jesus?"

Highway Rockin', various artists, mixing:
Allman Brothers Band, "One Way Out"

70s Rock Hits, various artists, producer, engineer:
Allman Brothers Band, "Southbound"

1998 Sampler, various artists, producer, engineer, mixing:
Jupiter Coyote, "Confusionville," "Good Thang"

1999
Delbert McClinton, *The Ultimate Collection*, producer, bass:
"B Boxcar Movie," "Shot from the Saddle"

Southern Rock Essentials, various artists, producer:
Allman Brothers, "Ramblin' Man"; Gregg Allman, "Midnight Rider"; Elvin
    Bishop, "Travelin' Shoes"

Alex Taylor, *Dinnertime* (re-release)

Elvin Bishop, *Juke Joint Jump* (re-release)

White Witch, *White Witch* (re-release)

Celebrate the Season, T. J. Martell Christmas Album, producer, mixing:
Chuck Leavell, "Please Come Home for Christmas"

Allman Brothers Band, *Classic Allman Brothers, The Universal Masters Collection*,
    producer:
"Ramblin' Man," "Jessica," "Southbound," "Win, Lose or Draw"

2000
Allman Brothers Band, *20th Century Masters, The Millennium Collection, The Best of
    the Allman Brothers*, producer:
"Ramblin' Man," "Jessica"

Mac Davis, *The Best of Mac Davis*, engineer:
"Kiss It and Make It Better"

Larry Gatlin/Gatlin Brothers, *Houston to Denver/Not Guilty*, engineer:
"Houston (Means I'm One Day Closer to You)," "Dream That Got a Little Out of Hand," "Daylight Lovin'," "It Takes One to Know One," "When the Night Closes In," "Denver," "Not Tonight, I've Got a Heartache," "If You're Ever Down and Out," "It's Me," "Lady Takes the Cowboy Every Time"

The 70s, Original NBC Movie Soundtrack, various artists, producer:
Allman Brothers Band, "Jessica"

2001
HourGlass, re-release

Allman Brothers Band, *The Road Goes on Forever* (re-release)

Gregg Allman, *Laid Back* (re-release)

Jerry Reed, *RCA Country Legends*, engineer:
"She Got the Goldmine, I Got the Shaft"

Goin' South, various artists, producer, engineer:
Allman Brothers Band, "Ramblin' Man"

Southern Rock, various artists, producer, engineer:
Allman Brothers Band, "Ramblin' Man," "Midnight Rider"

2002
Delbert McClinton, *Second Wind/Keeper of the Flame* (re-release)

Gregg Allman, *20th Century Masters, The Millennium Collection, The Best of Gregg Allman*, producer, bass:
"Midnight Rider," "Queen of Hearts," "These Days," "Multi-Colored Lady," "Please Call Home"

Gregg Allman, *No Stranger to the Dark, The Best of Gregg Allman*, producer, original recording producer:
"Island," "Melissa," "House of Blues," "Dark End of the Street," "I've Got News for You," "These Days"

Elvin Bishop, *20th Century Masters, The Millennium Collection, The Best of Elvin Bishop*, producer, electric guitar, tambourine:
"Let It Flow," "Ground Hog," "Stealin' Watermelons," "Travelin' Shoes," "Juke Joint Jump," "Sure Feels Good"

Katy Moffett, *Kissin' in the California Sun*, producer 3 tracks (re-release)

2003
Wet Willie, *20th Century Masters, the Millennium Collection*, producer:
"Grits Ain't Groceries"

Swamp Dogg, *If I Ever Kiss It, He Can Kiss It Goodbye*, drums:
"Wham Bam, Thank You Mam"

Delbert McClinton, *20th Century Masters, The Millennium Collection, The Best of Delbert McClinton*, producer, bass:
"Two More Bottles of Wine," "'B' Movie Boxcar Blues"

The Marshall Tucker Band, *The Marshall Tucker Band*, with bonus track, remix consultant:
"Take the Highway," "Can't You See," "Losing You," "Hillbilly Band," "See You Later, I'm Gone," "Ramblin," "My Jesus Told Me So," "AB's Song," "Everyday (I Have the Blues)"

Eric Clapton, *Martin Scorsese Presents the Blues: Eric Clapton*, producer: (listed but did not play or produce anything on the album)

Allman Brothers Band, *Martin Scorsese Presents the Blues, The Allman Brothers*, producer:
"Trouble No More," "Can't Lose What You Never Had"

Jerry Reed, *All American Country*, engineer:
"She Got the Goldmine, I Got the Shaft"

2004
Bonnie Bramlett, *It's Time/Lady's Choice* (re-release)

HourGlass, *Southbound*, re-release of original albums

Allman Brothers Band, *Stand Back, The Anthology*, producer:
"Ain't Wastin' Time No More," "Wasted Words," "Ramblin' Man," "Come and
  Go Blues," "Southbound," "Jessica," "Can't Lose What You Never Had,"
  "Win, Lose or Draw"

In The Mood For Memphis, various artists, engineering, mixing:
Dan Penn, "Memphis Women and Chicken"

2005
Eddie Hinton Anthology 1969–1993: A Mighty Field of Vision, producer, performer:
"Here I Am," "Sad Song," "Three Hundred Pounds of Hongry," "What Would I
  Do without You," "Cry and Moan," "Bottom of the Well"

Eddie Hinton, *Beautiful Dreams Sessions Vol. 3*, drums:
"Blue Blue Feeling," "Neighbor, Neighbor," "Walking with Mr. Lee," "Turn on
  Your Love Light"

Country Got Soul Vol. 2, various artists, producer, engineer, mixing:
Eddie Hinton, "I Can't Be Me"; Bonnie Bramlett, "Your Kind of Kindness"

Blues from the Heart of Dixie, various artists, producer, engineer:
Topper Price, "I Can't Hold Out," Microwave Dave, "Don't Throw Away My
  Baby"

Dickey Betts & Great Southern, *Atlanta Burning Down*, mixing:
"Out to Get Me," "Run Gypsy Run," "Sweet Virginia," "The Way Love Goes,"
  "Nothing You Can Do," "California Blues," "Bougainvillea"

Allman Brothers Band, *Gold*, producer, recording supervisor, acoustic guitar,
  percussion:
"Ramblin' Man," "Southbound," "Jessica"

Peach State Blues: A Collection of Contemporary Blues, various artists, engineer:
Reddog, "Honest Man"

Southern Rock Gold, various artists, producer:

"Ramblin Man," "Midnight Rider," "Travelin' Shoes," "Please Be With Me"

Larry Gatlin, *Best of Larry Gatlin & the Gatlin Brothers*, engineer:
"Houston (Means I'm One Day Closer to You)"

This Is Southern Rock, various artists, artist:

HourGlass, "Southbound"

2006

Jimmy Hall, *Rendezvous with the Blues* (re-release)with bonus tracks:
"That Did It Baby," "Night Time Is the Right Time," "Duck Soup"

Doug Kershaw, *Collectables Classics* (Box Set), producer, acoustic guitar,
    percussion:
"You Won't Let Me," "Rag Mama Rag," "Louisiana Blues," "Flip, Flop & Fly,"
    "Twenty-Three," "You Won't Let Me 2," "I'm Walkin'," "Bad News," "Black
    Rose," "I'm a Loser," "Kershaw's Two Step"

The Look, *Collection for the Record*, producer:
"We're Gonna Rock," "Do U Want Me Too?," "Don't let Me Be Misunderstood"

Delbert McClinton, *Definitive Collection*, producer:
"I Received a Letter," "Two More Bottles of Wine," "Ain't What You Eat but
    How You Chew It," "Take It Easy," "'B' Movie Boxcar Blues," "A Mess of
    Blues," "Plain Old Makin' Love"

Doug Kershaw, *Fais Do Do: The Music of the Bayou: 1969–1978*, producer:
"Rag Mama Rag," "Flip, Flop & Fly," "Black Rose," "I'm a Loser"

Dickey Betts, *Very Best of Dickey Betts: 1973–1978 Bougainvilleas Collection*,
    producer:
"Long Time Gone," "Rain," "Highway Call," "Let Nature Song," "Out to Get
    Me," "Run Gypsy Run," "Sweet Virginia," "Bougainvillea"

Mac Davis, *20th Century Masters, the Millennium Collection, The Best of Mac Davis*,
    engineer:
"You're My Bestest Friend," "Midnight Crazy," "Shame on the Moon"

John McAndrew, *I'll Play All Night Long*, overdub engineer

In the Beginning, various artists, drums:
Gregg Allman, "I Can Stand Alone"

Martin Mull, *No Hits, Four Errors: The Best of Martin Mull*, producer (credited, but
    I did not work on this album)

Martin Mull, *Normal*, re-release

Raw Spitt, *Raw Spitt*, re-release

South's Greatest Hits, various artists, producer:
Richard Betts, "Jessica"

Betty Wright, *I Love How You Love Me*, guitar, drums:
"I Love How You Love Me"

2007
Goin' South, various artists, producer:
Allman Brothers Band, "Ramblin' Man"; Richard Betts, "Long Time Gone"

Choice Cuts: The Capricorn Years 1991, 1999, Widespread Panic, producer

Ah Feel Like Ahcid!, 24 American Psychedelic Artifacts from the EMI Vaults, various
    artists, artist:
HourGlass, "Bells"

2008
Johnny Jenkins, *Ton Ton Macoute*, producer, engineer, drums, remixing

Bonnie Bramlett, *Piece of My Heart, The Best of 1969–1978*, producer:
"Your Kind of Kindness," "(Your Love Has Brought Me from a) Mighty Long
    Way," "Oncoming Traffic," "Two Steps from the Blues," "Forever Young"

2009

Gregg Allman, *The Solo Years* 1973, 1997, *One More Silver Dollar*, producer, engineer, bass, percussion:

"Midnight Rider," "Queen of Hearts," "Don't Mess Up a Good Thing," "Please Call Home," "These Days," "Feel so Bad," "Two Steps from the Blues," "Whipping Post," "Dark End of the Street"

Elvin Bishop, *Juke Joint Jump/Struttin' My Stuff*, producer, acoustic & electric guitar, percussion, remixing:

"Juke Joint Jump," "Calling All Cows," "Rollin' Home," "Wide River," "Sure Feels Good," "Arkansas Line," "Hold On," "Crawling King Snake," "Do Nobody Wrong"

UNRELEASED RECORDINGS AND DEMOS

(This is only a partial list as there is no longer any way to check the Capricorn vaults to determine which demo sessions may have been played on during that period.)

1962

The Impacts, Spar Music session, guitar:
"My Starter Won't Start"

1966

5 Men-Its, Boutwell Studio session, drums:
"You Can't Do That," "Blue, Blue Feeling," "The Night Before," "You're Gonna Lose That Girl," "Hey Girl"

1967

HourGlass, garage tapes, drums:
"Mustang Sally," "These Arms of Mine," "Love Light," "Outside Looking In," "Feel So Bad," "Stormy Monday"

HourGlass, St. Louis gig recordings, drums:
"Are You Lonely for Me," "Knock on Wood," "A Change Is Gonna Come," "Love Light," "These Arms of Mine," "Feel So Bad," "Outside Looking In," "Love Makes the World Go Round," "Spoonful," "My Girl," "Midnight Hour," "Give Me Some Lovin'," "Stormy Monday," (break song)

HourGlass, Boutwell Studio session, drums:
"Whatcha Gonna Do," "Changing of the Guard," "Richmond"

HourGlass, Troubadour rehearsal tape, drums:
"Try A Little Tenderness," "B. B. King Medley," "Slim Jenkins' Place"

1969
Duane Allman: FAME Recording Sessions, February 1969
   Duane Allman recorded tracks for a never-released solo album at FAME
   Recording Studios in Muscle Shoals, Alabama, in February 1969 with the help
   of Berry Oakley (bass), Paul Hornsby (piano, organ) and Johnny Sandlin
   (drums). Jaimoe played drums at the rehearsals, but not on the actual
   recordings.
   "Goin' Down Slow," "No Money Down," "Happily Married Man," "Down
   along The Cove" (instrumental), "Steal Away," "Dimples," "Bad News,"
   "Neighbor, Neighbor"

1970
Allman Brothers Band, demos for *Idlewild South*, producer:
"Midnight Rider," "Elizabeth Reed" (and others)

1973
Watkins Glen, Allman Brothers Band, live recording, producer:
"Wasted Words," "Done Somebody Wrong," "Southbound," "Blue Sky,"
   "Ramblin' Man," "Jessica," "Midnight Rider"

1977
Katy Moffett, *California Sun*, producer (songs listed that were recorded but didn't
   make the album plus three that did):
"Didn't We Have Love," "Walking after Midnight," "Kansas City Morning,"
   "(Waitin' For) The Real Thing," "Take Me Back to Texas," "Armadillo
   Mama," "Makin' the Best of Love," "California Blues," "Sea Song," "Good
   Ole Days to Come," "Let Her Down Easy," "Broke Down Engine Blues,"
   "Dock of the Bay," "Green Door," "Walkin' Home in the Rain," "You Don't
   Mean the Things You Say"

1980

Basics, producer:
"Beggin' For Beer," "Slow Motion Suicide," "Sexual Object," "Dawn of the
Dread," "Bad Guru"

Fountainhead, producer:
"Man of the World," "Hard Man," "Red Hot"

1982
Ronnie Dunn, producer, engineer, mixing:
"Poor Girl on the Rise," "Sweet Virginia," "Heart to Heart," "Jesse," "Come Back
to Me"

Delbert McClinton, producer:
"Thin Ice," "Married Man," "Never Say Never," "None of That Like Before,"
"Never Say Never"

1991
Dryer Brothers, producer:
"Wake Up Mama," "Psy Cowboy," "Snake"

Cowboy, producer:
"All Roads Lead Back Home," "Deal With the Deal," "Got Down in Mississippi,"
"Table of the Lord"

1995
Gregg Allman, producer, engineer:
"Between Now and Then"

1996
Northern Lights, *Northern Lights*, producer, engineer:
"Juice," "Kurtis," "You Don't Wanna Breathe," "Queen Bee," "Diggin' My Well,"
"Overwhelming Thoughts," "Man's Future," "A/B Positive," "Una Nova,"
"Think Suite: A. Overpass, B. Think, C. Tank"

1997
Kozmic Mama, producer:
"I Got Something," "What She Don't Know," "Friend Appeal," "Kalamazoo"

Holly Allen, the Decatur sessions, producer:
"Love Come between Us," "Three Chord Country Song," "Slick Enough to Slide," "Her Place"

Oteil Burbridge, producer, engineer:
"Subterranea," "Monk Funk," "Listen Bart," "Church," "A-2 Fay," "Barri's Song," "Ankh," "Memnon," "Overcast"

2000
Studio Brothers, producer, bass:
"Midnight Rider"

2001
Ultraphonic, producer, engineer, mixing:
"10,000 Years," "Old Man," "Complications," "Underground," "Weight of the World," "Why?," "Reasons," "We Are the Youth," "Ways of Religion," "Knock, Knock', 'Hammer," "All Good," "Our World," "Way to Go," "Near but Far"

TSS, producer, engineer, bass:
"The Got Song," "Getaway Cars"

2006
Lefty Collins, *Dancin' in the Heat*, producer, engineer:
"Having Faith," "I Love These Blues," "I Can't Go Back," "If I Had My Way," "Looking at the Sky," "Dancin' in The Heat," "Sneakin' Around," "Leave Your Man," "Guilt by Association," "Everything Will Be All Right," "Light of Day"

2009
Bonnie Bramlett, producer, engineer (in progress):
"King Jesus," "Hope in a Hopeless World," "He Is," "Like the Rain," "Can't No Grave Can Hold My Body Down," "Strange Things Happen Every Day," "Grandma's Hands," "Saved," "I'm Gonna Live Forever," "When There's Nothing Left but God"

Undated: *All Meat (Burbank's Finest)*, compilation, producer:
Elvin Bishop, Juke Joint Jump

Index

Aaberg, Phil, 179
Acker, Mike, 27, 32
Acosta, Kenny, 301
Akbar, 301
Alaimo, Steve, 73, 75, 78
Aldridge, Ava, 258
Aldridge, Walt, 218, 303
Allgood, 226, 235, 236, 246
Allman-Act, 28, 36
Allman Brothers Band, 27, 28, 47, 70, 75,
    76, 77, 79, 83, 89, 91, 95, 98, 101, 104,
    106, 107, 111, 113, 114, 115, 121, 124,
    125, 126, 127, 128, 130, 131, 133, 134,
    135, 137, 138, 140, 142, 143, 144, 145,
    150, 153, 160, 161, 163, 166, 168, 169,
    170, 171, 173, 175, 179, 183, 187, 189,
    195, 198, 214, 225, 238, 265, 268, 299,
    305, 308
Allman, Donna, 131
Allman, Duane, 20, 21, 22, 24, 25, 26, 27,
    28, 29, 30, 31, 32, 33, 35, 37, 38, 39, 40,
    41, 44, 45, 46, 47, 51, 52, 53, 54, 55, 56,
    57, 58, 59, 60, 62, 63, 65, 66, 68, 70, 71,
    72, 75, 76, 78, 83, 85, 89, 90, 91, 97,
    101, 102, 103, 104, 106, 111, 114, 115,
    118, 123, 124, 125, 126, 127, 129, 130,
    131, 132, 133, 134, 135, 137, 139, 140,
    141, 142, 145, 151, 171, 175, 178, 180,
    188, 194, 211, 214, 237, 241, 273, 285,
    299, 305, 306, 308
Allman, Galadrielle, 131, 284, 299
Allman, Gregg, 21, 22, 24, 25, 26, 27, 28,
    29, 30, 31, 32, 33, 35, 36, 37, 38, 39, 41,
    42, 44, 45, 46, 47, 50, 51, 53, 55, 56, 59,
    60, 63, 65, 66, 67, 68, 70, 75, 83, 84,
    102, 103, 104, 113, 114, 127, 129, 135,
    137, 138, 139, 143, 144, 145, 149, 150,
    151, 152, 153, 154, 155, 163, 168, 172,
    173, 174, 175, 178, 179, 180, 183, 184,
    185, 186, 187, 189, 193, 194, 198, 200,
    201, 202, 203, 207, 223, 225, 258, 259,
    260, 261, 264, 265, 266, 267, 268, 269,
    270, 274, 292, 294, 299, 305
Allman Joys, 19, 20, 21, 26, 27 , 28, 36, 46,
    64, 65
Amazing Rhythm Aces, the, 281, 294

Anderson, Warren 'Bunky', 261, 262,
    263, 265
Andrews, 'Punch', 205
Anthony, John, 162
Aquarium Rescue Unit, 237, 238, 241,
    249
Arline, Calvin, 203
Armstrong, Tippy, 70
Avalon Ballroom, 48
Avery, Ella, 93, 173,
Avery, Jackie, 83, 88, 90, 91, 93, 94, 285,
    288
Aykroyd, Dan, 211

Badanjek, Johnny, 205, 206
Bailey, Don, 24
Baldwin, Don, 179
Ballenger, Paul, 15, 17, 18, 270
Band, the, 166
Barrineau, Chris, 255
Baron, Aaron, 161
Beckett, Barry, 13, 20, 22, 72, 123, 192,
    207, 272
Beckmeier, Stevie, 201
Bell, John (J.B.), 227, 245, 246, 247
Bell, Laura, 254, 256
Belushi, John, 211, 254, 255, 256
Belz, Gary, 230, 231
Betts, Dickey, 27, 72, 76, 83, 104, 111,
    114, 128, 133, 134, 135, 138, 143, 144,
    145, 146, 147, 163, 168, 169, 179, 180,
    183, 184, 186, 187, 188, 193, 194, 195,
    196, 197, 198, 204, 241, 268, 269, 299,
    305
Bickerstaff, Jim, 239, 242
Billy Karloff & the Extremes, 215
Birdwatcher, Bobby, 73, 75
Bishop, Elvin, 178, 179, 187, 188
Blackburn, Bill, 10,
Blaine, Hal, 39
Blazek, Alan, 188
Bloodkin, 227, 254, 255
Blue Law, 48
Boutwell, Ed, 30
Boutwell Studio, 30
Bowen, Jimmy, 217

Boyer, Scott, 70, 75, 97, 98, 100, 110, 123, 124, 125, 140, 149, 150, 151, 157, 172, 173, 174, 181, 182, 190, 223, 224, 225, 234, 235, 256, 259, 260, 264, 265, 266, 287, 289, 291, 294, 295, 305
Boyer – Talton, 182
Bradley, Madison 'Red', 212
Bramblett, Randall, 174, 181, 274, 303
Bramlett, Bonnie, 29, 121, 131, 180, 181, 190, 191, 192, 193, 194, 286, 293, 294, 302, 305, 308
Brasfield, Tommy, 218
Briggs, David, 8, 9, 10, 18, 224, 258
Brock, Michael, 179
Brooks, Danny, 301
Brown, Bobby, 250, 251
Brown, Carolyn, 78, 79, 145, 220, 285, 299
Brown, David, 70, 73, 75, 174, 234
Brown, James, 305
Brown, Nappy, 281
Brown, Owen, 217, 222, 233, 271, 272
Brown, T. Graham, 281
Browne, Jackson, 33
Buckins, Beverly, 285
Buckins, Mickey, 284, 285
Buffalo Springfield, 47
Burbridge, Kofi, 274
Burbridge, Oteil, 238, 239, 251, 252, 254, 274, 305
Burdon, Eric, 45, 61
Burnside, DeWayne, 281
Butterfield, Paul, 45, 61
Bryant, Jen, 255

Caldwell, Bobby, 131, 156
Callahan, Mike, 141
Calloway, Harrison, 207
Cameron, Duncan, 223
Campbell, Charlie, 8, 12, 15, 16, 17, 18, 19
Campbell, Larry 'Red Dog', 128
Canned Heat, 48
Caplan, Michael, 265
Capricorn Rhythm Section (see CRS)
Captain Beyond, 156
Carr, Pete, 24, 32, 49, 52, 56, 59, 63, 68, 73, 74, 75, 82, 83, 88, 89, 95, 112, 199, 286

Carrigan, Jerry, 8, 10, 13, 15, 18, 70, 224, 258, 294, 305
Carter, Eric, 255
Carter, Jimmy, 195, 196, 299
Carter, John, 226, 293
Cartwright, Angela, 55
Cason, Buzz, 258
Cauthen, Ella, 308
Cauthen, Gray, 308
Cauthen, Leigh, 285
Cauthen, Reid, 308
Champion, Hollis, 6
Cheetah, the, 47, 48
Cher, 186, 200, 201, 202, 207, 223
Cicala, Roy, 151
Clapton, Eric, 139, 199
Clark, George, 97, 98, 124
Clear Light, 75
Clements, Vassar, 179, 180
Cline, Patsy, 5
Cocker, Joe, 192, 193
Codetalkers, the, 279
Comic Book Club, 64
Compton, Barbara, 285
Compton, Tommy, 27, 33, 237, 238, 285
Conley, Arthur, 86, 87, 88
Connell, Bill, 19, 21,
Coppage, Jeff, 232
Cowboy, 97, 98, 100, 101, 123, 140, 172, 174, 175, 181, 182, 238
Crawford, Hank, 266, 267
Creason, Sammy, 160
CRS, 290, 292, 293, 294, 295, 302, 305
Curtis, King, 109

Daigle, Tony, 289
Danko, Rick, 166, 167
Davis, Chalmers, 234, 254
Davis, Don, 94
Davis, Jesse Ed,
Davis, Mac, 221
Dawson, Jack, 255
Decoys, the 222, 223, 224, 225, 234, 235, 277, 281, 284, 287, 288, 293, 294, 305
Dilbeck, Boyce, 7
Dillon, Mike, 224, 287
Dixie, 127,
Dixie Dregs, 144, 228, 242
Dixie Hummingbirds, 150
Doors, the, 44

Donahue, Tom, 169
Dorffman, Lee, 156
Dowd, Tom, 95, 100, 104, 108, 113, 114, 133, 135, 136, 137, 161, 266, 268, 288, 306
Dr. John (see Rebennack, Mack)
Duck and the Bear, 72
Dudek, Les, 150
Dunn, Ronnie, 217, 218, 286

Easy, 100
Edmonds, Bin, 101
Electric Flag, 48
Emmons, Bobby, 258
English, Joe, 190, 191
Ezell, Ralph, 218

5 Men-Its, 14, 15, 17, 18, 285
5 Minutes, 19, 21, 160
FAME, 10, 11, 12, 17, 62, , 221
Faye, Barry, 199
Feiten, Buzzy, 150
Fenter, Frank, 79, 83, 88, 91, 94, 104, 106, 107, 110, 113, 114, 116, 120, 123, 126, 153, 154, 159, 175, 178, 189, 191, 197, 207, 219, 220
Fillmore, the, 46, 47, 61
Fisher, Beau, 160
Floyd the janitor, 99, 100
Floyd, Eddie, 95
Flye, Tom, 139, 170, 171, 174, 210, 213
Freeman, Ed, 15, 153, 154, 155, 201
Fritts, Donnie, 10, 270, 271, 272, 281, 286, 293, 294, 305
Fuller, Clay, 226

Gallaher, Microwave Dave, 256, 257, 281, 288, 294, 301
Gatlin Brothers, the, 221
Ghoul, the, 56
Gilbert, David, 206
Goedert, Ronn, 159, 160
Goldstein, Ron, 203
Gooch, Josh, 305
Graham, Bill, 47, 166, 171
Graham, Sandlin, 285, 308
Graham, Zach, 308
Gray, Byron, 27
Gray, Randy, 27

Grateful Dead, 152, 165, 166
Greene, Marlin, 8, 9, 12, 18, 50, 101, 284
Gunter, Marsha, 285

Hale, Owen, 218
Hall, Jack, 162
Hall, Jimmy, 160, 162, 258, 259, 260, 262, 263, 264, 281, 293, 303
Hall, Rick, 9, 10, 11, 12, 17, 38, 39, 62, 67, 70, 71, 89, 108, 175, 217, 218, 221
Hamm, Bill, 227
Hampton, Col. Bruce, 227, 237, 238, 239, 251, 252, 253, 274, 279, 281, 299
Harrelson, Allison, 285
Harrelson, Mark, 258 , 259, 264, 270, 285
Harris, Carolyn, 148
Havely, Dan, 8, 9, 224
Hawkins, Jim, 80, 81, 82, 84, 108, 121, 158, 284, 287
Hawkins, Roger, 13, 32, 69, 70, 123, 157, 191, 207, 208, 247, 258, 272, 273, 274, 305
Hayward, Charlie, 70, 82, 118, 157, 181, 191, 294
Healey, Dan, 166
Hedley, Tom, 232, 296
Herman, John (Jo Jo), 246, 248
Herring, Jimmy, 238, 239, 241, 250, 274
Herring, Scooter, 185, 186, 187, 194
Hicks, Earl, 259
Higdon, Mike, 222
Highly Kind, 281, 303
Hinton, Eddie, 9, 18, 19, 20, 22, 23, 24, 25, 27, 30, 33, 38, 39, 50, 62, 63, 66, 69, 71, 73, 87, 124, 133, 134, 233, 234, 270, 271, 272, 273, 285, 308
Hirsch, Ricky, 162, 190
Hodges, Jimmy Ray, 6, 7
Hodges, Robert, 6
Holly, Kelvin, 223, 224, 234, 254, 259, 262, 287, 301, 305
Hood, David, 13, 72, 123, 192, 206, 224, 247, 258, 259, 261, 262, 264, 270, 272, 274, 284, 287, 295, 301, 305
Hood, Judy, 287
Horn, Jim, 259, 261
Hornsby, Paul, 15, 17, 18, 20, 21, 22, 24, 26, 27, 31, 33, 35, 46, 58, 59, 60, 63, 66, 68, 70, 71, 76, 82, 83, 87, 88, 89, 93, 95, 107, 110, 111, 112, 120, 134, 139, 157,

160, 175, 176, 178, 238, 275, 285, 286, 289, 291, 292, 295
HourGlass, the, 25, 27, 36, 47, 50, 55, 65, 67, 69, 71, 72, 75, 76, 84, 102, 144, 149, 169, 171, 173, 181, 226, 238, 251, 260, 266, 305
Houser, Barbette, 232
Houser, Mike, 227, 231, 232, 244, 245, 248
Houston, Cissy, 151
Hubach, Frank, 151, 166
Hug, John, 207, 208, 209, 210
Hughes, Frank, 178, 188,
Hughes, Jimmy, 11
Hughey, John, 176, 179, 180
Hullabaloo Club, 43, 44
Hutchens, Danny, 227, 254, 255
Hydra, 178, 188

Iehle, Phil, 108
Impacts, the, 6, 7, 10, 13, 26, 285
Iron Butterfly, 65
Ivey, Clayton, 217, 218, 259, 26, 272, 274

Jackson, Al, Jr, 305
Jackson, Randy, 274
Jackson, Wayne, 72, 258
Jaeger, Rick, 205
Jaimoe, 71, 72, 76, 89, 93, 135, 138, 142, 143, 163, 173, 174, 183, 184, 185, 187, 305, 308
Jarvis, John, 208, 210, 218, 219
Jefferson Airplane, 46
Jenkins, Johnny, 88, 89, 90, 91, 92, 94, 165, 274, 275, 276
Johnson, David, 224
Johnson, Howard, 275
Johnson, Jimmy, 63, 66, 70, 123, 192, 203, 207, 258, 270, 272
Jones, Corky, 226
Jones, George, 3
Joseph, Jerry, 254, 255, 256, 271
Joplin, Janis, 45, 61, 65

Kaleidoscope, the, 48
Kane, Terry, 84, 121, 158, 159
Kashida, Kunio, 286, 287
Kashida, Masao, 286
Kaylan, Diana, 8
Keene, John, 229

Keith, Mike, 285, 296
Keith, Patrice, 285
Keller, Bob, 21, 46, 48, 49, 52, 59, 60
Keller, Ricky, 249, 250
Kellgren, Gary, 135, 154, 205, 213
Kendricks, Eddie, 216
Kershaw, Doug, 203
Kiel Auditorium, 65
Killen, Carolyn (see Carolyn Brown)
Kinzel, Kurt, 152
Kirshner, Don, 163, 168
Kite, E.G., 281
Knight, Ronnie, 275, 276, 285
Kopp, Kerry, 228
Kowalke, Pete, 97, 98, 124
Kurtz, Rick, 294
L
Landau, Jon, 95, 96
Landreth, Sonny, 289
Lang, Corky, 199
Lanier, Sam, 226, 254
Larson, Neil, 182, 191, 201, .203, 204
LaRue, Dave, 242
Lavitz, T (no period), 144, 242, 244, 245, 246, 284
Lazar, Gary, 205, 215
Leavell, Chuck, 70, 93, 112, 122, 139, 143, 149, 150, 157, 163, 174, 179, 180, 183, 184, 187, 190, 234, 252, 286
LeBlanc, Lenny, 258
Levy, Ron, 233, 234
Lewis, Jerry Lee, 4, 5, 6
Light, Don, 213
Little Richard, 299
Lockhart, June, 55
Lombar, Dru, 190, 281
Look, the, 215
Lopate, Mitch, 301
Lost in Space, 55
Love, Andrew, 72
Lowery, Henry, 33
Lyndon, Twiggs, 128, 214
Lynyrd Skynyrd, 64, 189

Macon (the band), 95
Magic Mushroom, the, 57
Mama Louise, 294
Manning, Terry, 87
Margolin, Bob, 281
Mark V, 8, 11, 12, 13, 15, 18, 225, 238

Marshal Tucker Band, 106, 107, 195, 197
Martin, Kathy, 133, 288, 289
Martin, Matt, 288
Masterson, Pruett, 4
Mathis, Jimbo, 281
Mazer, Elliot, 168
M'Butu, Count, 259, 274
McAnally, Mac, 218 ·
McCain, Jerry 'Boogie', 279, 280
McCallister, Kooster, 240, 242
McCarty, Jim, 206
McClinton, Delbert, 207, 208, 209, 210,
    212, 213, 218, 219, 258
McCutchen, Tom, 2
McEuen, Bill, 29, 30, 31, 32, 35, 36, 41, 43,
    44, 45, 61, 62, 63, 64
McKendree, Kevin, 301
McKinney, Mabron, 22, 26, 27, 29, 46, 52
Meadows, Glenn, 231, 232
Melting Pot, 107
Melvoin, Mike, 39
Merino, George, 116, 117, 136, 146, 153,
    162, 168
Merv Griffith Show, 42
Microwave Dave (see Dave Gallaher)
Miles, Buddy, 48
Miles, Floyd, 84, 86
Mims, Kenny, 218
Minutes, the, 20, 22, 26, 27
Missy, 251
Mitchell, Jimmy, 22
Mitchell, Joni, 109
Mitchell, Price, 22
Moffet, Doug, 258
Moffett, Katy, 199, 200
Montgomery, Peanut, 10
Morgenstein, Rod, 242
Morris, Doug, 199
Morse, Steve, 239, 242, 243
Mull, Martin, 120, 172
Mullenix, Lou, 70, 93, 112, 157
Mumy, Billy, 55
Mundy, Matt, 238, 239, 251
Murray, Bill, 209

Nalls, Jimmy, 157
Nalls, Steve, 288
Nalls, Wishy, 288
Nance, Todd, 227, 230, 244, 248
Newman, David 'Fathead', 266

Newmark, Andy, 207.208
Newton, Bert (Chigger), 288
Nichols, Adam, 278, 285
Nicholson, Gary, 258
Nighthawks, 281
Nitty Gritty Dirt Band, 29, 34, 35, 36, 54

Oakley, Berry, 70, 71, 72, 91, 104, 106,
    111, 118, 129, 134, 136, 139, 140, 141,
    142, 143, 144, 163, 165, 171, 194,
    211.214, 305, 306, 308
Oakley, Brittany, 140
Oakley, Candace, 140,
Oakley, Linda, 127, 140
Odom, Bunky, 79, 80, 145, 169
Offord, Eddie, 159, 160
Oldaker, Jamie, 286
Oldham, Spooner, 10, 11, 22, 50, 258,
    259, 260, 261, 271, 272, 294, 305
One Percent, 64
O'Rourke, Sean, 274
Ortiz, Domingo 'Sonny', 227, 230
Osborne, John, 216
Osmond, Marie, 221
Otis Redding Memorial Studio, 80
Owens, Butch, 6, 19, 32
Owings, Brian (BO), 224, 234, 254

Pallbearers, the, 18, 224, 225
Parnell, Lee Roy, 287, 289, 291, 293
Paulson, Pat, 44
Parker, Jeriel, 5
Pastorius, Jaco, 211
Paul, Jean, 109
Payne, Kim, 128
Pearson, Jack, 262, 264, 275, 281
Pendergrass, Buddy, 160
Penn, Dan, 10, 12, 13, 18, 21, 22, 50, 224,
    225, 258, 259, 260, 261, 272, 294, 305
Perkins, Deanie, 270, 271, 272, 273, 285
Perkins, Paul, 270, 272, 285
Perry, Bill, 281
Petty, Joe Dan, 128
Pier, the, 66
Pillmore, Bill, 97
Pinkston, Carol, 287
Pinkston, David, 212, 271, 287
Poco, 170
Popper, John, 252

Popwell, Robert 'Pops', 83, 88, 89, 93, 95, 112, 285, 288
Pousson, Walter Jr. (see Walter, Jr.)
Prestapino, Paul, 240
Price, Topper, 223, 259, 294
Pruet, Charlie, 226
Pucci, Mark, 295, 302
Purcell, Denny, 153, 168, 263
Putman, Bill, 80
Putnam, Norbert, 8, 9, 10, 18, 224

Rambos, the, 180
Rebennack, Mack (Dr. John), 39, 120, 121, 131, 203, 204
Reed, Jerry, 221
Reid, Clarence, 73
Reinhardt, Larry 'Rhino', 156
Rhoden, Chuck, 19
Rhythm Rockets, the, 4
Richards, Randy, 215, 216
Richardson, Buddy, 160
Rico, Yon, 274
Robbins, Dennis, 206
Rockets, the, 205, 213
Rose, Charles, 258, 272
Rosenthal, Jay, 268, 269
Ross, Lewis, 162
Rudd, Joe, 70, 110, 111, 112
Rudolph, Van, 6, 7, 10,
Russell, Carla, 288, 301
Russell, Jonathan, 168, 232
Russell, Leon, 282

Sain, Mike, 226
Salazarte, Alberto, 226
Sanders, Billy, 207, 208, 209, 210
Sandlin, Ann, 27, 217, 219, 221, 222, 226, 227, 245, 248, 252, 254, 256, 262, 266, 270, 275, 279, 280, 284, 289, 293, 294, 297, 301, 302
Sandlin, Big John, 1, 70
Sandlin, Lucille, 1, 70
Santa Monica Civic Auditorium, 47
Santana, 170
Sawyer, Wayne, 244
Saylor, Jerry, 8, 9, 12
Scaggs, Boz, 106
Scalded Dogs, 287
Schilling, Art, 223

Schmitzerle, Don, 195, 196, 226, 227, 243
Schneider, John, 289
Schools, Dave, 227
Schulman, Alan, 229
Schroeder, Papa Don, 22
Secrets, the, 5
Seger, Bob, 205
Senters, Ted, 195, 196
Shapiro, Brad, 74
Sharpe, Andrew, 278, 281, 301
Sharpe, Antony, 281
Shea, Bobby, 160
Sibley, Brent, 292
Shirley, Dwight, 6
Simpson, Albert, 303
Simpson, Jeff, 271, 272
Sims, Earl 'Speedo', 110
Sipe, Jeff, 238, 239, 274
Skeeters, the, 281, 288
Sledge, Percy, 284, 285, 293
Sloan, Allen, 242
Smith, Barry, 6
Smith, Billy, 5, 6
Smith, Dallas, 36, 38, 39, 40, 50, 51, 74
Soule', George, 258
South, Joe, 18
Spain, Avonlea, 308
Spain, Noah, 308
Spar Studio, 10
Sparks, Ovie, 158
Spoonful James, 48
Stan, 193
Standells, the, 47
Stanley, Owsley, 165
Starr, Frankie, 3
Steele, Dottie, 127
Steiner, Armin, 39, 40, 50
Stephens, Gretchen, 285
Stephens, Jeremy, 278, 282, 284, 285
Stephens, Lewis, 207
Stewart, Bill, 93, 110, 111, 149, 157, 157, 173, 174, 181, 182, 184, 190, 191, 201, 203, 205, 209, 210, 212, 233, 259, 262, 264, 272, 289, 291, 294, 295, 301, 305
Stiles, Fred, 15, 16, 17, 21, 22, 270, 285
Stills, Stephen, 47, 53
Stone, Chris, 116, 117, 151, 152, 156, 202, 205, 213, 214
Stone, Henry, 73, 74, 75
Straton, 'Stray', 179, 180

Strawberry Alarm Clock, 46, 46
Sunshine Company, the, 36, 46
Szymczyk, Bill, 28, 188, 204

Talton, Patti, 284
Talton, Tommy, 97, 98, 100, 101, 124,
    149, 150, 173, 174, 175, 181, 182, 190,
    191, 223, 238, 239, 284, 289, 291, 295,
    305
Talton, Sandlin Stewart (T.S.S), 190
Taylor, Alex, 96, 108, 109, 110, 111, 112,
    151, 157, 158
Taylor, Dennis, 260
Taylor, Dolphin, 216
Taylor, James, 109
Taylor, Livingston, 95, 96, 108
Thames, Bill, 293
Thames, Patti, 293
Thomas, Mickey, 179, 188
Thompson, Diana, 272, 287
Thompson, Harvey, 233, 234, 258, 272
Thompson, Peter, 271, 272, 273, 287
Thompson, Ronnie 'Machine Gun', 86
Thompson, Terry, 10, 11, 12
Thorn, Paul, 294
Thornton, Billy Bob, 240, 241, 286
Thornton, Buddy, 6, 7, 28, 204, 285
Thornton, Maureen, 285
Thurman, N.C., 224, 287
Tibbetts, Kenny, 173
Tillisch, Steve, 232, 243
Tony, Oscar, Jr., 288
Toy Shop, 278, 281
Troubadour, the, 48
Trucks, Butch, 70, 72, 73, 76, 89, 90, 111,
    135, 143, 144, 145, 163, 183, 184, 185,
    225, 234, 305, 308
Trucks, Derek, 274, 275, 289, 303
Trucks, Duane, 303
Turberville, Danny, 122, 151, 178
Tuffy, 128

Van Zant, Ronnie, 64
Vee, Bobby, 40
Vernazza, Johnny, 179, 188
Voorman, Klaus, 201

Walden, Alan, 78, 94
Walden, G. Scott, 245, 253
Walden, Peggy, 79, 105, 198, 243

Walden, Phil, 71, 75, 78, 79, 82, 83, 84, 85,
    86, 88, 89, 90, 92, 93, 94, 95, 96, 97, 98,
    101, 103, 104, 105, 106, 107, 109, 110,
    112, 113, 114, 116, 120, 121, 122, 123,
    126, 130.133, 134, 135, 137, 147, 153,
    154, 156, 159, 160, 163, 165, 169, 175,
    177, 178, 181, 185, 189, 190, 191, 192,
    193, 194, 195, 196, 197, 198, 199, 207,
    219, 225, 226, 227, 228, 235, 236, 237,
    238, 239, 240, 241, 242, 243, 245, 246,
    248, 249, 252, 253, 254, 263, 272, 274,
    285, 296, 297, 298, 299, 300, 302, 308
Walden, Phillip, 263
Walk, Joe, 4, 5, 32, 190, 208, 221, 222, 223,
    224, 233, 234, 272, 287, 288, 308
Walker, Cindy Richards, 258
Wallace, Bobby, 106, 126
Walshaw, David, 179, 180
Walter, Jr., 281, 288, 289
Wasley, Jerry, 286
Watters, Harry, 277
Watters, Ken, 277
Weaver, Carl, 222, 277, 278, 279, 280,
    281, 282, 283, 284, 291, 292, 293, 301,
    302, 303, 304
Webb, Jimmy, 40
Weeks, Willie, 201
Weisberg, Tim, 204, 205
Wells, Kitty, 175, 176, 177, 178, 189
Westfield, Kenyatta, 274
Wet Willie, 110, 160, 161, 162, 168, 169
Wexler, Jerry, 71, 79, 86, 95, 130, 299
Wheeler, Bryan 'BW, 223, 287, 288, 308
Whiskey a Go Go, 45, 48
Whiskey Howl, 121
White Witch, 158, 159, 160
Whiteside, Sam, 148, 191, 198
Whitley, Jackie, 5
Whitley, Johnny, 5
Whitlock, Bobby, 286
Whitsett, Carson, 258
Widespread Panic, 158, 226, 227, 228,
    229, 231, 232, 235, 237, 240, 241, 242,
    244, 245, 246, 247, 255
Willis, John, 223
Williams, Jerry 'Swamp Dogg', 83, 84,
    86, 87
Williams, Lamar, 142, 183, 184, 187
Williams, Marcus, 274
Williams, Woody, 274

Woodard, Jerry, 20
Woodford, Terry, 217
Wooley, Dick, 222, 287
Wooten, Regi, 274
Wright, Betty, 73
Wright, Johnny, 176, 177
Wynn, Tom, 97, 98, 124

Young, Neil, 47, 53
Young, Reggie, 258

Zoo, the, 74